The Transition to Language

Studies in the Evolution of Language

General Editors
James R. Hurford, *University of Edinburgh*
Frederick J. Newmeyer, *University of Washington*

This series provides a forum for work in linguistics and related fields that seeks answers to questions about the origins and evolution of language. It places a premium on sound scholarship, rational thought, and readable writing.

Published

The Transition to Language
Edited by Alison Wray

The Origins of Vowel Systems
Bart de Boer

Published in Association with the Series

Language Diversity
Daniel Nettle

Function, Selection, and Innateness:
The Emergence of Language Universals
Simon Kirby

The Origins of Complex Language:
An Inquiry into the Evolutionary Beginnings of Sentences, Syllables, and Truth
Andrew Carstairs-McCarthy

In Preparation

Language Evolution:
The States of the Art
Edited by Morten Christiansen and Simon Kirby

The Transition to Language

Edited by
Alison Wray

OXFORD
UNIVERSITY PRESS

OXFORD

UNIVERSITY PRESS

Great Clarendon Street, Oxford OX2 6DP

Oxford University Press is a department of the University of Oxford.
It furthers the University's objective of excellence in research, scholarship,
and education by publishing worldwide in

Oxford New York

Auckland Bangkok Bogotá Buenos Aires Cape Town Chennai
Dar es Salaam Delhi Hong Kong Istanbul Karachi Kolkata
Kuala Lumpur Madrid Melbourne Mexico City Mumbai Nairobi
São Paulo Shanghai Singapore Taipei Tokyo Toronto

and associated companies in Berlin Ibadan

Oxford is a registered trade mark of Oxford University Press
in the UK and in certain other countries

Published in the United States
by Oxford University Press Inc., New York

British Library Cataloguing in Publication Data

Data available

Library of Congress Cataloging in Publication Data

Data applied for

ISBN 0–19–925065–0
ISBN 0–19–925066–9 (Pbk.)

10 9 8 7 6 5 4 3 2 1

Typeset in Minion
by Peter Kahrel
Printed in Great Britain
on acid-free paper by
Biddles Ltd., Guildford & King's Lynn

Contents

Preface and Acknowledgements

The aim of this book is to examine the theme of transition from a number of different angles, and to raise issues and new challenges regarding the ways in which we, as researchers in the field, perceive our evolving task. As my introductory chapter makes clear, I view the future as one of cross-disciplinary collaboration, and the reconciliation of individual scenarios within a larger, consistent picture. The book includes contributions from the fields of anthropology, archaeology, artificial intelligence, biology, genetics, linguistics, primatology, and psychology. I hope that this broad range of perspectives will contribute to a fuller recognition of what seems to me an undoubted fact about this field of enquiry: none of us has purchase on the whole of the answer to the question, 'How did language evolve?'

The chapters of this book are a small sample of the papers presented at the Third International Conference on the Evolution of Language, held in April 2000 at the École Nationale Supérieure des Télécommunications in Paris. The organizing team for the conference was led by Jean-Louis Dessalles and Laleh Ghadakpour, and it was generously sponsored by the École Nationale Supérieure des Télécommunications, the Sony Computer Science Laboratory, France Telecom R&D, the Centre Nationale de la Recherche Scientifique, the Department of Sociology and Anthropology at the University of East London, and the Fondation Louis Leprince-Ringuet.

The various rounds of anonymous refereeing, for the conference and for the book, relied on the generosity of the individuals who gave their time to read and comment on the proposals and papers. A particular debt of gratitude is owed to the referees who participated in the final stage, providing detailed and insightful notes on the papers short-listed for inclusion in the book. I should also like to thank the authors themselves, who stuck to some tough deadlines and indulged me as I pestered them over fiddly bits of detail.

The book owes much of its identity, and perhaps its very existence, to the efforts of Jean-Louis Dessalles, whom I particularly thank for his invaluable contribution in the months after the conference. The series editors,

Jim Hurford and Fritz Newmeyer, have been a strong support to me, as has John Davey of Oxford University Press. I should also like to extend my heartfelt thanks to Chris Knight for his thoughtful advice, support, and example. Finally, my own work on the book would not have been possible without the time afforded by my Senior Research Fellowship at Cardiff University, and the patience and encouragement of my partner, Mike Wallace.

A.W.

Cardiff
July 2001

List of Figures

List of Tables

1 Introduction: Conceptualizing Transition in an Evolving Field

ALISON WRAY

1.1 Transition and Transitions

A book entitled *The Transition to Language* could give the impression that there was a single event at some point in prehistory before which there was no language and after which there was language. But that is far from the case. The constituent properties of human language—its mediums of transmission, its micro- and macro-structure, the mechanisms that process it, the manner in which it is used to convey messages—all entail independent, or partially independent, developments of physical, mental, and/or social configurations. Each such development can be conceptualized in terms of a transition. A transition may be sudden or gradual. That is, it may be the result of one event with major consequences for the species, or a slow accumulation of relatively unimportant small changes that ultimately effect a combined impact.

1.1.1 *The Challenge of Complexity*

The evolution of language as a whole must, in either case, be construed as a complex event-sequence essentially driven by the dynamics of chance. It behoves us to remember that there was no advance plan, and we should not impose upon our accounts too strong an impression of our retrospective standpoint. We do not know how else language might have turned out, and how different our conception of grammar, words, or effective communication might have been if some other combination of factors had taken our ancestors down a slightly different path. We do not know how many times one or another component of language *nearly* emerged, or emerged briefly but died out. We do not know which, if any, components emerged more than once and survive to this day as separate routes to the same outcome. Our aim as researchers is to trace a continuous line of events that culminates in our use of syntactic language for a range of interactive purposes, but in the course of our backwards reconstruction, the line may cross or tangle with others, or become obscured so that we can no longer be sure of where it goes next.

Some indication of the intrinsic complexity and the role of chance is evident in the computer simulations reported by Tonkes and Wiles and by Steels *et al.* in this volume, as also elsewhere, by Kirby (e.g. 1998, 2000), Batali (e.g. 1998) and others. When effective language-like systems emerge in these trials, each is a macro-pattern arising, after many iterations, out of a soup of random and semi-random events. This kind of modelling takes for granted the 'noise', whereby pretty well any configuration may occur once or many times, without ultimately prevailing. A coherent story emerges only out of a very large body of data. For those using other investigatory means it is, in general, extremely difficult to accommodate the full scope of the likely complications of the original scenario. Yet, unless we are careful in our visualizations of the events about which we hypothesize, we risk making over-precipitous assumptions, which may have far-reaching implications. This is what Davidson's chapter warns us of, as he reveals the potential dangers of too readily imposing onto data *post-hoc* rationales which then discount the residue of evidence.

1.1.2 *The Challenge to Open-Mindedness*

It is unquestionably necessary to locate any proposal within a solid context of existing theory. However, this presents us with a further, and difficult, challenge, because it means that a coherent account of how a given part of the linguistic package evolved can only be developed in relation to a particular hypothesis about the 'before' and 'after' states. In other words, answering the question of *how* and *why* a change occurred depends entirely on your position regarding *what* changed into *what*. The problem is that, as a result, each stage in the construction of a model of complex transition becomes, itself, a variable within the model as a whole. That is, it feeds into the investigator's perception of the transition event, determining the directions in which the account can evolve, and excluding other routes as incompatible. The risk is that assumptions made too readily at one point will deflect attention from lines of investigation that, in the final count, turn out to be of considerable significance.

The remedy is the continual reappraisal of the assumptions we make about language, but that is harder than it sounds, because the assumptions run so deep. The very conceptualization of what constitutes a transition event in the first place is dependent on adopting a committed position regarding the overall nature of language and, in particular, the order in which various components of the language 'package' evolved. A fundamental transition within one model of language evolution may simply evaporate in another. For instance, a model such as Bickerton's (e.g. 1996, 1998, this volume; Calvin and Bickerton 2000), in which full syntax developed out of a simpler spoken protolanguage, automatically entails that a previous transition also occurred, whereby agrammatical semantic representation became united with controlled phonetic vocalization. In contrast, the model that Corballis (this volume) proposes sees fully syntactic messages delivered through the medium of sign, long before speech was adopted. Such a view does not entail a transition to phonetic words without grammar, and envisages the unification of vocal delivery with an already fully-fledged grammatical language system.

Even the apparently fundamental assumption that the 'word' existed before the complex message can be challenged, when one asks just what the function of the 'word' could have been before there was syntax. If, as Terrace and Wray both propose in this book, the basic unit of expression was not referential but manipulative, then the 'translation' of so-called simple one-word messages reveals them not to be so simple after all. Just as the vervet's alarm call (Cheney and Seyfarth 1990) is more usefully glossed not as *eagle* but as *behave in a manner appropriate to my having seen an eagle*, so, in our ancestors, we might be forced to gloss a 'one-word' utterance not as *meat*, so much as *behave in some appropriate way in relation to me and the meat*. That, in turn, challenges our view on just what kind of expressive complexity syntax delivered for the first time, and what complexity it just repackaged.

1.1.3 *Types of Evidence*

If, from our perspective as adept users of an integrated linguistic system, it is very difficult to ascertain which parts of the language package came before others, it is even harder to work out whether a precursor should be viewed as prerequisite. Each assumption about the order in which our ancestors developed the various capacities necessary for language needs to be scrutinized and evaluated in the light of at least two types of evidence. One is internal consistency. From what we understand of language as a system, is it possible, or likely, that there was syntax before there were words, as Okanoya proposes? Is the apparatus of speech more likely to be the foundation of linguistic expression, or a response to it? Just how mentally adept at problem-solving could we have become *without* developing language? The other kind of evidence is comparative. Do other species, whether closely or not so closely related to our own, display skills and behavioural patterns that belie common assumptions about the order in which the constituent parts of language evolved, and why they did? Since there are in principle so many different position statements, each of which will support a different account of the events, the major challenge to any researcher of language evolution is to find independent support for the assumptions underpinning the given hypothesis. Without it, a model is little more than idle speculation.

1.2 Themes in Researching Transition

Since, as already pointed out, there is no single story of transition, or transitions, to tell, there is inevitably no entirely simple way to allocate a set of studies to thematic sections. The structure chosen for this book reflects three aspects of transition, without directly imposing a chronological ordering on them. These aspects may be characterized as the run-up to transition, the immediate triggers of transition, and their aftermath. But in each case, it is not necessarily the same transition that is under discussion. In other words, rather than attempting to map out, through the sequencing of chapters in the book, the story of how language might have evolved, the sections aim to focus on the issues arising out of these three faces of transition as a phenomenon.

1.2.1 *Part I. Making Ready for Language: Necessary, but not Sufficient*

Human language primarily uses the *vocal-auditory channel* (Hockett 1960), though as Ragir's account of sign languages (in Ch. 13) makes plain, it does not need to. Of course, humans are far from the only creatures to use this channel, but the units transmitted in human language are phonetic. Phonetic production requires a particular configuration of the vocal tract and this is the focus of Ch. 2, as Fitch seeks to separate out fundamental from non-fundamental features of that configuration. Fitch challenges some long-held beliefs about the uniqueness of the human vocal tract, beliefs that have led to associations between physical attributes and linguistic capabilities. He demonstrates, for instance, that although humans differ from apes in possessing a low larynx, the significance of this fact has been exaggerated. He draws on evidence from several species to argue that our unusual laryngeal arrangement is likely to have evolved for reasons other than the articulation of linguistic forms. Similarly, he shows that other animals can perceive formant patterns comparable with those characterizing human vowels, which suggests that language harnessed this channel because we could already discriminate within it, rather than the reverse.

The study of finch song, Okanoya argues in Ch. 3, can give us important insights into another aspect of language evolution, the relationship between syntax and semantics. The standard assumption, and one that is made in several chapters in this volume, is that syntax subserves the expression of meaning, so that semantics is assumed to predate and underpin the evolution of grammar. Okanoya's work on the song of the Bengalese finch demonstrates that syntax, albeit less complex than that in human language, can evolve independently of meaning. Moreover, the peculiar circumstances under which this finch has developed complexity in its song are such that it is possible to make direct links between syntactic prowess and sexual selection. Okanoya shows that while complexity in the male song correlates with increased female reproductive activity, in the wild the effects of preferential selection by females of mates with complex songs are countermanded by the increased vulnerability of good singers to predation. Only in a captive species, where predation no longer affects survival patterns, does sexual selection override natural selection, leading to the evolution of ever more complex song. Okanoya proposes that syntax might have evolved in a similar manner in humans, independently of message meanings, for the purpose of sexual display.

One of the characteristics of the human capacity for interacting with the world is a clear distinction between procedural knowledge (knowing *how*) and declarative knowledge (knowing *that*). Since declarative knowledge is so closely tied into information exchange, and information exchange is most efficiently achieved using language, there has been a tendency to assume that non-human animals do not possess it. All animal behaviour has been assumed to be grounded in procedural knowledge. Terrace (Ch. 4) directly challenges this assumption. He reports an experiment in which monkeys were trained to select sequences of images in a particular order, even though the images were differently positioned on the screen in different trials. The only way for them to achieve success—which they did—was to learn the sequence of images independently of their position in presentation, thus ruling out an automatic procedural response based on physical movements. They had to know *that* a particular image came in a particular place in the sequence, and tests demonstrated that they did indeed know the serial positions of the items, both relative to each other and in absolute terms. Terrace uses this evidence to conclude that declarative knowledge is independent of linguistic expression, and that we must look elsewhere to explain why humans are the only species to have developed language. In his view, the key difference between humans and other animals is that animals only ever use symbols manipulatively, in pursuit of a reward. In contrast, humans are also capable of using symbols referentially, that is, to talk about the world for its own sake.

1.2.2   *Part II. Internal Triggers to Transition: Genes, Processing, Culture, Gesture, and Technology*

If one assumes a general level of stability for a species in its environment, it is as well to look for both internal and external triggers when accounting for a transition. Stability will tend to impose the biological equivalent of the maxim 'if it ain't broken, don't fix it', so that most random genetic changes, even if they might be construed as beneficial, will not be necessary, and so will not be favoured by natural selection. Only when the organism lives within a sufficiently challenging environment will a small change to its physical or mental capabilities make a real difference to its survival chances. Meanwhile, a change in external factors, if it does not coincide with relevant variation within the species, will exert the same pressure on all individuals, and so will not precipitate selective survival. In the case of natural selection, then, transition will come about when the internal stage is set for certain individuals to respond better to new external circumstances, or vice versa. Alongside natural selection, however, operates sexual selection (cf. Okanoya, Ch. 3), whereby a genetic pattern is successful because its carriers are preferred as mates. There are undoubtedly some strong correlations between sexually selected traits and the overall capacity to survive—not least because it makes sense to prefer a mate who is strong and capable. Nevertheless, it may not always be possible fully to understand just what it is about an apparently irrelevant trait—or indeed, as with the peacock's tail or the complex songs of Okanoya's finches, one that is a veritable liability—that makes it so attractive to the opposite sex.

Crow (Ch. 5) focuses on the possibility that one particular gene, ProtocadherinXY, may be responsible for a significant internal transition: the shifting of hemispheric dominance to, in most individuals, the left. While ProtocadherinXY should not be construed as a gene for language, he considers whether it may have provided a developmental platform for other changes. Key to his account are two observations. The first is that linguistic skills are gender-sensitive: boys and girls develop their language differently and at slightly different ages. This suggests that some part of the genetic code for language capabilities must be represented on the sex chromosomes. The second is that this code must be present on both the X and the Y chromosome, as indicated by comparisons of normal males and females with individuals who have an extra, or a missing, X chromosome. The process of transition that he describes entails the chance copying, in a single male individual, of part of the X chromosome onto the Y chromosome, doubling the dose. Since this mutation subsequently spread across the entire ancestry of modern humans, we may assume that it delivered a powerful advantage. An augmentation in communicative capabilities is a plausible candidate. Crow proposes that the mechanism of spread across the population was sexual selection, as females preferred mates with the trait over those without it. Meanwhile, females had always had two copies of this genetic material, since they possess two X chromosomes, but one copy would normally be suppressed. This dormant second dose offers an explanation for how women might also have developed the trait. Although the mechanisms are still not understood, it seems likely that variation in the degree of suppression of this second dose might have been open to sexual selection, as males, in their turn, preferred females in whom the trait was expressed. As mentioned earlier, Okanoya (Ch. 3) also favours sexual selection over natural selection for the proliferation of genes linked to linguistic abilities.

Chapter 6 concerns the transition to a mode of communication that used referential words. In line with Terrace (Ch. 4), Wray views reference as a late, rather than an early, stage in the evolution of language. She argues that a plausible explanation for the long stagnation of culture and technology between 1.4 and 0.5 million years ago is that there were no names for things or actions.

During that period, she proposes, communication was manipulative only, and was achieved using holistic messages with only generic reference. She likens this to the phenomenon of formulaic language today, whereby speakers can opt to reduce their, and/or their hearer's, processing by using prefabricated word strings with agreed holistic meanings, particularly in routine interactional situations. By tracing the inherent limitations of holistic messages as the only system of communication (whereas today it is one of two), she shows how, finally, words for people and things would come about incidentally, leading, in turn, to words for actions. The result would be that these new individual words could be juxtaposed, agrammatically, to express novel, but highly ambiguous messages, much as Bickerton (e.g. 1998) envisages for his protolanguage. Wray proposes that the word-based system did not replace the pre-existing holistic one, but rather worked alongside it, in a cooperative arrangement that survives to this day.

Knight (Ch. 7) presents a powerful account of the transition to linguistic expression as a sequence of causes and effects. As human physiology evolved, especially brain-size, women were occupied with an ever-longer period of pregnancy and nursing. Consequently, they were increasingly dependent on their mates to provide food and protection, yet also increasingly vulnerable to their infidelity. Knight builds on previous proposals (e.g. Knight 1998; Power 1998) to suggest that this led to familial alliances between women, focused on rituals that confused the external signals of sexual maturity and availability and drew male family members into a collective responsibility for protecting all the women. The combined context of social pacts, egalitarianism, and ritual make-believe provided, he argues, a context for the development of language that was safe from the inherent dangers of deliberate deception (see sect. 1.2.3 below).

Corballis (Ch. 8) proposes that the trigger to spoken language was the adoption of tool-making practices and, in particular, the need to offer instruction in tool-making. The link between work and transitions in man's evolution has been made before (e.g. Engels 1895/1977), but in Corballis's case there is a particular significance in associating manual activity with speech, since he proposes that the full human language capacity had first developed within the medium of manual signing. He reasons that there is a more plausible link between the development of semantic representation and the physical medium of iconic gesture than there is between semantics and vocal expression, which is, in all other species—and still in our own outside of language—subcortical and reflexive. Similarly, there would be much more scope for a gradual implementation of grammar onto gesture, to create a primitive or even fully-fledged grammatical language that was then appropriated to the vocal medium when the physical limitations of signing came into conflict with other activities. Like Wray (Ch. 6), he proposes that the development of technology might actually have been inhibited by the current linguistic system—in his case because of the incompatibility of tool-making and signing.

Although Corballis's proposal is unusual, it very clearly highlights the need for concrete evidence from archaeology regarding the nature of tool-making technology in different eras. Specifically, as Davidson (Ch. 9) points out, the making of tools, when it involves several steps, is likely to indicate a capacity for language of some kind, because both entail the ability to embody an idea in a form that is only indirectly linked to it. Davidson's chapter impacts on our need chronologically to locate the transition to symbolic representation using archaeological evidence. He argues against the strong hypothesis, prevailing in the literature (see, for instance, Mithen 1996: 117 ff.), that the physical structure of Acheulean hand-axes (made *c.*1.4 million years ago) necessarily indicates that their makers were capable of sequential planning and symbolic thought (see Terrace, Ch. 4, though, for evidence of these capacities in monkeys). One of his contentions is that the archaeologists' selection of fashioned stones for the category 'hand-axe' has been too exclusive, being based upon pre-existing expectations of how, and why, they were made. A more inclusive analysis casts doubt, Davidson argues, on the intention of the tool-makers to shape a single stone through several stages towards a planned end-product, something which, in turn, undermines the claim that such conceptualization was possible.

1.2.3 *Part III. External Triggers to Transition: Environment, Population, and Social Context*

Bickerton (Ch. 10) argues that although social intelligence, an internal variable, was undoubtedly relevant in the transition to full human language, the earlier transition to protolanguage is unlikely to have been triggered by social factors (compare Calvin and Bickerton 2000: 123). Rather, he looks to the impetus of the savannah environment which our ancestors inhabited from around 3 million years ago. In Bickerton's view, it was the need to convey information about food sources that spurred hominids into linguistic expression, first using isolated words in agrammatical arrangements, and only much later imposing a hierarchical syntactic structure. Thus, in his account, the dynamic of language emergence is natural selection in a context of intense survival pressure, not, as Okanoya (Ch. 3) and Crow (Ch. 5) both propose, sexual selection. Bickerton argues that his account offers a solution to the problem of deceit. It has been observed (e.g. Knight 1998; Power 1998) that once language is used to impart information not already known to, or immediately checkable by, the hearer, there is the potential for the speaker to gain advantages by deception. Why, for instance, tell others about a food source, which one will then have to share, or even entirely surrender to them, when one can lie to them to get them out of the way while one eats the food oneself? The logical problem, then, is how language was able to emerge without immediately spiralling into self-destruction, as the credibility of its content was consistently undermined. For Power, Knight, and others, the key is the establishment of trust, and the apportioning of status and its rewards to those who act in the interests of the whole group. Bickerton, however, focuses not on the social context but on the pragmatics of communicating about food sources. He argues that although food source information is not always *immediately* checkable, it is certainly checkable in the short term, so that deception would be quickly detected. Any temporary gain would be strongly countermanded by the consequences of being found out.

The chapters by Tonkes and Wiles (Ch. 11) and by Steels *et al.* (Ch. 12) explore computer simulations of simple communication. In both cases, clear evidence is found for the spontaneous emergence of 'language' from representations of ideas in random codes. Tonkes and Wiles show that a community of speakers will converge on a vocabulary if new individuals first learn a small part of the language from their neighbours. They show that the speed of turnover in a population, the size of the population, the amount of learning undergone, and the part that poor learners are allowed to play in the teaching of others, are all variables capable of affecting the success with which the population settles into an agreed system of communication. Steels *et al.* report on their experiments with robots, in which effective communication using a shared vocabulary emerges in these entirely naïve organisms, provided they share a conceptual space. The experiments involve a robot choosing a visually defined item and attempting to tell another robot what it is. They, too, found that crucial variables are the amount of feedback and the size and stability of the population and environment.

Drawing on evidence from a quite different source, Ragir (Ch. 13) argues that, for individuals with the full genetic capacity for language, the trigger to its emergence is a suitable social environment. She compares a number of instances of fully structural sign languages emerging, or not emerging, from home sign pidgins. The situations in which sign language did not emerge were those in which (1) signers were viewed as outsiders or as deficient, and so were not integrated into the wider community, (2) the population was static, rather than continually refreshed by new members, or (3) the individuals were too geographically distant to function as a speech community. As in the computer simulation studies, emerging grammar seemed to be a natural product of negotiated meaning.

1.2.4 *Part IV. The Onward Journey: Determining the Shape of Language*

The hierarchical syntax of full human language represents the zenith of what Hockett (1960) terms 'productivity'. Syntactic theory demonstrates that human syntax is recursive, which means that constituents can be embedded into other constituents without destroying the overall grammatical structure. This in turn is the cornerstone of creativity, since it permits the use of a finite set of units to express an infinite number of potential messages, which are immediately comprehensible to a hearer who knows the language.

The significant final step, then, is the transition from no, or limited, productivity to full productivity, through the adoption of the full set of syntactic principles that characterize the world's languages. In this final part of the book, attention is paid to examining assumptions that have been made about the nature of this transition and, in particular, whether it is to be seen as a single event now past, or a continuing process. The chapters all consider which features of language, as we conceive of it today, are immutable and hard-wired, and which, of those that are, are language-specific, rather than a by-product of other mental faculties. An important theme is the extent to which we should view language as shaped by the general capabilities of the human brain and/or our communicative priorities, rather than, as Chomsky has proposed, an independently defined system with which the other modules of the human brain, and the pragmatic demands of communication, have to cope as best they can. All the chapters express scepticism about some aspect of the Chomskian concept of a *universal grammar*. In some cases, this extends to challenging the related idea that all languages are intrinsically the same in nature, conforming to a single *uniformitarian* structure.

Burling (Ch. 14) draws on evidence from language acquisition in children to challenge the oft-made claim that syntax constitutes a bundle of features that belong together and come as a package. He refutes an implication of this position, that children suddenly develop the entire package, and therefore do not make syntactic errors over the longer time-frame. He argues that there is ample evidence for a very slow development of syntactic capabilities in children, often overlooked because it is considerably masked by their ability to cope with input way beyond their production capabilities, and their tendency to avoid producing forms at the limit of their abilities. Although he concedes that patterns of acquisition in children do not necessarily tell us anything about how language evolved, his point is that child language should not be invoked as indicative of the potential for syntax to appear as a bundle in human evolution.

In Ch. 15, Hurford tackles the question of whether linguistic structure is more appropriately viewed as a product of mental representation, on the one hand, or of how we externalize our thoughts in the act of communication, on the other. He argues for the latter. In doing so, he contests the implications of the Chomskian model, and also, more directly, Bickerton's (1990) account of the transition from protolanguage to fully syntactic language. With Pinker and Bloom (1990) and Sampson (1997), he favours the view that the structure of language arose largely independently of the way we organize thought. Rather, it is to be attributed to the demands of expressing thought effectively to others.

In similar vein, Christiansen and Ellefson (Ch. 16) argue that language structures reflect practical constraints on processing, particularly the handling of complex sequences—compare Tonkes and Wiles (Ch. 11), and also Okanoya (Ch. 3) and Terrace (Ch. 4), on the importance of being able to deal with complex configurations. For instance, they offer experimental evidence, from artificial language learning, that constructions violating principles of universal grammar, such as subjacency, will be naturally edited out of a language on the basis of their poor learnability. Thus, there is no need to invoke a pre-existing, hard-wired, specifically linguistic determinant of universal grammatical constraints. Furthermore, although language undoubtedly offers advantages sufficient to effect selectional pressures in humans, it must also be seen as, itself, adaptive. That is, features compatible with the constraints of the human brain are selected in preference to features that are less easily processed.

Chapters 17 and 18, by Newmeyer and by Heine and Kuteva respectively, examine evidence for language continuing to evolve, and challenge the claim that the transition to full human language, through the acquisition of universal grammar, was a single and discrete event. Their findings challenge the assumption, known as uniformitarianism, that all human languages, across ancient and modern time, have been equal in complexity. Both chapters present arguments based on evidence for unidirectionality in language change. Newmeyer considers the potential effects on language of the changing communicational needs of speakers, and their processing options, including, in more recent times, those made available by literacy. Heine and Kuteva home in on evidence for grammaticalization as a unidirectional force in language change. The logical corollary of their argument is that the noun and verb classes are the most ancient, and other properties of language have evolved from them.

1.3 A Field in Transition

An evolving field of research such as this one quickly takes stock of the known, and explores ever new ways of identifying the most robust frameworks for proceeding into the unknown. Two immediate challenges offer themselves to us. Meeting them is a prerequisite, if research into the evolution of language is to undergo its own future transitions.

1.3.1 *The Challenge of Interdisciplinarity*

It is both a strength and a weakness of research into the evolution of language that the questions it addresses are fundamentally cross-disciplinary. The weakness lies in the difficulty that individuals may have in fully taking into account, let alone satisfactorily evaluating, the work of those in other fields of investigation. It is not uncommon to find that a carefully thought-out theory based on research in one area draws relatively indiscriminately on claims from another, often on the basis of their visibility, currency, or comprehensibility, rather than their robustness. Linguists, for instance, are often frustrated by the failure of those in other fields to appreciate just how complex language is, and amazed at how its emergence can be portrayed by non-linguists as unproblematic. Experts in primatology are similarly disappointed by the glib comments and simplified descriptions of ape behaviour given by those who have never observed it in detail, and palaeontologists would no doubt argue that only they fully appreciate the difficulties in ascertaining how the different parts of the fossil evidence fit together.

Gatherings such as the Evolution of Language conferences in Edinburgh (1996), London (1998), and Paris (2000) certainly have made it easier for researchers to familiarize themselves with each others' work, while books like this and its predecessors (Hurford *et al.* 1998; Knight *et al.* 2000), along with other series such as *Studies in Language Origins* (Wind *et al.* 1989, 1994; Von Raffler-Engel *et al.* 1991), and *Archaeology and Language* (Blench and Spriggs 1999) offer a forum for chapters to be juxtaposed in ways that would not be possible under the auspices of a single discipline. Nevertheless, there is still too little true cross-fertilization of ideas. Since few individuals have the time or resources needed to become an expert in half a dozen different disciplines, the solution must lie in more opportunities for collaborative interdisciplinary work.

1.3.2 *Joined-Up Theory*

A further challenge for the field is to make the set of individual accounts more 'joined-up'. Many hypotheses will not be properly tested until they are juxtaposed with hypotheses dealing with other parts of the evolution story. Although individuals may, and do, point to aspects of compatibility between their own and another's account, a more methodical approach is needed. Almost all theories, of necessity, have to place themselves, explicitly or implicitly, somewhere on the time line between the present and 5 million years ago, when humans and chimpanzees shared a common ancestor. Similarly, each one makes some sort of statement about the scope of its coverage, and which aspects of language evolution it most relates to. It should, therefore, be possible to evaluate whole sets of accounts relative to each other, at least at the broad level. Putting this into practice is not easy, but surely is a worthwhile pursuit. To flesh out the idea, let us consider one such potential macro-scenario, drawing mostly on the collection in this book for illustration.

Since most researchers will be interested in seeking support for their own hypotheses, the practical way to construct a macro-scenario is to identify a focal point: one account that is taken, for the purposes of the exercise, to be correct. From here, other accounts are tested on the basis of their compatibility with it and, as one or more is identified as compatible, each of these is used as the basis for testing others. The aim is to map out a set of potential routes through the entire period of interest, and to articulate, for each hypothesis under assessment, what, precisely, about it makes it compatible, or incompatible, with the focal account.

In this example, the focal point is Corballis's proposal, in this volume, that words and syntax developed first in the context of manual signing, and only much later shifted to the vocal medium. Taking this scenario to be true, how must the rest of the macro-scenario shape up around it? The questions that we might ask include:

- Which existing accounts of the development of the articulatory mechanisms are most compatible with their not being employed for linguistic communication until 150,000 years ago, or later? Is Fitch's account of which properties of the vocal tract are *not* peculiar to humans equally valid in the context of speech or sign as the prevailing medium until evolutionarily modern times?
- Does Davidson's proposed downgrading of the skill entailed in hand-axe making in the Acheulean period support the idea that tool-making technology was inhibited by the use of the hands for communication? Or does his claim regarding the absence of planning in hand-axe making contradict the idea that its makers possessed a fully structured, albeit signed, language?
- Was there a signed protolanguage first? If so, can descriptions of protolanguage such as those of Bickerton and Wray simply be applied to sign, or are they too dependent on the vocal medium to be compatible?
- How would the first signs have originated? Can the shorthand 'nursing poke' and 'raised hand' gestures of the chimp (Tomasello *et al.* 1994; Tomasello and Call 1997), which Knight discusses, be viewed as the first step towards a fully symbolic gesture set under cultural transmission? Indeed, is there a direct parallel between a model of onomatopoeic sounds becoming words and iconic gestures becoming signs?
- Is Okanoya's suggestion, that syntax developed as a meaningless vocal display, transferable to the medium of gesture?
- Given what is known about the left lateralization of sign language (e.g. Hickok, Bellugi, and Klima 2001), can Crow's account of a genetic basis for transition apply to the adoption of sign language as easily as to spoken language?
- How does Corballis's account relate to Ragir's findings about the spontaneous development of grammatical sign languages today?

- How long should we be imagining syntactic sign language to have existed before speech took over, and what light might this throw on the question of whether universal grammar is a stable or evolving feature of language?
- Can computers simulate the boot-strapped emergence of gestures from random attempts to communicate, in precisely the same way as they simulate the emergence of spoken communication?

According to how each of these questions is answered, the map of events will become filled in differently. Each answer will generate its own questions, the answers to which, in turn, fill in more of the picture. One type of outcome could be a multilevel time-line, which depicts such events as the transitions to symbolic communication, cultural transmission, vocal articulation, and syntax, relative to changes in technological practices, neurological and psychological organization, social behaviour, demographic balance, and environmental circumstances.

By placing different hypotheses, from different disciplines, into the 'focal' position, and examining the way in which they impact on other hypotheses, it should slowly become clear which proposals are the most tolerant of the evidence from elsewhere. These are the accounts that we should take most seriously. However, the others should not be lightly discarded. Thinking around an idea, as is proposed here, should place us in a better position to judge how an account that seems intractable at present could re-enter the frame if one variable is changed, as may happen when, say, a new fossil is discovered, a new gene is identified, or a bonobo reveals new capacities for language-like behaviour. In short, the purpose of seeking joined-up accounts is to establish a more sophisticated cross-disciplinary framework within which to assess new ideas, so that the many lines of research can support each other in their quest for better models of language evolution.

FURTHER READING

There is not as yet an impartial, comprehensive overview of the current research in language evolution, and the best way to become familiar with the major ideas in the field is to read the research papers themselves. The following collections and journals are a useful starting-point, Harris's book being a collection of old and out of print papers:

BLENCH, R., and SPRIGGS, M. (1999), *Archaeology and Language* (4 vols.; London: Routledge).

HARRIS, R. (1996) (ed.), *The Origin of Language* (Bristol: Thoemmes Press).

HURFORD, J. R., STUDDERT-KENNEDY, M., and KNIGHT, C. (1998) (eds.), *Approaches to the Evolution of Language* (Cambridge: Cambridge University Press).

KNIGHT, C., STUDDERT-KENNEDY, M., and HURFORD, J. R. (2000) (eds.), *The Evolutionary Emergence of Language* (Cambridge: Cambridge University Press).

VON RAFFLER-ENGEL, W., WIND, J., and JONKER, A. (1991) (eds.), *Studies in Language Origins*, ii (Amsterdam: John Benjamins).

WIND, J., JONKER, A., ALLOTT, R., and ROLFE, L. (1994) (eds.), *Studies in Language Origins*, iii (Amsterdam: John Benjamins).

WIND, J., PULLEYBANK, E. G., DEGROLIER, E., and BICHAKJIAN, B. H. (1989) (eds.), *Studies in Language Origins*, i (Amsterdam: John Benjamins).

REFERENCES

BATALI, J. (1998), 'Computational Simulations of the Emergence of Grammar', in Hurford *et al.* (1998: 405–26).

BICKERTON, D. (1990), *Language and Species* (Chicago: University of Chicago Press).

—— (1996), *Language and Human Behaviour* (London: UCL Press).

—— (1998), 'Catastrophic Evolution: The Case for a Single Step from Protolanguage to Full Human Language', in Hurford *et al.* (1998: 341–58).

BLENCH, R. and SPRIGGS, M. (1999), *Archaeology and Language* (4 vols.; London: Routledge).

CALVIN, W. H., and BICKERTON, D. (2000), *Lingua ex Machina* (Cambridge, Mass.: MIT Press).

CHENEY, D. L., and SEYFARTH, R. M. (1990), *How Monkeys See the World* (Chicago: University of Chicago Press).

ENGELS, F. (1895), 'Anteil der Arbeit an der Menschwerdung des Affen', *Die Neue Zeit* (Stuttgart) 14/2: 545–54, reprinted in the Kleine Bücherei des Marxismus-Leninismus series (1977) (Berlin: Dietz Verlag).

HICKOK, G., BELLUGI, U., and KLIMA, E. S. (2001), 'Sign Language in the Brain', *Scientific American* 284/6: 42–9.

HOCKETT, C. F. (1960), 'The Origin of Speech', *Scientific American*, 203/3: 89–96.

HURFORD, J. R., STUDDERT-KENNEDY, M., and KNIGHT, C. (1998) (eds.), *Approaches to the Evolution of Language: Social and Cognitive Bases* (Cambridge: Cambridge University Press).

KIRBY, S. (1998), 'Fitness and the Selective Adaptation of Language', in Hurford *et al.* (1998: 359–83).

—— (2000), 'Syntax without Natural Selection: How Compositionality Emerges from Vocabulary in a Population of Learners', in Knight *et al.* (2000: 303–23).

KNIGHT, C. (1998), 'Ritual/Speech Coevolution: A Solution to the Problem of Deception', in Hurford *et al.* (1998: 68–91).

KNIGHT, C., STUDDERT-KENNEDY, M., and HURFORD, J. R. (2000) (eds.), *The Evolutionary Emergence of Language: Social Function and the Origins of Linguistic Form* (Cambridge: Cambridge University Press).

MITHEN, S. (1997), *The Prehistory of the Mind* (London: Thames & Hudson).

PINKER, S., and BLOOM, P. (1990), 'Natural Language and Natural Selection', *Behavioral and Brain Sciences*, 13/4: 707–27.

POWER, C. (1998), 'Old Wives' Tales: The Gossip Hypothesis and the Reliability of Cheap Signals', in Hurford *et al.* (1998: 111–29).

SAMPSON, G. (1997), *Educating Eve: The 'Language Instinct' Debate* (London: Cassell).

TOMASELLO, MICHAEL, and CALL, J. (1997), *Primate Cognition* (New York and Oxford: Oxford University Press).

——NAGELL, K., OLGUIN, R., and CARPENTER, M. (1994), 'The Learning and Use of Gestural Signals by Young Chimpanzees: A Trans-generational Study', *Primates* 35: 137–54.

VON RAFFLER-ENGEL, W., WIND, J., and JONKER, A. (1991) (eds.), *Studies in Language Origins*, ii (Amsterdam: John Benjamins).

WIND, J., JONKER, A., ALLOTT, R., and ROLFE, L. (1994) (eds.), *Studies in Language Origins*, iii (Amsterdam: John Benjamins).

——PULLEYBANK, E. G., DEGROLIER, E., and BICHAKJIAN, B. H. (1989) (eds.), *Studies in Language Origins*, i (Amsterdam: John Benjamins).

PART I

Making Ready for Language:
Necessary, but not Sufficient

2 Comparative Vocal Production and the Evolution of Speech: Reinterpreting the Descent of the Larynx

W. Tecumseh Fitch

2.1 Introduction

2.1.1 *The Importance of Comparative Data*

Since Darwin the comparative method has been recognized as one of the most powerful tools for deriving and testing hypotheses about evolution. The comparative method provides a principled way to use empirical data from living animals to deduce the behavioural abilities of extinct common ancestors, along with clues to the adaptive function of those abilities. For example, in the study of the evolution of speech, analysis of the vocal behaviour of non-human primates can help identify homologies (characteristics shared by common descent), which in turn allow us to infer the presence or absence of particular characteristics in shared ancestors. Second, examples of convergent evolution (where similar traits have evolved independently in different lineages, presumably due to similar selective forces) can provide clues to the types of problems that particular morphological or behavioural mechanisms are 'designed' to solve. Unfortunately, we know much more about human speech than we do about vocal communication in any other species, and thus the empirical database for comparative study is weaker than desirable. However, interest in non-human vocal production has exploded recently, in terms of both peripheral factors and central ner-

The extremely helpful comments of Alison Wray and an anonymous reviewer on an earlier version of this manuscript are gratefully acknowledged. Takeshi Nishimura, Kyoto Primate Research Institute, Japan, graciously provided the MRI image of the chimpanzee in Fig. 2.1. Megan, A. W. Crompton's dog, barked for Fig. 2.2.

vous control, and we can look forward to rapid advances in the near future.

The other major approach to analysing the evolutionary history of a trait is based on the fossil record. Analyses of fossils can provide information about the order in which different traits were acquired during phylogeny (e.g. large brains and bipedalism in hominid evolution, or feathers and flight in birds), and thus place important constraints upon evolutionary hypotheses. Fossils can also provide dating information, thus allowing collation with data from other fossils and sites, and inferences about the climate, ecology, and competitors faced by the fossilized organism when alive.

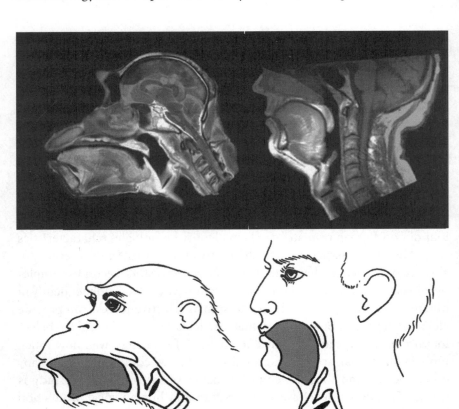

Unfortunately, the fossil record is notoriously incomplete, and there are no guarantees that any individuals in key transitional stages in evolution will have been preserved. More importantly, fossils typically preserve only skeletal morphology, and thus provide reliable indicators of behaviour only when the behaviour in question requires unambiguous morphological modifications (as habitual bipedalism and powered flight do).

For the last thirty years, fossil analysis has been the dominant approach to the study of the evolution of speech. Paleoanthropologists have attempted to use the hominid fossil record to deduce the timing and order of speech-related adaptations such as the descent of the larynx and enlargement of cortical regions. This approach was initiated by the seminal observation by P. Lieberman *et al.* (1969) that the human vocal tract differs from that in other primates in having a lowered larynx (Fig. 2.1), a configuration that allows humans to make a wider variety of vowels that other primate species. Soon afterward, P. Lieberman and Crelin (1971) used a reconstruction of the Neanderthal soft tissue vocal tract, based on basicranial anatomy and some comparative data, to infer that larynx position in Neanderthals was closer to that of other primates than of modern humans. This suggested that Neanderthals could not make certain speech sounds that are typical of modern human languages. Although those authors never claimed that Neanderthals lacked language entirely, the paper spurred a vigorous (and still ongoing) debate about the speech and language capacities of Neanderthals, and extinct hominids in general (Falk 1975; DuBrul 1976; Arensburg *et al.* 1989, 1990). A review of this literature makes clear that there is still no general agreement about when articulate speech came to play the crucial role that it subserves in modern human language. This is not surprising, because the vocal tract is largely made up of soft tissue that does not fossilize, and thus there are no obvious skeletal indicators that would provide unambiguous evidence for speech. Thus, despite many years of hard work, new fossils, and creative new approaches to analysis, the currently available fossil data are inconclusive.

Meanwhile, the comparative approach to the evolution of speech has languished. Despite some early work on the anatomy and physiology of vocal production in non-human primates that adopted an explicitly comparative approach (P. Lieberman 1968; P. Lieberman *et al.* 1969), there has been very little further work in this vein until recently. In this chapter I will review these recent comparative data on vocal production in non-human animals and explore their implications for theories of the evolution of the human vocal tract and speech capabilities. After some terminological preliminaries, I first review results from the comparative study of primate vocal communication, which provide crucial insights into the primitive features of primate communication systems that were inherited by our early hominid ancestors. I then turn to recent anatomical and physiological data on animal vocal production. These data demonstrate great mobility of the larynx in non-human mammals, and cast doubt upon the notion that skeletal features could provide unambiguous cues to vocal capabilities. The animal data also suggest alternative hypotheses for the descent of the larynx in human evolution. I conclude that the comparative approach provides a rich source of hypotheses and predictions about vocal evolution, and in some cases the means for testing them empirically.

2.1.2 Terminology

Language and Speech

'Language' is a system for representing and communicating complex conceptual structures, irrespective of modality. Theoretically, language might have originally been encoded gesturally rather than vocally (Hewes 1973; Falk 1980; Corballis 1992, and this volume). Signed languages and the written word are contemporary examples of non-spoken language. In contrast, 'speech' refers to the particular auditory/vocal medium typically used by humans to convey language. Although speech and language are closely linked today, their evolution may not have been, and in any case their component mechanisms can be analysed separately. The evolution of language presumably entailed complex conceptual structures, a drive to represent and communicate them, and systems of rules to encode them. The evolution of speech required vocalizations of adequate complexity to serve these linguistic needs, entailing a capacity for vocal imitation and learning, and a vocal tract with a wide phonetic range. The evolution of human speech may also have required perceptual specializations (Liberman and Mattingly 1985; P. Lieberman 1984; Hauser 1996), but there are currently no clear candidates for human-specific speech perception mechanisms, and in this chapter I will focus mainly on speech production.

One of the great problems in studying the evolution of language from a comparative viewpoint is the lack of clear homologues to human language in the communication systems of other animals, most glaringly in other non-human primates. Fortunately, this limitation does not apply in the realm of speech. Most peripheral aspects of human vocal production are shared with other mammals, allowing us to analyse the evolution of speech by studying these aspects from a comparative perspective. The acoustics, musculature, innervation, and peripheral motor control of human and animal vocal tracts are fundamentally similar, and are all open to experimental investigation. Such investigations have revealed a few key differences between human vocal production abilities and those underlying animal vocalizations, as detailed below.

Phonetics and Phonology
When discussing the evolution of speech, a key distinction is that between the mechanisms underlying human phonetic capabilities (the physiological capacity to make the wide variety of speech sounds used in contemporary human languages), and phonological capabilities (the neural capacities that underlie critical organizational structures of speech). While some researchers might consider the latter problem as part of speech evolution, others view it as an aspect of language evolution. This decision seems largely a matter of taste, as long as the distinction is made, and the topic at hand clearly defined. In the current review I focus exclusively on phonetic evolution, considering the evolution of phonology as an important problem in the evolution of language *per se*. For a Darwinian approach to phonology and the evolution of syllabic structure, see MacNeilage (1998).

2.2 Formants in Animal Communication

In this section I review recent work in the comparative vein that addresses the issue of potential evolutionary homologies between human speech and animal communication systems. I focus on the unquestioned importance of formants in human speech, and the much more sparse and recent data on the role of formants in animal communication. These new data unambiguously demonstrate that a wide variety of vertebrates, including many species of mammals and birds, both produce and perceive formants. This suggests that the use of formants in animal communication has a long evolutionary history, predating humans by millions of years, that can be readily explored with the comparative method.

Formants (from Latin *formare*, to shape) are the natural modes (or resonances) of the air contained in the vocal tract (Titze 1994; P. Lieberman and

Blumstein 1988). The pattern and movements of formants provide the most important acoustic cues in human speech. Each individual formant acts like a bandpass filter, letting certain frequencies pass through it unchanged in amplitude, while damping out all other frequencies. A single formant is thus specified by its centre frequency and a bandwidth. The formant centre frequency (typically shortened to just 'formant frequency') is the frequency that the formant allows to pass through with maximal amplitude. The bandwidth gives a measure of the breadth of this 'spectral sweet spot'. Perceptual experiments with humans indicate that formant bandwidth plays a relatively minor role in the perception of vowels and other formant-defined sounds, so most discussions of formants in human speech focus on their frequency. There is no non-technical word for the perceptual quality of formants, though it is generally one aspect of 'timbre'. None the less, formants are quite salient: the difference between 'beet' and 'boot' spoken at one pitch, is a difference in formants alone (corresponding to the vowels /i/ and /u/). Note that there is no relationship between formants and voice pitch (which is determined by the fundamental frequency, or vibration rate of the vocal 'cords' in the larynx): their independence is one of the central tenets of modern speech science. Thus it is a serious but regrettably common error to confuse formants with pitch.

A single vocal tract has many formants, which together define the vocal tract transfer function: the complex, multi-peaked filter created by the combination of all formants. In general it is possible to measure at least six formants in a human transfer function, but only the bottom three are necessary for most human phonetic distinctions to be preserved. The overall pattern of these formants is critical in speech (as opposed to the frequency of any single formant). The single most important determinant of the transfer function is the length of the vocal tract that produces it: long vocal tracts produce low-frequency, densely packed formant patterns. Thus all the formants of large men are shifted to lower frequencies relative to those of smaller men, or children (Fitch and Giedd 1999). Additionally, modifications in the overall shape of the vocal tract modify the frequencies of the lower formants, shifting them from their default position in a simple tube. These time-varying changes in formant pattern provide the most fundamental acoustic cues in human speech. Synthesized signals that preserve the time-varying pattern of formant frequencies, but eliminate all other acoustic cues, are understandable as speech by most listeners (Remez *et al.* 1981).

2.2.1 *Formants in Animal Vocalizations*

Given the vast literature on formant production and perception in speech and singing (Fant 1960; P. Lieberman and Blumstein 1988; Sundberg 1987; and Titze 1994 provide reviews), the literature on formants in animal communication is extremely limited. However, recent comparative data provide a clear indication that formant frequencies are prominent in the vocalizations of many diverse vertebrate species, and suggest that they may be more important functionally than previously recognized. In this section I briefly review these data, and their implications for the ancestral use of formants in primate communication (see Fitch and Hauser forthcoming for more detail).

P. Lieberman (1968; P. Lieberman *et al.* 1969) was the first to analyse formants in the vocalizations of non-human primates, focusing mainly on the relatively restricted frequency range and lack of temporal variability of formants in primate calls. Except for a spectrographic analysis by Richman (1976), and some prescient comments by Andrew (1976), work on formants in primate communication ceased for almost twenty years. During that period, the work of Suthers and colleagues on bats (Suthers and Fattu 1973; Suthers *et al.* 1988) and birds (Suthers and Hector 1988; Suthers 1994) provided abundant documentation of the importance of vocal tract resonances in vocal production in those groups. Further exploration of the role of formants in birdsong was provided by Nowicki (1987) and Brittan-Powell *et al.* (1997).

The 1990s saw a renaissance of interest in the role of formants in primate vocal production. Hauser *et al.* (1993) used audio-video analysis to demonstrate a correlation between lip position and formants in rhesus macaques (as suggested by P. Lieberman 1968). Because lip protrusion lengthens the vocal tract, it lowers formants. Hauser and Schön Ybarra (1994) went on to demonstrate the causal link between the two by experimentally eliminating lip movements with xylocaine injections. Shipley *et al.* (1991) described similar findings in domestic cats. Fitch and Hauser (1995) explored the significance of formants in the evolution of primate communication and their possible use as cues to body size. The first unambiguous demonstration that spectral peaks in primate vocalizations represent formants was provided by Fitch's (1997) work demonstrating a correlation between formant frequencies and vocal tract length. This work also showed that formants correlate with body size in macaques, confirming that formants could provide a reliable cue to body size (similar correlations were found in dogs by Riede and Fitch 1999). Owren *et al.* (1997), in a study of formants in baboon grunts, verified that these calls have an extremely restricted formant space relative to human speech, as argued for macaques by P. Lieberman *et al.* (1969). In sum, this work makes it clear that formants play an important role in vocal production in a diverse set of primates, and suggests that formants could convey useful information about body size in mammals. Do other members of the same species perceive this information?

2.2.2 Formant Perception in Animals

There is a long history of using animals as subjects in speech perception experiments. In general, these studies indicate that, given appropriate training, animals can learn to use formants to discriminate among different human speech sounds. This ability has been demonstrated in both birds (Hienz *et al.* 1981; Dooling and Brown 1990; Dooling 1992) and mammals (baboons: Hienz and Brady 1988; dogs: Baru 1975; cats: Dewson 1964). However, the relevance of these studies to animal communication is limited by the facts that (1) human voice parameters were used, and these may not tap into the same auditory perceptual systems or resources that animals have evolved for perceiving their own vocalizations, and (2) the animals received extensive training in these studies, and the results thus tell us less about pre-existing auditory capabilities than about skills the animals can acquire. In addition, 'talking' birds such as parrots and mynahs can imitate human formants (Klatt and Stefanski 1974; Nottebohm 1976; Warren *et al.* 1996) which implies an ability to perceive these cues in speech without training. In summary, while these studies show that many species have a latent ability to perceive formants, they do not show that this ability is used in their species-specific communication systems.

More conclusive evidence was provided by Owren's groundbreaking work with vervet monkeys. Owren and Bernacki (1988) used linear predictive coding (LPC) analysis of vervet 'snake' and 'eagle' alarm calls to separate characteristics of source waveform, presumed vocal tract filtering functions, and temporal patterning which distinguished these calls. Owren (1990) then used an operant paradigm to test classification of synthetic calls in which each of these characteristics was modified independently. The results indicated that changes in the spectrum played the dominant perceptual role in distinguishing the two call types, raising the possibility that changes in vocal tract shape convey distinctive information in these calls. However, Owren did not isolate these spectral cues to ensure that they derived from formants rather than other sources (e.g. frication noise, laryngeal source, etc.). Another recent study (Sommers *et al.* 1992) compared the formant perception abilities of humans and macaques directly, and found that the monkeys perceived formants in synthesized signals as accurately as do humans. In both of these studies the use of an operant paradigm, with trained animals pressing levers in a laboratory setting, still allowed extensive learning to take place.

To overcome these difficulties, we developed (Fitch and Kelley 2000) a naturalistic testing paradigm to examine the spontaneous reaction of naïve birds and primates to conspecific calls that varied only in formant frequency. Loudspeakers were hidden in bushes or behind blinds and thus invisible to the subjects. Using a habituation/dishabituation paradigm, a set of sounds was played repeatedly until the animal habituated (no longer showed a vigilant head-raise or head-turn response). Then, we played a resynthesized version of one of these calls that differed from the original only in its formant frequencies. These formant-shifted calls elicited a renewed response ('dishabituation') in most cases. A control playback showed that subjects were not responding to artefacts induced by synthesis. These studies demonstrate that non-human subjects, with no training, responded to changes in formant frequency in conspecific calls. Together, the findings reviewed here indicate that formant perception is not an evolutionary novelty evolved by humans, or by primates, and suggest that formants may play an important role in the communication systems of many non-human vertebrates.

2.2.3 *The Evolution of Formant Perception*

Understanding how formants came to assume their central role in human speech demands an understanding of the role they played in pre-linguistic hominids. Data from non-human mammals allow us to reconstruct several non-exclusive possibilities for the ancestral role of formants in acoustic communication. The first is that formants play a role in individual identification (Hauser 1992; Owren 1996; Rendall *et al.* 1996). Because each individual's vocal tract differs slightly in length, shape, nasal cavity dimensions, and other anatomical features, differences in formant frequencies or bandwidths could provide cues to the identity of a vocalizer. Many vertebrates can distinguish the voices of different individuals, such as their offspring (or parents), or familiar and unfamiliar neighbours. Thus, a role for formants as a component of 'vocal signatures' could be widespread in vertebrate communication systems.

Formants also provide an indication of the body size of a vocalizer. Vocal tract length is positively correlated with body size in humans, monkeys, and dogs (Fitch 1997; Fitch and Giedd 1999; Riede and Fitch 1999). In turn, formant frequencies are closely tied to vocal tract length: large individuals with long vocal tracts have low formant frequencies. (This formant cue is completely independent from voice pitch, which in fact has no correlation with body size in adult humans; Künzel 1989.) These correlations are surprisingly strong (r = −0.88 in macaques), suggesting that our mammalian ancestors could have used formant frequencies to estimate body size accurately from vocalizations. This would be useful in many contexts, e.g. gauging the size of a stranger in darkness or dense foliage. Perceptual mechanisms for judging size may in turn have provided a pre-adaptation for 'vocal tract normalization' (Fitch 1997), a critical aspect of speech perception whereby sounds from different-sized speakers are 'normalized' to yield equivalent percepts (Ladefoged and Broadbent 1957; Nearey 1978; P. Lieberman 1984). Such normalization allows us to recognize the /i/ vowel of a child and an adult as 'the same', despite significant differences in formant frequencies.

Summarizing this section, there is no doubt that the vocalizations of many different vertebrate species possess formants. It follows from the basic physics of vocal production and the anatomy of the vocal tract that formants can provide cues to body size, and/or to individual identity. Furthermore, perceptual studies have shown that many vertebrates perceive formants, both in human speech and in conspecific calls. Direct comparisons of humans and monkeys show that monkeys perceive formants as accurately as human beings. Thus, rather than being in any way specific to human spoken language, formants have a long evolutionary history among mammals, and perhaps all terrestrial vertebrates, and we can expect that human speech perception was built upon this fundamental, shared primitive basis. This suggests that perceptual mechanisms previously believed to be unique to humans and evolved for speech (e.g. vocal tract normalization, P. Lieberman 1984) may in fact represent much more ancient adaptations.

2.3 Vocal Tract Anatomy and Physiology in Humans and Animals

A central puzzle in the evolution of speech revolves around the fact that human vocal tract anatomy differs from that of other primates. Fig. 2.1 shows MRI midsagittal sections through the heads of a chimpanzee and an adult human. It is evident that the human larynx rests much lower in the throat. Indeed, in most mammals, the larynx is located high enough in the throat to be engaged into the nasal passages, enabling simultaneous breathing and swallowing of fluids (Negus 1949; Crompton *et al.* 1997). This is also the case in human infants, who can suckle (orally) and breathe (nasally) simultaneously (Laitman and Reidenberg 1988). During human ontogeny, starting at about age 3 months, the larynx begins a slow descent to its lower adult position, which it reaches after three to four years (Sasaki *et al.* 1977; Senecail 1979; D. E. Lieberman *et al.* 2001). A second, smaller descent occurs in human males at puberty (Fant 1975; Fitch and Giedd 1999). A similar 'descent of the larynx' presumably occurred over the course of human evolution. Until recently, a descended larynx was believed to be unique to humans.

Although this difference between humans and animals has been known for more than a century (Bowles 1889; Howes 1889), it wasn't until the late 1960s that the acoustic significance of this configuration was recognized. Building upon advances in speech science, Lieberman and colleagues realized that the lowered larynx allows humans to produce a much wider range of formants than other mammals (P. Lieberman *et al.* 1969, 1972). The change in larynx position greatly expands our phonetic repertoire, because the human tongue can now move both vertically and horizontally within the vocal tract (this anatomical configuration, in the shape of an inverted L, is sometime termed a 'two-tube' vocal tract). By independently varying the area of the oral and pharyngeal tubes we can create a wide variety of vocal tract shapes and formant patterns. In contrast, a standard mammalian tongue rests flat in the long oral cavity, and cannot create vowels such as the /i/ in 'beet' or the /u/ in 'boot'. Such vowels are highly distinctive, found in virtually all languages (Maddieson 1984), and play an important role in allowing rapid, efficient speech communication to take place. These vowels require extreme constriction in some vocal tract regions, and dilation in others, which the two-tube configuration allows.

Since these early observations, the descent of the human larynx has played a central role in discussions of the evolution of speech. The high larynx position in the Neanderthal vocal tract reconstructed by Crelin (P. Lieberman and Crelin 1971) suggested that Neanderthal speech abilities were limited, relative to modern humans. It was also suggested that non-human mammals (and Neanderthals) were unable to close the velum completely, and thus produced only nasalized (and thus less discriminable vowels). Despite significant controversy (Morris 1974; Falk 1975; DuBrul 1976; Arensburg *et al.* 1990) this idea has been perennially cited since then (e.g. Diamond 1992). Recent researchers have emphasized the descent of the human larynx even further, suggesting that changes in our vocal anatomy represented the crucial first step towards particulate speech (Studdert-Kennedy 1998), or even syntax (Carstairs-McCarthy 1998).

Unfortunately, these interesting ideas have always rested upon an inadequate comparative database. The work on animal vocal anatomy dates mostly from the nineteenth century, and was based exclusively upon dissections of dead animals. By the time new techniques allowing anatomical visualization of living animals were developed, such as X-ray film (cineradiography) or MRI, the study of comparative anatomy had fallen from favour. Although occasional critics pointed out that the crucial issue is not the resting position of the larynx, but its position during vocalization (Nottebohm 1976), it is only recently that modern imaging techniques have been applied to live vocalizing mammals (Fitch 2000a). These data indicate that mammals lower the larynx as a matter of course during vocalization, in some cases approaching the 'two-tube' configuration typical of adult humans. Furthermore, new anatomical analyses show that we are not unique in our laryngeal position, because several other species also have a permanently descended larynx. These new comparative data, reviewed below, suggest that the importance of the descent of the larynx in speech evolution has been overemphasized.

2.3.1 *Cineradiographic Investigations of Animal Vocalization*

Fitch (2000a) presented X-ray video observations of vocalization in four mammal species (dogs, *Canis familiaris*; goats, *Capra hircus*; pigs, *Sus scrofa*; and cotton-top tamarins, *Saguinus oedipus*). The cineradiographic observations indicate that animal vocal tracts are surprisingly elastic and mobile, and that dead, formalin-fixed specimens provide a poor guide to the range of vocal movements available to the living animal. These data indicate that the vocal tract configuration of vocalizing animals, at least in dogs, pigs, goats, and monkeys, is more similar to that of human talkers than was previously inferred on the basis of dissections of dead animals. In particular, all four non-human species examined can and do lower their larynges into the oral cavity during loud vocalizations, either to a relatively minor degree (goats) or to a surprisingly extensive degree (dogs). Finally, all four species appear to raise the velum, closing off the nasal airway, during loud vocalizations.

Fig. 2.2 provides X-ray video stills from Fitch (2000*a*), illustrating the typical vocal tract movements during vocalization (in this case, a dog bark-

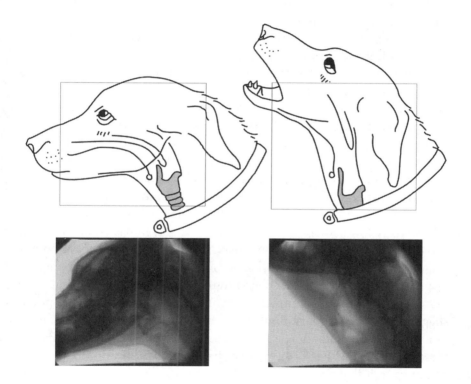

Fɪɢ. 2.2 Cineradiographic still images of dog barking. Left: resting breathing is through nasal cavity, larynx is in standard, high position. Right: during barking, the larynx is retracted deep into the pharynx, drawing the tongue body along, and the velum rises to close off the nasal cavity. See Fitch (2000*a*) for details.

ing). In the first frame, the larynx is in its resting position, high in the throat, and the epiglottis and velum are touching. Thus, the dog is breathing exclusively through its nose (as probably typical in mammals). In the second frame, the dog lowers the larynx considerably, raises the velum to close off the nasal cavity, and phonates. Thus the acoustic energy emanates from the oral cavity alone (the bark is not nasalized). The larynx is presumably lowered by contraction of the 'strap' muscles that stretch from the breastbone up to the larynx and hyoid (the sternohyoid and sternothyroid muscles). After ceasing phonation, the larynx rises again to a high position, but the epiglottis and velum are not re-engaged until the animal swallows. This sequence is typical of all the mammals examined in the study, and thus may represent the typical mammalian vocal gesture.

The most likely reason for the retraction of the larynx during vocalization in these species is that sounds emitted through the mouth are louder. This is because the nasal cavity, with its complex coiled turbinates and large surface area, absorbs sound more than the oral cavity (Fitch 2000a). In this context, it should be noted that the animals in this study were also able to produce purely nasal vocalizations, with no lowering of the larynx. This intranasal vocal configuration appears to be typical of quiet vocalizations (e.g., pig grunts, dog whines), supporting the loudness hypothesis.

These data have important implications for the evolution of speech. First of all, the surprising mobility of the larynx during vocalization suggests that static anatomy provides a poor indication of physiological capability. Thus, attempts to divine larynx position from the skeletal remains of fossil hominids must be viewed with suspicion. If dogs can achieve a substantially lowered larynx, without any changes in basicranial angle or hyoid morphology, it seems likely that Neanderthals, other fossil hominids, or chimpanzees could as well. Second, the fact that other mammals assume a two-tube vocal tract configuration during vocalization, but none the less do not produce complex formant movements or articulate speech, suggests that the primary limitations on their vocal ability result from limits on neural signalling rather than of peripheral anatomy. Finally, these data suggest that a lowered larynx during vocalization is in fact a primitive trait that we share with other mammals, rather than a uniquely human adaptation. What is unusual about our species is that the adult human larynx is permanently lowered, rather than dropping only during vocalization. However, other recent data show that even this difference is not uniquely human.

2.3.2 *Permanent Descent of Larynx in Non-human Mammals*

Although the cineradiographic data indicate that the low position of the human larynx may not be as significant as previously supposed, this config-uration is still unusual. But despite the claims of Negus (1949), this position is not unique to humans. In at least two species of deer, red deer (*Cervus elap-hus*) and fallow deer (*Dama dama*), the larynx of postpubertal males is per-manently lowered to a resting position comparable to that in humans (Fitch and Reby 2001). Both of these species of deer produce loud, low-pitched roars during the autumn rut that serve to intimidate rival males (Clutton-Brock and Albon 1979) and to entice and perhaps accelerate ovulation in females (McComb 1987, 1991). During these roars, the larynx is withdrawn as far as physiologically possible, to the inlet of the thorax, thus exaggerating the lowering of the larynx that accompanies vocalization in other mammals to an almost ridiculous extreme. Although the rest position of the larynx is similar to that of adult humans, there are some differences. First, the velum in males is greatly elongated, which probably allows them to have velar/epiglottic contact during resting breathing. Second, the linkage between the larynx and the hyoid bone in these deer is a formed by a highly elastic and extensible thyrohyoid ligament. Thus, while the larynx descends, the hyoid bone stays high in its normal resting position in these deer (unlike in humans, or dogs, where the hyoid descends along with the larynx). These data make it quite clear that the 'descent of the larynx' can no longer be con-sidered a uniquely human trait, and indicate that there must be other pos-sible adaptive reasons for laryngeal descent besides speech production.

It seems likely that some other species possess a similar ability to lower the larynx far beyond the normal mammalian level, or that of humans. The hyoid linkage of large cats of the genus *Panthera* (lions, tigers, leopards, jag-uars) has been known for more than a century to be quite unusual, in that it contains an elastic ligament that allows the hyoid and larynx to descend far from the base of the skull (Owen 1834; Pocock 1916; Hast 1989). Although cineradiographic observations of roaring lions are obviously difficult to obtain and not yet available, it seems likely that this unusual hyoid anatomy allows them to lower the larynx during vocalizations, like the deer described above. In Arabian camels (*Camelus dromedarius*), the hyoid anatomy is like that of red deer, with an elastic thyrohyoid ligament, suggesting that they too could lower the larynx during vocalization. Finally, the larynx occupies a permanently lowered position in koalas (*Phascolarctos cinereus*) (Sonntag

1921; Fitch, unpublished data). In koalas, the hyoid descends with the larynx, matching the human situation more closely than is the case with deer. These observations, although preliminary, suggest that extreme laryngeal lowering might be more common in mammals than one would have previously guessed. However, much more extensive comparative investigations of vocal production in a wide range of living mammals will be necessary before a comprehensive comparative appraisal of mammalian vocal anatomy and physiology is possible.

To summarize this section, recent comparative data suggest that the descent of the larynx in humans, though undeniably real and significant, has been overemphasized. The cineradiographic observations show that the position of the mammalian larynx (along with the hyoid and tongue) in the vocal tract is quite flexible, and the current data suggest that, in general, mammals lower the larynx when producing loud vocalizations. These observations also call into question the notion that static anatomy provides a valid indication of physiological (and thus phonetic) potential, and cast doubt on attempts to reconstruct vocal anatomy and speech capabilities on the basis of fossilized skeletal remains. In the next section I will briefly describe some of the more general implications of these data for the evolution of speech.

2.4 Implications of Comparative Data for the Evolution of Speech

2.4.1 *The Phonetic Importance of the Descended Larynx*

Although the observations above suggest that the descent of the larynx may not have played the crucial role in the evolution of humans posited by some theorists, the fact remains that the human larynx is unusual (though not unique) among mammals. Furthermore, the fundamental observation of P. Lieberman and colleagues (1969) still appears to hold true: humans produce a much wider range of formant frequencies than any other mammal species that has been analysed (e.g. Owren *et al.* 1997). I suggest that a modified form of Lieberman's account for this fact is still the best explanation for the descended larynx in modern humans: the two-tube vocal tract allows us to produce a wider range of vowels, and probably other speech sounds, than would a single-tube tract. I propose two modifications to Lieberman's original hypothesis that make it consonant with the new comparative data reviewed above.

The first proposed modification is that animal vocal tracts, with a high laryngeal resting position, do not provide an absolute anatomical barrier to a variety of vocal tract shapes, as was previously believed. Rather, with some muscular effort, a mammal such as a dog (or chimp) can pull the larynx down into a humanlike position, and then in principle have a much wider range of vocal tract shapes available. Indeed it seems likely that this is precisely how early hominids spoke: by retracting the larynx as needed during vocalization, and then returning it to a resting intranarial position. Once the larynx is temporarily lowered, there is no obvious anatomical or physiological barrier to the kind of rapid articulatory movements characteristic of modern human speech. In seeking to understand why neither dogs or chimps in fact perform such movements, it appears that more attention will need to be paid in the future to the phonetic needs of their vocal communication system, and to the neural mechanisms that control the articulators. From this neuroethological viewpoint, there is an obvious gradualistic path from the temporarily descended larynx typical of mammals to a permanently low larynx as in humans: for organisms which do a lot of talking (as we do) it may simply become more energetically efficient to leave the larynx low than to continually raise and lower it. A vocal tract that rests in the vocalization position may also aid in speed and accuracy of articulation, for example providing a solid and constant basis for the precise control necessary to make fricatives.

The second modification is that the current utility of the descended larynx (providing phonetic virtuosity) need not be identical to its original function at an earlier stage of phylogeny. Thus, some authors have proposed that the original descent of the larynx was an incidental byproduct of upright posture (DuBrul 1976), or of the facial retraction typical of hominid evolution. I do not personally find such arguments convincing (why don't other habitually upright mammals such as kangaroos or gibbons have a descended larynx? Why is the larynx still high in domestic animals bred to have short snouts, such as Pekingese dogs or Persian cats?) However, the form of the underlying argument seems sound: once the larynx attained a permanently low position, for whatever reason, the new vocal anatomy could be 'exapted' for its phonetic utility. I will now explore another possible evolutionary route to a low larynx, that is consistent with available data on vocal anatomy and acoustics, and can also explain the presence of a low larynx in species such as deer, where speech is lacking.

2.4.2 The Size Exaggeration Hypothesis for Descent of the Larynx

An alternative hypothesis for the descent of the larynx takes as its starting-point the fact mentioned earlier that formants are correlated with body size (Fitch 1997; Fitch and Giedd 1999; Riede and Fitch 1999). One effect of a lowered larynx is to increase vocal tract length (and consequently, to decrease formant frequencies). Thus, an animal with a lowered larynx can duplicate the vocalizations of a larger animal that lacks this ability, exaggerating the impression of size conveyed by its vocalizations. According to this hypothesis the original selective advantage of laryngeal lowering was to exaggerate size and had nothing to do with speech. This remains the sole function of the extreme laryngeal descent observed in male deer (and probably other mammals, such as lions, as well). Although Ohala (1983, 1984) initially offered a similar proposal, focusing on human males, as a refutation of Lieberman's hypothesis, I suggest that the two are compatible, with size exaggeration providing a pre-adaptation for the evolution of speech. Once the larynx was lowered, the increased range of possible formant patterns was co-opted for use in speech. Consistent with the size exaggeration hypothesis, a second descent of the larynx occurs at puberty in humans, but only in males (Fitch and Giedd 1999). This second descent, at least, appears to be part of a suite of sexually selected male pubertal changes that enhance apparent size, including shoulder broadening and facial hair growth.

The size exaggeration hypothesis is general, following from basic vocal anatomy and general acoustic principles, rather than being specific to hominids. This suggests that other taxa might show vocal tract elongation, and provide additional comparative insights into this phenomenon. A well-studied example is provided by a wide variety of bird species that possess an anatomical peculiarity called tracheal elongation. In these species, the trachea forms long loops or coils within the body. Because the bird sound source, called the syrinx, rests at the base of the trachea, this greatly elongates the bird's vocal tract, lowering its formant frequencies. A recent analysis (Fitch 1999) suggests that this serves to exaggerate the impression of size conveyed by vocalizations. Such exaggeration may be highly effective in animals that vocalize at night or from dense foliage. It is interesting to note that tracheal elongation in birds is not restricted to males. In species where both males and females are territorial, both sexes have elongated trachea, and in one polyandrous species the trait is found only in females (Fitch 1999). These data suggest that Ohala's (1983) exclusive focus on laryngeal descent in human males, 'to improve the male's ability to protect the family unit' (p. 13) was too narrow. Given the role of females as primary caregivers in most primates, such a function might well be expected for a mother's voice as well.

If the size exaggeration hypothesis is correct, the descent of the human larynx is but one example of a pervasive phenomenon in evolution: convergent evolution of an anatomical mechanism to exaggerate their vocally projected size, by diverse species. In humans, by hypothesis, this provided a necessary pre-adaptation which, together with important changes in neural control mechanisms, allowed hominids to exploit the vocal domain for linguistic communication more richly.

2.5 Conclusions

The comparative data reviewed in this chapter make clear that the empirical study of living animals can provide a rich source of data, insights, and testable hypotheses about the evolution of human speech. Studies of animal formant production and perception have revealed that the most basic mechanisms underlying speech have a long evolutionary history, and suggest that certain perceptual mechanisms that were once believed uniquely human (e.g., vocal tract normalization) may in fact be part of the primitive perceptual toolkit inherited from our pre-linguistic ancestors. Work on animal vocal production has shown that the descent of the larynx may also represent the exploitation of a pre-existing adaptation (for making loud sounds) present in many mammals. Finally, data from non-human species with elongated vocal tracts suggests that the initial impetus for the descent of the larynx in early hominids may have had nothing to do with speech, but instead functioned to exaggerate body size. In all these cases, the comparative data allow us to identify and investigate examples of homology and analogy, and thus specify the starting-point, selective forces, and subsequent phylogenetic history of some critical components of modern human speech.

Despite this impressive start, there is still a dearth of comparative data relevant to speech evolution. One of the most pressing needs is for a better understanding of the neural control mechanisms that underlie our ability to produce and imitate speech sounds. The most prominent vocal ability that differentiates humans from other primates is vocal imitation. Humans, like many birds, seals, whales, and dolphins, can imitate the sounds they hear, but our nearest primate relatives almost completely lack this ability (Studdert-

Kennedy 1983; Janik and Slater 1997; Fitch 2000*b*). It is worth noting that Darwin (1871) appreciated the importance of imitation, an important component of his theory that adaptations for singing in early hominids provided a pre-adaptation for speech (pp. 56–62). Unfortunately, the neural basis of our imitative ability remains almost completely mysterious, even in humans. Given the obvious importance of this ability for the formation of large vocabularies (without which syntax would be valueless), we can only hope that more data on vocal imitation in humans and other mammals will become available.

The last few decades have seen an acceleration of theoretical speculation concerning the evolution of speech and language. Much of this theory is based upon scraps of evidence from fossil hominids. Given the limitations of these fossils, which are unable strongly to constrain hypotheses or test predictions about speech evolution, an obvious alternative source of data is the comparative study of living non-human species. However, besides the seminal work of Lieberman, and a few lone researchers such as Hauser, Owren, Suthers, and their colleagues, there has been surprisingly little modern research into mammalian vocal production, animal formant perception, or other topics extremely relevant to the evolution of speech. Almost all data on mammal vocal anatomy is fifty or more years old, and thus predates an adequate theory of vocal production. Thus aspects of vocal anatomy that can today be recognized as critical (e.g. descended larynges) went unnoticed or unmentioned by these anatomists. As a result, there is still a great deal to learn about animal vocal production. Modern visualization and signal processing tools developed to study speech are only now beginning to be applied to non-human mammals, and with some 4,000 species still unstudied, any sweeping generalizations about how mammals make and perceive sound are obviously premature. None the less, the data reviewed here clearly illustrate the value of an empirical, comparative approach to understanding the evolutionary precursors of human speech perception and production.

FURTHER READING

HAUSER, M. D., and KONISHI, M. (1999), *The Design of Animal Communication* (Cambridge, Mass: MIT Press/Bradford).

LIEBERMAN, P. (2000), Human Language and our Reptilian Brain: The Subcortical Bases of Speech, Syntax and Thought (Cambridge, Mass: Harvard University Press).

MACNEILAGE, P. F., and DAVIS, B. L. (2000), 'On the Origin of Internal Structure of Word Forms', *Science*, 288: 527–31.

REFERENCES

ANDREW, R. J. (1976), 'Use of Formants in the Grunts of Baboons and Other Nonhuman Primates', *Annals of the New York Academy of Sciences*, 280: 673–93.

ARENSBURG, B., SCHEPARTZ, L. A., TILLIER, A. M., VANDERMEERSCH, B., and RAK, Y. (1990), 'A Reappraisal of the Anatomical Basis for Speech in Middle Paleolithic Hominids', *American Journal of Physical Anthropology*, 83: 137–46.

——TILLIER, A. M., VANDERMEERSCH, B., DUDAY, H., SCHEPARTZ, L. A., and RAK, Y. (1989), 'A Middle Paleolithic Human Hyoid Bone', *Nature* 338, 758–60.

BARU, A. V. (1975), 'Discrimination of Synthesized Vowels [a] and [i] with Varying Parameters (Fundamental Frequency, Intensity, Duration and Number of Formants) in Dog', in G. Fant and M. A. A. Tatham (eds.), *Auditory Analysis and Perception of Speech* (New York: Academic Press).

BOWLES, R. L. (1889), 'Observations upon the Mammalian Pharynx, with Especial Reference to the Epiglottis', *Journal of Anatomy and Physiology* (London), 23: 606–15.

BRITTAN-POWELL, E. F., DOOLING, R. J., LARSEN, O. H., and HEATON, J. T. (1997), 'Mechanisms of Vocal Production in Budgerigars (*Melopsittacus undulatus*)', *Journal of the Acoustical Society of America*, 101: 578–89.

CARSTAIRS-MCCARTHY, A. (1998), 'Synonymy Avoidance, Phonology and the Origin of Syntax', in J. R. Hurford, M. Studdert-Kennedy, and C. Knight (eds.), *Approaches to the Evolution of Language: Social and Cognitive Bases* (New York: Cambridge University Press).

CLUTTON-BROCK, T. H., and ALBON, S. D. (1979), 'The Roaring of Red Deer and the Evolution of Honest Advertising', *Behaviour*, 69: 145–70.

CORBALLIS, M. (1992), 'On the Evolution of Language and Generativity', *Cognition*, 44: 197–226.

CROMPTON, A. W., GERMAN, R. Z., and THEXTON, A. J. (1997), 'Mechanisms of Swallowing and Airway Protection in Infant Mammals (*Sus domesticus* and *Macaca fasicularis*)', *Journal of Zoology* (London) 241: 89–102.

DARWIN, C. (1871), *The Descent of Man and Selection in Relation to Sex* (London: John Murray).

DEWSON, J. H. (1964), 'Speech Sound Discrimination by Cats', *Science*, 141: 555–6.

DIAMOND, J. (1992), *The Third Chimpanzee* (New York: HarperCollins).

DOOLING, R. J. (1992), 'Hearing in Birds', in D. B. Webster, R. F. Fay, and A. N. Popper (eds.), *The Evolutionary Biology of Hearing* (New York: Springer-Verlag), 545–60.

——and BROWN, S. D. (1990), 'Speech Perception by Budgerigars (*Melopsittacus undulatus*): Spoken Vowels', *Perception & Psychophysics*, 47: 568–74.

DUBRUL, E. L. (1976), 'Biomechanics of Speech Sounds', *Annals of the New York Academy of Sciences*, 280: 631–42.

FALK, D. (1975), 'Comparative Anatomy of the Larynx in Man and the Chimpanzee: Implications for Language in Neanderthal', *American Journal of Physical Anthropology*, 49: 171–8.

FALK, D. (1980), 'Language, Handedness, and Primate Brains: Did the Australopithecines Sign?', *American Anthropologist*, 82: 72–8.

FANT, G. (1960), *Acoustic Theory of Speech Production* (The Hague: Mouton & Co.).

——(1975), 'Non-uniform Vowel Normalization', *Speech Transactions Laboratory Quarterly Progress and Status Report*, 2–3: 1–19.

FITCH, W. T. (1997), 'Vocal Tract Length and Formant Frequency Dispersion Correlate with Body Size in Rhesus Macaques', *Journal of the Acoustical Society of America*, 102: 1213–22.

——(1999), 'Acoustic Exaggeration of Size in Birds by Tracheal Elongation: Comparative and Theoretical Analyses', *Journal of Zoology* (London) 248: 31–49.

——(2000a), 'The Phonetic Potential of Nonhuman Vocal Tracts: Comparative Cineradiographic Observations of Vocalizing Animals', *Phonetica*, 57: 205–18.

——(2000b), 'The Evolution of Speech: A Comparative Review', *Trends in Cognitive Sciences*, 4: 258–67.

——and GIEDD, J. (1999), 'Morphology and Development of the Human Vocal Tract: A Study Using Magnetic Resonance Imaging', *Journal of the Acoustical Society of America*, 106: 1511–22.

——and HAUSER, M. D. (1995), 'Vocal Production in Nonhuman Primates: Acoustics, Physiology, and Functional Constraints on "Honest Advertisement"', *American Journal of Primatology*, 37: 191–219.

—— —— (forthcoming), 'Unpacking "Honesty": Vertebrate Vocal Production and the Evolution of Acoustic Signals', in A. Simmons, R. R. Fay, and A. N. Popper (eds.), *Acoustic Communications* (New York: Springer).

——and KELLEY, J. P. (2000), 'Perception of Vocal Tract Resonances by Whooping Cranes, *Grus americana*', *Ethology*, 106: 559–74.

——and REBY, D. (2001), 'The Descended Larynx Is Not Uniquely Human', *Proceedings of the Royal Society, B*, 268: 1669–75.

HAST, M. (1989), 'The Larynx of Roaring and Non-roaring Cats', *Journal of Anatomy*, 163: 117–21.

HAUSER, M. D. (1992), 'Articulatory and Social Factors Influence the Acoustic Structure of Rhesus Monkey Vocalizations: A Learned Mode of Production?', *Journal of the Acoustic Society of America*, 91: 2175–9.

——(1996), *The Evolution of Communication* (Cambridge, Mass.: MIT Press).

——and SCHÖN YBARRA, M. (1994), 'The Role of Lip Configuration in Monkey Vocalizations: Experiments Using Xylocaine as a Nerve Block', *Brain and Language*, 46: 232–44.

——EVANS, C. S., and MARLER, P. (1993), 'The Role of Articulation in the Production of Rhesus Monkey (*Macaca mulatta*) Vocalizations', *Animal Behaviour*, 45: 423–33.

HEWES, G. W. (1973), 'Primate Communication and the Gestural Origin of Language', *Current Anthropology*, 14: 5–24.

HIENZ, R. D., and BRADY, J. V. (1988), 'The Acquisition of Vowel Discriminations by Nonhuman Primates', *Journal of the Acoustical Society of America*, 84: 186–94.

——SACHS, M. B., and SINNOTT, J. M. (1981), 'Discrimination of Steady-State Vowels by Blackbirds and Pigeons', *Journal of the Acoustical Society of America*, 70: 699–706.

HOWES, G. B. (1889), 'Rabbit with an Intra-Narial Epiglottis, with a Suggestion Concerning the Phylogeny of the Mammalian Respiratory Apparatus', *Journal of Anatomy and Physiology* (London) 23: 263–72, 587–97.

JANIK, V. M., and SLATER, P. B. (1997), 'Vocal Learning in Mammals', *Advances in the Study of Behavior*, 26: 59–99.

KLATT, D. H., and STEFANSKI, R. A. (1974), 'How Does a Mynah Bird Imitate Human Speech?', *Journal of the Acoustical Society of America*, 55: 822–32.

KÜNZEL, H. J. (1989), 'How Well Does Average Fundamental Frequency Correlate with Speaker Height and Weight?', *Phonetica*, 46: 117–25.

LADEFOGED, P., and BROADBENT, D. E. (1957), 'Information Conveyed by Vowels', *Journal of the Acoustical Society of America*, 29: 98–104.

LAITMAN, J. T., and REIDENBERG, J. S. (1988), 'Advances in Understanding the Relationship Between the Skull Base and Larynx with Comments on the Origins of Speech', *Journal of Human Evolution*, 3: 99–109.

LIBERMAN, A. M., and MATTINGLY, I. G. (1985), 'The Motor Theory of Speech Perception Revised', *Cognition*, 21: 1–36.

LIEBERMAN, D. E., McCARTHY, R. C., HIIEMAE, K. M., and PALMER, J. B. (2001), 'Ontogeny of Postnatal Hyoid and Larynx Descent in Humans', *Archives of Oral Biology*, 2001: 117–28.

LIEBERMAN, P. (1968), 'Primate Vocalization and Human Linguistic Ability', *Journal of the Acoustical Society of America*, 44: 1574–84.

——(1984), *The Biology and Evolution of Language* (Cambridge, Mass.: Harvard University Press).

——and BLUMSTEIN, S. E. (1988), *Speech Physiology, Speech Perception, and Acoustic Phonetics* (Cambridge: Cambridge University Press).

——and CRELIN, E. S. (1971), 'On the Speech of Neanderthal Man', *Linguistic Inquiry*, 2: 203–22.

——CRELIN, E. S., and KLATT, D. H. (1972), 'Phonetic Ability and Related Anatomy of the Newborn and Adult Human, Neanderthal Man, and the Chimpanzee', *American Anthropologist*, 74: 287–307.

——KLATT, D. H., and WILSON, W. H. (1969), 'Vocal Tract Limitations on the Vowel Repertoires of Rhesus Monkeys and Other Nonhuman Primates', *Science*, 164: 1185–7.

McCOMB, K. (1987), 'Roaring by Red Deer Stags Advances Date of Oestrous in Hinds', *Nature*, 330: 648–9.

——(1991), 'Female Choice for High Roaring Rates in Red Deer, *Cervus elaphus*', *Animal Behaviour*, 41: 79–88.

MacNeilage, P. F. (1998), 'The Frame/Content Theory of Evolution of Speech Production', *Behavioral and Brain Sciences*, 21: 499–546.

Maddieson, I. (1984), *Patterns of Sounds* (Cambridge: Cambridge University Press).

Morris, D. H. (1974), 'Neanderthal Speech', *Linguistic Inquiry*, 5: 144–50.

Nearey, T. (1978), *Phonetic Features for Vowels* (Bloomington: Indiana University Linguistics Club).

Negus, V. E. (1949), *The Comparative Anatomy and Physiology of the Larynx* (New York: Hafner).

Nottebohm, F. (1976), 'Vocal Tract and Brain: A Search for Evolutionary Bottlenecks', *Annals of the New York Academy of Sciences*, 280: 643–9.

Nowicki, S. (1987), 'Vocal Tract Resonances in Oscine Bird Sound Production: Evidence from Birdsongs in a Helium Atmosphere', *Nature*, 325: 53–5.

Ohala, J. J. (1983), 'Cross-language Use of Pitch: An Ethological View', *Phonetica*, 40: 1–18.

——(1984), 'An Ethological Perspective on Common Cross-language Utilization of Fø of Voice', *Phonetica*, 41: 1–16.

Owen, R. (1834), 'On the Anatomy of the Cheetah, Felis jubata', *Transactions of the Zoological Society* (London) 1: 129–36.

Owren, M. J. (1990), 'Acoustic Classification of Alarm Calls by Vervet Monkeys (*Cercopithecus aethiops*) and Humans: II. Synthetic Calls', *Journal of Comparative Psychology*, 104: 29–40.

——(1996), 'An "Acoustic-Signature" Model of Speech Evolution', *Journal of the Acoustical Society of America*, 99: 2258.

——and Bernacki, R. (1988), 'The Acoustic Features of Vervet Monkey (*Cercopithecus aethiops*) Alarm Calls', *Journal of the Acoustical Society of America*, 83: 1927–35.

——Seyfarth, R. M., and Cheney, D. L. (1997), 'The Acoustic Features of Vowel-like *Grunt* Calls in Chacma Baboons (*Papio cyncephalus ursinus*): Implications for Production Processes and Functions', *Journal of the Acoustical Society of America*, 101: 2951–63.

Pocock, R. I. (1916), 'On the Hyoidean Apparatus of the Lion (*F. Leo*) and Related Species of Felidae', *The Annals and Magazine of Natural History*, 8: 222–9.

Remez, R. E., Rubin, P. E., Pisoni, D. B., and Carrell, T. D. (1981), 'Speech Perception Without Traditional Speech Cues', *Science*, 212: 947–50.

Rendall, D., Rodman, P. S., and Emond, R. E. (1996), 'Vocal Recognition of Individuals and Kin in Free-ranging Rhesus Monkeys', *Animal Behaviour*, 51: 1007–15.

Richman, B. (1976), 'Some Vocal Distinctive Features Used by Gelada Monkeys', *Journal of the Acoustical Society of America*, 60: 718–24.

Riede, T., and Fitch, W. T. (1999), 'Vocal Tract Length and Acoustics of Vocalization in the Domestic Dog *Canis familiaris*', *Journal of Experimental Biology*, 202: 2859–67.

SASAKI, C. T., LEVINE, P. A., LAITMAN, J. T., and CRELIN, E. S. (1977), 'Postnatal Descent of the Epiglottis in Man', *Archives of Otolaryngology*, 103: 169–71.

SENECAIL, B. (1979), *L'os hyoide: Introduction anatomique a l'étude de certains mecanismes de la phonation* (Paris: Faculté de Médicine de Paris).

SHIPLEY, C., CARTERETTE, E. C., and BUCHWALD, J. S. (1991), 'The Effects of Articulation on the Acoustical Structure of Feline Vocalizations', *Journal of the Acoustical Society of America*, 89: 902–9.

SOMMERS, M. S., MOODY, D. B., PROSEN, C. A., and STEBBINS, W. C. (1992), 'Formant Frequency Discrimination by Japanese Macaques (*Macaca fuscata*)', *Journal of the Acoustical Society of America*, 91: 3499–510.

SONNTAG, C. F. (1921), 'The Comparative Anatomy of the Koala (*Phascolarctos cinereus*) and Vulpine Phalanger (*Trichosurus vulpecula*)', *Proceedings of the Zoological Society of London*, 39: 547–77.

STUDDERT-KENNEDY, M. (1983), 'On Learning to Speak', *Human Neurobiology*, 2: 191–5.

——(1998), 'The Particulate Origins of Language Generativity: From Syllable to Gesture', in J. R. Hurford, M. Studdert-Kennedy, and C. Knight (eds.), *Approaches to the Evolution of Language: Social and Cognitive Bases* (Cambridge: Cambridge University Press).

SUNDBERG, J. (1987), *The Science of the Singing Voice* (Dekalb, Ill.: Northern Illinois University Press).

SUTHERS, R. A. (1994), 'Variable Asymmetry and Resonance in the Avian Vocal Tract: A Structural Basis for Individually Distinct Vocalizations', *Journal of Comparative Physiology*, 175: 457–66.

——and FATTU, J. M. (1973), 'Mechanisms of Sound Production in Echolocating Bats', *American Zoologist*, 13: 1215–26.

——and HECTOR, D. H. (1988), 'Individual Variation in Vocal Tract Resonance May Assist Oilbirds in Recognizing Echoes of Their Own Sonar Clicks', in P. E. Nachtigall and P. W. B. Moore (eds.), *Animal Sonar: Processes and Performances* (New York: Plenum Press), 87–91.

——HARTLEY, D. J., and WENSTRUP, J. J. (1988), 'The Acoustic Role of Tracheal Chambers and Nasal Cavities in the Production of Sonar Pulses by the Horseshoe Bat, *Rhilophus hildebrandti*', *Journal of Comparative Physiology, A*, 162: 799–813.

TITZE, I. R. (1994), *Principles of Voice Production* (Englewood Cliffs, N.J.: Prentice Hall).

WARREN, D. K., PATTERSON, D. K., and PEPPERBERG, I. M. (1996), 'Mechanisms of American English Vowel Production in a Gray Parrot (*Psittacus erithacus*)', *The Auk*, 113: 41–58.

3 Sexual Display as a Syntactical Vehicle: The Evolution of Syntax in Birdsong and Human Language through Sexual Selection

KAZUO OKANOYA

3.1 Introduction

In addition to natural selection, sexual selection is another Darwinian force that enables evolution. Sexual selection functions when a member of one sex selects an individual of the other sex as their reproductive partner based on particular traits. The traits do not necessarily have survival value: an arbitrary trait without survival value could evolve by sexual selection, just because one sex prefers that trait in the other sex. The idea of sexual selection was first presented by Darwin (1871), and was advanced by Fisher, Hamilton, and Zahavi, among others (Cronin 1991). Darwin saw the possibility of applying this idea to explain the origin of language, but until recently there have been few attempts to pursue this. Where, in recent years, sexual selection has been invoked, it has focused on functional properties (Dunbar 1996; Miller 2000), not syntactic ones.

Here I present a hypothesis for the evolution of syntax that can reconcile the Darwinian process of gradual evolution and the Chomskian view of catastrophism: what was gradual was the evolution of syntax in sexual display and what was catastrophic was the appropriation of syntactical form for semantic purposes. This hypothesis was inspired by our research into birdsong syntax. I argue that sexual display could be a pre-adaptation for syntax, that sexual display first evolved a finite-state syntax, and that seman-

I am grateful to Alison Wray for her valuable comments on how to improve this chapter. Chris Knight also gave me inspiring suggestions. The research was supported by PRESTO, the Japan Science and Technology Corporation. Much of the experimental evidence and ideas described here are the result of collaboration with students and fellow researchers at Chiba University.

tic tokens were later inserted as elements of this finite-state syntax. In other words, sexual display effected the evolution of syntax, and syntax then became a vehicle for linguistic expression. I advance this argument because sexual selection is good at shaping complex, arbitrary behaviour that lacks survival significance.

Nativists deny the gradual evolution of syntax because the significance of rudimentary syntax in survival is not clear (Chomsky 1996). In their view, language is functional only in its complete form. However, presuming that sexual selection shaped the rudiments of syntax, we can assume that syntax evolved without significance in survival. This argument can solve several important questions regarding the origin of language, such as why only humans have language and how protolanguage acquired syntax.

3.2 Birdsong and Human Language

Most studies that take a gradualist view of the evolution of language seem unnecessarily constrained from a phylogenic perspective. For these studies, the evolution of language is the evolution of language-like behaviour in primates and hominids. True, our language is uniquely human and, arguably, evolved only once in our species. However, this narrow focus severely impedes the study of language evolution by largely excluding the examination of animal behaviour, regardless of phylogeny, that has common features with human language. In so far as such behaviours are likely to have evolved via similar selection pressures as those that drove the evolution of human language, they could provide clues to the origin of language.

Here, birdsong is the subject of choice. Birdsong has several features in common with human language (Marler 1970). Both are complex behaviours requiring the control of breath, articulatory movements, and voice-producing organs (Suthers 1999). Both behaviours are known to be lateralized, i.e. each side of the brain functions differently when producing (Nottebohm 1971) and perceiving (Okanoya *et al.* 2001*b*) them. Both require two stages of learning: first, young animals have to hear and remember conspecific vocalizations; next, they have to train their own vocal apparatus so that they can vocalize sounds similar to those that they remember (Konishi 1985). Furthermore, we found an additional important feature common to human language and birdsong. Both have systematic, but not stereotyped, arrangements of sound elements: syntax.

3.3 Finite-State Syntax in Bengalese Finch Song

In passerine birds, song is a learned behaviour used by males to attract females and to protect territories (Catchpole and Slater 1996). Generally, a song is composed of several different song notes (elements), and the order of these notes is stereotyped. The number of song notes and the length of the stereotyped sequence vary between species. However, unlike most song-birds studied to date, Bengalese finches (*Lonchura striata* var. *domestica*) sing non-deterministic songs that can be described by a finite-state syntax.

Bengalese finches critically depend upon auditory feedback when singing (Okanoya and Yamaguchi 1997). When deprived of auditory feedback, the temporal organization of the song deteriorates immediately. No animals except humans rely as heavily on immediate auditory feedback when vocalizing. This critical dependence on auditory feedback may be closely related to the unique complexity of their song; Bengalese finches must listen to their own songs in real time in order to produce immediate varieties of a song.

Each male Bengalese finch sings a unique song with a unique set of song elements and an individual-specific finite-state syntax. In their songs, two to five song elements are organized into a 'chunk'. Several chunks are further organized into phrases by parsing through a finite-state syntax. A Bengalese finch can produce an infinite variety of songs by taking different paths in the finite-state automaton.

To find the finite-state syntax from a Bengalese finch song, we first denote each unique note in the sequence with a unique letter of the alphabet. Thus, a song sequence can be expressed as a string of letters. Suppose a bird sings the following songs:

S1: dddefghidddefghidddefhiabcdddefghiabcdddefghidddefghidddef

S2: dddefghidddefghidddefghidddefghidddefghiabgdddefghiabcdddde fghidddefghidddefghidddefghiabcdddef

S3: aababdddefghidddefghiabcdddefghidddefghidddefghidddefghidd defghiabcdddefghidddefbcdddefghidddef

If we have more such data, we can rewrite the above strings by utilizing rules such as:

Rule 1: dddef → 1, Rule 2: ghi → 2, Rule 3: abc → 3

Using these rules, we obtain:

S1:   12121hi312312121
S2:   1212121212abg1231212121231
S3:   aabab1212312121212123121bc121

When applying these rewrite rules, we can rewrite the original strings into chunk-strings by ignoring less than 5 per cent of the original notes. Using these chunk-strings, we can obtain a finite-state syntax that produces the sequences S1, S2, S3, and so on. Within these sequences, we can identify phrases, such as 1–2, 1–2–1, 1–2–3–1, and so on.

This particular bird does not manifest any examples that we consider to constitute 'embedding', though it could be argued that in a sequence such as 121212312 the 3 has been embedded into a repetitive string of 1s and 2s. However embedding is certainly evident in some other birds, such as the one whose sequences are represented in Fig. 3.1 (upper part). In this bird, the sequence 'im' or 'ε' was inserted between the sequences 'bcd' and 'fg'. This

Bengalese finch

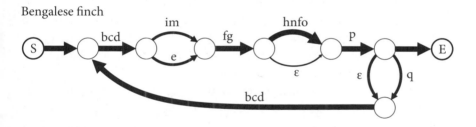

White-backed munia

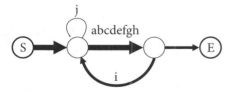

FIG. 3.1 Transition diagrams obtained from a Bengalese finch song (upper) and a white-backed munia song (lower). Each letter denotes an acoustically distinct song note, but the use of letters was arbitrary. 'a, b, c . . .' in the upper diagram do not indicate the same acoustic elements as 'a, b, c . . .' in the lower diagram. Note that the temporal organization of the Bengalese finch song is much more complex than that of the white-backed munia.

type of embedding of a sequence within a larger sequence is observed in the songs of about 30 per cent of these birds.

Why do Bengalese finches sing such complex songs? We tried to answer this question from four perspectives, including its mechanism, development, function, and evolution (Tinbergen 1963). During this process, we tried to extract principles that could be applied both to human language evolution and birdsong evolution. The sexual selection origin of syntax was deduced through these processes.

3.4 Brain Hierarchy and Behavioural Hierarchy

The song control system in the forebrain of songbirds consists of a set of discrete nuclei including the NIf, HVc, and RA (Margoliash 1997). The NIf receives auditory input from Field L, an avian primary auditory cortex, and receives motor input from thalamic nuclei. The HVc receives auditory/ motor input via the NIf and auditory input directly from Field L, and then it sends motor/auditory output to the RA. The RA directly controls the hypoglossal nucleus that innervates the syrinx, the avian vocal organ. We hypothesized that each of these nuclei might control the hierarchical structure of Bengalese finch song.

When the NIf was lesioned bilaterally, the song lost phrase level variability; that is, the complex song changed into a simple, stereotyped ordering of linear syntax (Hosino and Okanoya 2000). This implies that the NIf is responsible for phrase-to-phrase transition. The effect of HVc lesions was side dependent: a left HVc lesion resulted in total disturbance of song, while pre-operative songs recovered completely after a right HVc lesion. When the left HVc was partially lesioned, a particular state transition disappeared, but all song elements were preserved (Uno and Okanoya 1998). Thus, the HVc seems to be responsible for chunk-level variability. A partial lesion of the RA resulted in deletion of a certain song note from the song, but the overall finite-state syntax remained unchanged (Okanoya *et al.* 2001*a*). Thus, the RA appears to be responsible for producing each note.

Combined, we found that the finite-state syntax is expressed in hierarchically organized brain nuclei in Bengalese finches. Neurons in the HVc responded to particular combinations of song notes (Okanoya and Nakamura 2000). The combination selectivity of these neurons was correlated with the complexity of an individual's songs. On the other hand, neurons in the RA responded to each note independently (Okanoya, Nakamura, and Hirata 2001). These electrophysiological data supplement the lesion data.

Hierarchical control of human language has not been examined in this much detail, but at least nouns are topographically organized, and syntactical operations are conducted in different anatomical loci from those used for nouns. Based on a study of 127 adults with a localized brain lesion, Damasio *et al.* (1996) suggested that, in humans, nouns are categorically localized in the left lateral lobe, excluding Wernicke's area. On the other hand, lesions within and around Broca's area, and within Wernicke's area, produce various types of agrammatism without causing a naming deficit (Grodzinsky *et al.* 2000). More recently, the anterior Rolandic operculum, the region adjacent to Broca's area, was identified as a locus of syntactical operation during the real-time production of speech (Indefrey *et al.* 2001).

From these data, we can conclude that the control of each token and the control of syntactical arrangements of tokens are processed independently in the brains of both humans and birds. In humans, semantic and syntactical processing are independently mapped on the brain (Ullman *et al.* 1997) and each token is semantically represented with multiple corticocortical associations (Calvin and Bickerton 2000).

3.5 Cortical-Basal Ganglia Loop and Vocal Control

In both humans and birds, corticocortical networks govern real-time control of vocal production. In addition, other subcortical systems are required in the learning and real-time maintenance of vocalization. The basal ganglia are involved in the acquisition of skilled motor movement. The basal ganglia calculate the degree of error between an expected motor movement and the movement performed (Lawrence 2000). In humans, higher levels of activity were found in the basal ganglia when speaking a second language than when speaking the first language (Klein *et al.* 1994).

In addition to the direct pathway described in sect. 3.4, the HVc and RA in songbirds are also connected by an indirect pathway, the anterior forebrain pathway (Jarvis *et al.* 1998). This pathway begins at the HVc, and projects to the nucleus of the basal ganglia, Area X. From there, projections return to another cortical nucleus, lMAN, via a thalamic nucleus. lMAN then projects to the RA, completing an indirect pathway between the HVc and RA. In

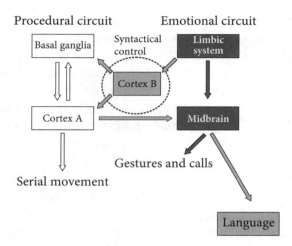

Fig. 3.2 Hypothetical neuro-anatomical substrates for syntax and semantics. Syntactical and semantic aspects of language evolved independently in separate brain circuits. Syntax evolved in the procedural, basal ganglia-cortex circuit and semantics evolved in the emotional, limbic-midbrain circuit. When another cortical region was involved in the procedural circuit, a finite-state syntax became possible. The emotional circuit is used for gestural and call communication in apes. When the emotional circuit establishes mutual projections with the intervening cortical structure, a finite-state syntax with some semantic contents becomes possible.

humans, the locus of syntactical operation for real-time speech production, the anterior Rolandic operculum, also receives projections from the basal ganglia (Indefrey *et al.* 2001).

Songbirds sing solo songs and sing courtship rituals. The function of solo song is enigmatic, but a recent study utilizing gene expression[1] gives us a clue to its function. They compared the levels of gene expression in the brains of male zebra finches after solo singing and courtship singing. In both cases, there were high levels of gene expression in the cortical structures, the HVc and RA. However, strong gene expression was also detected in the basal ganglia after solo singing, but the expression was not as great after courtship singing (Jarvis *et al.* 1998). The results imply that the function of solo singing

---

[1] 'Gene expression' here means transcription of a part of DNA into mRNA in response to particular neural activity. mRNA levels are measured by hybridizing complementally DNA with the mRNA or using the antigen to the protein synthesized by the mRNA.

is to maintain the spectro-temporal structures of learned song by utilizing the basal ganglia-cortex pathway.

Lesioning part of the basal ganglia in Bengalese finches resulted in 'stuttering' in song production. Birds stuttered the same song notes several times before proceeding to the next song note (Kobayashi *et al.* 2001). This is similar to a syndrome observed in patients with Parkinson's disease or basal ganglia lesions (Fabbro *et al.* 1996; Lawrence 2000).

These anatomical substrates are shown schematically on the left in Fig. 3.2. The basic vocal control pathway is shown on the right in the figure (emotional circuit). The internal state of the animal is conveyed to the midbrain, which controls vocal output directly. Therefore, in apes, internal emotional states are directly reflected in vocal expression. A basal ganglia-cortex loop (procedural circuit) controls serially ordered behaviour in both mammals and birds (Lawrence 2000). In addition, songbirds and humans have added an additional cortical control to this system (Cortex B), presumably through sexual selection. This enables complex serial patterning of behaviour. In these animals, vocal control is partially taken over by this circuit (Deacon 1997).

3.6 Development of Syntactical Control in Birds and Humans

Human infants begin vocalizing right after birth, but 'cooing' vowel-like sounds begins at 3 months of age. At 7 months, canonical babbling, consisting of consonants and vowels, begins. The first words are produced at around 12 months of age. At 16 months, infants typically produce 50 words, most of them nouns. When the vocabulary exceeds 250, words are first organized into syntactical structures. The minimal syntactical utterance of two-word sentences begins at around 24 months of age (Boysson-Bardies 1999).

In male Bengalese finches, primitive song begins at around day 30 after hatching. Vocalization at this stage is more or less a train of noises. At this stage, each song is called a 'subsong'. Between days 50 and 100 or so, the acoustical morphology of each note stabilizes. After day 80, almost all the notes used in the adult song are present, but the sequence, the finite-state rule, of the song is not stabilized. Nevertheless, several chunks that appear in the adult song can be identified at this stage. The song at this stage is called a 'plastic song'. Full crystallization of the song is usually attained at around day 120.

In this fashion, Bengalese finches and humans follow similar developmental paths. In both species, phonological development precedes syntactical development.

3.7 Functions of the Finite-State Song Syntax: A Handicap Process

Why do Bengalese finches develop such complex songs? We examined the reproductive behaviour of females when stimulated with complex or simple syntax songs. Song recordings obtained from a male Bengalese finch were analysed, and four distinctive song phrases were identified. In this bird's song, these four phrases were organized so that phrases A or B were repeated several times, and phrases C or D followed this repetition, but these phrases were never repeated. After C or D was sung once, phrases A or B were again repeated. We wrote software that produced this sequence of song phrases ('complex syntax song'), or that only repeated phrase B ('simple syntax song'). Phrase B included most of the song notes included in phrases A, C, and D.

Three groups of female Bengalese finches were studied. Each group consisted of four finches, separately caged, and kept together in a sound isolation box. The first group was stimulated with the complex syntax song, the second group with the simple syntax song, and the third group was not stimulated. The number of items of nesting material carried each day when stimulated with complex or simple syntax songs was counted and compared. Female finches carried more nesting material and had higher oestrogen levels when stimulated with the complex song.

Thus, we showed that a song with a complex syntax effectively stimulated the reproductive system of females. From this, we postulate that complex song patterning should be more attractive to female birds, and, therefore, the song syntax in Bengalese finches may have evolved through the process of sexual selection (Darwin 1871).

The ability to sing a complex song may be an honest signal that advertises the potency of the singer (Zahavi and Zahavi 1997), since singing a complex song may require (1) higher testosterone levels, (2) a greater cognitive load, and (3) more brain space. We tested one of the above hypotheses by disrupting an ongoing song by shining a flashlight at the bird. Birds that were singing more complex songs were less prone to stop singing (Nakamura and Okanoya 2000). The data support the hypothesis that singing a complex song probably requires a greater cognitive load and makes the animal less careful about potentially dangerous situations. Therefore, although a complex song may be disadvantageous for the bird's survival, the singer is preferred by females because the disadvantage of complexity reflects the potency of the singer.

3.8 Evolution of the Finite-State Syntax

We described Bengalese finch songs using a finite-state syntax. The syntax of human language is context-free, allowing self-embedding structures that cannot be expressed by a finite-state syntax. Although Bengalese finch songs do not show self-embedding, they do show simple, one-step embedding structures (Fig. 3.1, upper part). Still, there is a fundamental difference between human syntax and Bengalese finch song syntax. In order to argue that human syntax also evolved via sexual selection, we need to present a hypothesis that explains how a finite-state syntax could evolve into a context-free grammar.

One of the rationales for the following argument is that a finite-state grammar, in its elaborate form, approximates a context-free grammar (Pereira and Wright 1998). Our second rationale is that finite-state syntax, although fundamentally different from the syntax of modern humans, could still be regarded as the rudiment of human syntax, because an elaborate finite-state syntax could establish a communicative and representational ability close to that of a context-free grammar. Thus, our ancestors could have used a finite-state syntax during the process of syntax evolution. Finally, the main theme of the following argument, the independent evolution of syntax and semantics, holds equally for finite-state syntax and context-free grammar.

3.8.1 *Female Choice and the Evolution of Song Syntax*

Bengalese finches (*Lonchura striata* var. *domestica*) are the domesticated strain of the wild white-backed munia (*Lonchura striata*). White-backed munias were imported to Japan about 250 years ago, and were subsequently domesticated. Japanese aviculturists selected white-backed munias based on their parental abilities and for white mutations. There are no records in the avicultural literature indicating that Bengalese finches were selected for their songs. Nevertheless, we found that the complex song syntax is absent in the white-backed munia, the ancestor species (Honda and Okanoya 1999; Fig. 3.1)

To compare song complexity between the ancestor species and Bengalese finches, the following index of song linearity was devised. Let N be the number of unique song notes and P be the number of note-to-note transition patterns, then song linearity $= N/P$. Song linearity defined in this way varies from 1.0 (when the song is completely linear and deterministic) to $N/N^2 = 1/N$ (when the song is completely random, so that each note can be followed by all note types, in this case $P = N^2$). The average number of song notes used by white-backed munias and Bengalese finches is the same (around 8). However, the average linearity is significantly lower in Bengalese finches (around 0.4) than in white-backed munias (around 0.8). Fig. 3.1 shows examples of transition diagrams obtained from a Bengalese finch and a white-backed munia. The finite-state song syntax in Bengalese finches must have evolved in the past 250 years. This might look a short time, but 250 years means 1,000 generations for Bengalese finches, and this corresponds to roughly 20,000 years for humans.

We hypothesize that sexual selection acted in the evolution of finite-state syntax. That is, females of the ancestor species preferred complex songs, but the ability of males of the ancestor species to develop and sing complex songs was limited by constraints in nature, including predation risk and foraging cost. We retested this hypothesis by examining reproductive behaviour in the ancestor species. A simple, linear song of a white-backed munia male was spliced into song notes, and the finite-state syntax from a Bengalese finch that used the same number of song notes was applied to the song notes of the white-backed munia. Thus, we composed a new song that had the phonology of the white-backed munia, and the syntax of the Bengalese finch. We played either the original simple munia song, or the 'hybrid' song. Nesting behaviour was much greater when stimulated with the hybrid song.

3.8.2 *Self-Domestication and the Evolution of Syntax in Humans*

White-backed munias developed a finite-state syntax after domestication freed them from predation pressure and other pressures associated with life in the wild. In such a protected environment, song structure can develop as a result of female choice. Syntactical complication will then continue, to fulfil females' perceptual preferences (Ryan *et al.* 1990).

Bickerton argued that, for humans, a savannah environment increased predation risk and simultaneously decreases foraging efficiency. Our ancestors had to develop tool-making, fire use, co-operative hunting, and language as additional armours to cope with the new environmental pressures (Bickerton 1995).

My suggestion differs slightly, but significantly, from that of Bickerton. Since a savannah environment forced our ancestors to develop tools for protection, they became somewhat protected from environmental pressures that were once very threatening. This led to self-domestication. In such an environment, sexual selection was able to play a greater role in shaping our evolution than natural selection.

Based on these results, we discuss the evolution of complex behaviour and associated changes in the brain. Bengalese finches presumably developed a finite-state syntax through the process of sexual selection. However, each token in a Bengalese finch song lacks associated semantics, and the finite-state syntax in Bengalese finch song does not convey any meaning. Thus, a finite-state syntax can evolve without meaning.

3.9 Independent Evolution of Form and Content

3.9.1 *Semantic Grounding Can Prevent Syntactical Evolution: Knight's Seesaw*

Language did not evolve in primates other than humans. Why? Chris Knight thinks, 'apes are too clever for words' (Knight 1998: 72). By this, he means that for a communication system to evolve, signals must be honest. Signals under limbic control (e.g. a cat's hiss when threatened) are honest. They occur as reflexes to outside stimuli and are not under voluntary control. They also, however, do not have any 'meaning' other than that of a natural and immediate response to a stimulus. Signals take on a meaning when they can be divorced from the immediate environment of a stimulus and used to refer to some aspect of that stimulus–response event, while not actually evoking it. This requires voluntary control, and is therefore cognitive. Such behaviour emanates from the 'higher' brain, the cortex. As soon as a signal is under voluntary control, it can be produced both honestly and for the purposes of deceit. Thus, it is no longer *reliably* honest like a reflex, limbic signal is. It follows that there is no possibility of creating voluntary strings of semantic tokens (that is, meaningful language) without sacrificing the guarantee of honesty. As a result, the problem of honest tokens places, indirectly, a constraint on the development of syntax, *if syntax is conceived of as an extension of semantic expression.*

On the other hand, songbirds are in the opposite situation. In Bengalese finches, each token forming their song has no meaning. Thus, syntactical development has enough room to experiment with various types of complexity. In Bengalese finches, syntactical complexity alone is the subject of sexual selection. That is, *syntax is grounded to sexual selection and bears no survival value.* As long as this situation continues, each token is prohibited from having semantics. Once tokens begin to have individual meanings, it matters how they are arranged, and so sexual selection is no longer free to operate on a structure-only basis.

Specifically referring to our studies of Bengalese finches as exemplary of the wider logical problem, Knight (personal communication) has likened the incompatibility of simultaneous syntactic and semantic evolution to a seesaw. As our findings show, advance in one is incompatible with advance in the other (see also Knight 1998). However, Knight's seesaw problem can be solved for human language if we assume that the syntactical faculty developed independently, in the domain of sexual display.

3.9.2 *Evolution of Syntactical and Semantic Competence*

Most authors arguing about the origin of language assume that protolanguage, with symbolic content but no syntactical structure, evolved first; then, the protolanguage somehow evolved into a true language with syntax (e.g. Bickerton 1995; Pinker 1994). In this standard view of language evolution, state-dependent reflex signalling presumably evolved through natural selection into symbolic representation (e.g. Munn 1986), and thence, somehow, the capacity for context-free grammar arose.

How the protolanguage acquired syntax is the hardest question to answer when considering the origin of language (for a recent hypothesis, see Calvin and Bickerton 2000). Through analyses of Bengalese finch songs, we developed the hypothesis that syntactical behaviour evolves without the need for semantics, and, thus, without the need for survival value.

We propose that the symbolic and syntactical aspects of human language evolved independently (Fig. 3.3). As in Bengalese finch songs, in humans too, the rudiment of syntax might have evolved through sexual selection; in

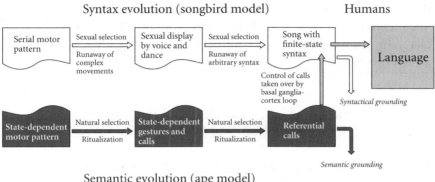

Fig. 3.3 Independent evolution of semantics and syntax. The syntactical faculty evolved by sexual selection in the domain of body movement. The vocal aspects of body movement evolved to produce a finite-state syntax. The semantic faculty originally evolved by natural selection from state-dependent, emotional body movements. Such body movements were ritualized through natural selection to signal the specific internal state of the animal. This produced gestures. Vocalizations associated with gestures were used in sexual displays with a finite-state syntax.

this case, mutual sexual display using song and dance involving males and females was a pre-adaptation for syntax. An animal with a serially ordered courtship display could evolve into an animal with a finite-state syntax for sexual display, simply by sexual selection for sequence complexity.

Once such a species independently established competence for symbolic representations, symbolic tokens might be used within a finite-state sexual display. If simple embedding was used in such display, that display might express the stronger fitness of the performer.

As we saw earlier, the voluntary control over symbolic representation could prevent the simultaneous evolution of syntax and semantics, and this would be true for our account too, if syntax and semantics operated in the same domain. We have proposed several hypotheses that deal with this problem. However, if syntax and semantics evolved in different behavioural domains, the difficulty is avoided. For example, suppose the semantic faculty evolved in the gestural domain and the syntactical faculty developed in the vocal domain. Then, since the final behavioural output differed—voice and gesture—semantic grounding would not prevent syntactical complication. In such a case, independent evolution could continue to a certain degree.

With this scheme we need to assume a merging process. One way to attain this merging is to assume that the brain programs that control the vocal hierarchy ultimately took over control of the semantically grounded vocal production (Fig. 3.2).

3.10 Conclusion: A Sexual Selection Scenario of Syntax Evolution

Anatomical, physiological, and developmental evidence suggests that bird-song and human language share common perceptual-motor properties. Sexual selection has shaped complex syntactical behaviour in Bengalese finches. If human language syntax also evolved by sexual selection, we can devise the following scenario. The self-domestication that occurred after ancestral humans adapted to a savannah environment freed humans from some of the risks of predation. This permitted the elaboration of sexual displays, including dancing and singing. Since the ability to dance and sing is an honest indicator of the performer's sexual proficiency, and singing is more effective than dancing for broadcasting, singing evolved through sexual selection until it obtained a finite-state syntax (Fig. 3.3, upper stream).

In parallel with the evolution of syntax, some of the state-dependent gestures were gradually replaced by calls through natural selection, because calls could be simultaneously addressed to multiple colony members. After syntactical singing and semantic calls were independently established, the acoustic tokens used in singing were sometimes replaced with calls that had a particular semantic content. Initially, the semantic content of the calls was erased in the context of singing, because the performance was not message-carrying—it was syntactically, not semantically, grounded. Gradually, however, a string of semantic tokens sometimes assumed the role of a public address in addition to its sexual display role. This could have been the beginning of syntactical language. Such vocalizations would be rather fictional or poetic, because syntactical grounding would dilute the semantic content. Or, to put it another way, the semantics of a display message would be ritualistic and not tied into the immediate temporal environment and, hence, more honest than the news-bearing communication that dominates language today (compare Knight 1998). Additional factors, such as social calculus and neuroanatomical topography (Calvin and Bickerton 2000), would then have modified the simple finite-state language into true language.

Since apes did not evolve singing as a sexual display, their ability to sequentially present different vocal signals and to form finite-state syntax was limited. Instead, their ability to reference particular situations using particular gestures evolved. Since such signals had to be honest ones, the meaning of each signal was grounded and could not be freely modified.

FURTHER READING

CALVIN, W. H., and BICKERTON, D. (2000), *Lingua ex Machina: Reconciling Darwin and Chomsky with the Human Brain* (Cambridge, Mass.: MIT Press).

CATCHPOLE, C. K., and SLATER, P. J. B. (1996), *Bird Song: Biological Themes and Variations* (Cambridge: Cambridge University Press).

CRONIN, H. (1991), *The Ant and the Peacock: Altruism and Sexual Selection from Darwin to Today* (Cambridge: Cambridge University Press).

DEACON, T. (1997), *The Symbolic Species: The Co-evolution of Language and The Human Brain* (New York: Norton).

MILLER, G. (2000), *The Mating Mind: How Sexual Choice Shaped the Evolution of Human Nature* (New York: Doubleday).

ZAHAVI, A., and ZAHAVI, A. (1997), *The Handicap Principle* (Princeton: Princeton University Press).

REFERENCES

BICKERTON, D. (1995), *Language and Human Behavior* (Seattle: University of Washington Press).

BOYSSON-BARDIES, B. DE (1999), *How Language Comes to Children: from Birth to Two Years* (Cambridge, Mass.: MIT Press).

CALVIN, W. H., and BICKERTON, D. (2000), *Lingua ex Machina: Reconciling Darwin and Chomsky with the Human Brain* (Cambridge, Mass.: MIT Press).

CATCHPOLE, C. K., and SLATER, P. J. B. (1996), *Bird Song: Biological Themes and Variations* (Cambridge: Cambridge University Press).

CHOMSKY, N. (1996), *The Minimalist Program* (Cambridge, Mass.: MIT Press).

CRONIN, H. (1991), *The Ant and the Peacock: Altruism and Sexual Selection from Darwin to Today* (Cambridge: Cambridge University Press).

DAMASIO, H., GRABOWSKI, T. J., TRANEL, D., HICHWA, R. D., and DAMASIO, A. R. (1996), 'A Neural Basis for Lexical Retrieval', *Nature*, 380: 499–505.

DARWIN, C. (1871), *The Descent of Man and Selection in Relation to Sex* (London: John Murray).

DEACON, T. (1997), *The Symbolic Species: The Co-evolution of Language and the Brain* (New York: Norton).

DUNBAR, R. (1996), *Grooming, Gossip, and the Evolution of Language* (Cambridge, Mass.: Harvard University Press).

FABBRO, F., CLARICI, A., and BAVA, A. (1996), 'Effects of Left Basal Ganglia Lesions on Language', *Perception and Motor Skills*, 82: 1291–8.

GRODZINSKY, Y., SHAPIRO, L., and SWINNEY, D. (2000) (eds.), *Language and the Brain: Representation and Processing* (New York: Academic Press).

HONDA, E., and OKANOYA, K. (1999), 'Acoustical and Syntactical Comparisons Between Songs of the White-Backed Munia (*Lonchura striata*) and its Domesticated Strain, the Bengalese Finch (*Lonchura striata* var. *domestica*)', *Zoological Science*, 16: 319–26.

HOSINO, T., and OKANOYA, K. (2000), 'Lesion of a Higher-order Song Control Nucleus Disrupts Phrase-level Complexity in Bengalese Finches', *NeuroReport*, 11: 2091–2095.

INDEFREY, P., BROWN, C. M., HELLWIG, F., AMUNTS, K., HERZOG, H., SEITZ, R. J., and HAGOORT, P. (2001), 'A Neural Correlate of Syntactic Encoding During Speech Production', *Proceedings of the National Academy of Sciences of the U.S.A.*, 98: 5933–6.

JARVIS, E. D., SCHARFF, C., GROSSMAN, M. R., RAMOS, J. A., and NOTTEBOHM, F. (1998), 'For Whom the Bird Sings: Context-Dependent Gene Expression', *Neuron*, 21: 775–88.

KLEIN, D., ZATORRE, R. J., MILNER, B., MEYER, E., and EVANS, A. C. (1994), 'Left Putaminal Activation When Speaking a Second Language', *NeuroReport*, 21: 2295–7.

KNIGHT, C. (1998), 'Ritual/Speech Coevolution: A Solution to the Problem of Deception', in J. R. Hurford, M. S. Studdert-Kennedy, and C. Knight (eds.), *Approaches to the Evolution of Language: Social and Cognitive Bases* (Cambridge: Cambridge University Press), 68–91.

KOBAYASHI, K., UNO, H., and OKANOYA, K. (2001), 'Partial Lesions in the Anterior Forebrain Pathway Affect Song Production in Bengalese Finches', *NeuroReport*, 12: 353–8.

KONISHI, M. (1985), 'Birdsong: From Behavior to Neuron', in W. M. Cowan (ed.), *Annual Review of Neuroscience* (Palo Alto: Annual Review, Inc), viii.125–70.

LAWRENCE, A. D. (2000), 'Error Correction and the Basal Ganglia: Similar Computations for Action, Cognition, and Emotion?', *Trends in Cognitive Science*, 4: 365–7.

MARGOLIASH, D. (1997), 'Distributed Time-Domain Representations in the Birdsong System', *Neuron*, 19: 963–6.

MARLER, P. (1970), 'Birdsong and Speech Development: Could There Be Parallels?', *American Scientist*, 58: 669–73.

MILLER, G. (2000), *The Mating Mind: How Sexual Choice Shaped the Evolution of Human Nature* (New York: Doubleday).

MUNN, C. A. (1986), 'Birds That "Cry Wolf"', *Nature*, 306: 583–4.

NAKAMURA, K., and OKANOYA, K. (2000), 'Measuring the Cognitive Cost of Voco-Auditory Behavior: A Case of Bengalese Finch Song', *Transactions on Technical*

Committee of Psychological and Physiological Acoustics (Tokyo: The Acoustical Society of Japan), H-99–100: 1–6.

NOTTEBOHM, F. (1971), 'Neural Lateralization of Vocal Control in a Passerine Bird', *Journal of Experimental Zoology*, 177: 229–62.

OKANOYA, K., and NAKAMURA, K. (2000), 'Song Complexity Correlates Temporal Combination Selectivity of HVc Auditory Neurons in Bengalese Finches', *Proceedings of the Seventh Western Pacific Regional Acoustics Conference* (Tokyo: Acoustical Society of Japan), 227–32.

——and YAMAGUCHI, A. (1997), 'Adult Bengalese Finches (*Lonchura striata* var. *domestica*) Require Real-time Auditory Feedback to Produce Normal Song Syntax', *Journal of Neurobiology*, 33: 343–56.

——NAKAMURA, K., and HIRATA, N. (2001a), 'Motor and Perceptual Properties of Nucleus RA in Bengalese Finches', *Society for Neuroscience Abstracts*, 31: 318.5.

——IKEBUCHI, M., UNO, H., and WATANABE, S. (2001b), 'Left-side Dominance for Song Discrimination in Bengalese Finches (*Lonchura striata* var. *domestica*)', *Animal Cognition*, 4: 241–5.

PEREIRA, F. C. N., and WRIGHT, R. N. (1998), 'Finite-state Approximation of Phrase-Structure Grammars', in E. Roche and Y. Schabes (eds.), *Finite-State Language Processing* (Cambridge, Mass.: MIT Press), 149–74.

PINKER, S. (1994), *The Language Instinct* (New York: William Morrow).

RYAN, M., FOX, J. H., WILCZYNSKI, W., and RAND, A. S. (1990), 'Sexual Selection for Sensory Exploitation in the Frog *Physalaemus pustulosus*', *Nature*, 343: 66–7.

SUTHERS, R. A. (1999), 'The Motor Basis of Vocal Performance in Songbirds', in M. Hauser and M. Konishi (eds.), *The Design of Animal Communication* (Cambridge, Mass.: MIT Press), 37–62.

TINBERGEN, N. (1963), 'On Aims and Methods of Ethology', *Zeitschrift für Tierpsychologie*, 20: 410–33.

ULLMAN, M. T., CORKIN, C., COPPOLA, M., HICKOK, G., GROWDON, J. H., KOROSHETZ, W. J., and PINKER, S. (1997), 'A Neural Dissociation Within Language: Evidence That the Mental Dictionary Is Part of Declarative Memory and That Grammatical Rules Are Processed by the Procedural System', *Journal of Cognitive Neuroscience*, 9: 266–76.

UNO, H., and OKANOYA, K. (1998), 'Partial Lesions of HVc Disrupt Note Chunking in Bengalese Finches', *Society for Neuroscience Abstracts*, 24: 1187.

ZAHAVI, A., and ZAHAVI, A. (1997), *The Handicap Principle* (Princeton: Princeton University Press).

4 Serial Expertise and the Evolution of Language

H. S. Terrace

4.1 Introduction

'An army of monkeys strumming on typewriters writ[ing] all the books in the British Museum' (Eddington 1928) is a well-known metaphor for an absurdly unlikely event. A similar point could be made, albeit less dramatically, about the vanishingly small likelihood of a monkey producing any linguistic sequence. Monkeys can, however, learn non-grammatical sequences. The goal of this chapter is to describe the remarkable expertise of monkeys to master non-linguistic sequences, and to indicate how a monkey's serial expertise can broaden our understanding of the evolution of language.

What makes a monkey's serial expertise relevant to the evolution of language is the opportunity it provides to dissociate thought from language. In humans, language and thought are inextricably entwined. However, as is evident from the growing literature on animal cognition, animals think without language. For example, animals readily master such cognitive tasks as concept formation (Wasserman and Bhatt 1992; Hernstein *et al.* 1976), delayed, symbolic, and successive matching-to-sample (Kendrick *et al.* 1981; Wright *et al.* 1984), numerical reasoning (Boysen 1993; Biro and Matsuzawa 1999; Brannon and Terrace 1998; Hauser *et al.* 1996), timing (Meck and Church 1983; Breukelaar and Dalrymple-Alford 1998) and serial learning (Terrace 1987; Chen *et al.* 2000; Swartz *et al.* 1991; Chen *et al.* 1997; Sands and Wright 1980).

The literature on animal cognition has succeeded admirably in identifying a variety of cognitive abilities that overlap with those of humans, and in

The research reported in this chapter was supported by NIMH grant MH40462 to H. S. Terrace.

revealing the weaknesses of theories of animal behaviour that make no pro-vision for cognitive processes. However, the cognitive skills that have been documented in animals are the skills of a novice, and whether an animal can acquire expertise at performing a cognitive task has remained an open ques-tion. Expertise presupposes cognitive ability, but the converse is not neces-sarily true. To demonstrate expertise it is necessary to show an increase in the efficiency with which a subject performs a cognitive task as new exem-plars of that task are learned.

In contrast to the extensive literature on human expertise (Chi *et al.* 1988), the literature on animal expertise is virtually nil. The major exception is Har-low's classic experiments on 'learning sets' in which monkeys learned to dis-criminate two novel objects (Harlow 1950). (See Hunter and Kamil 1971 and Eichenbaum *et al.* 1986 for similar experiments on korvids and rats.) To establish a learning set, the subject is presented with new exemplars of a particular type of problem irrespective of its performance on the current exemplar of that problem. Consider, for example, a simple discrimination problem in which a monkey is presented with two 3-dimensional objects, for example, a red cylinder and a blue rocket. In the trials with this pair of objects, a peanut is consistently hidden under one of them, say, always the blue rocket, but the position of the objects is changed randomly from trial to trial. Subsequent problems would pit a green star against a blue cube, a red car against a blue fish, and so on. Logically, the monkey should always chose the correct object on the second trial by applying the simple rule, 'if A, then always A; if B, then always B'. However, the monkey has to be trained on a few hundred different pairs of objects before he uses that logic consistently. During the first block of 8 problems the monkey will choose the correct item on the second trial only 55 per cent of the time; after 100 problems, 85 per cent of the time; after 200 problems, 90 per cent of the time, and so on. It takes that long because the monkey has to learn to ignore features of the objects not relevant to its decision.

The difference between the literatures on human and animal expertise is not just one of relative size. The extensive literature on human expertise (e.g. Chi *et al.* 1988) characterizes differences in the *strategies* used by experts and novices while attempting to solve novel exemplars of different types of problem, including mathematics and physics (Schoenfeld and Hermann 1982; Larkin *et al.* 1980; Chi *et al.* 1981), chess (Simon and Chase 1973), serial memory (Chase and Ericsson 1981), and medicine (Lesgold *et al.* 1988). Experiments on human expertise also presuppose an ability to plan and execute novel *sequences* (Miller *et al.* 1960). The few experiments performed on animal expertise required subjects to make but a *single* response (as, indeed, do most experiments on animal learning and memory).

If convincing evidence of animal expertise could be found, it would pose an intriguing dilemma for theories of cognition. What kind of knowledge could an animal expert be using? Philosophers have distinguished between two types of human knowledge: 'knowing how' to execute some motor skill (for example, riding a bicycle), and 'knowing that' certain facts are true—for example, an elephant is bigger than a dog and a dog is bigger than a fly (Ryle 1949). Psychologists have drawn an analogous distinction in the definitions of procedural and declarative memory (Squire 1994). Procedural memory is acquired slowly, by conditioning, and is inflexible and unconscious. Declarative memory is acquired rapidly, is flexible, and is expressed consciously as verbal facts (Tulving and Schachter 1990).

The distinction between procedural and declarative memory, which was formulated to account for various phenomena of human cognition, presupposes linguistic ability, specifically, the ability to *declare* particular facts. If linguistic ability were used as a litmus test for declarative knowledge, it would follow that animals are limited to procedural knowledge. That conclusion may be appropriate in the case of simple conditioning, but it is not clear how it would apply to instances of animal cognition. The serial expertise of monkeys that will be described in this chapter is a case in point. Procedural memory cannot explain the serial expertise of monkeys who learned, by trial and error, to produce arbitrary 7-item lists on which the chance probability of guessing the correct order is 1/5040. Similarly, procedural memory cannot account for the monkeys' ability to solve new problems, on a *first* trial basis, by applying the serial knowledge they acquired while learning 7-item lists.

4.2 Training Monkeys to Learn Lists

The subjects of this experiment were four juvenile male rhesus macaques (Benedict, Macduff, Oberon, and Rosencrantz).[1] Subjects were trained on

---

[1] The subjects were raised in the same native social group (in Yemasee, South Carolina) from their birth (in 1995) until they were 1.5 years old. In 1996, they were transported to the animal facility at the New York State Psychiatric Institute where they were pair-housed

lists composed of novel photographs of natural objects, e.g. the 7 items in panel A of Fig. 4.1. All items in a given list were displayed simultaneously on a touch-sensitive video monitor. The subject's task was to touch the items in a particular order (A → B → C → D → E → F → G). As shown in Fig. 4.1, panel B, a new configuration of the list items was presented on each trial. That prevented subjects from representing the required sequence as procedural knowledge, that is, as a fixed-motor pattern of responses to specific external cues.

Any error resulted in the immediate termination of the trial. All correct responses were followed by brief visual and auditory feedback. That feedback, which informed the subject that his response was detected, provided no information as to the identity of the next item. For example, during training on a 7-item list, the feedback for responding correctly to item B provided no information that the next response should be directed to item C (as opposed to items D, E, F, or G).

4.2.1 *Simultaneous Chaining Paradigm*

The *simultaneous chaining* paradigm used in this experiment differs radically from the *successive chaining* paradigm, the traditional method used to train sequential behaviour (e.g. maze learning). In a successive chaining paradigm, subjects can rely on external stimuli (e.g. the choice points of a maze) as discriminative stimuli for making a particular sequence of responses (e.g. turn left, turn right, turn right, etc.). To execute a simultaneous chain, on the other hand, subjects have to generate *internal* cues to define their position in the sequence before making each response (Terrace 1984). The following thought experiment, based on a 7-item simultaneous chain, shows why.

Imagine trying to enter your 7-digit personal identification number (PIN), say *9–2–1–5–8–4–7*, at a cash machine on which the positions of the numbers were changed each time you tried to obtain cash. You could not enter

---

in adjoining cages to promote psychological well-being. Members of each pair were separated and restricted to their respective cages prior to an experimental session by inserting a metal partition on one side of the cage. At the start of this experiment, the subjects were 2 years old. The subjects, who were neither food nor water deprived, were maintained throughout the experiment in accordance with NIH guidelines. Following training on 4-item lists, Rosencrantz, Benedict, and Macduff served in two experiments on numerical sequences (Brannon and Terrace 1998, 2000). For these subjects, training on 7-item sequences began immediately after the experiments on numerical sequences.

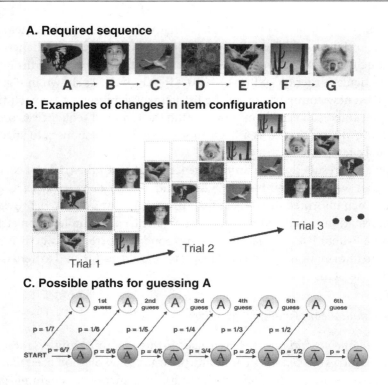

A. Required sequence

A → B → C → D → E → F → G

B. Examples of changes in item configuration

Trial 1   Trial 2   Trial 3 • • •

C. Possible paths for guessing A

Note: A colour version of the above figure can be viewed at the following address: www.oup.com/uk/pdf/figure4_1.pdf

FIG. 4.1 Simultaneous chaining paradigm: *A. Example of a 7-item list.* Subjects are required to respond to each colour photograph in a prescribed order (A → B → C → D → E → F → G). The photographs were selected arbitrarily from a library of approximately 5,000 photographs. *B. Variation of the configuration of list items.* List items were presented on a touch-sensitive video monitor. The task was to touch the items in the prescribed order irrespective of their position on the monitor. Prior to each trial, a new configuration was selected at random from the more than 5.8 million configurations that could be generated by presenting 7 items in any of 16 positions. *C. Determining the ordinal position of a list item.* At the beginning of training on each list subjects had to make 'logical guesses' or search errors to determine the ordinal position of each item by trial and error. The minimum number of search errors is the sum of the product of two variables: the number of search errors that can be made at each position of the sequence and the probability of making each type of logical guess. For example, the probability of identifying A on the first guess is $1/7$; on the second guess, it is $6/7 \times 1/6 = 1/7$; on the third guess, it is $6/7 \times 5/6 \times 1/5 = 1/7$, and so on. After 6 incorrect guesses, A is the only item that remains to be chosen. The probability of that outcome is also $1/7$: $(6/7 \times 5/6 \times 4/5 \times 3/4 \times 2/3 \times 1/2$

that (or any) PIN by executing a sequence of distinctive motor movements, i.e. first pressing the button in the lower right corner of the number pad to enter 9, then the button in the upper middle position to enter 2, and so on. Instead, you would have to search for each number and mentally keep track of your position in the sequence as you pressed different buttons. As difficult as that task may seem, it would be far more difficult if you had to determine your PIN number by *trial and error*. Any error would terminate a trial and result in a new trial on which the digits were displayed in a different configuration. To determine your PIN, you would have to recall the consequences of any of the 36 types of logical errors you could make while attempting to produce the required sequence—21 types of forward (anticipatory) errors and 15 types of backward (reiterative) errors (see later). Further, you would have to learn the first 6 digits without getting any money from the cash machine. With but two exceptions, this is precisely the problem the monkeys had to solve at the start of training on each of the four 7-item lists on which they were trained. Instead of numerals, the monkeys had to respond to photographs. Instead of cash, they were given banana pellets.

4.2.2 *Experimental Procedure*

List training for each monkey began immediately after he learned to obtain a banana pellet by touching a small photograph displayed on a touch-sensitive video monitor.[2] Each daily session consisted of 60 trials. The same

[2] Training and testing were conducted in the monkey's home cage with the aid of a touch-sensitive 15-inch video monitor that was positioned in front of the cage prior to each session. Each of the digitized colour photographs that were used as list items measured 1.5×1.5 inches, and could be displayed in any of the 16 positions defined by a 4×4 matrix. Photographs (rather than colours or geometric forms) were used as list items to

(FIG. 4.1 *cont.*)
$\times 1/1$). If the monkey selects A with the first guess, he will have made 0 search errors; with the second guess, 1 search error, with the third guess, 2 search errors, and so on. The maximum number of search errors is the sum of the possible search errors leading up to a logical guess. For example, guessing A after 2 search errors could result from any sequence in which the monkey responds to two different items other than A (B and C, C and D, B and E, etc.). Thus the maximum number of search errors needed to determine A is $0 + 1 + 2 + 3 + 4 + 5 + 6 = 21$. The expected number of logical errors needed to determine A is $21 \times 1/7 = 3$; to determine B, $15 \times 1/6 = 2.5$; to determine C, $10 \times 1/5 = 2$, and so on. The value of the expected number of logical errors at each position decreases linearly, 0.5 guesses at each position, until it reaches a value of 0 at item F.

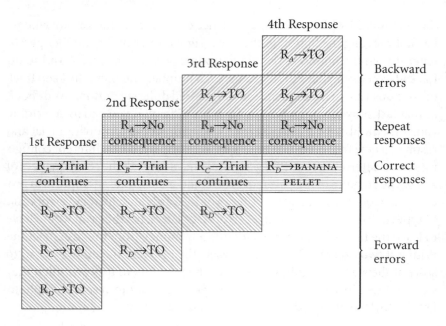

FIG. 4.2 Types of responses and their consequences on a 4-item list (A → B → C → D).

list items were presented on each trial, in a different configuration on each trial. Once the subject satisfied the training criterion on a particular list (see below), a new list was introduced at the start of the next session. Each subject learned 22 lists in the following order: seven 3-item lists (Lists 1–7), eleven 4-item lists (Lists 8–18), and four 7-item lists (Lists 19–22). Thus, the number of list items (n) was increased in two steps, from 3 to 4 items, and from 4 to 7 items. Each list was composed of different colour photographs selected arbitrarily from the following categories: animals, humans, scenery, foods, flowers, and various man-made objects. All list items were presented from the start of training on each list.

The following contingencies for errors and correct responses were in effect on each trial. Any error terminated the trial and initiated an 8-second

provide a large set of highly discriminable stimuli for generating lists of novel items. No assumptions were made as to what a subject perceived in the photographs (i.e. natural objects or discriminable collages of coloured pixels (Herrnstein *et al.* 1976; Wasserman and Bhatt 1992)).

time-out during which the video monitor was dark. A correct response allowed the trial to continue and also produced brief secondary reinforcement (a 0.5 cm wide green border, that surrounded the photograph the subject selected, and a 1200 Hz tone, both presented simultaneously for 0.3 sec.). Food reward (a banana-flavoured pellet) was provided only if the subject responded in the correct order to each of the n items. To learn the first $n-1$ items of each list, subjects had to rely exclusively on secondary reinforcement (the feedback that followed each response). Thus, on a new 4-item list, the subjects had to learn the correct order in which to respond to items A, B, and C before they could obtain any food reward; on a new 7-item list, the correct order in which to respond to items A, B, C, D, E, and F.

Fig. 4.2 shows all the correct responses and errors that can occur as a subject attempts to learn a new 4-item list. Correct responses appear in the cells with horizontal shading; errors, in the cells with diagonal shading. Errors were classified as *forward* or *backward*. Forward errors (diagonal down shading) are responses to an item beyond the currently correct item (e.g. a response to C at the beginning of a trial, a response to D after a correct response to A, etc.). Backward errors (diagonal up shading) are responses to a previously correct item (e.g. a response to A after the subject had responded to A and B). Repeat responses to the same item, which were rare, had no consequences (cells with cross-hatched shading). As shown in Fig. 4.3, the number of possible errors (both forward and backward) increases exponentially as list length increases.[3] As a consequence, the process of guessing the positions of the first $n-1$ items by trial and error becomes exponentially more difficult as n increases.

The primary goal of 3- and 4-item training was to develop skills for determining the correct order in which to respond to a new set of list items by trial and error (as opposed to achieving a high level of accuracy on any particular list). With the 3- and 4-item lists, subjects were advanced to a new list each time they completed at least 65 per cent of the trials correctly during

---

[3] On 3-, 4-, and 7-item lists, the subjects could make, respectively, 4, 9, and 36 forward and backward errors. Given the conservative assumption that the subjects make no backward errors during the execution of a sequence (sampling without replacement), the probability of responding to the items of a new list correctly by chance was $1/n!$ where $n =$ the number of items of the list and $!$ indicates that n should be expanded as a factorial, so that $3! = 3 \times 2 \times 1 = 6$ and $7! = 7 \times 6 \times 5 \times 4 \times 3 \times 2 \times 1 = 5040$. For 3-, 4-, and 7-item sequences, the chance probabilities of completing a new list correctly were .17, .04, and 00002 (cf. Fig. 4.2).

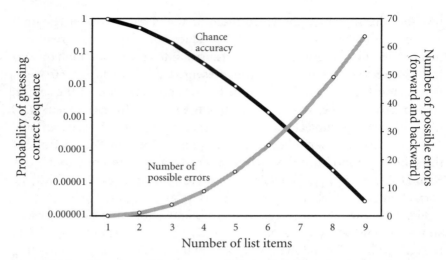

FIG. 4.3 Number of possible errors and the probability of guessing the correct sequence on simultaneous chains of varying length: the number of possible forward and backward errors grows exponentially as list length increases. Examples of all possible forward and backward errors on a 4-item list are shown in Fig. 4.2. As the number of possible errors increases, the probability of guessing the correct sequence decreases.

a daily session *or* after 3 days of training on a particular list.[4] Exceptionally, however, on their *first* 3- and 4-item lists, the subjects were trained until they completed 65 per cent of the trials correctly in a single session, irrespective of how many days it took to reach that point. This ensured that they had mastered at least one 3- and one 4-item list.

As can be seen in Fig. 4.3, the shift to 7-item lists, during the last phase of training, entailed a large increment in list difficulty. The likelihood of guessing the order in which to respond correctly to each item of a new 7-item list (1/5040) is more than 200 times less than the likelihood of guessing the order in which to respond correctly on a new 4-item list (1/24). Thus, the subjects' ability to master a 7-item list was a strong test of any serial expertise they acquired while learning 3- and 4-item lists. The subjects were trained

---

[4] The subjects were required to complete 65% of the trials during one session on their first 3- and 4-item lists because different strategies are needed to encode list items in each instance. A 3-item list has two salient end items and one interior item. The latter could be encoded by default. A default rule would not work for a 4-item list because it has two interior items.

on each of the four 7-item lists until they completed 65 per cent of the trials correctly during a single session.

4.3 Serial Expertise

4.3.1 *Accuracy and Trials to Criterion*

Compelling evidence of serial expertise was observed at each stage of training. Accuracy of responding increased progressively during the course of learning new 3-, 4-, and 7-item lists, as did subjects' efficiency in determining the ordinal position of list items on each new list. Fig. 4.4 (Panels A and B) shows the mean accuracy of responding on successive 3- and 4-item lists during the first and last sessions of training on each list.[5] None of the subjects exceeded the chance level of accuracy (.17) during the *first* session of training on their first 3-item list. However, all subjects exceeded that level of accuracy during the first session of training on at least 5 of the 7 remaining lists.[6] Benedict and Oberon exceeded the chance level of accuracy (.04) during the first session of training on *all* 4-item lists; Rosencrantz and Macduff, on approximately two-thirds of those lists. The mean accuracy level during the last session of training on 3-item lists was approximately 57 per cent. On 4-item lists, the mean level of accuracy during the last session of training increased steadily from 46 to 61 per cent.

The strongest evidence of serial expertise was the subjects' mastery of 7-item lists. Each monkey learned each of the four 7-item lists on which they were trained and required progressively fewer sessions to satisfy the accuracy criterion on each new list. As shown in Fig. 4.4 (panel C), the subjects needed an average of 31.5, 17.5, 13 and 12.25 sessions, respectively, to satisfy the accuracy criterion on their first, second, third and fourth 7-item lists (ranges: 21–55, 11–25, 11–19, and 7–17, respectively). Those 7-item lists were only the nineteenth, twentieth, twenty-first and twenty-second lists (of any length) on which the subjects were trained. Similar reductions in the amount of training needed to satisfy an accuracy criterion have been observed in experiments in which adult human subjects were trained to memorize successive lists of arbitrarily selected words (Keppel *et al.* 1968).

---

[5] Data from the first 3- and 4-item lists are not shown because the subjects were trained to a criterion of completing at least 65% of the trials correctly during one session.

[6] Oberon exceeded the chance level of accuracy on six of the seven 3-item lists; Macduff, Rosencrantz, and Benedict, on five of those lists.

As compared to the monkeys trained in this experiment, human subjects had learned thousands of lists prior to their experimental training.

The data shown in Fig. 4.4 underestimate the subjects' knowledge of the ordinal position of particular items because they are based on the subjects' ability to respond correctly to *all* the items on a particular trial. No credit was given for partially completed trials. For example, a trial on which a subject made an error after responding correctly to items A, B, C, and D, is, by definition, an incorrectly completed trial. The conditional probability of respond-

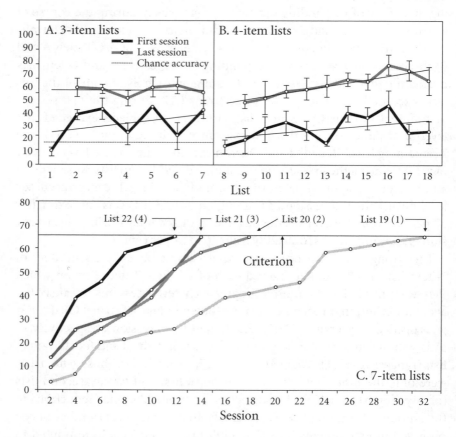

FIG. 4.4 Learning curves for 3-, 4-, and 7-item lists: *A and B*: each panel shows the percentage of correctly completed trials during the first and the last (lower and upper functions, respectively) sessions of training on 3-item lists (A) and 4-item lists (B). *C*: each function shows the mean accuracy of responding on each 7-item list during even-numbered sessions. Note that the x-axis of Panel C is Session (not List).

ing correctly at *each* position is a more sensitive measure of serial knowledge. In the previous example, responding correctly to A at the start of the trial would count as a correct response. So would responding correctly to B, given a correct response to A; responding correctly to C, given a correct response to B, and so on. Fig. 4.5 shows the conditional probability of responding correctly to each item during the first session of training on the last 4-item list and during the first session of training on the first and the last of the 7-item lists. These data provide evidence of primacy and recency effects and of the development of the subjects' expertise at learning new lists (see below).

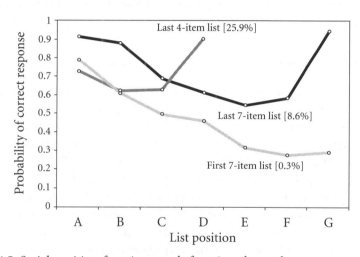

FIG. 4.5 Serial position functions: each function shows the average conditional probability of a correct response at each position during initial training on the last 4-item list (overall list no. 18), and the first and the last 7-item lists (overall lists nos. 19 and 22). The conditional probabilities of responding correctly to individual items should not be confused with the probability of responding correctly to all the items on a particular trial (a correctly completed trial). As shown by the numbers in brackets to the right of each function, the probability of correctly responding to all the items on a particular trial is the product of the conditional probabilities of responding correctly to each item. For example, even though the conditional probabilities of a correct response to A, B, C, and D during the first session of training on the last 4-item list were, respectively, 73%, 62%, 63%, and 91%, subjects completed only 25.9% of the trials correctly.

4.3.2. *Primacy Effect*

A primacy effect is obtained when subjects respond more accurately to items from the start of the list than to items from the middle of the list. The magnitude of the primacy effect increased markedly between the first and the last 7-item list. Of greater significance were the high absolute levels of accuracy at positions A and B at the start of training on the last 7-item list. On the *first* 7-item list, accuracy at positions A and B was respectively 79 per cent and 62 per cent; on the *last* 7-item list, 92 per cent and 88 per cent. On average, the subjects made only 4.5 and 9 errors respectively at positions A and B during the *first* session of training on the *last* 7-item list. During the first session of training on the last *4-item* list, accuracy of responding to items A and B was, respectively, only 73 per cent and 62 per cent. During that session, the average number of errors at positions A and B was respectively 14.25 and 37.

4.3.3 *Ideal List-Learner*

The few errors that the subjects made at positions A and B during the first session of training on their last 7-item list barely exceeded the minimum number of 'logical guesses' needed to identify those items. Logical guesses are necessary to the extent that subjects tend not to guess an item's ordinal position correctly with their *first* response to that item (see Figs. 4.1C and 4.3). To return to the example of guessing a 7-item PIN, an ideal list-learner would need an average of 3 logical guesses to identify A; 2.5 logical guesses to identify B; 2 logical guesses to identify C, and so on. An ideal list-learner learns a new list with the fewest possible errors. To achieve that level of exper-tise, a subject would have to remember the consequences of each error at a particular position and never repeat those errors. If, for example, an ideal list-learner responded to B, D, or G at the first position of a new 7-item list, she would not respond to any of those items at the start of subsequent trials. The extent to which the subjects' accuracy approximated that of an ideal list-learner is a measure of their expertise at learning new lists, for example, the subjects' accuracy at positions A and B at the start of training on the fourth 7-item list.

4.3.4 *Recency Effect*

A recency effect on a simultaneous chain would occur if the subjects learned to respond to the last item by default, because they knew it was the only item they had not already selected. For this, the subjects would have to store in working memory the first $n-1$ items to which they had responded on a given trial. Although a clear recency effect was observed at the end of training on 4-item lists, none was apparent at the start of training on 7-item lists. The relevant data are shown in Fig. 4.5. At the start of training on the subjects' last 4-item list (List 18), accuracy of responding to the last item (D) was 92 per cent. At the start of training on the *first* 7-item list, there was little difference between the low levels of accuracy at the last two positions (F: 27 per cent and G: 29 per cent). However, a strong recency effect was observed during the first session of training on the *last* 7-item list. While the subjects responded correctly at position F on 59 per cent of the opportunities to do so, they responded correctly at position G on 92 per cent of the opportunities to do so.[7] During the first session of training on their last 7-item list, the subjects made an average of only 0.5 of an error at position F (two monkeys made no errors at all, and two made one error each).

4.3.5 *Knowledge of Ordinal Position*

What did the monkeys actually *know* about these lists? The simplest representation of an arbitrary list, one that can be described as procedural knowledge, is a sequence of item–item associations between adjacent items, e.g. on a 7-item list, A–B, B–C, C–D, D–E, E–F, and F–G (Ebbinghaus 1964). However, they might also have learned the absolute positions for the items (i.e. A-position$_1$, B-position$_2$ . . . G-position$_7$). Evidence that monkeys can acquire such item-position associations during training on one or more lists has been obtained from experiments in which the subjects were given within-list subset tests (D'Amato and Colombo 1988), wild-card tests (D'Amato and Colombo 1989), derived list tests (Chen *et al.* 1997), and ordinal-position distractor tests (Orlov *et al.* 2000). Just as with the present experiment, in none of those experiments was there a requirement to learn associations between an item and its ordinal position. Thus, the subjects' knowledge of item-position associations was acquired incidentally.

   In the present experiment, ordinal knowledge was evaluated on a subset test composed of two types of trials. All 28 items used during training on the four 7-item lists were used in the subset test. As in previous experiments on ordinal knowledge, *within*-list trials were composed of items from a particular list (e.g. the subsets A_3B_3, A_3C_3, A_3D_3, A_3E_3, A_3F_3, A_3G_3, B_3C_3, B_3D_3 . . .

---

[7] An opportunity to respond at F occurred only when A, B, C, D, E had been correctly selected, and at G only when A, B, C, D, E, F had been correctly selected.

E_3F_3, E_3G_3, F_3G_3, from the third of the 7-item lists). The present experiment also included *between*-list trials on which subsets were composed of items drawn from *different* 7-item lists (e.g. the subsets A_2B_4, C_3F_4, E_1G_3, B_1E_2, and so on). The subset test was administered after the subjects mastered their fourth 7-item list.[8]

The subjects' performance on the subset test provided clear evidence that they could retrieve the ordinal position of all list items. Accuracy of responding to the first item, both on within- and between-list subsets, was almost perfect on the *first* presentation of each subset type. On average, the subjects responded correctly on 94 per cent of the trials on which a particular token of a within-list subset was presented for the first time (range across the subjects: 92–96 per cent) and on 91 per cent of the trials on which a particular token of a between-list subset was presented for the first time (range across the subjects: 89–96 per cent). The lowest levels of accuracy to a within- and a between-list subset were, respectively, 80 and 71 per cent. These data are significant because they show that each monkey represented, in long-term memory, the ordinal position of items from each of the four 7-item lists they learned and that they were able to compare, in working memory, the ordinal positions of any two items from any of the 7-item lists on the first occasion on which these items were presented. The ability to perform such comparisons on a first trial basis cannot be characterized as procedural knowledge.

4.3.6 *Distance and Magnitude Effects*

Two other features of the subjects' performance that cannot be characterized as procedural knowledge have been referred to as a 'distance' and 'magnitude' effects (Moyer and Landauer 1967; Banks 1977; Holyoak and Patterson 1981). A distance effect is obtained when some measure of performance varies with the ordinal distance between the positions in the original list of the two items used in the sub-test. A magnitude effect is obtained when

---

[8] Following the acquisition of List 4, each subject was retrained on Lists 1–4 to a criterion of completing 80% of the trials correctly in one session. They were then given a 2-item subset test (Swartz *et al.* 1991; Ohshiba 1997) containing each of the 84 within-list and 252 between-list 2-item subsets that could be drawn from the 28 items used to construct Lists 1–4. The subset test was given over five sessions. The subjects were rewarded for responding to the subset items in the order in which they appeared on the original list(s). For example, on a within-list trial on which items C and E from List 3 were presented, the subjects were rewarded for responding in the order $C_3 \rightarrow E_3$. Similarly, on a between-list trial on which item B from List 4 was presented with item D from List 1 the subjects were rewarded for responding in the order $B_4 \rightarrow D_1$.

some measure of performance varies with the absolute ordinal position in the original list of the first sub-set item. The accuracy functions in the upper portion of Fig. 4.6 provide evidence of a distance effect for accuracy of responding. Evidence of a magnitude effect for reaction times (RTs) is presented in the lower panel.

The distance between the items of a given subset pair is defined as the number of list positions that intervene between those items when the ordinal positions of the *original* lists are compared. Thus, all subsets containing the items C and D, whether composed of C_4D_3, C_2D_1, C_1D_1, etc. are considered to be separated by a distance of 1; all subsets containing the items BD, whether composed of B_2D_2, B_3D_1, etc. are considered to have a distance of 2, and so on. Here, we can contrast two different types of learning theory, which predict different outcomes. *Associative* theories of serial learning would predict that accuracy of responding to subset pairs would *decrease* as the distance between the items increased because associative strength between items decreases with distance. Theories of *serial learning* based on spatial representations of lists (e.g. Holyoak and Patterson 1981) would predict that accuracy would *increase* as the distance between the items increases because larger distances are more discriminable than smaller distances.

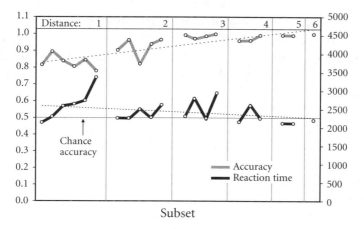

FIG. 4.6 Accuracy and reaction times on subset test: the upper functions show accuracy to each type of subset at distances 1–6. The lower functions show the median reaction time to the first item of each subset at distances 1–6. The dashed lines show the best-fit linear models.

Even though accuracy of responding was nearly perfect on many subset types, the upper set of functions shown in Fig. 4.6 provide clear evidence of a distance effect. At a distance of 1, the mean level of accuracy was 83 per cent; at distance of 2, 92 per cent. For distances greater than 2, the average level of accuracy was 99 per cent for all subsets. Were it not for this ceiling effect, it is likely that further increases in distance would have exerted an even stronger influence on accuracy.

An analysis of RTs of correct responses to the first item on subset tests revealed a strong magnitude effect at distance 1. That is, it took less time for the subjects to decide, say, that A came before B than to decide that F came before G. The relevant data are shown in the lower set of functions in Fig. 4.6. The median RT to the first item on AB trials was 2,180 msec. On FG trials, it was 3,374 msec. At distance 1, RTs increased approximately 470 msec for each increment in ordinal position. Analogous reaction time functions have been obtained from human subjects in experiments on the discriminability of adjacent pairs of letters of the alphabet when the alphabetical position of the first item is varied from trial to trial (Lovelace and Snodgrass 1971; Hamilton and Sanford 1978).

The distance and magnitude effects shown in Fig. 4.6 suggest that there were two processes for deciding which item of a subset pair came first. That decision was equally easy, and hence equally rapid, when the distance between items exceeded 1. At distance 1, however, the subjects are unable to perceive the ordinal position of each item directly. Instead, they attempt to do so by an iterative process in which they compared each item with a representation of the initial item on the original lists. The more advanced the first item is on the original list, the longer it took to determine its ordinal position.

4.4 Serial Expertise and Declarative Memory

The sequences that Rosencrantz, Macduff, Benedict, and Oberon learned are by far the most difficult lists mastered by any non-human primate, including those trained in experiments on the linguistic and numerical abilities of apes (Rumbaugh 1977; Premack 1976; Matsuzawa 1985; Boysen et al. 1993). It is doubtful, however, that the performance described in this study reflects the upper limit of a monkey's serial capacity. The ease with which these monkeys learned 7-item lists and the steady decrease in the number of sessions needed to master new lists suggests that they could learn them in fewer than 7 sessions and that they could also master longer lists.

What sort of memory is needed to perform these tasks with expertise accrued from learning? The monkey's serial expertise reveals a serious limitation in models of memory that are based on the distinction between declarative and procedural knowledge—'knowing that' C comes before E, but after B, etc., as opposed to 'knowing how' to execute a fixed motor sequence (Ryle 1949; Squire 1994; Schachter and Tulving 1994). As currently defined, neither category of knowledge is useful in explaining a monkey's serial expertise. Declarative knowledge presupposes the ability to encode knowledge as linguistic propositions. Procedural knowledge cannot account for sequences that are executed with physically different responses on each trial. Procedural knowledge is also unable to account for a monkey's ability to ascertain an item's ordinal position on a new list with almost maximal logical efficiency or its ability to compare the ordinal positions of items from different lists on a first-trial basis.

To account for a monkey's serial expertise, theories of declarative memory have to make provision for non-verbal knowledge.[9] One candidate is a memory system in which information is encoded as images in an analogical format (Kosslyn 1980; Lashley 1951; Paivio 1975). Analogical theories of cognition have been criticized on the grounds that images convey less information than propositional representations (Pylyshyn 1981). That criticism may be valid in the case of human cognition, but it does not apply to monkeys. Indeed, it is the utter irrelevance of propositional representations that argues for analogical representation as an explanation of the accuracy and reaction time functions shown in Fig. 4.6.

From an evolutionary perspective, definitions of declarative knowledge that rely on linguistic propositions make little sense. Aside from the results of the present experiment, there is a considerable body of evidence suggesting that declarative knowledge evolved before language (Bickerton 1995;

---

[9] Theories of declarative memory would also have to accommodate unconscious thought. A discussion of that issue would make for too large a digression. It should be noted, however, that an analysis of human cognition of *any* type also questions the validity of definitions of declarative memory that use consciousness as a defining criterion. The logic of Freud's theory of unconscious thought applies as much to rational thought as it does to irrational thought. A case in point is Chomsky's (1957) distinction between surface and deep structure. People are not conscious of deep structure when they speak but that fact has never been used to argue that grammar should be regarded as procedural rather than declarative knowledge.

Reber 1993). For example, a monkey's ability to judge the relative social rank of other monkeys in their living groups requires declarative knowledge (Harcourt and de Waal 1992). Such judgements presuppose the ability to represent the ordinal position of other monkeys, in different combinations, in a manner similar to that observed on the subset tests administered in this experiment. Another non-verbal precursor of declarative knowledge is suggested by an animal's ability to represent spatial information and to use that information to solve a problem (Gallistel 1992). By encoding an item's ordinal position as a spatial position during list learning, a monkey could compare the ordinal position of items from various lists with respect to pre-existing spatial co-ordinates. That hypothesis is supported by the reaction time data obtained on within- and between-list subset tests.

4.5 Serial Expertise, Reference, and Grammatical Ability

But what does expertise in serial memory tell us about language? Edding-ton's imaginary 'army of monkeys ... strumming on typewriters' lacked the serial expertise of the subjects of this experiment. However, serial expertise *per se* would not have increased the likelihood of any linguistic output. The ability to produce arbitrary sequences is a necessary condition for learning any human language, but it is not sufficient. The sequences in question must also *refer* to particular events or objects.

Recent ape language projects provide an instructive example of the kind of confusion that results when serial skills are equated with linguistic skills. The goal of the ape language projects reflected the Chomskian *Zeitgeist* in which 'mere' vocabulary was considered less important than grammar as the defining feature of language. The ability to learn a finite set of words, one at a time, was considered qualitatively simpler than the ability to combine them into novel sentences. On this view, evidence that an ape could learn to produce simple sequences would provide a basis for claiming that apes could learn language.

Although claims about the grammaticality of an ape's sequences (Gardner and Gardner 1975; Premack 1976) have been widely criticized (Terrace *et al.* 1979; Pinker 1994), it is generally assumed that an ape can acquire a sizeable vocabulary (Gardner and Gardner 1973; Rumbaugh 1977; Premack 1976; Patterson 1978). Because an ape's ability to learn words has been viewed as less controversial than its grammatical ability, the meanings of the words of an ape's vocabulary have undergone less scrutiny than claims about grammar. It is easy to show, however, that the meanings of the words of an ape's vocabulary have been greatly exaggerated. There is no evidence that any of those words were used to *refer* to objects or events or that they had any function other than to request some reward.

Skinner (1957) distinguished between two kinds of verbal behaviour in young children. *Mands*, the first verbal utterances of a child,[10] are requests for *primary* reinforcers. For example, *ice cream, hug, more*, are uttered in order to elicit concrete events through the agency of the listener—in these cases, getting ice cream, a hug, or a second helping. *Tacts* call attention to particular objects, for example *car, moon, doggie*.

The spontaneous requests of apes for particular rewards are mands, e.g. a chimp signing *eat, drink, tickle*, etc., or touching the lexigrams *eat* or *drink* on a computer keyboard. Whether apes use tacts, however, is less clear. Symbols used in the presence of particular stimuli to earn a reward are not tacts. The function of a tact is to inform, not to beg. To qualify as a tact, a symbol has to be used by a speaker to convey information to a listener about some object or event, in the absence of primary reinforcement. By that criterion, there is no evidence that apes tact.

The achievements of Kanzi and other bonobo chimpanzees (*Pan paniscus*) provide an example of the problems inherent in the interpretation of an ape's use of symbols. Savage-Rumbaugh has shown that, unlike common chimpanzees (*Pan troglodytes*), bonobo chimpanzees acquire vocabularies of ASL, lexigrams, and spoken English by observational learning. *Pan troglodytes* learn to use symbols only after extensive training by their human teachers. *Pan paniscus* can learn to use the same symbols simply by observing how their teachers use them. This suggests a real difference between *P. troglodytes* and *P. paniscus* with respect to their ability to imitate the actions of their human caretakers. The question remains, however, why do bonobos imitate their teachers? Are they attempting to communicate their perceptions of the world, or are they simply doing what's expected of them to ensure a steady flow of primary reinforcers? There is no evidence that bonobos would continue to use their extensive vocabularies in an environment in which their

---

[10] Skinner has argued that children learn to use mands before they learn to use tacts because mands were 'pure' operants that were emitted in a wide variety of contexts and because they were not under the control of particular discriminative stimuli. As Nelson (1996) and others have noted, however, there is no empirical evidence that mands are learned before tacts.

caretakers did not provide food, drinks, or games of chase and tickle. Until that obvious interpretation of an ape's use of symbols can be ruled out, it is premature to argue that the symbols apes learn to use function as tacts (Terrace 1985).

If, as all the available evidence suggests, apes do not use symbols referentially, questions about their grammatical ability are premature. The same can be said of theories of the evolution of language that use grammatical ability as a criterion for distinguishing between human and non-human primates. Paradoxically, the hard question about the evolution of language is not at the level of syntax or serial expertise, but at the level of the word. The ability to use arbitrary symbols to solve a discrimination problem and to learn arbitrary lists of symbols are impressive intellectual achievements. Those achievements should not, however, be confused with grammatical ability. A grammar provides speakers with a mechanism for creating particular *meanings* by arranging *meaningful* symbols into particular sequences. A grammar also provides listeners with a mechanism for comprehending the *meaning* of symbolic sequences (Chomsky 1957, 1965). Meaning is not a factor, however, either in the mastery of symbolic discrimination problems, or in the development of serial expertise.

4.6 The Evolution of Language

Whether our ancestors' first linguistic utterances consisted of single words or grammatical sequences remains a matter of considerable controversy (Bickerton 1995; Deacon 1997). What is clear, however, is that before human or non-human primates could communicate with language, they would have to be able to assume both the roles of a speaker and a listener (Terrace 1985). To understand the meaning of a word, both the speaker and the listener must know that the word in question *refers* to a particular object or event. It is therefore reasonable to assume that the social function of language evolved before the ability to arrange words grammatically (Terrace 1970; Bickerton 1995; Deacon 1997; Donald 1991). If a speaker and a listener are unable to share the meaning of a word, how could they share the meaning of a sentence?

Like referential ability, grammatical ability is uniquely human. However, grammatical ability appears to be the endpoint of a long process of cognitive development that began when some ancestral group of primates discovered how to partake in social exchanges in which speakers registered whether their listeners understood their messages and listeners solicited a speaker's attention if the speaker's message was not understood. To ignore that process is to create a gap between extant forms of primate communication and language that cannot be filled by a single cognitive mutation.

It is encouraging that many candidates for filling this gap other than grammatical ability have been suggested in recent discussions of criteria for distinguishing *Homo sapiens* from other primates. These include the intentional use of individual symbols—whether sounds, manual signs, mimetic movements—mimesis (Donald 1991), 'on-line' vs. 'off-line' thinking (Bickerton 1995), a 'theory of mind' (Dunbar 1998), and the relaxation of the social structure of primate groups to allow subordinates to differ with more dominant members of a group (Byrne and Whiten 1988; Barker *et al.* 1992).

It is by no means clear how these antecedents evolved and how they eventually coalesced into language. What is clear is that theories of the evolution of language no longer need to be limited to positions that George Miller described as the 'miraculous' and the 'impossible' views of language (Bruner 1983: 34). The former, a strictly nativist account, assumes an abrupt change in the structure of the brain that resulted in language (Pinker and Bloom 1990); the latter, that language can be reduced to a set of learned associations between various symbols and responses (e.g. Skinner 1957). As the Edinburgh, London, and Paris conferences on the evolution of language have made clear, the miraculous view of language has begun to lose its appeal in the face of more focused questions about the functional constituents of language and their origins. Answers to those questions, including the significance of serial expertise in monkeys, will contribute to better definitions of the kinds of changes in primate intelligence and communication that gave rise to language.

FURTHER READING

BRANNON, E. M. and TERRACE, H. S. (2000), 'Representation of the Numerosities 1–9 by Rhesus Monkeys', *Journal of Experimental Psychology: Animal Behavioral Processes*, 25: 31–49.

ROBERTS, W. A. (1998), *Principles of Animal Cognition* (New York: McGraw-Hill).

SHETTLEWORTH, S. J. (1998), *Cognition, Evolution, and Behaviour* (Oxford & New York: Oxford University Press).

TERRACE, H. S. (1985), 'Animal Cognition: Thinking without Languages', *Philosophical Transactions of the Royal Society, London*, B308: 113–28.

TERRACE, H. S. (1985), 'In the Beginning Was the Name', *American Psychologist*, 40: 1011–28.

REFERENCES

BANKS, W. P. (1977), 'Encoding and Processing of Symbolic Information in Comparative Judgments', *The Psychology of Learning and Motivation*, 11: 101–59.

BARKER, J. H., COSMIDES, L., and TOOBY, J. (1992), *The Adapted Mind: Evolutionary Psychology and the Generation of Culture* (New York: Oxford University Press).

BICKERTON, D. (1995), *Language and Human Behavior* (Seattle: University of Washington Press).

BIRO, D., and MATSUZAWA, T. (1999), 'Numerical Ordering in a Chimpanzee (Pan troglodytes): Planning, Executing and Monitoring', *Journal of Comparative Psychology*, 113/2: 178–85.

BOYSEN, S. T. (1993), 'Counting in Chimpanzees: Nonhuman Principles and Emergent Properties of Number', in S. T. B. E. J. Capaldi (ed.), *The Development of Numerical Competence Animal and Human Models* (New Jersey: Lawrence Erlbaum), 39–59.

—— BERNSTON, G. G., SHREYER, T. A., and QUIGLEY, K. S. (1993), 'Processing of Ordinality and Transitivity by Chimpanzees (Pan troglodytes)', *Journal of Comparative Psychology*, 107/2: 208–15.

BRANNON, E. M., and TERRACE, H. S. (1998), 'Ordering of the Numerosities 1–9 by Monkeys', *Science*, 282: 746–9.

—— —— (2000), 'Representation of the Numerosities 1–9 by Rhesus Monkeys', *Journal of Experimental Psychology: Animal Behavioral Processes*, 25: 31–49.

BREUKELAAR, J. W. C., and DALRYMPLE-ALFORD, J. C. (1998), 'Timing Ability and Numerical Competence in Rats', *Journal of Experimental Psychology: Animal Behavior Processes*, 24/1: 84–97.

BRUNER, J. S. (1983), *Child's Talk: Learning to Use Language* (New York: W. W. Norton).

BYRNE, R. W., and WHITEN, A. (1988), *Machiavellian Intelligence: Social Expertise and the Evolution of Intellect in Monkeys* (Oxford: Clarendon Press).

CHASE, W. G., and ERICSSON, K. A. (1981), 'Skilled Memory', in J. R. Anderson (ed.), *Cognitive Skills and Their Acquisition* (Hillsdale, NJ: Lawrence Erlbaum).

CHEN, S., SWARTZ, K., and TERRACE, H. S. (1997), 'Knowledge of the Ordinal Position of List Items in Rhesus Monkeys', *Psychological Science*, 8: 80–6.

—— —— —— (2000), 'Serial Learning by Rhesus Monkeys: II. Learning 4-item Lists by Trial and Error', *Journal of Experimental Psychology: Animal Behavioral Processes*, 26: 274–85.

CHI, M. T. H., FELTOVICH, P. J., and GLASER, R. (1981), 'Categorization and Representation of Physics Problems by Experts and Novices', *Cognitive Science*, 5/2: 121–52.

—— GLASER, R., and FARR, M. (1988), *The Nature of Expertise* (Hillsdale, NJ: Lawrence Erlbaum).

CHOMSKY, N. (1957), *Syntactic Structures* (The Hague: Mouton).

—— (1965), *Aspects of the Theory of Syntax* (Cambridge, Mass.: MIT Press).

D'AMATO, M. R., and COLOMBO, M. (1988), 'Representation of Serial Order in Monkeys (*Cebus apella*)', *Journal of Experimental Psychology*, 14: 131–9.

—— —— (1989), 'Serial Learning with Wild Card Items by Monkeys Cebus apella: Implications for Knowledge of Ordinal Position', *Journal of Comparative Psychology*, 15/3: 252–61.

DEACON, T. W. (1997), *The Symbolic Species* (New York: W. W. Norton).

DONALD, M. (1991), *Origins of the Modern Mind* (Cambridge, Mass.: Harvard University Press).

DUNBAR, R. (1998), 'Theory of Mind and the Evolution of Language', in J. R. Hurford, M. Studdert-Kennedy, and C. Knight (eds.), *Approaches to the Evolution of Language* (Cambridge: Cambridge University Press), 92–110.

EBBINGHAUS, H. (1964), *Memory: A Contribution to Experimental Psychology* (first published 1885; transl. 1913) (New York: Dover).

EDDINGTON, A. S. (1928), *The Nature of the Physical World* (Cambridge: Cambridge University Press).

EICHENBAUM, H., FAGAN, A., and COHEN, N. J. (1986), 'Normal Olfactory Discrimination Learning Set and Facilitation of Reversal After Medial-Temporal Damage in Rats: Implications for an Account of Preserved Learning Abilities in Amnesia', *Journal of Neuroscience*, 6: 1876–84.

GALLISTEL, C. R. (1992), *Animal Cognition* (Cambridge, Mass.: MIT Press).

GARDNER, B. T., and GARDNER, R. A. (1973), *Teaching Sign Language to the Chimpanzee: Washoe* (University Park, Pa.: The Psychological Cinema Register).

—— —— (1975), 'Evidence for Sentence Constituents in the Early Utterances of Child Chimpanzees', *Journal of Experimental Psychology*, 104: 244–67.

HAMILTON, J. M. E., and SANFORD, A. J. (1978), 'The Symbolic Distance Effect for Alphabetic Order Judgments: A Subjective Report and Reaction Time Analysis', *Quarterly Journal of Experimental Psychology*, 30: 33–43.

HARCOURT, A. H., and DE WAAL, F. B. M. (1992), 'Coalitions and Alliances: Are Primates More Complex Than Non-primates?', in A. H. Harcourt and F. B. M. de Waal (eds.), *Coalitions and Alliances in Humans and Other Animals* (New York: Oxford University Press).

HARLOW, H. F. (1950), 'Analysis of Discrimination Learning by Monkeys'. *Journal of Experimental Psychology*, 40: 26–39.

HAUSER, M. D., MACNEILAGE, P., and WARE, M. (1996), 'Numerical Representations in Primates', *Proceedings of the National Academy of Science*, 93: 1514–17.

HERRNSTEIN, R. J., LOVELAND, D. H., and CABLE, C. (1976), 'Natural Concepts in Pigeons', *Journal of Experimental Psychology: Animal Behavior Processes*, 2: 285–302.

HOLYOAK, K. J., and PATTERSON, K. K. (1981), 'A Positional Discriminability Model of Linear-Order Judgments', *Journal of Experimental Psychology*, 7/6: 1283–302.

HUNTER, M. W., III, and KAMIL, A. C. (1971), 'Object Discrimination Learning Set and Hypothesis Behavior in the Northern Blue Jay (*Cyanocitta cristata*)', *Psychonomic Science*, 22: 271–3.

KENDRICK, D., RILLING, M., and STONEBRAKER, T. (1981), 'Stimulus Control of Delayed Matching in Pigeons: Directed Forgetting', *Journal of the Experimental Analysis of Behavior*, 36/2: 241–51.

KEPPEL, G., POSTMAN, L., and ZAVORTINK, B. (1968), 'Studies of Learning to Learn: VIII. The Influence of Massive Amounts of Training upon the Learning and Retention of Paired-Associate Lists', *Journal of Verbal Learning and Verbal Behavior*, 7: 790–6.

KOSSLYN, S. (1980), *Image and Mind* (Cambridge, Mass.: Harvard University Press).

LARKIN, J. H., McDERMOTT, J., SIMON, D. P., and SIMON, H. A. (1980), 'Expert and Novice Performance in Solving Physics Problems', *Science*, 208: 1335–42.

LASHLEY, K. S. (1951), 'The Problem of Serial Order in Behavior', in L. A. Jeffries (ed.), *Cerebral Mechanisms in Behavior* (New York: John Wiley), 112–36.

LESGOLD, A., ROBINSON, H., FELTOVITCH, P., GLASER, R., KLOPFER, D., and WANG, Y. (1988) (eds.), *Expertise in a Complex Skill: Diagnosing X-ray Pictures* (Hillsdale, NJ: Lawrence Erlbaum).

LOVELACE, E. A., and SNODGRASS, R. D. (1971), 'Decision Times for Alphabetic Order of Letter Pairs', *Journal of Experimental Psychology*, 88/2: 258–64.

MATSUZAWA, T. (1985), 'Use of Numbers by a Chimpanzee', *Nature*, 315/6014: 57–9.

MECK, W. H., and CHURCH, R. M. (1983), 'A Mode Control Model of Counting and Timing Processes', *Journal of Experimental Psychology: Animal Behavior Processes*, 9/3: 320–34.

MILLER, G. A., GALANTER, E., and PRIBRAM, K. H. (1960), *Plans and the Structure of Behavior* (New York: Holt Rhinehart & Winston).

MOYER, R. S., and LANDAUER, T. K. (1967), 'Time Required for Judgments of Numerical Inequality', *Nature*, 215: 1519–20.

NELSON, K. (1996), *Language in Cognitive Development* (Cambridge: Cambridge University Press).

OHSHIBA, N. (1997), 'Memorization of Serial Items by Japanese Monkeys, a Chimpanzee, and Humans', *Japanese Psychological Research*, 39: 236–52.

ORLOV, T., YAKOVLEV, B., HOCHSTEIN, S., and ZOHARY, E. (2000), 'Macaque Monkeys Categorize Images by Their Ordinal Number', *Nature*, 404: 77–80.

PAIVIO, A. (1975), 'Perceptual Comparisons Through the Mind's Eye', *Memory and Cognition*, 3: 635–47.

PATTERSON, F. G. (1978), 'The Gestures of a Gorilla: Language Acquisition by Another Pongid', *Brain and Language*, 12: 72–97.

PINKER, S. (1994), *The Language Instinct* (New York: William Morrow).

—— and BLOOM, P. (1990), 'Natural Language and Natural Selection', *Behavioral and Brain Sciences*, 13: 704–84.

PREMACK, D. (1976), *Intelligence in Ape and Man* (Hillsdale, NJ: Lawrence Erlbaum).

PYLYSHYN, Z. (1981), 'The Imagery Debate: Analogue Versus Tacit Knowledge', *Psychological Review*, 88: 16–45.

REBER, A. S. (1993), *Implicit Learning and Tacit Knowledge: An Essay on the Cognitive Unconscious* (New York: Oxford University Press).

RUMBAUGH, D. M. (1977), *Language Learning by a Chimpanzee: The Lana Project* (New York: Academic Press).

RYLE, G. (1949), *The Concept of Mind* (New York: Barnes & Noble).

SANDS, S. F., and WRIGHT, A. A. (1980), 'Serial Probe Recognition Performance by a Rhesus Monkey and a Human with 10- and 20-Item Lists', *Journal of Experimental Psychology: Animal Behavior Processes*, 6: 386–96.

SAVAGE-RUMBAUGH, E. S. (1994), *Kanzi: The Ape at the Brink of the Human Mind* (New York: Wiley).

SCHACHTER, D. L., and TULVING, E. (1994), *What are the Memory Systems of 1994?* (Cambridge, Mass.: MIT Press).

SCHOENFELD, A. H., and HERRMANN, D. J. (1982), 'Problem Perception and Knowledge Structure in Expert and Novice Mathematical Problem Solvers', *Journal of Experimental Psychology: Learning, Memory, and Cognition*, 8/5: 484–94.

SIMON, H. A., and CHASE, W. G. (1973), 'Skill in Chess', *American Scientist*, 61: 394–403.

SKINNER, B. F. (1957), *Verbal Behavior* (New York: Appleton-Century-Crofts).

SQUIRE, L. R. (1994), 'Declarative and Nondeclarative Memory', in D. L. Schachter and E. Tulving (eds.), *Memory Systems 1994* (Cambridge, Mass.: MIT Press), 204–31.

SWARTZ, K. B., CHEN, S., and TERRACE, H. S. (1991), 'Serial Learning by Rhesus Monkeys. I: Acquisition and Retention of Multiple Four-item Lists'. *Journal of Experimental Psychology: Animal Behavior Processes*, 17: 396–410.

TERRACE, H. S. (1970), 'Towards a Doctrine of Radical Behaviorism', *Contemporary Psychology*, 15: 531–5.

—— (1984), 'Simultaneous Chaining: The Problem it Poses for Traditional Chaining Theory', in M. L. Commons, R. J. Herrnstein, and A. R. Wagner (eds.), *Quantitative Analyses of Behavior: Discrimination Processes* (Cambridge, Mass.: Ballinger), 115–38.

—— (1985), 'In the Beginning Was the Name', *American Psychologist*, 40: 1011–28.

—— (1987), 'Chunking by a Pigeon in a Serial Learning Task', *Nature*, 325: 149–51.

—— PETITTO, L. A., SANDERS, R. J., and BEVER, T. G. (1979), 'Can an Ape Create a Sentence?', *Science*, 206: 891–902.

TULVING, E., and SCHACHTER, D. L. (1990), 'Priming and Human Memory Systems', *Science*, 247: 301–6.

WASSERMAN, E., and BHATT, A. (1992), 'Conceptualization of Natural and Artificial Stimuli by Pigeons', in W. Honig and K. Fetterman (eds.), *Cognitive Aspects of Stimulus Control* (Hillsdale, NJ: Lawrence Erlbaum), 203–23.

WRIGHT, A. A., SANTIAGO, HECTOR C., and SANDS, STEPHEN F. (1984), 'Monkey Memory: *Same/Different* Concept Learning, Serial Probe Acquisition, and Probe Delay Effects', *Journal of Experimental Psychology: Animal Behavior Processes*, 10/4: 513–29.

PART II

Internal Triggers to Transition: Genes, Processing, Culture, Gesture, and Technology

5   ProtocadherinXY: A Candidate Gene for Cerebral Asymmetry and Language

T. J. CROW

5.1 The Problem for Evolutionary Theory

'Human language is an embarrassment for evolutionary theory', perhaps, as Premack (1985: 283) suggested, 'because it is vastly more powerful than one can account for in terms of selective fitness', but also as Chomsky (1972) had pointed out, in language we have a faculty without clear precedent in other primates (see also Penner 2000). Bickerton (1995) has argued that language appeared suddenly and recently. Evidence, such as rock art, for a representational capacity that might parallel possession of language, can be traced back, with some difficulty, to around 90,000 years (Noble and Davidson 1996; Mellars 1998). Such capacity is absent in the archaeological record that relates to the Neanderthals (Mellars 1998), as also in the longer record that relates to *Homo erectus* (Bickerton 1995; Noble and Davidson 1996). While these hominid species are credited with protolanguage, the components of language (e.g. grammatical elements and structure, embedding and sub-categorization of verbs) characteristic of modern humans are assumed to have been absent. Thus the acquisition of the capacity for language represents a recent, and datable, discontinuity in hominid evolution. The parsimonious conclusion (because it links the distinctive characteristic of the species to its genetic origin) is that the origin of language coincided with the transition to modern *Homo sapiens* dated to somewhere between 100,000 and 150,000 years ago (Stringer and McKie 1996).

This conclusion forces us to take sides in a long-running dispute about the nature of the evolutionary process, particularly as it relates to speciation. The focus of the debate is on what genetic change accounts for the transition from one species to another and by what selective process it is retained.

5.1.1 Gradualism in Evolution

The prevailing view within evolutionary theory—the Biological or Isolation Species Concept—is that populations separate, become subject to different environmental selective pressures, and acquire genetic variation that leads to reproductive isolation (Mayr 1963; Dobzhansky 1937). This view is consistent with Darwin's original concept, represented, for example, in the only figure that appears in the *Origin of Species* (Darwin 1859: ch. 4). The figure indicates that over the passage of thousands of generations variations accumulate and lineages separate. Some lineages are extinguished, and those that survive may be widely separated in geography and perhaps also in adaptive characteristics. Darwin was anxious to emphasize the continuity of the variation within and between species. No qualitative distinction was drawn.

In the case of the origin of language, viewed as a speciation event, however, two problems arise with this view. The first is that there is no evidence of a gradual accumulation of linguistic capabilities over a long period. The second is that the dispersal and geographical isolation of modern humans must have occurred *after* the appearance of language, with the propensity for language being present in all humans *despite* that dispersal and isolation. The alternative would be to assume that such changes occurred independently but with the same effect in populations that had already separated. To suggest this is to invoke an implausible process of parallel evolution in separate continents. Clearly the genetic events being considered here, as also those that define any species, must be limited in time. But *how* restricted in time and space a speciation event may be expected to be is the subject of debate within evolutionary theory (see, for instance, Otte and Endler 1989; Howard and Berlocher 1998; Coyne and Orr 1998; Magurran and May 1999).

5.1.2 Discontinuity in Evolution

Discontinuity theory thus challenges Darwinian gradualism. Amongst the earliest proponents of discontinuity were Bateson (1894), and, in the wake of the rediscovery of Mendelian principles, de Vries (1905). A radical attack was mounted by Goldschmidt (1940) with his concept of 'hopeful monsters', the outcome of macromutations that generated innovations in a single step. With reference to the time course of evolutionary change in the fossil record,

Eldredge and Gould (1972) reintroduced the question of discontinuity with their concept of 'punctuated equilibria'.

Theories of discontinuity face two general problems of their own, however. (1) How is sudden change selected? If change is not gradual as Darwin supposed, by what new principle does speciation occur? The problem can be illustrated with reference to Goldschmidt's 'hopeful monsters'. How can a radical departure from a body plan previously adjusted by a long process of environmental selection be an adaptational improvement? (2) By what genetic mechanism is 'between-species' to be distinguished from 'within-species' variations?

One answer (Goldschmidt's solution) to the second question is that the critical changes that distinguish one species from another relate particularly to chromosomal change, that is, to structural rearrangements of the chromosomal complement. These would affect the capacity for successful reproduction between individuals having the different arrangements, by leading to infertility, or sterility of the offspring. While this mechanism has been strongly promoted by some authors (e.g. White 1973; King 1993) others (e.g. Coyne and Orr 1998) are unconvinced of any necessary relation between chromosomal change and species transitions. For example it is argued that inter-species hybrid sterility may be present when no structural changes are detectable, and that some within-species variations in chromosomal structure are unassociated with a reduction in fertility. Where obvious structural differences between species are present there is the possibility that these accumulated after, rather than at the time of, the speciation event.

In this chapter I shall suggest (following Crow 1993*a*,*b*; 1996; 1998*a*,*b*; 2000) that consideration of language and its relation to the speciation of modern *Homo sapiens* offers a possible solution to these problems—specifically that it is a subset of chromosomal changes, those relating to the sex chromosomes—that has particular relevance to species transitions, and that this is the case because such changes (perhaps particularly those relating to regions of homology, i.e. DNA sequence similarity, between the two sex chromosomes) can be subject to a process of sexual selection, a process that refines and adapts the consequences of the primary change. Sexual selection is the process of mate choice that Darwin distinguished from natural selection to explain features such as the deer's antlers and the peacock's tail that differentiate one sex from the other within a species. The sequence of events in which a chromosomal change is followed by sexual selection is consistent with the implication of Darwin's (1871) juxtaposition of his treatise on the *Descent of Man* with his theory of sexual selection—that *Homo sapiens* had evolved by some process of sexual selection, although this implication seems not to have been made explicit.

5.1.3 *The Out-of-Africa Hypothesis*

The current context of discussions of human evolution is the Out-of-Africa hypothesis—the theory that modern *Homo sapiens* originated some time between 100,000 and 150,000 years ago as a result of a genetic change that occurred in a population somewhere in East Africa (Stringer and McKie 1996; see Fig. 5.1). A parsimonious view is that it was that change that accounted for the transition from protolanguage to full human language and that it is the latter capacity that accounts for the extraordinary biological success of *Homo sapiens* compared to precursor primate and hominid species. That language is the defining feature of humanity seems first to have been clearly stated by de Condillac (1746). The universality of the capacity for language to human populations (as appreciated by Sapir 1921) reflects the genetic identity of the species, an identity that is invariant with respect to the environment.

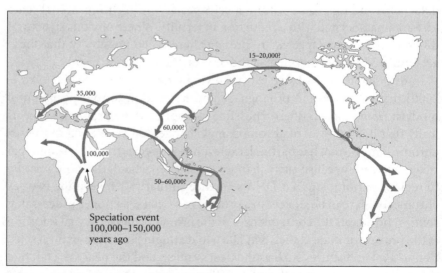

FIG. 5.1 The diaspora of modern *Homo sapiens* (adapted from Stringer and McKie 1996: 169) to emphasize the significance of the genetic change (here designated a speciation event) that enabled the transition from a prior hominid species.

But what could that change have been? There are few candidates, but the one that has been available at least since the observations of Broca 135 years ago is that the brain lateralized, and that some component of language was confined to the dominant hemisphere. The singularity of brain lateralization is strongly supported by cross-species comparison within primates. Handedness, the outward manifestation of hemispheric dominance, is strongly skewed to the right in human populations (Perelle and Ehrman 1994; Provins *et al.* 1982) and Annett (1985) has argued that it can be accounted for by a single gene. In contrast, according to the observations of Marchant and McGrew (1996) of 38 chimpanzees in the wild in the Gombe National Park, while hand preference to the right or to the left may be a characteristic of the individual, directional bias at the level of the population is absent. No other index so clearly distinguishes the two species (Fig. 5.2).

It appears that directional handedness is an outward manifestation of an anatomical asymmetry in the human brain that is probably best represented as a 'torque' (Fig. 5.3). In most individuals the right frontal lobe is wider than the left and the left occipital lobe is wider than the right. Frontal and occipital asymmetries are intercorrelated (Bear *et al.* 1986) and are reflected in the

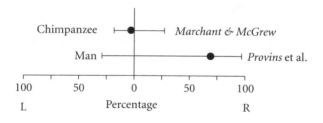

	Number of individuals	activities
Chimpanzee	38	46
Man	1960	75

Fig. 5.2 Hand preference in chimpanzees and *Homo sapiens* compared. Data for chimpanzees refer to a community of 38 animals (*Pan troglodytes schweinfurthii*) observed in the Gombe National Park by Marchant and McGrew (1996). Data for *Homo sapiens* were collected by questionnaire from populations of undergraduate psychology students in Scotland and Australia by Provins *et al.* (1982). In each case the data relate to a wide range of everyday activities. Medians and boundary values (horizontal bars) for 95% of the population have been extracted from graphs in the original publications.

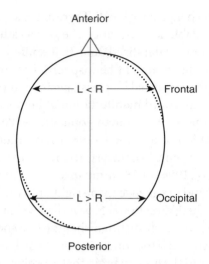

FIG. 5.3 The anatomical 'torque' in the human
brain from right frontal to left occipital.

asymmetry of the planum temporale described by Geschwind and Levitsky
(1968). A correlate at the cellular level has been uncovered by Buxhoeveden
and Casanova (2000). They report that the mean distance between the col-
umns of pyramidal cells in the superior temporal gyrus (Wernicke's area),
asymmetrical to the left in the human brain, does not differ between the
hemispheres in the chimpanzee.

5.2 Sex Differences and X–Y Linkage

Sex has a major influence on the development of language (Maccoby and
Jacklin 1975; Halpern 1992). Girls talk at an earlier age than boys (Moore
1967) and have greater verbal ability (Butler 1984). What explains this sex
difference? One possibility is that lateralization for language is related to
sex. In an examination of the UK National Child Development cohort it was
found that at the age of 11 years, on an index of relative hand skill, girls were
more strongly lateralized than boys. Furthermore, degree of lateralization
predicted verbal ability (Crow et al. 1998). Those close to the point of 'hemispheric indecision' (equal hand skill) were impaired in the acquisition of
words relative to the rest of the population. Girls at this age had significantly
more words than boys but the relationship of verbal ability to hand skill

was the same in the two sexes. Thus the acquisition of words may reflect the rate at which dominance is established in one hemisphere, girls being more lateralized or lateralizing faster than boys (Shucard *et al.* 1987). It is of interest that, as far as is known, this difference in the acquisition of words is not accompanied by a sex difference in grammatical ability.

A clue to the genetic mechanism comes from observations of individuals with sex chromosome aneuploidies (a deficit or an excess of sex chromosomes relative to the normal two—XX in a female and XY in a male). Individuals who lack an X chromosome (Turner's syndrome) have relative impairments of non-dominant hemisphere ability whilst those who have an extra X (XXY, Klinefelter's, or XXX syndromes) have dominant hemisphere deficits. This strongly suggests that an asymmetry determinant (the 'right shift factor' to use Annett's (1985) term for the cerebral dominance gene) is present on the X. However, the fact that normal males (XY) do not have deficits in non-dominant, that is, spatial, ability comparable to those that are seen in Turner's syndrome, indicates that the presence of the Y chromosome must complement the influence of a single X chromosome—i.e. the gene must also be present on the Y. Thus it can be concluded that the gene is in the relatively select class that is present in homologous form on both the X and the Y chromosome (Crow 1993*b*; see Netley 1998). Evidence consistent with X–Y linkage was obtained from a family study (Corballis *et al.* 1996); X linkage is supported by a recent analysis of the literature and a new family collection (McKeever 2000).

X–Y homologous genes are an unusual class, most being generated by translocations of blocks of sequences on the X to the Y chromosome; that is, there is a duplication on the Y of sequences that were previously present only on the X (see Fig. 5.4). These translocations can be dated in the course of mammalian evolution (Lambson *et al.* 1992). Those of greatest interest are the two events that have occurred since the separation of the chimpanzee and hominid lineages:

1. A translocation from the X chromosome long arm (the Xq21.3 region) to the Y chromosome short arm (Yp) that is estimated to have taken place 2 to 3 million years ago (Sargent *et al.* 1996). The translocated segment on Yp was split by a subsequent paracentric inversion that left two blocks in Yp that are homologous to the original block in Xq21.3. The paracentric inversion has not been dated (Mumm *et al.* 1997; Schwartz *et al.* 1998) although this is a question of great interest (see Laval *et al.* 1998 for evidence of linkage of handedness to the Xq21.3 region).

2. The generation of the second pseudoautosomal region at the telomeres (ends) of the long arms of the X and Y chromosomes (Freije *et al.* 1992).

The Xq21.3/Yp translocation (as probably also the events relating to the second pseudoautosomal region) created new Y-linked representations of X-linked genes and thereby generated a balance of control of these genes between the sexes that was not previously present. Such an event occurred in a single male. The immediate effect was to double the dose of the relevant genes in that individual (relative to other males, and to females, in

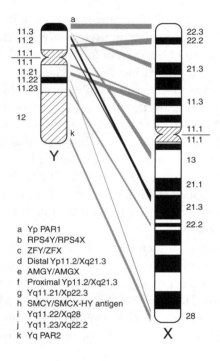

a Yp PAR1
b RPS4Y/RPS4X
c ZFY/ZFX
d Distal Yp11.2/Xq21.3
e AMGY/AMGX
f Proximal Yp11.2/Xq21.3
g Yq11.21/Xp22.3
h SMCY/SMCX-HY antigen
i Yq11.22/Xq28
j Yq11.23/Xq22.2
k Yq PAR2

FIG. 5.4 Regions of homology between the X and the Y chromosome. Bands of homology are labelled from a to k on the Y chromosome. The dark band indicates the Xq21.3 region that is homologous to two blocks (d and f) on Yp (the Y short arm); k indicates the long arm (Yq) pseudoautosomal region (YqPAR2). Both these regions of homology are present in humans but not in earlier primates. The short arm (YpPAR1) pseudoautosomal region was created earlier in evolution, as also were the other regions of homology. The region of the centromere is cross-hatched. Genes within established homologues on X and Y are identified by acronyms (RPS4X/Y, ZFX/Y, AMGX/Y, SMCX/Y). Adapted from Affara *et al.* (1996).

whom the genes on one of the two X chromosomes are normally 'inactivated', a presumed mechanism of 'dosage compensation' between males and females). For such a translocation to become universal in the human population the characteristic coded for by the gene clearly must have been selected. Because the new or accentuated characteristic was present in males, this selection may have been sexual, that is, males with the characteristic would have been preferentially selected by females as mates.

But since the gene was already present on the X chromosome, males now expressing the gene in double dose may, in turn, have subjected the relevant characteristic in females to a new selective force. Thus one can envisage an escalating process whereby a characteristic first selected in males was then selected in females. The quantitative expression of the trait would differ between the sexes, as a function of two variables: (1) variation in the extent of inactivation of the copy of the gene on the inactivated X chromosome in females, and (2) variation in the gene sequence on the X and the Y chromosome (see below in relation to ProtocadherinXY). Thus the disruption of a previous equilibrium by a single X to Y translocation (a discrete 'saltational' change) has the potential to have generated a process of sexual selection that led to the progressive refinement of a single feature to define a new species.

In the case of lateralization, the initial step towards either protolanguage at an earlier stage, or towards full language in the case of modern *Homo sapiens*, could be honed by mate selection on a simple parameter such as the point of maturation (Crow 1998a; see Figs. 5.5 and 5.6).

One can raise the question of why, if two doses of the gene are advantageous after the translocation from the X to the Y, such adjustment could not have taken place when the gene was present only on the X. Because genes on one X chromosome in females are subject to inactivation (the dosage compensation mechanism referred to above) the gene sequence and the expression of the gene are the same in both sexes. Only after the gene has been reduplicated on the Y chromosome do the possibility of differential expression in males and females, and the potential influence of mate choice (sexual selection) arise. It seems possible that it is the process of sexual selection, acting at least in part by modifying the state of dosage compensation of genes on the X, that establishes the new evolutionary equilibrium. The difficulty in understanding the mechanism is that it is presently unclear how (in what appears to be a general rule for mammals) genes on the X with a homologue on the Y become protected from the process of X inactivation in females. One proposal is that pairing of X and Y sequences in male meiosis plays a role (Crow 1991). Investigating the phenomenon of protection from X inactivation across mammalian orders, Jegalian and Page (1998) suggest that, following the establishment of the sequence on the Y chromosome, change in gene sequence and inactivation status occurs by selective pressure first on the male and then on the female, consistent with a role for sexual selection. The proposal, therefore, is that a gene within the Xq21.3/Yp11.2 region of homology (ProtocadherinXY is the specific candidate) has been subject to sexual selection in hominids, including modern *Homo sapiens*, because it is present on the Y chromosome as well as the X whereas in the great Apes it is present only on the X, and that changes in gene sequence on the Y and inactivation status on the X have been intimately involved in this process.

5.3 Sexual Selection and Speciation

A relationship between sexual selection and speciation is in agreement with proposals arising from work in other species. For example, it has been suggested that speciation in *Drosophila* takes place particularly in relation to the appearance of novel sexual dimorphisms that are then subjected to a process of sexual selection (Kaneshiro 1980; Kaneshiro and Boake 1987; Carson 1997). Somewhat similar suggestions have been made for the colour changes that accompany the rapid speciation of cichlid fish that has taken place in the lakes of East Africa (Dominey 1984; McKaye 1991) and in relation to changes between species in song morphology and plumage in birds (Price 1998; Okanoya, Chapter 3 above). In each case the focus of the speciation process is a sexual dimorphism (a difference in some physical or behavioural characteristic between the sexes).

Thus the evolution of language in *Homo sapiens* (Crow 1996, 1998*a*,*b*) may be a specific case of a more general phenomenon. In *Homo sapiens* it is proposed (Crow 1993*b*) that the primary change (the change that led to language) occurred in a gene that influenced the relative development of the two hemispheres and that this had an effect on the rate of brain growth. It is established that the rate of brain growth in man is different in the two sexes (e.g. Fig. 5.5). Whether this sex difference is related to differences in the sequence of the gene on the X and the Y (such as are known to be present in the case of ProtocadherinXY) or to differences in residual inactivation on the X remains to be investigated.

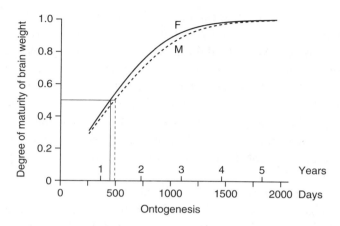

FIG. 5.5 The sex difference in the rate of brain growth according to the data of Marchand reproduced from Kretschmann *et al.* (1979).

If the relative development of the two hemispheres is regulated by an X–Y homologous gene this implies that the trajectory of brain growth is susceptible to differential modification in the two sexes. The target of selection is presumably related to the plateau of brain growth (Fig. 5.5), the stage at which maturation of the brain is reached. The point of selection as a mate of males by females may be assumed to be later than that of females by males as reflected by the consistency across populations of the two- to three-year difference in age at marriage (Crow 1993*b*)—males are older than females at the time of marriage.

The preference of females for older males is consistent with the assumption that the peak of lateralization and verbal ability occurs later in males than in females. If the target of selection is verbal ability, it appears that females select a mate whose linguistic prowess matches their own, and that they are thereby determining the latest point at which optimal lateralization may occur. With the introduction of the key dimension of lateralization, strong selection of the linguistically able over the less able has the potential over time to bring about big changes in the point of plateau in brain growth.

Here one can see there are three interacting variables—degree of lateralization, age of being selected as a mate, and the rate (perhaps determining the plateau) of brain growth. For each of these variables the difference between the sexes may reflect differences in the sequence or expression of a gene on the X and the Y chromosome. At what stage in hominid evolution were these

sex differences introduced? It can be envisaged that the primary translocation from the X to the Y (occurring between 2 to 3 million years ago; Sargent *et al.* 1996), which doubled the gene dosage in males, prolonged brain
maturation and initiated a sequence of changes including one affecting the
inactivation status of the genes in this region on the inactive X chromosome
in females. There is some evidence for asymmetry in *Homo erectus* (Steele
1998) and this change might be relevant. One can speculate that the paracentric inversion that came later (but cannot be precisely dated; Schwartz *et al.*
1998) was more relevant to the change that brought about modern *Homo
sapiens.*

Thus, a sequence of hypotheses can be formulated. First, lateralization is
the critical change that defines the human brain and has conferred upon it
the capacity for language (Annett 1985; Corballis 1991). Second, this change

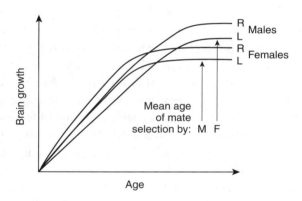

FIG. 5.6 Hypothetical trajectories of growth of the cerebral hemispheres in humans
under the influence of an asymmetry determinant (Annett's 'right shift factor' or
the cerebral dominance gene—located in homologous form on the X and the
Y chromosome) acting early in development. Genetic (or epigenetic, that is, gene
expression rather than gene sequence) variation is associated with different trajectories of relative growth of the left (L) and right (R) hemispheres, the degree of
asymmetry being determined by variation on the X and Y chromosomes. Note
that the asymmetry of the human brain is, in reality, more complex than a simple
right–left difference; it is better represented as a 'torque' (a bias or twist; see Fig. 5.3)
across the antero-posterior axis from right frontal to left occipital. Mean age at
mate choice differs between the sexes; females choose mates who are generally
older than themselves and males choose females who are younger than themselves
(see Crow 1993*b*).

occurred in the course of hominid evolution (Marchant and McGrew 1996; Buxhoeveden and Casanova 2000). Third, given the neuropsychological findings in sex chromosomal aneuploidies outlined above, the change was the consequence of a change on the sex chromosomes. Fourth, the evolutionary history of these chromosomes points to the Xq21.3 to Y translocation as the key event. Whether or not lateralization followed the original translocation or occurred later (for instance, at the time of the paracentric inversion) the presence of the gene on the Y chromosome introduced the possibility of differential modification in the two sexes. The important point is that a change that creates a new region of homology between the X and the Y chromosomes establishes a new sexual dimorphism and sets up a situation in which sexual selection can act first on males and then on females to modify the relevant characteristic. This, it is proposed, is what happened following the Xq21.3/Yp translocation and its subsequent modifications, to generate hemispheric differentiation and the capacity for language. The fact that there are language anomalies as well as hemispheric deviations in the sex chromosome aneuploidies (Money 1993) reinforces the general case that language is related to an X–Y homologous gene.

Thus, the evolution of language in *Homo sapiens* may be an exemplar of a general rule that links sex linkage, sexual selection, and speciation. According to this rule, a primary change in the Y copy of an X–Y homologous gene, (1) generates a new sexual dimorphism, and (2) is subject to female choice. The X–Y difference can then become the target of runaway (Fisherian) sexual selection.

5.4 ProtocadherinXY

Of the 30,000 estimated genes in the genome, any gene within the 3.5Mb region (approximately 0.2% of the genome) in the Xq21.3 block that translocated to the Y chromosome after the separation of the hominid lineage would be of interest in relation to distinctively human characteristics, because the expression of such a gene will have changed relative to its expression in the great Apes. With the case outlined above for an asymmetry determinant in the X–Y homologous class, this region acquires increased interest in relation to the evolution of the cerebral cortex. Given the paucity of genes on the Y chromosome, few functional genes would be predicted, and there is no a priori reason to expect any one gene within this region to be expressed

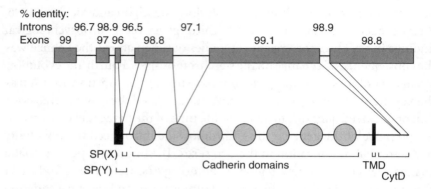

% identity:
Introns   96.7 98.9 96.5   97.1   98.9
Exons   99   97 96   98.8   99.1   98.8

SP(X)   TMD
SP(Y)   Cadherin domains   CytD

FIG. 5.7 The structure of ProtocadherinXY. In the DNA structure (upper part of diagram) there are six exons (thick bars representing the part of the molecule that is transcribed into RNA and then translated into protein) separated by five introns (thin horizontal lines) each with between 96 and 99.1% homology between X and Y copies. In protein structure (lower part of diagram) there are seven extracellular cadherin domains (filled circles, representing the part of the molecule on the cell surface that interacts with a similar molecule on the surface of another cell), a signal peptide (SP—concerned with the delivery of the molecule to its proper location on the cell membrane) that differs between the X and the Y copies, a transmembrane domain (TMD) that crosses the cell membrane, and a cytoplasmic domain (CytD—the mediator of effects within the cell) that again differs in termination sequence between X and Y copies. Each of the differences between X and Y forms of the protein has the potential to explain a difference between the sexes (figure adapted from Blanco *et al.* 2000).

in the brain. However, in the course of sequencing the region, one gene has been found to be expressed in the brain, *and* to have characteristics relevant to nervous system growth and development. This gene (ProtocadherinXY, see Fig. 5.7) belongs to a class that codes for proteins that are expressed on the surface of subsets of neurones to act as axon guidance molecules (Blanco *et al.* 2000). Protocadherins are a subfamily of the cadherins, molecules that are expressed in a regionally specific manner in the central nervous system to identify specific brain nuclei, fibre tracts, and layers within structures such as the cerebral cortex. They contribute to morphogenesis and tract formation in part in a species-specific manner (see e.g. Redies 2000; Yagi and Takeichi 2000).

It is clear from its location in the genome that the control and expression of ProtocadherinXY changed in the course of human evolution, and this must have had consequences for the structure of the human brain. Given the background of evidence for an X–Y homologous determinant of cerebral asymmetry it is plausible, although it remains to be demonstrated by studies of variations in gene sequence and expression, that these changes were critical in the evolution of language. On the basis of its location, inferred function, and evolutionary history, ProtocadherinXY is a candidate for a central role in the evolution of language.

5.5 Conclusions

1. Language is an embarrassment for gradualist evolutionary theory because, according to some authors, it requires a saltation, that is, a discontinuous 'speciation event'.

2. Cerebral asymmetry is present in *Homo sapiens* but absent in the chimpanzee.

3. There is a case that a gene for asymmetry is present in homologous form on both the X and the Y chromosome.

4. A chromosomal change between the chimpanzee and *Homo sapiens* established a new region of homology between the X and the Y chromosome; it constitutes a saltational change of a type that would be expected to be subject to sexual selection.

5. Within that region (Xq21.3/Yp) a protocadherin gene with forms that now differ on the X and Y has been identified.

6. This gene would be expected to influence brain development differently in the two sexes; it could be relevant to the mean faster brain growth and development of verbal ability in females.

7. The role of language in *Homo sapiens* elucidates a putative general role of sex chromosomal change and sexual selection in transitions to specific mate recognition systems.

FURTHER READING

BICKERTON, D. (1995), *Language and Human Behavior* (Seattle: University of Washington).

CROW, T. J. (1998), 'Nuclear Schizophrenic Symptoms as a Window on the Relationship between Thought and Speech', *British Jornal of Psychiatry*, 173: 103–9.

—— (1998), 'Sexual Selection, Timing and the *Descent of Man*: A Theory of the Genetic Origins of Language', *Current Psychology of Cognition*, 17: 1079–114.

CROW, T. J. (1998), 'Why Cerebral Asymmetry is the Key to the Origin of Homo sapiens: How to Find the Gene or Eliminate the Theory', *Current Psychology of Cognition*, 17: 1237–77.

SARGENT, C. A., BRIGGS, H., CHALMERS, I. J., LAMBSON, B., WALKER, E., and AFFARA, N. A. (1996), 'The Sequence Organization of Yp/proximal Xq Regions of the Human Sex Chromosomes is Highly Conserved', *Genomics*, 32: 200–9.

REFERENCES

AFFARA, N., BISHOP, C., BROWN, W., COOKE, H., DAVEY, P., ELLIS, N., GRAVES, J. M., JONES, M., MITCHELL, M., RAPPOLD, G., TYLER-SMITH, C., YEN, P., and LAU, Y. C. (1996), 'Report of the Second International Workshop on Y Chromosome Mapping 1995', *Cytogenetics and Cell Genetics*, 73: 33–76.

ANNETT, M. (1985), *Left, Right, Hand and Brain: The Right Shift Theory* (London: Lawrence Erlbaum).

BATESON, W. (1894), *Materials for the Study of Variation, Treated with Especial Regard to Discontinuity* (New York: Macmillan).

BEAR, D. M., SCHIFF, D., SAVER, M., GREENBERG, R., and FREEMAN, R. (1986), 'Quantitative Analysis of Cerebral Asymmetry; Fronto-occipital Correlation, Sexual Dimorphism and Association with Handedness', *Archives of Neurology*, 43: 598–603.

BICKERTON, D. (1995), *Language and Human Behavior* (Seattle: University of Washington).

BLANCO, P., SARGENT, C. A., BOUCHER, C., MITCHELL, M., AFFARA, N. A (2000), 'Conservation of PCDHXY in Mammals: Expression of Human X/Y Genes Predominantly in Brain', *Mammalian Genome*, 11: 906–14.

BUTLER, S. (1984), 'Sex Differences in Human Cerebral Function', *Progress in Brain Research*, 61: 443–54.

BUXHOEVEDEN, D., and CASANOVA, M. (2000), 'Comparative Lateralization Patterns in the Language Area of Normal Human, Chimpanzee, and Rhesus Monkey Brain', *Laterality*, 5: 315–30.

CARSON, H. L. (1997), 'Sexual Selection: Driver of Genetic Change in Hawaiian Drosophila', *Journal of Heredity*, 88: 343–52.

DE CONDILLAC, E. B. (1746), *Essai sur l'origine des connaissances humaines*, trans. T. Nugent as *Essay in the Origin of Human Knowledge* (New York: AMS Press), 1974.

CHOMSKY, N. (1972), *Language and Mind* (San Diego: Harcourt, Brace, Jovanovich).

CORBALLIS, M. C. (1991), *The Lop-sided Ape: Evolution of the Generative Mind* (New York: Oxford University Press).

——LEE, K., MCMANUS, I. C., and CROW, T. J. (1996), 'Location of the Handedness Gene on the X and Y Chromosomes', *American Journal of Medical Genetics (Neuropsychiatric Genetics)*, 67: 50–2.

COYNE, J. A., and ORR, H. A. (1998), 'The Evolutionary Genetics of Speciation', *Philosophical Transactions of the Royal Society London B*, 353: 287–305.

CROW, T. J. (1991), 'Protection from X Inactivation', *Nature*, 353: 710.

——(1993*a*), 'Origins of Psychosis and the Evolution of Human Language and Communication', in S. Langer, J. Mendlewicz, and J. Racagni (eds.), *New Generation of Antipsychotic Drugs: Novel Mechanisms of Action* (Basle: Karger), 39–61.

—— (1993*b*), 'Sexual Selection, Machiavellian Intelligence and the Origins of Psychosis', *Lancet*, 342: 594–8.

——(1996), 'Language and Psychosis: Common Evolutionary Origins', *Endeavour*, 20: 105–9.

——(1998*a*), 'Sexual Selection, Timing and the *Descent of Man*: A Theory of the Genetic Origins of Language', *Current Psychology of Cognition*, 17: 1079–114.

——(1998*b*), 'Why Cerebral Asymmetry is the Key to the Origin of Homo sapiens: How to Find the Gene or Eliminate the Theory', *Current Psychology of Cognition*, 17: 1237–77.

——(2000), 'Did Homo sapiens Speciate on the Y Chromosome?', *Psycoloquy* 11(001). http://www.cogsci.soton.ac.uk/cgi/psyc/newpsy?11.001.

—— CROW, L. R., DONE, D. J., and LEASK, S. J. (1998), 'Relative Hand Skill Predicts Academic Ability: Global Deficits at the Point of Hemispheric Indecision', *Neuropsychologia*, 36: 1275–82.

DARWIN, C. (1859), *The Origin of Species by Means of Natural Selection or the Preservation of Favoured Races in the Struggle for Life* (London: John Murray).

——(1871), *The Descent of Man, and Selection in Relation to Sex* (London: J. Murray); reissued in facsimile 1981 (New Jersey: Princeton University Press).

DOBZHANSKY, T. (1937), *Genetics and the Origin of Species* (New York: Columbia University Press).

DOMINEY, W. J. (1984), 'Effects of Sexual Selection and Life Histories on Speciation: Species Flocks in African Cichlids and Hawaiian Drosophila', in A. A. Echelle and I. Kornfield (eds.), *Evolution of Fish Species Flocks* (Orono, Me.: Orono Press), 231–49.

ELDREDGE, N., and GOULD, S. J. (1972), 'Punctuated Equilibria: An Alternative to Phyletic Gradualism', in T. M. Schopf (ed.), *Models in Palaeobiology* (San Francisco: Freeman, Cooper), 82–115.

FREIJE, D., HELMS, C., WATSON, M. S., and DONIS-KELLER, H. (1992), 'Identification of a Second Pseudoautosomal Region Near the Xq and Yq Telomeres', *Science*, 258: 1784–7.

GESCHWIND, N., and LEVITSKY, W. (1968), 'Left–Right Asymmetry in Temporal Speech Region', *Science*, 161: 186–7.

GOLDSCHMIDT, R. (1940), *The Material Basis of Evolution* (New Haven: Yale University Press).

HALPERN, D. F. (1992), *Sex Differences in Cognitive Abilities* (Mahwah, NJ: Lawrence Erlbaum).

HOWARD, D. J., and BERLOCHER, S. H. (1998) (eds.), *Endless Forms: Species and Speciation* (Oxford: Oxford University Press).

JEGALIAN, K., and PAGE, D. C. (1998), 'A Proposed Mechanism by Which Genes Common to Mammalian X and Y Chromosomes Evolve to Become X Inactivated', *Nature*, 394: 776–80.

KANESHIRO, K. Y. (1980), 'Sexual Isolation, Speciation and the Direction of Evolution', *Evolution*, 34: 437–44.

—— and BOAKE, C. R. B. (1987), 'Sexual Selection: Issues Raised by Hawaiian Drosophila', *Trends in Ecology and Evolution*, 2: 207–11.

KING, M. (1993), *Species Evolution: The Role of Chromosome Change* (Cambridge: Cambridge University Press).

KRETSCHMANN, H.-J., SCHLEICHER A., WINGERT F., ZILLES K., and LOEBLICH, H.-J. (1979), 'Human Brain Growth in the 19th and 20th Century', *Journal of the Neurological Sciences*, 40: 169–88.

LAMBSON, B., AFFARA, N. A., MITCHELL, M., and FERGUSON-SMITH, M. A. (1992), 'Evolution of DNA Sequence Homologies Between the Sex Chromosomes in Pprimate Species', *Genomics*, 14: 1032–40.

LAVAL, S. H., DANN, J., BUTLER, R. J., LOFTUS, J., RUE, J., LEASK, S. J., BASS, N., COMAZZI, M., VITA, A., NANKO, S., SHAW, S., PETERSON, P., SHIELDS, G., SMITH, A. B., STEWART, J., DELISI, L. E., and CROW, T. J. (1998), 'Evidence for Linkage to Psychosis and Cerebral Asymmetry (Relative Hand Skill) on the X Chromosome', *American Journal of Medical Genetics (Neuropsychiatric Genetics)*, 81: 420–7.

MCKAYE, K. R. (1991), 'Sexual Selection and the Evolution of the Cichlid Fishes of Lake Malawi, Africa', in M. H. A. Keenleyside (ed.), *Cichlid Fish: Behavior, Ecology & Evolution* (London: Chapman and Hall), 241–57.

MCKEEVER, W. F. (2000), 'A New Family Handedness Sample with Findings Consistent With X-linked Transmission', *British Journal of Psychology*, 91: 21–39.

MACCOBY, E. E., and JACKLIN, C. N. (1975), *The Psychology of Sex Differences* (Oxford: Oxford University Press).

MAGURRAN, A. E., and MAY, R. M. (1999) (eds.), *Evolution of Biological Diversity* (Oxford: Oxford University Press).

MARCHANT, L. F., and MCGREW, W. C. (1996), 'Laterality of Limb Function in Wild Chimpanzees of Gombe National Park: Comprehensive Study of Spontaneous Activities', *Journal of Human Evolution*, 30: 427–43.

MAYR, E. (1963), *Animal Species and Evolution* (Cambridge, Mass.: Harvard University Press).

MELLARS, P. (1998), 'Neanderthals, Modern Humans and the Archaeological Evidence for Language', *Memoirs of the California Academy of Sciences*, 24: 89–115.

MONEY, J. (1993), 'Specific Neurocognitional Impairments Associated with Turner (45,X) and Klinefelter (47,XXY) Syndromes: A Review', *Social Biology*, 40: 147–51.

MOORE, T. (1967), 'Language and Intelligence: A Longitudinal Study of the First Eight Years', *Human Development*, 10: 88–106.

MUMM, S., MOLINI, B., TERRELL, J., SRIVASTAVA, A., and SCHLESSINGER, D. (1997), 'Evolutionary Features of the 4Mb Xq21.3 XY Homology Region Revealed by a Map at 60-Kb Resolution', *Genome Research*, 7: 307–14.

NETLEY, C. (1998), 'Sex Chromosome Aneuploidy and Cognitive Development', *Current Psychology of Cognition*, 17: 1190–7.

NOBLE, W., and DAVIDSON, I. (1996), *Human Evolution, Language and Mind* (Cambridge: Cambridge University Press).

OTTE, D., and ENDLER, J. A. (1989) (eds.), *Speciation and its Consequences* (Sunderland, Mass.: Sinauer).

PENNER, J. G. (2000), *Evolution Challenged by Language and Speech* (London: Minerva).

PERELLE, I. B., and EHRMAN, L. (1994), 'An International Study of Human Handedness: The Data', *Behavior Genetics*, 24: 217–27.

PREMACK, D. (1985), '"Gavagai" or the Future History of the Language Controversy', *Cognition*, 19: 207–96.

PRICE, T. (1998), 'Sexual Selection and Natural Selection in Bird Speciation', *Philosophical Transactions of the Royal Society London [Biology]*, 353: 251–60.

PROVINS, K. A., MILNER, A. D., and KERR, P. (1982), 'Asymmetry of Manual Preference and Performance', *Perceptual and Motor Skills*, 54: 179–94.

REDIES, C. (2000), 'Cadherins in the Central Nervous System', *Progress in Neurobiology*, 61: 611–48.

SAPIR, E. (1921), *Language: an Introduction to the Study of Speech* (New York: Harcourt Brace Jovanovic).

SARGENT, C. A., BRIGGS, H., CHALMERS, I. J., LAMBSON, B., WALKER, E., and AFFARA, N. A. (1996), 'The Sequence Organization of Yp/proximal Xq Regions of the Human Sex Chromosomes is Highly Conserved', *Genomics*, 32: 200–9.

SCHWARTZ, A., CHAN, D. C., BROWN, L. G., ALAGAPPAN, R., PETTAY, D., DISTECHE, C., McGILLIVRAY, B., DE LA CHAPELLE, A., and PAGE, D. C. (1998), 'Reconstructing Hominid Evolution: X-Homologous Block, Created by X–Y Transposition, was Disrupted by Yp Inversion Through LINE-LINE Recombination', *Human Molecular Genetics*, 7: 1–11.

SHUCARD, D. W., SHUCARD, J. L., and THOMAS, D. G. (1987), 'Sex Differences in Electrophysiological Activity in Infancy: Possible Implications for Language Development', in S. U. Philips, S. Steele, and C. Tanz (eds.), *Language, Gender and Sex in Comparative Perspective* (Cambridge: Cambridge University Press), 489–502.

STEELE, J. (1998), 'Cerebral Asymmetry, Cognitive Laterality, and Human Evolution', *Current Psychology of Cognition*, 16: 1202–14.

STRINGER, C., and McKIE, R. (1996), *African Exodus: The Origins of Modern Humanity* (London: Jonathan Cape).

DE VRIES, H. (1905), *Species and Varieties, Their Origin by Mutation* (Chicago: Open Court).

WHITE, M. J. D. (1973), *Modes of Speciation* (San Francisco: W. H. Freeman).

YAGI, T., and TAKEICHI, M. (2000), 'Cadherin Superfamily Genes: Functions, Genomic Organization, and Neurologic Diversity', *Genes and Development*, 14: 1169–80.

6   Dual Processing in Protolanguage:
        Performance without Competence

6.1. Introduction

6.1.1 *Two Strategies in Language Processing*

There is a considerable body of research on formulaicity in language, span-
ning over 150 years and encompassing adult and child, native and non-
native, normal and aphasic speech and writing (see Wray 1999 and 2002 for
reviews). A plausible way of accounting for the linguistic patterns revealed
by this research is to recognize two distinct processing strategies (e.g. Becker
1975; Bolinger 1976; Ellis 1996; Langacker 1987; Sinclair 1991; Wray 1992).
An analytic[1] strategy combines individual morphemes and words by means
of grammatical rules to offer us the scope to say anything that we might ever
wish to, whether or not we have said, or encountered, it before. This strategy
underlies our 'grammatical competence'. A holistic strategy takes from the

I am grateful to Jim Hurford, Frederick Newmeyer, Chris Knight and members of the team
of anonymous reviewers for many helpful and challenging comments on versions of this
chapter. I should also like to thank Simon Kirby, Stevan Harnad, and Michael Tomasello,
who raised important and thought-provoking issues when I presented the original paper
in Paris.

    [1] In line with standard practice in this field, 'analytic' here refers to the processes by
which individual morphemes and words are assembled into longer strings, and longer
strings are broken down into morphemes and words. As indicated in the text, 'analytic' is,
therefore, in opposition with 'holistic'. This usage contrasts with another (e.g. Hurford 2000:
225), in which 'analytic' processing is the rule-governed breaking down of large units into
smaller ones, while 'synthetic' processing is the rule-governed construction of larger units
out of smaller ones. In my usage, both of these processes are contained within the term 'analytic' but, in addition (and crucially for the coming discussion of human protolanguage), I
use the term to refer to *any* string made out of component units, even if the arrangement
is not rule-governed.

lexicon prefabricated strings of morphemes, words, phrases, clauses, or sentences—even whole texts—and reproduces them without recourse to the analytic strategy. In other words, a complete phrase or sentence, with an agreed meaning—and often also a layer of associated pragmatics or metaphor—is processed as if it were a single irreducible item. A compromise between the two systems occurs when partially prefabricated 'frames' are customized to the situation through the insertion of individual morphemes and words (Wray 2002: chs. 1–3). In such frames we have a natural and flexible mixture of formulaicity, carrying the bulk of the interactional message, and discrete topic reference, fitting it for its specific purpose.

A significant effect of the holistic strategy is that certain ways of expressing an idea become fixed as the preferred ones in the speech community. The remainder of the grammatically possible and meaningful combinations that could express the same idea are rarely heard, and may be judged as unidiomatic and non-native (Pawley and Syder 1983). Idioms are a good example of word strings that must be holistically processed, since the meaning of the parts is at odds with the meaning of the whole. Evidence from phonology, corpus research, and language pathology, however, indicates that the range of formulaic language extends well beyond just idioms, to include the preferred expression of many common ideas of regular construction and meaning (e.g. *fancy seeing you here*; *have a good trip*; *the ADJ-er the better*). Such idiomatic strings, it seems, are usually produced and understood holistically, even though they *can* be analysed, and indeed may be in certain circumstances.

A striking proportion of formulaic expressions are used to manipulate others into physical, emotional, and perceptual reactions. Examples include: *watch where you're going* and *keep off the grass* (physical manipulation), and *I'm sorry* and *I hate you* (emotional manipulation). Manipulating the hearer perceptually is achieved by using expressions that mark in- or out-group status, preface information as new (e.g. *you'll never guess what's happened*), indicate power relations (e.g. *how dare you!*), and so on.[2] Of course, most of these functions can be achieved non-formulaically too, but the

---

[2] There are obvious parallels with Searle's (1965, 1979) Speech Acts, particularly *directives* and *expressives*, but to adopt Searle's terms and all their implications would be misleading, since his interest lies in exploring the illocutionary effects of speech events, irrespective of their form, whereas my purpose here is to note that a given form (that is, the formulaic string) happens often, though not always, to be associated with certain illocutionary functions.

effect can be somewhat bizarre. I have proposed (Wray 1999, 2000*b*, 2002; Wray and Perkins 2000) that while non-manipulative formulaic strings, such as directly referential formulaic expressions (e.g. *a long time ago; right at the top of NP*) and those used for discourse management[3] (e.g. *and another thing; if I could just butt in here*), are geared to reducing the speaker's processing effort, manipulative messages aim to make the *hearer's* processing easier, since that increases the likelihood of swift comprehension and appropriate action. This remains true even for expressions that are lengthy and which, if analysed, would be complex (e.g. *I wonder if you would be so kind as to VP*). Provided the hearer recognizes the string and decodes it holistically, its length and internal construction are no hindrance to swift processing.

6.1.2 *Holistic 'Survival' Communication in the Protolanguage*

The manipulative functions of our formulaic language correspond closely with those observed in the communicative behaviour of chimpanzees in the wild (Reiss 1989; cf. also Terrace, this volume, sect. 4.5). On the basis of this parallel, and other indicators, I have proposed (Wray 1998, 2000*a*) that the holistic strategy for expressing manipulative messages in phonetic form may be considerably more ancient than the analytic strategy. I have suggested that the holistic cries and gestures of our pre-human ancestors were transformed, over a long period of time, into a phonetically expressed set of holistic message strings, each with a manipulative function such as greeting, warning, commanding, threatening, requesting, appeasing, etc. The holistic delivery of such messages is something that we still prefer, though, clearly, our holistic forms today are not direct descendants of those original ones. Today, our formulaic language is formed out of smaller, meaningful components—though the extent to which this is a supplementary, rather than a central, feature of them is subject to question (Wray 2002). What we have inherited is not the forms themselves, but the *strategy* of using holistic linguistic material to achieve these key interactive functions. We resolve modern problems of interaction (including that of getting the hearer to

---

[3] Referential and discourse-managing formulaic strings are seen, in this model, as an innovation of full human language, a response to the processing demands of the full analytic system. As a result, we shall not consider them in the context of protolanguage, where, it is proposed, all the formulaic expressions are manipulative.

react in a desired way) in part by using an ancient holistic processing strategy, applied to our modern linguistic formulations. Thus, a key issue in understanding language evolution is how the second, analytic strategy arose, and how it integrated with the existing holistic one.

6.1.3 *Dual Processing Strategies in the Protolanguage*

This chapter explores the possibility that the analytic system arose during the protolanguage period, supplementing and enhancing, in a limited way, the capacity of the holistic message inventory to effect manipulative communication, and creating a new, though somewhat restricted, means of expressing novel messages. I shall demonstrate that the interaction of these two systems, in the absence of hierarchical grammar, is a convincing match for existing grammarless language systems, such as those of Kanzi, very young children, aphasic people, and foreign tourists. Bickerton (e.g. 1996: 28 f., 71) associates these systems with his own protolanguage model, but I shall argue that the present model captures significant additional features. In sect. 6.2 Bickerton's protolanguage model is adopted as a plausible realization of the analytic strategy in the protolanguage period. In sect. 6.3 we shall consider the nature of the holistic system that I propose pre-existed and provided the context for the emergence of the analytic system. It will then be possible, in sect. 6.4, to see how the two systems could beneficially operate together.

6.2 A Simple Analytic Protolanguage

Bickerton (e.g. 1998, 2000; Calvin and Bickerton 2000) proposes that full human language emerged through a process of argument-assignment, maybe around 150,000 years ago (Calvin and Bickerton 2000: 143). This process worked on a relatively small set of pre-existing referential words, mostly for objects and actions, that constituted a primitive protolanguage. Bickerton suggests that this protolanguage may have existed for as much as a million years (ibid. 103), though I shall suggest a shorter period. The words could be placed together in short strings (perhaps no more than three at a time), but their arrangement would have been a 'random concatenation' (Bickerton 1998: 349) rather than grammatically structured.

Bickerton's scenario for language evolution is reasonable. It makes sense that complex analytic syntax emerged from something more simple, and that a simple word-based protolanguage should feature, predominantly if not exclusively, the prototypes of what, in a grammatical system, would be nouns and verbs. However, I have always been concerned about one aspect of the scenario as Bickerton depicts it. As he fully acknowledges, such a protolanguage would be only a rough and ready means of expression, lacking subtlety, and subject to large measures of ambiguity. Although it would be better than anything that had existed before for exchanging referential information, this is only part of the communication story. My difficulty lies in the capacity for such a protolanguage successfully to convey the *other* kinds of messages—those relating to physical, emotional, and perceptual manipulation. As is clear from what we know about communication in other species,[4] these are not only of central importance, but also subtle and sensitive: it is important that the message is correctly understood, and received as intended. Bickerton's protolanguage would be a poor vessel for the kind of subtle and complex social messages that we must assume the protolanguage speakers required for marshalling their lives within their society (e.g. Dunbar 1996; Worden 1998).

Importantly, though, this poor fit is two-edged. On the one hand, Bickerton's protolanguage, by arranging words agrammatically, creates a level of ambiguity that is incompatible with the successful expression of the routine manipulative messages necessary for a community to function. In this regard, his system is too *weak* for the communication that we assume took place. Yet, at the same time, the system is too *powerful* for such communication. The strength of an analytic protolanguage, however simple and agrammatical, is that the existence of individual referential words permits the construction of novel messages. But the social communication that both we and other animals achieve holistically is *not* novel. It is a closed set of messages that are repeated as routines.[5] While Bickerton's system places a heavy

---

[4] Primate communication is usually mentioned in this context. An interesting supplement is elephant communication. Kigotho (2001) reports work by Joyce Poole of the Kenya Wildlife Service, indicating that calls are used to 'reinforce bonds between relatives and friends, to take care of youngsters and to reconcile differences among friends' (p. 19). Other calls relate to 'coalitions against aggressors' and the bull's advertising of his 'sexual state, identity and rank' (ibid.). Notably, the glosses provided for these calls are all indicative of a manipulative intent: 'I'm hungry, I need to suckle', 'let's go this way', 'No way, I don't like what you're doing. Leave me alone for now', 'I am here, where are you?', and 'Please come this way. I am over here' (ibid.).

[5] Of course, because we can apply our analytic system to our formulaic material, we have the scope to edit holistic strings, whether for play or flexibility (e.g. *happy unbirthday*;

burden on the hearer to work out the meaning of a message using context and pragmatics, the messages of social routine have value only if they are swiftly understood and reacted to. Efficient delivery and comprehension are best achieved when only minimal processing is required, that is, if the messages are entirely, or largely, holistic (Wray 2002).

In sect. 6.4, I shall argue that there is a place for a simple analytic protolanguage of the kind that Bickerton proposes, but not as the sole medium of communication. My argument will parallel that for dual-systems processing in our language today, whereby a Chomskian-style analytic grammar is most compatible with the evidence for formulaicity in language if it is viewed as one of two processing approaches (see e.g. Wray 2002: chs. 1, 14). First, though, I shall explore in more detail the holistic protolanguage that I propose coexisted with—and preceded—the simple analytic system from which our modern grammatical capability developed.

6.3 A Holistic Protolanguage

The model used here is described in more detail in Wray (1998, 2000*a*). In this holistic protolanguage the messages are semantically complex and agrammatical. Being holistic, a complete message is uniquely associated with an arbitrary form that is, crucially, not made out of smaller recombinable units of meaning.[6] In my earlier work I have illustrated this with the examples *tebima* and *mutapi* which I gloss there as 'give that to her' and 'give that to me' respectively. The arbitrary nature of the form relative to the message means that 'there is no phonological similarity between sequences with similar meanings . . . There is no part of *tebima* that means "give" or "her". Simply, the whole thing means the whole thing' (Wray 2000*a*: 294). Whereas the English string *give that to her* can be represented in a word-for-

---

watch where you're writing!). See Hudson (1998), Moon (1998), and Nunberg *et al.* (1994), for explorations of the capacity for formulaic strings to tolerate variation in form.

[6] In the transition to a word-centred, grammatically governed system, such utterances contribute to the emerging lexicon and grammar by being segmented into a *post-hoc* structure (compare the account of segmentation in first-language acquisition, sect. 6.5.1). This leads to agreed meanings for parts of the original whole form, mapped onto parts of the original whole meaning (Wray 1998, 2000*a*). This natural emergence of lexical forms and grammatical rules from holistic messages is elegantly demonstrated in Kirby's (1999*a*,*b*, 2000) computer simulations.

word gloss of the speaker's semantic representations (Fig. 6.1a), the proto-language equivalent has no such correspondence (Fig. 6.1b). Although the speaker possesses the *semantic* level categories, they are not discretely represented linguistically. Lest this seem odd, Figs. 6.1c and 6.1d remind us that formulaic expressions often do this too.

This method of glossing, however, could still tempt the unwary to consider that *tebima* is somehow structurally composed of the meanings in the gloss. In order to create a more satisfactory distance between the form and the meaning, in this chapter I adopt a different style of gloss, that uses the prefix device, 'What I say when I want you to _', shortened to 'W I S W I W Y T _' for convenience. In this notation, *tebima* is 'What I say when I want you to give a specified object (distant) to a specified female person' and *mutapi* is 'W I S W I W Y T give a specified object (distant) to me'. Although more cum-

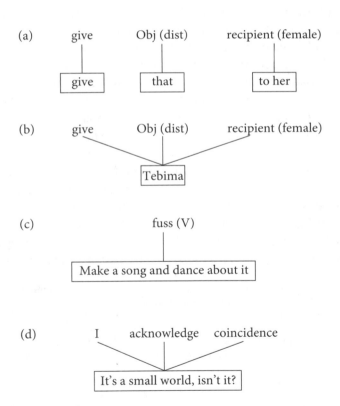

FIG. 6.1 Mappings of meanings to words and word strings.

bersome, this style of message glossing helps to retain the sense of functional meanings that are not directly linked to form.[7]

6.3.1 *Constraints on a Holistic Protolanguage*

In the above glosses, the denotation is generic, featuring terms such as 'object' and 'female person'. We shall explore the reasons for this now, since they are central to the explanation for an ultimate integration of the analytic and holistic protolanguage systems. In principle, you can have a holistic message with any meaning you like, from 'come here' to 'five minutes ago I saw a buck rabbit behind the stone at the top of the hill'. However, two inherent limitations on a holistic system, when operating alone, place severe constraints on the quality and type of message that can be sustained.

The first limitation determines the total number of messages that the system can support. Each message must be kept distinct, since its holistic form is the sole means of conveying the associated meaning. If, as we shall assume here, distinctiveness is achieved using phonetic contrasts, then the number of possible distinct messages will depend on two things. One is the speakers' ability to pronounce, and the hearers' to perceive, sufficient phonetic distinctions. The other is memory capacity, which will determine both how many strings can be easily recalled (long-term memory), and how long each one can be (working memory).

The second limitation creates a threshold on the frequency with which a given string is used. It is only through a string's use that it can be acquired by new speakers and refreshed in the memory of everyone else. With no possibility of internal morphological clues, a little-used string will not be reconstructable once forgotten. It will simply drop out of memory and be lost.[8] To stay in the inventory, a message must establish a balance between

---

[7] The usefulness of message glossing can be seen in the following examples, where the linguistic form is not identical to the message: *mind your backs* = 'WISWIWYT avoid stepping backwards because I am passing behind you' (physical manipulation); *how do you do?* = 'WISWIWYT accept my formal greeting at our first ever meeting' (emotional manipulation); *NP [+human] will see you now* = (a) 'WISWIWYT know that NP (dominant party) is ready for the appointment' (perceptual manipulation); (b) 'WISWIWYT go to NP's location' (physical manipulation).

[8] Note that this frequency threshold is no different than it is for any of our own monomorphemic words, or for any polymorphemic words, or multiword strings, that are not customarily analysed (see Wray 2002 for a full exploration of 'morpheme equivalence' in internally complex items).

specificity and resultant frequency. Suppose a message needs to be said ten times a month for it to remain active in the protolanguage. Many specific messages will not reach the threshold, because the circumstances for their appropriacy will not arise that often. So, each of 'w i s w i w y t stay with Mary'; 'w i s w i w y t stay with Joyce'; 'w i s w i w y t stay with Sally' and so on, might be unviable. In contrast, a generic message that we might gloss as 'w i s w i w y t stay with specified female person', encompassing all pragmatically possible female referents, would apply to the combined individual circumstances, and more easily remain active.[9] The specified person would, of course, need to be indicated through, say, a gesture (see next section).

The level of specificity in denotation can vary, provided the frequency requirements are still met. For instance, there might be sufficient discussion of hunting for there to exist separate messages for 'w i s w i w y t hunt antelope with me'; '... hunt duck...'; '... hunt rabbit...' After all, it would be quite useful to possess the ability to differentiate between potential quarries.[10] In some circumstances, a message might be so commonly used for it to apply to a set of one, e.g. 'w i s w i w y t sit in the centre of the circle'; 'w i s w i w y t honour Mary'. Finally, certain generic messages entail unequivocal specific reference, such as 'w i s w i w y t give specified object (distant) to me', where the identity of the recipient is reliably indexed with the identity of the speaker. This exploitation of natural sets is one way in which the overall limitations on the message inventory can be accommodated.

Generic denotation[11] could feasibly affect the linguistic and wider behaviour of the speaker group. Consider, for instance, 'w i s w i w y t meet me/us at the ridge'. Like other message forms, its survival in the message inventory would depend upon its frequent use. The viability of individual messages would be maximized by having, say, three messages used for agreeing on meeting places, each of which was used often, rather than ten or twenty used rarely. Since the messages would determine the behaviour of the group, this enforced reductionism would restrict the range of pre-planned actions, encouraging habit over innovation. In other words, rather than the capacity for thinking about absent objects and locations forcing the language into

[9] In choosing 'female person' I am assuming that this constitutes a reliable perceived set.
[10] Even here, of course, the messages still apply to natural sets, since there are many individual examples of each animal.
[11] Cf. also Hurford's (2001) rather more philosophical account of why individual denotation was not present in protolanguage, and Ragir's observation (this volume, sect. 13.3), that the pidgins of Providence and Grand Cayman did not have names for people or places.

greater displaced reference, the reverse could happen. This is just one constraint of expression that would be substantially alleviated by the presence of referential words, though, as we shall see, the restrictions on innovation would not go away entirely.

6.3.2 *The Problem of Displaced Reference*

Generic denotation creates a problem. In the case of 'w ɪ s w ɪ w ʏ т stay with specified female person', how is the hearer to know which female is meant? If she is nearby and visible to the speaker and hearer, pragmatics and/or a simple gesture will be sufficient to disambiguate. But in other circumstances there could be considerable problems with ambiguity. Significantly, this ambiguity resides in *reference*, the one thing that a Bickertonian protolanguage is good at. In contrast, Bickerton's protolanguage is ambiguous in message transmission, where the holistic protolanguage would be clear. This gives us our first hint of the compatibility of the two systems (sect. 6.4).

The problem for the holistic system is most acute in cases where the message is pragmatically associated with an absent referent, such as 'w ɪ s w ɪ-w ʏ т fetch specified female person'. 'Fetch X' is a very plausible manipulative message, and it is one that really does need individual denotation, since, when the person in question is absent, gestures and context may not suffice. Yet individual denotation in holistic messages is so costly that if there was much of it, it would soon undermine the entire system.

6.3.3 *Resolving the Problem of Displaced Reference*

There are two possible solutions. One is that individual denotation is not an option, and so certain kinds of displaced reference simply cannot be achieved. This, I propose, characterized the first, and most lengthy, part of the protolanguage period, when the holistic system operated alone. The result would have been (a) severe limitations on thought and action, as already mentioned above, (b) a level of expressional vagueness that would tend to undermine planning, and, of course, (c) a severely restricted capacity for creativity, due to the inherent absence of novel expression. All these are consistent with Mithen's (1996) observation that there was virtually no technological innovation for more than a million years after the invention of the hand-axe around 1.4 million years ago. Specifically, he identifies four features of this technological stagnation: the failure to adopt bone, antler and ivory as raw materials, the failure to make tools for specific purposes, the failure to make multi-component tools, and the very limited degree of variation in stone tools across time and space (pp. 116–23).

It is not a question of laying this lack of progress *directly* at the door of language, but rather of identifying ways in which the design of a holistic protolanguage would support conservatism in a way that an analytic language, even of limited scope, would not, since the latter is inherently designed to facilitate novel expression, albeit only of a rudimentary kind. Looked at in this way, the stability of a holistic protolanguage is entirely compatible with Mithen's proposal that the early human mind was not "joined up" that is, 'a cognitive barrier prevented the integration of knowledge' (ibid. 131). The absence of novel linguistic expression would conspire with cognitive tunnel vision to impede the making of connections between ideas and expressing such ideas to others. Meanwhile, the existence of a reliable set of holistic expressions with agreed manipulative meanings would reinforce habit and maintain social relationships, supporting the survival of individuals as group members. Since, as Mithen points out (e.g. ibid.), there was certainly sufficient environmental pressure for innovation to be useful, we may not attribute its failure to occur to an easy existence. By identifying holistic protolanguage as an impediment to the expression of new ideas, it is easier to explain how early humans could have failed for so long to undergo natural selection for a more integrated intelligence.

The second solution to the problem of individual denotation is that it is accommodated. This is what I suggest came to pass at some point during the protolanguage period. The impetus could have been a small but significant increase in memory capacity, a cognitive change that made irresistible the expression of new connections between ideas, and/or environmental pressure to extend the scope of the protolanguage system. In all cases, the consequence would be a minor—but not a major—revolution in expression, opening the way to an analytic system, though not yet to syntax.

6.3.4 *The Emergence of Words*

In order to see how the first individual words could emerge, let us imagine that the frequency with which 'fetch' messages for individuals are needed is sufficient to support individual designation, and that the system can handle it. The message inventory will include a separate message form for each of 'WISWIWYT fetch N', where N is every member of the group (or at least every member that might be fetched). In other words, there is a distinct phonetic form associated with each individual in the group, for the context of 'fetch that person'. Once you have *any* message for which each individual has his or her own personal referential form, you have attained proper names by the back door, even if, in the first instance, there is additional message material tagged on.

Let us next imagine that a speaker wishes to get a hearer to give an apple to Mary, but, though the apple is in plain view, Mary is not present and so cannot be indicated by gesture. The speaker resolves the problem by saying first *baku*, 'WISWIWYT fetch Mary', and then *tebima*, 'WISWIWYT give specified object (distant) to specified female person'. Since only one of the two variable referents (the apple) has been indicated by gesture, the hearer is seeking local information that will indicate who the recipient of the apple is. Provided *baku* is viewed as somehow relevant to this quest, the effect (whether on this first occasion or only after repeated usage) will be to interpret 'WISWIWYT fetch Mary' as a perceptual rather than physical manipulator ('conjure up an image of Mary'), or indeed, simply to understand *baku* as 'What I say when I mean Mary' ('WISWIM Mary'), a straightforward referential name. There is no difficulty in extending the process that creates words for people to provide a limited number of words for things.[12]

The innovation of WISWIM messages, that is, messages whose purpose is to refer rather than to manipulate, is of considerable significance. Referring for its own sake is the key to breaking out of the stranglehold of pre-existing messages, because it enables the discrete mention of topics. It is the crucial step into the communication of novel ideas. But to create novel messages, you need more than just names for people and things. You also need words for actions. And these, it turns out, come for free. In order to see why, we need to consider the semantics of *baku tebima*.

6.3.5   *Topic Focus and the Emergence of Verbs*

Even though, in *baku tebima*, two previously independent messages have been juxtaposed, nothing grammatical need be entailed. The simplest model that fits this scenario, and the one that we shall assume here, is that *baku* acts as a topicalizer, entirely dependent for its relationship to *tebima* on the pragmatics of the situation. In this case, as we saw, the hearer interprets *baku*

---

[12] *Pace* Bickerton (Calvin and Bickerton 2000: 105), 'getting names doesn't necessarily buy you words'.

as indicative of the missing recipient, both because no one else is gestured towards, and because *baku* is associated with Mary, who is absent.

But now suppose that the speaker's use of *baku tebima* is inconsistent with that reading because both the apple and a recipient (Joyce) have either been indicated or are understood from context. How is the hearer to interpret the speaker's message? If the role of *baku* is as topicalizer, then the hearer will apply pragmatics to deduce an alternative reading, assuming only that Mary has been mentioned for some reason relevant to the interpretation of *tebima*. One participant in *tebima* is still unspecified. The agent of *tebima* is, by default, the hearer, because it is a manipulative utterance. But if, in the absence of any alternative, the topicalizer can displace the normal second-person agent, then a raft of interesting things follow.

First, a manipulative message that is given a different agent than the addressee loses its imperative status, and becomes referential. So while *tebima* means, by default, 'w ɪ s w ɪ w ʏ ᴛ give specified object (distant) to specified female person', when combined with the topicalizer *baku*, interpreted as specifying the agent, it means: 'w ɪ s w ɪ ᴍ Mary is giving/gave/will give/should give specified object (distant) to specified female person'. In other words, in the context of a referential item in agent role (pragmatically, not grammatically, assigned), a manipulative string is transformed from 'What I say when I want you to _' to 'What I say when I mean _'.

Give or take levels of specificity in generic reference, 'w ɪ s w ɪ ᴍ [topic] give thing to person' looks very similar to the specification for a verb, since the semantics of 'give' naturally entail an agent, object, and recipient. Of course, we are not dealing here with verbs *per se* because there is no grammatical framework for them, but we certainly would seem to have arrived at 'proto-verbs' of the kind that Bickerton proposes for his analytic protolanguage. Bickerton's proto-verbs carry a semantic entailment of arguments at a generic level,[13] and these arguments are not explicit unless there is a reason for making them so (Bickerton 1998: 349). Since items are randomly ordered (ibid.), in a string such as *Ig take* (Calvin and Bickerton 2000: 137), Ig could be the agent or object of the action. This seems to be the equivalent of *baku tebima*. Just as for Bickerton, the unnamed arguments are subject to

---

[13] Bickerton, of course, has no reason to identify generic subsets such as object (distant), object (proximate), person (male), person (female). Subsets fall out of the story here only because I have explored the middle ground between totally generic reference and possible measures of explicitness. The workable level of sets could be more specific than I have proposed (e.g. subdividing for age as well as gender, for size or shape as well as proximity), or less specific (e.g. a single message 'w ɪ s w ɪ w ʏ ᴛ give specified object to specified person' or even 'w ɪ s w ɪ w ʏ ᴛ give X to Y'), without any impact on the system as I have defined it.

clarification by other means, such as gesture or context, and, furthermore, if too little is specified, there is tremendous scope for ambiguity. *Baku tebima* could mean, in different circumstances, 'WISWIWYT give specified object (distant) to Mary', 'WISWIWYT give Mary to specified female person' or 'WISWIM Mary is giving/gave/will give/should give specified object (distant) to specified female person'. The correct interpretation of the message will be highly contingent upon the clarity of the context and the attention-focus of the hearer.

There are, however, two important, though subtle, differences. The first relates to the question of ambiguity just raised. In Bickerton's model, the simple analytic protolanguage is all there is, and so the ambiguity is endemic and unavoidable. In the present model, however, there is a strategy for minimizing ambiguity: the well-established manipulative interpretation remains the default, and topicalizers are introduced primarily for displaced reference of objects, not for specifying agents. This comes about because the primary purpose of linguistic communication remains manipulative (see sect. 6.4). The effect is that speakers and hearers start from, and return to, a manipulative interpretation, which grounds the message and makes an agreed reading of it more likely. Note that we, too, default to a manipulative interpretation when unable to identify the relevance of a referential statement (when, for instance, we interpret *the door's open* as a request rather than a contextually stranded observation; cf. Grice 1975; Sperber and Wilson 1995).

The second difference between the WISWIM derivative of a manipulative message and a Bickertonian proto-verb is that the latter possesses no linguistic means of anchoring, through structure, the semantic arguments, even though they must exist cognitively. In contrast, in the holistic strings there *is* a linguistic expression of the semantic arguments, because the messages are inherently complete, even if the denotation is generic, and therefore vague. Where Bickerton's proto-verb *give* carries no obligatory elements, a holistic message equivalent, *tebima*, could be represented, semantically, as a semi-fixed frame: 'WISWIM _ give _ to _' with the gaps filled by compulsory gestures or contextual cues. In short, while the proto-verb *give* is only a word, *tebima* is a whole message.

These differences mean that our account is much more than a just-so story about how the analytic protolanguage got its first words. In the next section I shall show that it does not make sense to assume that once a few simple words arrived on the scene they took on all the communicative functions previously achieved by other, holistic means (even if these did *not* include a holistic message system as described here). I shall demonstrate how, given that there *was* a pre-existing holistic message system, it would not only *not* be thrown over in favour of the analytic system, but would continue to exert expressive conservatism, balanced by social subtlety and explicitness. And while the two systems found ways of supporting each other in expanding the scope for the expression of messages, this would not unleash the capacity for analyticity to create truly useful novel utterances.

6.4 Dual Systems in Protolanguage

Both the holistic and analytic protolanguages have inherent weaknesses as modes of communication, but each offers some measure of compensation for the other. As noted earlier, simply stringing together random sequences of two or three referential object- and action-words would be a poor means of delivering urgent survival messages, because they would be inherently ambiguous and demand a great deal of processing. Furthermore, such strings would be novel configurations for highly predictable messages, and these messages do not need to be constructed anew each time. On the other hand, naming would greatly enhance the scope of the holistic message system to apply its existing messages to non-present referents. In addition, the random stringing together of referential words *would* be of value in invoking new ideas, that is, ones not provided for in the holistic inventory.

The scenario that I propose, then, is one in which holistic messages continue to be used for manipulative purposes, that is, to service the routine interactions of the group, while the new, analytic system takes on two functions. The first is to provide some limited specificity for the holistic messages, as demonstrated above. This would free up the range of reference while continuing to offer an easy processing solution to the problem of how to express semantically complex but repetitive and predictable messages. The other function is as an independent means of achieving non-manipulative messages dedicated to information exchange.

The forte of the analytic protolanguage would be the juxtaposition of novel combinations of words into simple non-hierarchical strings, to stimulate the hearer into a corresponding juxtaposition of the ideas they express. A successful outcome would be when speaker and hearer succeeded in sharing the same image of the relationship between the ideas, something that would rely heavily on the hearer's application of pragmatics, since the messages would be inherently ambiguous in the absence of relational words and grammatical structure. Despite its imprecision, the analytic protolanguage would be a genuinely valuable tool for the new function of information exchange. We may fully align this account with Bickerton's own of the workings of an analytic protolanguage, except for one thing.

Because of the continuation of the holistic system, the analytic system would not carry the entire burden of communication. It would not convey the routine manipulative functions, including social exchange, to which it is, in any case, least well-suited (see sect. 6.2). As a result, the problem would not arise of how such a simple and ambiguous means of communication could support social interaction. Instead of ending up as a poor substitute for whatever system of social interaction preceded it, it would not replace it at all, but rather supplement it.

This non-essential role for the analytic system in protolanguage offers some explanatory advantages. First, it can arise slowly, and falteringly, perhaps failing and restarting many times, rather than needing to be up and running from the start, in order to be worth selecting for.[14] Second, its advent does not need to be marked by any major technological or cultural revolution (see discussion in sect. 6.3.3). If survival interaction was achieved holistically, then the free-standing analytic system would not be operating at the cutting edge of survival, and its messages would be regarded as trivial relative to the important holistic ones.

This, in turn, provides a solution to the problems of deception and checkability that arise if the analytic system is seen as the sole means of communication. Bickerton (this volume) and others (e.g. Deacon 1997; Knight 1998, 2000, this volume; Power 1998) recognize the problem that, once one can talk about things, one can lie about them too, and is likely to do so if it is to one's advantage. For instance, a speaker could say '(there is) honey (in a) tree (on the) ridge', when it was not true, if the intention was to deceive the hearer for some reason. The puzzle is how an analytic protolanguage could ever get off the ground, for hearers would not be able to trust that the input data conveyed what they believed it to. The entire problem hinges, however, on the analytic protolanguage being used for manipulative and social communication, where the consequences of deception are potentially catastrophic for the hearer or, if found out, for the speaker.

---

[14] Indeed, it could be subject to sexual, rather than natural, selection (cf. Okanoya, this volume).

But if holistic messages continued to service the manipulative survival communication, the problem becomes only minor. Manipulative messages do not have truth values. While it is certainly possible to produce 'W I S W I - W Y T meet me/us at the ridge' when you have no intention of being there, or else of lying in ambush, it is not the message that is untrue, just the intention that leads to its production. In other words, while we can still imagine the speakers to be capable of deception, this will not have the same consequences for trusting the holistic message system as it has for trusting the information-conveying analytic one. In the less vital context of information exchange for its own sake, to which the analytic system is relegated in this account, there is less need to deceive. This nicely aligns with Knight's proposal (1998, 2000, this volume) that referential language could only take hold at all if it was restricted in use to fiction, ritual, and play.

To recap, several characteristics differentiate the dual-systems model proposed here from Bickerton's protolanguage. First, the survival messages are more semantically complex and socially sensitive than simple agrammatical arrangements of referential words could produce. Second, the holistic frames are all characterized by a default 'W I S W I W Y T _' interpretation, that is, they are understood to be manipulative of the hearer unless pragmatics force a 'W I S W I M _' reading. Third, there is much less ambiguity because the meaning of the holistic strings is constant and reliable. On the other hand there is a consequent absence of flexibility in meaning beyond that made possible by the semantic 'gaps' of generic denotation. The holistic system constrains its users only to express messages they have expressed before, though, with the help of names, they express them with explicit reference to a wider range of people and objects. True novel expression is possible, as for Bickerton's protolanguage, in the unsystematic association of single referential items to represent new ideas, and it is every bit as cumbersome as he describes. But this exercise is restricted to non-survival contexts, where the consequences of deceit are minimal and the inherent ambiguity is not life-threatening.

6.5 When Performance Outstrips Competence

When the holistic and analytic systems operate together, performance can outstrip competence if the holistic system makes available messages that the analytic system is not equipped to handle. In our protolanguage this would mean that the capacity for the speakers and hearers to achieve a high level

of effective communication would far exceed the expectations of an agrammatical system. In terms of Chomsky's (1965: 4) definitions it is impossible
for performance to outstrip competence because all grammatical language
is a product of analytic knowledge. Chomsky focuses on the 'ideal speaker-
listener' (p. 3) in order to examine the purest form of this knowledge,
uncorrupted by the effects of distraction, change of tack, and so on. Our performance, then, is normally perceived as a poor reflection of what we actually know about our language, and certainly could not qualitatively exceed
that knowledge. However, a range of evidence challenges the usefulness of
this narrow view of performance.

6.5.1 *First-Language Acquisition*

Despite an overriding emphasis in the published research on the acquisition
of language via single-word and two-word utterances, this is only one of two
strategies that young children employ. The other is a holistic strategy. In the
very first stages of acquisition—where this strategy is least disputed—children deliver, with convincing intonation, approximations of common messages, most if not all of which are manipulative (compare Foster 1990: 39).
As they get older, children appear to diversify in style,[15] some adopting a
predominantly analytic strategy to acquisition, and others favouring a continuation of the holistic strategy, to the extent that they may learn and appropriately use complete sentences for some time before they really engage with
breaking them down. When they do, they may not automatically home in on
words and morphemes, but rather segment lengthy strings into shorter, but
still internally complex, holistic units (Bates *et al.* 1995; Peters 1977, 1983;
Plunkett 1993). Children favouring the holistic strategy can appear very
precocious, because their utterances correctly employ morphological and
pronominal particles, and a range of vocabulary well in advance of the age-
norm. These, however, are only present as part of the whole, and cannot be
used creatively. In other words, although they feature in the child's performance, they are not yet part of its analytic competence.

6.5.2 *Aphasia*

One of the most consistently observed features of non-fluent aphasia is

---

[15] For a review of research see Wray and Perkins (2000) and Wray (2002: chs. 6, 7).

the fluent production of common expressions of several words' length, and even of complete memorized texts such as rhymes and prayers, in otherwise agrammatical and hesitant speech. As early as the mid-nineteenth century Hughlings Jackson (Taylor 1958) remarked on this capability, and still today it is generally believed that the normal production of lexis and grammar in such utterances reflects not some temporary reprieve for the otherwise impaired analytic system, but rather the routine retrieval of prefabricated strings. The fluent production of grammatical strings, when the capacity to construct those strings from scratch has been lost, is a case of performance without competence. The fluent, grammatical output derives from the individual's pre-trauma formulaic inventory. This is confirmed by the aphasic person's inability to use in creative ways the linguistic material that they contain (see Wray 2002: ch. 12 for a full review of this phenomenon).

6.5.3 *Second-Language Learners*

Many foreign-language learners begin by mastering a few phrases that can enable them to express simple messages successfully, even before they can construct them from scratch. This strategy features in both taught and natural learners (Wray 2002: chs. 8–11). Subsequently, as reflected in phrase-books and in some classroom teaching, learners may identify some useful semi-fixed frames into which referential nouns or verbs can be inserted. This enables creativity to the extent that any number of new words can be learned and slotted into the memorized frames. But it does not permit a full range of novel expression, because the learner is not equipped to create new constructions. The extent to which a second language learner relies on a holistic strategy for an extended period will depend on a range of factors including learning situation, age, goals, and motivation (see Wray 1999, 2002 for fuller accounts of formulaic language in the second-language acquisition process). Memorizing and successfully employing phrases, in the absence of the linguistic knowledge required to construct them, constitutes performance without competence.

6.5.4 *Kanzi*

Savage-Rumbaugh has consistently argued (e.g. Savage-Rumbaugh *et al.* 1998), that the bonobo Kanzi has a much greater capacity for human language than formal tests indicate. Kanzi is able to respond appropriately to quite complex embedded commands, even without the help of context or being able to see the speaker. Kanzi's output, however, rarely extends beyond strings of two or three lexigram symbols, and there is little indication that he recognizes word order as a potential device for expressing relationships between the symbols, or that he has any capacity to create a hierarchical rather than a linear, structure for them. In the light of his production performance, outside commentators characteristically propose that Kanzi's comprehension processes comprise the identification of key nouns and verbs, using context and pragmatics to guess about their relationship (e.g. Calvin and Bickerton 2000: 40; Corballis this volume).

However, Kanzi's production is limited to what he can produce on his lexigram board of word-equivalent symbols. The board is designed around the assumption that all language is processed analytically, by putting together words one by one according to a set of internalized rules. But suppose that Kanzi is capable of, and indeed is already using when he can, a holistic processing strategy? In production he would be unable to do much in this regard other than create little routines of common symbol sequences, making their execution more fluent and less effortful. However, in comprehension, Kanzi might be capable of understanding, holistically, much more than his analytic abilities would ever reveal. Certainly, one aspect of this would be the identification of the content words that make the message unique. But he might also be understanding with some exactness the larger linguistic frame surrounding these words, treating it as a discontinuous single lexical item.

To understand a command like *Take the ball that's in the refrigerator and put it outside*, Kanzi would not, then, need to be capable of hierarchical structuring. He would need to know the referential words *ball, refrigerator, outside*, and the frame[16] *Take NP_1 that's in NP_2 and put it in NP_3*, which he could interpret as 'w I s w I w y T find a in b and take it to c'. His use of the holistic strategy, based around a frame and single referential items, could easily be overlooked, because the tests focus on the novel juxtaposition of words he knows in constructions he knows. That is, the messages are novel, but the constructions are not (Wray 2002: ch. 1).

For Kanzi there would be no quick way of learning a new lexical frame, as he would not have a sufficiently sophisticated analytic grammar to work out

---

[16] Although such a frame is hierarchical for us [take [NP_i [Rel BE [PP (Loc)]]] and [put [it_i] [PP (Loc)]], it would not need to be for Kanzi. Even the cross-referencing of the initial NP and the later pronoun does not need to be grammatically brokered, since the item you deliver to the new location is the one you've got in your hand.

what made it tick grammatically, but once he had learned it (by encounter-
ing sufficient examples to work out which words were changeable and which
were constant), he would be set up to understand as many novel formulations based upon it as testers could invent. Kanzi's inability to apply a humanlike analytic competence to language would become apparent only if he was
presented with a new construction, based on the same grammatical principles as one he knew, but not appearing in the same form. Even though it
was a logical product of the human analytic grammar, he would be at a loss
until he had been able to learn how to handle it. For instance, if he was taught
both active and passive forms for one construction, this would not lead to
a generalized ability to recognize the passive forms of constructions he had
only encountered in the active.

If this interpretation of Kanzi's linguistic behaviour is right, then it
explains why his interaction with Savage-Rumbaugh and other staff is so
much more convincingly language-like than his production and his test performances indicate.[17] It would mean that Kanzi is displaying, in his comprehension, performance capabilities in excess of his analytic competence. One
is left wondering whether this would extend to his production if he were
equipped with a means of producing holistic items with complex meanings.

6.6 Conclusion

In this chapter I have attempted to shed light on language evolution by drawing on recent research showing that formulaic language plays a central role
in our linguistic behaviour today. I have argued that the holistic processing
strategy that we use for achieving manipulative interaction may predate the
emergence of single referential words and the analytic grammar that combines them. I have proposed that our ancestors first communicated entirely
holistically, which limited them to using only a fixed set[18] of routine manipulative utterances. They then developed a second, analytic system, that ran

---

[17] In speech pathology, too, patients often perform very poorly on tests (which focus on
analytic processing) relative to their capabilities in real interaction (where holistic processing can more easily be employed as a support) (Wray 1992, 2002).

[18] Introducing new ones would be approximately as difficult as it is for us to coin a new
monomorphemic word for an abstract idea. In both cases, usage would be the main way
in which it was learned and passed on, though the protolanguage message could also be
deliberately demonstrated (being a manipulative message), whereas we would supplement
usage with a linguistic definition.

side by side with it. The impetus for the appearance of this system was the disambiguation of holistic messages, particularly those entailing displaced reference, through the introduction of words for people and things and, consequently, actions. This in turn made possible the independent expression of new, informative statements by juxtaposing these items, even though inherent ambiguity, deriving from the absence of grammar, constrained the power of this new means of expression. The analytic system would have been ill-suited for the subtle social interactions required for individual and group survival, and these messages would have continued to be holistically processed as, indeed, they largely are today.

If the holistic system is not taken into account when examining linguistic performance, its efficacy in delivering semantically complex messages at relatively little processing cost may be falsely interpreted as indicating a greater analytic competence in the language than actually exists. This is clear when we examine the performance of various types of speaker today who do not possess as much analytic competence as they appear to display in their (holistic) performance. For our ancestors, the same arrangement could have meant that, despite the absence of grammar, their interaction was both complex and subtle.

FURTHER READING

CALVIN, W., and BICKERTON, D. (2000), *Lingua ex Machina* (Cambridge, Mass.: MIT Press). (An account of Bickerton's non-holistic protolanguage model and its development into full human language, juxtaposed with accounts of the brain's role in language processing.)

KIRBY, S. (2000), 'Syntax without Natural Selection: How Compositionality Emerges from Vocabulary in a Population of Learners', in C. Knight, M. Studdert-Kennedy, and J. R. Hurford (eds.), *The Evolutionary Emergence of Language* (Cambridge: Cambridge University Press), 303–23. (Kirby's paper is a working model of the central process described in sect. 6.3 and Wray 2000*a*).

WRAY, A. (2000), 'Holistic Utterances in Protolanguage: The Link from Primates to Humans', in C. Knight, M. Studdert-Kennedy, and J. R. Hurford (eds.), *The Evolutionary Emergence of Language* (Cambridge: Cambridge University Press), 285–302. (Explores the process by which a holistic protolanguage could develop into our analytic, rule-governed full human language.)

——(2002), *Formulaic Language and the Lexicon* (Cambridge: Cambridge University Press). (Provides a detailed exploration of the nature of formulaic language and the implications of its existence for models of the lexicon.)

REFERENCES

BATES, E., DALE, P. S., and THAL, D. (1995), 'Individual Differences and their Implications for Theories of Language Development', in P. Fletcher and B. MacWhinney (eds.), *The Handbook of Child Language* (Oxford: Blackwell), 96–151.

BECKER, J. (1975). 'The Phrasal Lexicon', Bolt Beranek and Newman Report 3081, AI Report 28, repr. in R. Shank and B. L. Nash-Webber (eds.), *Theoretical Issues in Natural Language Processing* (Cambridge, Mass.: Bolt Beranek and Newman), 60–3.

BICKERTON, D. (1996), *Language and Human Behaviour* (London: University of London Press).

——(1998), 'Catastrophic Evolution: The Case for a Single Step from Protolanguage to Full Human Language', in Hurford *et al.* (1998: 341–58).

——(2000), 'How Protolanguage Became Language', in Knight *et al.* (2000: 264–84).

BOLINGER, D. (1976), 'Meaning and Memory', *Forum Linguisticum*, 1: 1–14.

CALVIN, W., and BICKERTON, D. (2000), *Lingua ex Machina* (Cambridge, Mass.: MIT Press).

CHOMSKY, N. (1965), *Aspects of the Theory of Syntax* (Cambridge, Mass.: MIT Press).

DEACON, T. (1997), *The Symbolic Species: The Co-evolution of Language and the Brain* (London: Penguin).

DUNBAR, R. (1996), *Grooming, Gossip, and the Evolution of Language* (London: Faber & Faber).

ELLIS, N. C. (1996), 'Sequencing in SLA: Phonological Memory, Chunking and Points of Order', *Studies in Second Language Acquisition*, 18: 91–126.

FOSTER, S. H. (1990), *The Communicative Competence of Young Children* (London and New York: Longman).

GRICE, H. P. (1975), 'Logic and conversation', in P. Cole and J. Morgan (eds.), *Syntax and Semantics*, iii. *Speech Acts* (New York: Academic Press), 41–58.

HUDSON, J. (1998), *Perspectives on Fixedness: Applied and Theoretical* (Lund: Lund University Press).

HURFORD, J. R. (2000), 'Introduction: The Emergence of Syntax', in Knight *et al.* (2000: 219–30).

——(2001), 'Protothought had No Logical Names', in J. Trabant (ed.), *New Essays on the Origin of Language* (Berlin: Mouton), 117–30.

—— STUDDERT-KENNEDY, M., and KNIGHT, C. (1998) (eds.), *Approaches to the Evolution of Language* (Cambridge: Cambridge University press).

KIGOTHO, W. (2001), 'If You Hear a Rumble in the Jungle It's Probably Just the Elephants Talking', *The Times Higher Education Supplement*, 20 Apr., p. 19.

KIRBY, S. (1999a), 'Syntax out of Learning: The Cultural Evolution of Structured Communication in a Population of Induction Algorithms', in D. Floreano, J.-D. Nicoud, and F. Mondada (eds.), *Advances in Artificial Life*. Lecture notes in

Computer Science, 1674 (Berlin: Springer), 694–703. www.ling.ed.ac.uk/~simon/ publications.html.

KIRBY, S. (1999*b*), 'Learning, Bottlenecks and Infinity: A Working Model of the Evolution of Syntactic Communication', in K. Dautenhahn and C. Nehaniv (eds.), *Proceedings of the AISB '99 Symposium on Imitation in Animals and Artifacts* (Sussex: Society for the Study of Artificial Intelligence and the Simulation of Behaviour), 55–63. www.ling.ed.ac.uk/~simon/publications.html

——(2000), 'Syntax Without Natural Selection: How Compositionality Emerges from Vocabulary in a Population of Learners', in Knight *et al.* (2000: 303–23).

KNIGHT, C. (1998), 'Ritual/Speech Coevolution: A Solution to the Problem of Deception', in Hurford *et al.* (1998: 68–91).

——(2000), 'Play as Precursor of Phonology and Syntax', in Knight *et al.* (2000: 99–119).

——STUDDERT-KENNEDY, M., and HURFORD, J. R. (2000) (eds.), *The Evolutionary Emergence of Language: Social Function and the Origins of Linguistic Form* (Cambridge: Cambridge University Press).

LANGACKER, R. H. (1987), *Foundations of Cognitive Grammar*, i. *Theoretical Prerequisites* (Stanford, Calif.: Stanford University Press).

MITHEN, S. (1996), *The Prehistory of the Mind* (London: Thames & Hudson).

MOON, R. (1998), *Fixed Expressions and Idioms in English* (Oxford: Clarendon Press).

NUNBERG, G., SAG, I., and WASOW, T. (1994), 'Idioms', *Language*, 70/3: 491–538.

PAWLEY, A., and SYDER, F. (1983), 'Two Puzzles for Linguistic Theory: Nativelike Selection and Nativelike Fluency', in J. C. Richards and R. W. Schmidt (eds.), *Language and Communication* (London and New York: Longman), 191–226.

PETERS, A. M. (1977), 'Language Learning Strategies: Does the Whole Equal the Sum of the Parts?', *Language*, 53/3: 560–73.

——(1983), *Units of Language Acquisition* (Cambridge: Cambridge University Press).

PLUNKETT, K. (1993), 'Lexical Segmentation and Vocabulary Growth in Early Language Acquisition', *Journal of Child Language*, 20: 43–60.

POWER, C. (1998), 'Old Wives' Tales: The Gossip Hypothesis and the Reliability of Cheap Signals', in Hurford *et al.* (1998: 111–29).

REISS, N. (1989), 'Speech Act Taxonomy, Chimpanzee Communication, and the Evolutionary Basis of Language', in J. Wind, E. G. Pulleybank, E. De Grolier, and B. H. Bichakjian (eds.), *Studies in Language Origins* (Amsterdam: John Benjamins), i. 283–304.

SAVAGE-RUMBAUGH, S., SHANKER, S. G., and TAYLOR, T. J. (1998), *Apes, Language, and the Human Mind* (New York: Oxford University Press).

SEARLE, J. R. (1965), 'What is a Speech Act?', in M. Black (ed.), *Philosophy in America* (Ithaca, NY: Cornell University Press), 221–39.

——(1979), 'A Taxonomy of Illocutionary Acts', in J. R. Searle, *Expression and Meaning* (New York: Cambridge University Press), 1–29.

SINCLAIR, J. McH. (1991), *Corpus, Concordance, Collocation* (Oxford: Oxford University Press).

SPERBER, D., and WILSON, D. (1995), *Relevance: Communication and Cognition*, 2nd edn. (Oxford: Blackwell).

TAYLOR, J. (1958) (ed.), *Selected Writings of John Hughlings Jackson* (London: Staples Press), vol. ii.

WORDEN, R. (1998), 'The Evolution of Language from Social Intelligence', in Hurford *et al.* (1998: 148–66).

WRAY, A. (1992), *The Focusing Hypothesis: The Theory of Left Hemisphere Lateralised Language Re-examined* (Amsterdam: John Benjamins).

——(1998), 'Protolanguage as a Holistic System for Social Interaction', *Language and Communication*, 18: 47–67.

——(1999), 'Formulaic Language in Learners and Native Speakers', *Language Teaching*, 32/4: 213–31.

——(2000a), 'Holistic Utterances in Protolanguage: The Link from Primates to Humans', in Knight *et al.* (2000: 285–302).

——(2000b), 'Formulaic Sequences in Second Language Teaching: Principles and Practice', *Applied Linguistics*, 21/4: 463–89.

——(2002), *Formulaic Language and the Lexicon* (Cambridge: Cambridge University Press).

——and PERKINS, M. R. (2000), 'The Functions of Formulaic Language: An Integrated Model', *Language and Communication*, 20/1: 1–28.

7 Language and Revolutionary Consciousness

CHRIS KNIGHT

> From the outset, 'spirit' is cursed with the 'burden' of matter, which appears in this case in the form of agitated layers of air, sounds, in short, of language. Language is as old as consciousness, language *is* practical consciousness, as it exists for other men, and thus as it really exists for myself as well. Language, like consciousness, only arises from the need, the necessity of intercourse with other men.
>
> (Karl Marx and Friedrich Engels 1845–6/1963: 85–6)

7.1 Chomsky's Model

Replying to his many critics, Chomsky (1979: 57) once accused them of not understanding science. To do science, Chomsky explained, 'you *must* abstract some object of study, you must eliminate those factors which are not pertinent . . .' The linguist—according to Chomsky—cannot study humans articulating their thoughts under concrete social conditions. Instead, you must replace reality with an abstract model. To deny this is to reject science altogether.

'Linguistic theory', in Chomsky's (1965: 3) well-known formulation, 'is primarily concerned with an ideal speaker-listener, in a completely homogenous speech-community, who knows its language perfectly and is unaffected by such grammatically irrelevant conditions as memory limitations, distractions, shifts of attention and interest, and errors (random or characteristic) in applying his knowledge of the language in actual performance.' In this deliberately simplified model, children acquire language in an instant (Chomsky 1976: 15). The evolution of language is also instantaneous (1998: 17, cited in Botha 1999: 245). Semantic representations are not socially constructed but innate and pre-existent (1988: 191; 1996: 20–30). Humans speak not for social reasons, but in expressing their genetic nature (1976: 57–69; 1980: 229–30). Speech is the natural, autonomous output of a specialized computational mechanism—the 'language organ'—unique to *Homo sapiens*.

In his capacity as a natural scientist, Chomsky (1976: 186) sees people as 'natural objects', their language a 'part of nature'. Linguistics 'falls naturally within human biology' (1976: 123). However, this is not biology as normally understood. Discussing the evolution of speech, Chomsky suggests: 'The answers may well lie not so much in the theory of natural selection as in molecular biology, in the study of what kinds of physical systems can develop under the conditions of life on earth . . .' (1988: 167). Language's features may be 'simply emergent physical properties of a brain that reaches a certain level of complexity under the specific conditions of human evolution' (1991: 50). More recently, Chomsky (1998: 17) has speculated that 'a mutation took place in the genetic instructions for the brain, which was then reorganized in accord with the laws of physics and chemistry to install a faculty of language'.

For Chomsky, linguistics can aspire to the precision of physics for a simple reason—language itself is a 'natural object' (2000: 106–33). As such, it approximates to a 'perfect system'—an optimal solution to the problem of relating sound and meaning. Biologists, according to Chomsky, do not expect such perfection, which is a distinctive hallmark of physics. He explains: 'In the study of the inorganic world, for mysterious reasons, it has been a valuable heuristic to assume that things are very elegant and beautiful.' Chomsky (1996: 30) continues: 'Recent work suggests that language is surprisingly "perfect" in this sense . . . Insofar as that is true, language seems unlike other objects of the biological world, which are typically a rather messy solution to some class of problems, given the physical constraints and the materials that history and accident have made available.' Language, according to Chomsky, lacks the messiness one would expect of an accumulation of accidents made good by evolutionary tinkering. Characterized by beauty bordering on perfection, it cannot have evolved in the normal biological way.

7.2 The Language Machine

On the eve of the computer-inspired 'cognitive revolution', Chomsky's *Syntactic Structures* (1957) excited and inspired a new generation of linguists because it chimed in with the spirit of the times. The book treated language not as a mass of empirical facts about locally variable linguistic forms and traditions, but as the output of a mechanical device whose design could be precisely specified. In science, according to Chomsky, less is more. If a theory is sufficiently powerful and simple, it should radically reduce the amount of knowledge needed to understand the relevant facts. *Syntactic Structures* infuriated established linguists—and delighted as many iconoclasts—because its message was that much of the profession's previous work had been a waste of time. Why laboriously collect and attempt to make sense of concrete, detailed observations as to how the world's variegated languages are spoken, if a simplifying short cut is available? In an ice-cool, starkly logical argument that magisterially brushed aside most current linguistic theory, *Syntactic Structures* evaluated some conceivable ways of constructing the ultimate 'language machine':

Suppose we have a machine that can be in any one of a finite number of different internal states . . . the machine begins in the initial state, runs through a sequence of states (producing a word with each transition), and ends in the final state. Then we call the sequence of words that has been produced a 'sentence'. Each such machine thus defines a certain language; namely the set of sentences that can be produced in this way.   (Chomsky 1957: 18)

As his argument unfolds, Chomsky rules out this first, crude design for his envisaged machine—it clearly would not work. Then by a process of elimination, he progressively narrows the range of designs which—on purely theoretical grounds—ought to work. Thrillingly, he opens up the prospect of discovering in effect the 'philosopher's stone'—the design specifications of a device capable of generating consistently grammatical sentences not only in English but, with appropriate modifications, in any language spoken (or capable of being spoken) on earth. This ultimate device, Chomsky reasons, must be the very one which, in real life, resides in the brain of every human being. Language, in this new perspective, is no longer a mass of variegated behavioural manifestations or locally observable regularities. It is the device enabling speaking to occur. The aim of linguistics is to expose this hidden object to view.

Chomsky's (1996: 31) ultimate dream is to integrate linguistics into an expanded version of physics: 'The world has many aspects: mechanical, chemical, optical, electrical and so on. Among these are its mental aspects. The thesis is that all should be studied in the same way, whether we are considering the motion of the planets, fields of force, structural formulas for complex molecules, or computational properties of the language faculty.' Consistently with this project, he defines language as 'an individual phenomenon, a system represented in the mind/brain of a particular individual' (1988: 36), contrasting this with the earlier view of language as 'a social phenomenon, a shared property of a community'. Saussure (1974 [1915]: 14) wrote of *langue*: 'It is the social side of speech, outside the individual who can never create nor modify it by himself; it exists only by virtue of a sort of contract signed by the members of a community.' The problem with such usage, Chomsky (1988: 36–7) complains, is that it 'involves obscure sociopolitical and normative factors'. His misgivings are clear. Where social factors are concerned, science must inevitably fail us. There simply *cannot be a social science*. Those who define language in social terms are therefore doomed to find the whole topic 'obscure'.

Chomsky denies the relevance of social factors even when considering language acquisition by the human child. The infant's linguistic capacities, he explains, cannot be taught. Instead, they must be 'allowed to function in the way in which they are designed to develop' (1988: 173). After briefly discussing this topic, he concludes: 'I emphasized biological facts, and I didn't say anything about historical and social facts. And I am going to say nothing about these elements in language acquisition. The reason is that I think they are relatively unimportant' (1988: 173). Superficial irrelevancies aside, Chomsky views language acquisition as independent of experience: 'No one would take seriously a proposal that the human organism learns through experience to have arms rather than wings, or that the basic structure of particular organs results from accidental experience. Rather, it is taken for granted that the physical structure of the organism is genetically determined ...' (1976: 9–10). Human mental structures develop in the same way. 'Acquisition of language', concludes Chomsky (1988: 174), 'is something that happens to you; it's not something that you do. Learning language is something like undergoing puberty. You don't learn to do it; you don't do it because you see other people doing it; you are just designed to do it at a certain time.'

7.3 A Stimulating and Loving Environment

Almost in the same breath, however, Chomsky makes an admission that appears striking in its humanity and self-evident force—and equally in its lack of fit with his other claims. 'Now a good system of raising children', he observes (1988: 173), 'puts them in a stimulating, loving environment in which their natural capacities will be able to flourish.'

This innocent-seeming observation in fact poses a puzzle. If experience is of secondary significance, why should it be important to love the child? Of course, without food and protection, the child may die. And without stimulation, its language organ may not develop. But beyond such basic neccessities, what does Chomsky mean by a 'loving' environment? His thinking is clarified when he imagines the alternative possibility: 'Now let's take a human child which is raised in an orphanage, and let's suppose the child is given the right medical care and food and has normal experience with the physical world. Nevertheless the child may be very restricted in its abilities. In fact, it may not learn the language properly' (ibid.). Chomsky does not quite specify the problem with this nameless institution. But he leaves us in little doubt. The child is afforded a physically secure yet *non*-loving, *non*-stimulating environment. Consequently, its natural capacities may *not* flourish. Chomsky here comes close to conceding that a social factor—namely, insufficient caring interaction or 'love'—might prevent an otherwise normal child from acquiring language despite its genetic endowment.

Let us agree, for the sake of argument, that language acquisition indeed depends on a 'loving, stimulating environment'. The suggestion seems hardly controversial. But what are the features required for an environment to count as 'loving'? Although he assumes some threshold level of linguistic stimulation, Chomsky has shown little interest in such 'external' issues. Developmental psychologists and anthropologists, however, have amassed detailed knowledge concerning precisely the conditions under which a human child—under varying cultural conditions—will optimally internalize its natal language (Ochs and Schieffelin 1984). A related body of research has revealed that even apes may acquire limited symbolic competence if cared for in humanlike ways (Savage-Rumbaugh and Rumbaugh 1993; Tomasello *et al.* 1993). Overall, the evidence suggests that co-operative mindreading—the solicitous interest of others—is indeed a critical variable in enabling normal linguistic competence to be acquired.

When happy in its social surroundings, a baby's playful gestures may communicate details of its cognitive states. When unhappy, it expresses mainly emotional and physiological states (Trevarthen 1979: 347 n.). A child pointing and gesturing for an apple within its mother's reach might naturally expect her to respond helpfully, preferably by providing the apple (Lock

1993: Fig. 12.1). But imagine a hungry mother whose response was to eat the desired item herself. The child would soon abandon cognitive transparency in favour of cries, attempts at physical snatching—or eventual silent withdrawal. Lack of a 'stimulating, loving environment' would in this way block the child's linguistic development.

Admittedly, such mother–infant competition would appear unusual, at least among humans. But what about other species? All mammals nurse their young, and most primates carry them, too. But primate mothers—differing in this respect from Kanzi's loving human carers (Savage-Rumbaugh and Rumbaugh 1993)—rarely offer foraging assistance after weaning. Macaque mothers in South India take food directly out of their infants' hands and mouths (Simonds 1965). Goodall (1990: 166) describes a chimpanzee mother who not only displaced her daughter from a termite-fishing nest but also seized the young female's tool for her own use.

Wild-living primates also appear relatively reluctant to share *information* of obvious value to their young. How should this be explained? Barbara King (1994) addressed this problem in her book, *The Information Continuum*. Her aim in this volume was to show that 'no critical watershed in social information transfer separates primates and humans' (p. 7). As her research proceeded, however, she encountered an unexpected result. Rarely do wild-living apes use volitional signals to donate foraging-related information to one another. Mothers often appear reluctant to give such information even to their own offspring. King comments: 'Adults do sometimes donate information to immatures . . . [but] it is puzzling that such instances are so infrequent . . . If a mother could help her offspring by donating information to it at relatively little cost to herself, why doesn't she? Primatologists have no true understanding of this situation' (p. 6).

Such apparent selfishness does indeed seem anomalous—but only if we accept human levels of trust and sociality as the norm. We naturally expect humans to seek social recognition by learning to speak in relevant ways (Dessalles 1998). But an ape intentionally divulging relevant information in public might lose rather than gain in status, as others took advantage of its honesty. Adult chimpanzees, admittedly, do emit co-operative signals—such as food-calls (Wrangham 1977). But, being irrepressible, these excited sounds are interpreted by listeners as audible *evidence* of the presence of food, regardless of cognitive intentions. The intention behind a food call would be of little interest to others. Ape facial expressions are potentially more transparent in this respect. By human standards, however, they remain inscrutable. In all primates except humans, the sclera—the tissue surrounding the dark-coloured iris of the eye—is dark rather than light or white. The consequent lack of contrast makes it difficult for others to infer direction of gaze (Kobayashi and Kohshima 2001). Like mobsters wearing sunglasses, mature apes are experts at being poker-faced, displaying no enthusiasm at all for having their minds read too easily (de Waal 1982).

A female gorilla was travelling in a party when she noticed a clump of edible vine. She paused as if intending to groom herself. When the others had unsuspectingly moved on, she took advantage of their ignorance—and ate the whole quantity undisturbed (Savage-Rumbaugh and McDonald 1988: 225, citing Fossey). This ape's intelligence led her to *avoid* divulging relevant information to others in her group. In pursuing this strategy, she faced minimal social costs. Even had her duplicity been exposed, she might have lost some share of the food—but not status in the eyes of her community. Primate social status is quite straightforwardly consistent with *concealing* relevant information. Why, then, should an ape mother foster in her offspring qualities such as honesty and transparency? These are human moral values, not those of Machiavellian primate politics (cf. Byrne and Whiten 1988).

Admittedly, apes are not simply Machiavellian as in 'completely unscrupulous'—they may display sociable impulses, including many suggestive of human 'moral' sensibilities (de Waal 1996). Still, the global political order remains founded on other principles. In all animals, effective parenting entails equipping the young to reach reproductive maturity, preparing them for the competitive challenges they may later face. To a human parent, donating relevant information to young offspring might appear unconditionally adaptive. But imagine a world in which adult success depended on primate-style competition for dominance. Would it then be adaptive to encourage dependency on easy-to-fake information received second-hand? Where group-level moral principles are non-existent, it may be best to leave youngsters to fend for themselves—as ape mothers indeed appear to do.

7.4 Signal Evolution: The Social Background

Human sobs tend automatically to trigger tears; laughter is intrinsically contagious. In such cases, stimulus and response are not cognitively mediated; little intellectual choice is involved. If only to facilitate deception, however, both primates and humans require at least some element of cognitive control over their species-specific 'gesture/calls' (Burling 1993), and such capacities have in many cases evolved. But there is always a paradox here. What is the value to anyone of a patently false smile? To be cognitively controlled is to be suspect—if a sign can be manipulated, it can be faked. Even where control is theoretically possible, therefore, the need to inspire trust will prompt signallers to fall back on more 'primitive' performances that are impossible to fake. Where trust cannot be assumed but must be generated via the signalling activity itself, cognitive control over signal-emission must inevitably be *selected against* (Knight 1998, 1999, 2000).

Much more than other primates, humans rely on signals that are patent fakes. 'Mimesis' is the term given by Donald (1991) to a category of signals lying somewhere between hard-to-fake primate gesture/calls and speechlike arbitrary signs. Mimetic culture, in Donald's terms, consists of emotionally expressive signals that to an extent can be deliberately manipulated—'faked'. Professional actors learn how to do this as part of their trade, but all humans can 'act' within limits. There is something socially provocative and risky about such signalling, however. The difficulty is that although fake sobs or tears may be switched on and off at will, human evolved responses remain to an extent emotionally governed and irrepressible. To drop one's guard when others are faking is to risk being seriously manipulated and controlled.

If 'information' is defined as 'that which permits choices to be made' (Smith 1977: 2), mimesis is not straightforwardly informative. Music, song, dance, and other forms of art tug at the emotions, seducing and in other ways persuading the target audience in manners that may seem cognitively unfair. To those in the know, however, collaborative faking can build confidence between the actors precisely because of the emotional and energetic costs entailed (cf. Power 1998, 2000). Among human hunter-gatherers, fiction-generating emotional performances—particularly initiation rituals— are staged to cement bonds and generate in-group confidence rather than to widen or enhance cognitive choice (Knight 1999).

Young children become immersed in mimesis from an early age. In middle-class Western nuclear family contexts (Ochs and Schieffelin 1984), a mother's songlike communication with her infant is not fundamentally informative. Instead, the typically exaggerated prosody has an instrumental function—the sounds have acoustic properties well designed to arouse, alert, soothe, or otherwise directly influence the child's psychology (Fernald 1992). In hunter-gatherer and other traditional cultures, child-rearing practices may differ substantially, yet functions of social bonding and control remain central to pre-verbal communication. Ritual ordeals experienced later in life—including initiation rites—are in a similar sense meaningful yet linguistically uninformative, being aimed more at narrowing personal choices than widening them (Power 2000; Rappaport 1999).

Speech is quite different, both in form and function. To the extent that infant-directed vocalizing becomes linguistic, something new and distinctively human begins to occur. In addition to alerting, soothing, or otherwise manipulating the infant's responses, the newly comprehensible words and sentences begin to affect *cognition*, dispassionately communicating aspects of the speaker's *thought*. Assuming the listener can make use of this information, its behavioural choices are thereby widened, not narrowed.

Dessalles (1998) has described how such contributions are valued and rewarded within human speech communities. Listeners motivate speakers to be 'relevant' by allocating status on that basis. Competition for linguistic status differs subtly yet fundamentally from primate-style competition for dominance. The key distinction is that linguistic status is *assigned* by the speaker's coalition or peer group, not extracted by physical, social, or resource-holding dominance at others' expense. An inescapably *moral* distinction is entailed here. 'When competing for relevance and for status', Dessalles (2000: 78) writes, 'individuals behave for the good of the group.' The most successful speakers are those best able to contribute—directly or indirectly—to in-group co-operative decision-making. Competition of this kind may be described, paradoxically, as 'competition to co-operate'.

The human child, correspondingly, acquires speech within a supportive and interactive milieu quite unlike the environment to which a young primate must adapt. In nurturing speech in the growing child, caregivers including playmates must display interests stretching beyond motives of one-sided manipulation or control. Far from striving to limit one another's behavioural choices, successful conversationalists must learn to widen them. In pursuing this goal, they typically exchange roles, rewarding their mutual co-operation, as each responds informatively to the other's intentionally transparent moves. The infant's part in all this begins with gurgling, mutual eye-contact, and smiling, develops into babbling, laughter, and imaginative play—and culminates in syntactically complex speech (Bates *et al.* 1979; Locke 1993). Such social engagement is not merely an external 'environment'. The intersubjectivity involved here is internal to and constitutive of the child's developing speech (Tomasello 1996).

7.5 Conventional Signalling among Primates

Animal signals are typically 'exaptations' (Gould and Vrba 1982) or 'derived activities' (Tinbergen 1952). Over evolutionary time, certain aspects of non-communicative behaviour assume a signalling function, becoming correspondingly specialized through a process known as 'ritualization'. Signal evolution begins when others read some aspect of normal behaviour as significant. If the subject of such surveillance can benefit from having its mind read or its behaviour anticipated, then over evolutionary time natural selection will accentuate the cues, reducing any ambiguity. By definition, such phylogenetic ritualization entails special elaboration and added costs.

The term 'ontogenetic ritualization' (Tomasello and Call 1997) has recently been coined to denote the learning-based process through which two or more individuals, following repeated encounters, may reduce a volitional gesture used in social interaction to a mutually understood shorthand. Since the final version in this case is actually *less* costly and elaborate than the original, I propose (following Burling 2000) to avoid the potentially confusing term 'ritualization' here, referring instead simply to 'conventionalization'.

Very often, the context of primate conventionalization is play (cf. Knight 2000). A juvenile chimp, for example, may slap an adult on the head while jumping onto its body. Suppose the juvenile regularly starts this game by raising one hand as if preparing to slap. On next recognizing this gesture, the adult may anticipate the whole performance, responding accordingly. Conventionalization is accomplished when, anticipating such comprehension, the juvenile raises its hand in a merely tokenistic way, no longer to perform the physical act of slapping but 'symbolically'—to invite participation in the game (Tomasello and Call 1997: 299–300).

In addition to co-operative play, the mother–infant nursing context may allow conventional signals to emerge. The chimpanzee infant 'nursing poke' (Tomasello *et al.* 1994) begins as a functional action: the infant pushes aside its mother's arm to reach her nipple. As mother and infant interact with one another over time, the poke becomes abbreviated, gradually assuming a unique, idiosyncratic form. Before long, the infant is tweaking or stroking its mother in its own special way, the shorthand now mutually understood as a request to suckle. The relation between the modified signal's form and its meaning is now partly dependent on agreement. Such conventionalization occurs because each infant has an interest in cutting the costs of requesting a feed, while mothers have a corresponding motive to satisfy their offspring while reducing the amount of poking endured. The outcome is a learned, intentional, discrete shorthand, falling outside the normal species-specific repertoire of emotionally expressive, hard-to-fake gesture-calls.

Conventionalization occurs when interests on both sides coincide, allowing tokenistic signalling to replace costly action or indexical display. Among primates, however, the tokens involved are of restricted scope. The nursing poke has no prospect of becoming circulated beyond the specific mother–infant relationship in which it first emerges. Each mother–infant dyad must re-invent the wheel, as it were, arriving independently at its own idiosyncratic version of the poke. Destined to survive only until that particular infant is weaned, each such token, correspondingly, has no prospect of becoming a cultural replicator or meme (cf. Dawkins 1989).

The nursing-poke and the raised-hand play-invitation are instances of volitional primate signalling displaying an element of conventionalization. Other possible examples are the head nod, head shake, wrist flap, and tap/poke—cognitively expressive gestures, each with its own meaning, used by immature apes in their playful interactions with one another (Blount 1990: 429). During sex, male bonobos may use a pointing gesture to direct females into the desired position (Savage-Rumbaugh *et al.* 1977). Arguably, this is shorthand for actually pushing the female into place. More subtle pointing through orientation of the head or eyes may play a role in other intimate relations between apes. But such signals are unlikely to become socially circulated or transmitted between generations in conventional form.

Where trust is not extended throughout a coalition or community, associated conventional signalling cannot be extended either. Instead, conventional signals will be confined within isolated, restricted pockets of social space where sufficient trust momentarily prevails. In their capacity as incipient memes, therefore, such signals lack prospects of achieving immortality. They may evolve, but without leaving any descendants. Consequently, neither linguistic nor more general symbolic cultural evolution can get under way.

7.6 Darwinian Versus Mechanistic Explanations of Language Origins

Why do chimpanzees not capitalize on the potential for symbolic communication which they evidently possess? The reasons are social. With apes as with humans, it is political conflict and anxiety—not individual 'nature'—that sets limits on the scope for playfulness and creativity in social interaction. Young apes engaged in playful antics are clearly enjoying themselves. Bonobos of all ages use sexual play as a means of bonding, particularly in relationships between females (Parish 1996). But among primates generally, scheming within a Machiavellian political framework (Byrne and Whiten 1988) sets up anxieties, conflicts, and corresponding defensive alliances which permeate and effectively constitute adult sociality at the global level. In the absence of any public framework for enforcing 'morality', the onset of sexual maturity confronts individuals with the Darwinian imperative to engage in potentially traumatic conflict with in-group conspecifics. If playfulness becomes less frequent as ape youngsters mature, it is because autonomous, freely creative expressivity is simply not compatible with a situation in which individuals feel sexually or in other ways anxious or threatened (Knight 2000).

If this is accepted, then the transition from primate gesture/call to linguistic sign was driven less by the emergence of novel mechanisms than by the evolution of novel strategies of social co-operation. Few today would wish to deny Chomsky's main point—humans, unlike apes, come into the world with genetically determined linguistic potential. But early *Homo* must also have possessed remarkable symbol-using capacities, long before speech as we know it had evolved. Bonobos such as Kanzi (Savage-Rumbaugh and Rumbaugh 1993) have demonstrated their ability to deploy and act upon conventional signs—if their human caregivers can be relied on to reward such behaviour. In the case of evolving humans, there were of course no external caregivers to give the necessary rewards. Rather, speakers and listeners had to place trust in one another in ways that would be maladaptive under conditions of Machiavellian primate politics.

7.7 The Human Symbolic Revolution

Deacon (1997) argues that language evolution was rooted in novel requirements for communication about social contracts. Non-human primates, in this view, are under no pressure to speak. Needing to communicate only about the currently perceptible world, an ape can always draw attention to some symptom or likeness of the intended referent. But a contract, Deacon observes, exists only as an idea shared among those committed to honouring and enforcing it. How, then, might information about it be conveyed? Since physical correlates—indices—in this case do not exist, Deacon argues that the only way to convey information about a contract would have been to establish a suitable symbol. This symbol—he suggests—would be likely to derive from some ritual action involved in cementing the contract (as a wedding ring might come to symbolize 'marriage'). With recurrent use, such ritual symbols became reduced to shorthands and eventually to words.

Using different lines of reasoning, Maynard Smith and Szathmáry (1995: 279–309) are persuasive in linking the evolution of language with the emergence of social co-operation at the level of the group, viewing this in turn as based on ritually cemented contractual understandings. Drawing on these insights, can we construct a model testable in the light of archaeological, palaeontological, genetic, and ethnographic data? The ancestors of modern humans had long monitored events in the physical and biological worlds, and additionally must have possessed sophisticated 'mind-reading' powers. But no amount of mind-reading ability will enable one to see a 'spirit'. How and why, then, did our ancestors shift to a novel cognitive preoccupation with 'institutional facts' (Searle 1996)—that is, with a domain of contractual fictions such as 'gods and underworlds' (Chase 1994)? According to one recent Darwinian model (Power and Aiello 1997; Power 1998, 1999), 'sham menstruation' (more usually known as 'female initiation') was a fiction-generating strategy in which newly fertile females were bonded in coalitionary alliance with their pregnant and nursing mothers, sisters, and other kin. I favour this model because, unlike some others that have been proposed, it sets out from premises in modern Darwinian theory.

As brain size increased dramatically during the later phases of human evolution, the heavily child-burdened human female needed to avoid being made pregnant and then abandoned by her mate. Females who secured increasing levels of continuous investment from males had improved fitness. A popular hypothesis in this context is that females solved their problems through 'sham oestrus' (Hill 1982). The evolving human female ceased to restrict sexual activity to the period around ovulation, instead dampening 'oestrus' and extending her receptivity beyond the fertile period. By withholding precise information about her true periods of fertility, the human female kept her mate sexually interested over an increasingly extended period.

Sham menstruation builds on this idea, but gives it an additional twist. Even where females have evolved continuous sexual receptivity, they still risk being exploited by philandering males. Once ovulation signals have been phased out, menstruation becomes one of the few indicators of fertility to remain externally detectable. This may help explain the extraordinary attention focused upon it in virtually all hunter-gatherer and other traditional cultures (Knight 1996). The human female menstruates considerably more copiously than any other primate. Unless countermeasures are taken, this risks divulging information that would allow philanderers to discriminate against pregnant or nursing mothers in favour of females who are visibly cycling—hence potentially available to be impregnated in the near future. Unless cultural factors intervene, we would expect a philanderer to monitor such information, attempting to seduce an imminently fertile (cycling) female at the expense of his already impregnated mate.

This threat—according to sham menstruation theory—provides the stimulus in response to which symbolic culture emerges. Recall that by starting to menstruate, a young female divulges her imminent fertility, attracting corresponding male attention. We would predict that pregnant and nursing females in the vicinity might perceive this as a threat. In the counter-strategy envisaged by Power and Aiello (1997), these females take collective action to deal with this threat. It would be difficult to hide the young female, denying her condition or existence. Hiding her would also mean failing to exploit her attractions—her potential value in extracting additional mating effort from males. Instead of hiding her, therefore, the young woman's real and/or fictional mothers, aunts, and sisters do just the reverse. Publicly advertising her condition, they seek by proximity to identify with her 'imminent fertility' and corresponding attractions. Bonding together closely, the young woman's female kin temporarily bar male sexual access to her and scramble her signal, packaging the released information in a form that philanderers cannot use.

Painting up with 'blood', the kinswomen dance and in other ways act in synchrony, asserting themselves as inseparable from their menstruating 'sister'. Defending against the threat of harassment, they draw jointly on their own and one another's male kin for support. As 'brothers' consequently become involved in physically defending their 'sisters', would-be philanderers are deterred from picking and choosing between one female and the next on the basis of biological signals. The fiction is broadcast that everyone just now is imminently fertile. Sexual harassment or violence remains, of course, an option for would-be philanderers. But under the new conditions, sexual rewards can more easily be earned by going away hunting and returning to camp with supplies of meat. In the arrangement that now begins to emerge—

known ethnographically as 'bride-service'—meat from the hunt is handed to senior figures within the bride's coalition. They then redistribute it among close and distant kin. To maximize provisions thereby obtained, kin-bonded females should logically maximize joint access to multiple in-married males. This in turn means ensuring that any male who already has a sexual partner is barred from monopolizing access to additional mates. Ideally, each young woman as she comes of age should bring in at least one additional 'bridegroom'—preferably a young man with a good reputation as a hunter.

For intrinsic reasons—since outgroup male harassment may at any time be attempted—this strategy must involve coalitionary control over women's bodies and availability (cf. Knight 1991: 122–53). This in turn depends on one fundamental precondition. When any female is signalling sexual resistance, her kin—both male and female—must support her in this and ensure that her message is understood. Females must schedule their action to maximum effect, appealing to male kin as necessary, synchronizing with sisters and ensuring that signals are salient and unambiguous. As each young female comes of age, she must be decisively and permanently initiated into the same coalition-based strategy.

Against this background, we can derive a prediction about the precise form of the basic cultural replicator or meme (cf. Dawkins 1989). The expected signature of sexual resistance can be inferred by recalling its theoretical antithesis in the form of primate sexual soliciting. We may conduct this reasoning in two steps:

1. A chimpanzee in oestrus signals her availability with a prominent genital swelling. This is a competitive signal, advertising to males in the vicinity that she is of the right (*same*) species, the right (*different*) sex—and that this is the right (*fertile*) time.
2. On this basis, sexual resistance should be displayed by collectively signalling wrong sex (male), wrong species (animal) and wrong time (menstruating).

Matching these predictions, gender- and species-ambivalent performances are in many traditions intrinsic to women's 'rituals of rebellion' (e.g. Gluckman 1954/1963). Throughout sub-Saharan Africa, females on such occasions paint up with cosmetics—especially brilliant reds—simultaneously playing male and/or animal roles (Power 2000). Cross-culturally, hunter-gatherer initiation ceremonies establish sexual inviolability in comparable ways (Knight *et al.* 1995; Power and Watts 1997).

Associated with the earliest appearance of anatomically modern *Homo sapiens* in sub-Saharan Africa—dating to between 100,000 and 130,000 years ago—archaeologists report evidence for the deliberate mining, selection, treatment, and artistic application of red ochre pigments. Arguably, this is evidence for the world's first 'art' (Watts 1999). Drawing on ethnographic data from the same region, the red ochre pigments have been interpreted as connoting blood, fertility, and the supernatural potency so widely attributed to menstruation (Power and Watts 1997; Watts 1999). Examples of more recent local rock art include therianthropes—creatures in which human and animal features are combined (Lewis-Williams and Dowson 1989). Khoisan traditions are of particular significance, since in their case strands of cultural, including ritual, continuity evidently stretch back into the Middle Stone Age (Watts 1999). In the Kalahari, a Ju/'hoansi maiden still celebrates her first menstruation by ceremonially bonding with female kin. While bleeding, she adopts the identity of the Eland Bull. Central to belief about this mythical creature is that he enjoys sexual relations with his multiple 'wives'—the maiden's kinswomen acting the part of eland cows. During the Eland Bull Dance—the ceremony held to celebrate a girl's first menstruation—such fictional sex is acted out by all concerned (Lewis-Williams 1981). Other hunter-gatherer representations of divinity—such as the Australian Aboriginal Rainbow Snake—illustrate the same logic of gender and species reversal (Knight 1983, 1988).

The 'human revolution' became consummated as coalitionary resistance to philandering drove up the costs of 'selfish' male strategies to the point where they were no longer affordable. With this source of internal conflict removed, enhanced community-wide trust transformed the context in which communication occurred. We have seen that signals may become conventionalized wherever trusting listeners can be assumed. The establishment of stable, 'blood'-symbolized kin-coalitions allowed 'brothers' and 'sisters' to trust one another as never before. Signallers no longer needed to ground each communicative performance in hard-to-fake displays whose *intrinsic* features inspired trust. Trust, in other words, no longer had to be generated signal by signal—it could be assumed. With this problem removed, even patent fictions could now be valued as evidence from which to reconstruct others' thoughts. Language consists entirely of fictions of this kind.

Humans who had undergone the revolution, then, no longer had to stage a 'song and dance' each time they needed to appear persuasive. Costly ritual performance remained necessary, but only because each individual's initiation into and subsequent commitment to the speech community could be signalled in no other way. Once such commitment had *already* been displayed, coalition members could cut their costs, replacing indexical display with a repertoire of conventionally agreed shorthands (see Knight 1998, 1999, 2000). Since these low-cost abbreviations—'words' or 'protowords'— were tokens in the first instance of group-level contractual phenomena, they could be honest without having to be grounded in anything real. Reality-defying performances upholding community-wide moral contracts are familiar to anthropologists as 'religion' (Rappaport 1999). Once humans had established such traditions, they found themselves communicating within a shared moral universe—a socially constructed virtual reality—of their own making.

7.8 Summary and conclusion

Chimpanzees have significant untapped potential for symbolic communication. During infancy, rudimentary symbolic skills may serve purposes in playful and mother–infant contexts. But with the approach of sexual maturity, such skills become increasingly marginal. Only if trusting, playful, and solicitous relationships were central in the *struggle for adult reproductive success* would mothers enhance their fitness by fostering sophisticated symbolic dependency in their offspring. As things are, chimpanzee mothers refrain from any such inappropriate parenting. Instead, chimpanzee infants are taught that most valuable of all lessons—how to fend for themselves.

Human children learn a different lesson. In their case, the importance of play is not that it prepares for an adult life of competitive conflict. It prepares instead for a life of engagement with symbols. In the human case, it is as if communal pretend-play were not confined to childhood but—in novel forms such as art, ritual, and religion—had become extended into adult life. Creative, playful, and imaginative symbolic performance is central to human social competence, playing a key role in alliance-formation, sexual courtship, and reproductive success (Knight 1999; Miller 1999; Power 1999).

Social theorist Pierre Bourdieu (1991: 430) derides Chomsky's model of a 'homogenous speech community', terming it the 'illusion of linguistic communism'. But this may be too dismissive. Chomsky identifies human linguistic creativity with social and political freedom. He is entitled to argue that where performance is distorted by external factors such as conflict or social inequality, these aberrations should not distort our picture of human speech as such. Anthropologists have confirmed that structures of one-sided political dominance indeed obstruct syntactical creativity, driving speakers to resort to syntactically impoverished, repetitive verbal clichés (Bloch 1975). During social revolutions, by contrast, as authoritarian pretensions are punctured through gossip, humour, and political conspiracy, the full creative possibilities of speech become explored.

The scenario I favour is that speech emerged out of a social revolution (Knight 1991, 1998, 1999, 2000; Knight *et al.* 1995). Consummated in sub-Saharan Africa some 130,000 years ago (Watts 1999), it inaugurated the most successful and stable system of human social organization to date—the egalitarian hunter-gatherer lifestyle. 'Communism in living' (Morgan 1881; Lee 1988) afforded ideal conditions for language's rapid evolution. In freeing our ancestors from their former competitive anxieties, it liberated human potential. Far from being marginal or external, as Chomsky suggests, distinctively human social strategies in this way gave rise to distinctively human speech.

FURTHER READING

Deacon, Terrence (1997), *The Symbolic Species: The Co-evolution of Language and The Human Brain* (London: Penguin). (Social contracts and the origins of language.)

Dunbar, Robin, Knight, Chris, and Power, Camilla (1999) (eds.), *The Evolution of Culture* (Edinburgh: Edinburgh University Press). (Interdisciplinary debates on the origins of language and symbolic culture.)

Knight, Chris (1991), *Blood Relations: Menstruation and the Origins of Culture* (New Haven and London: Yale University Press). (The human revolution.)

Kohn, Marek (1999), *As We Know It: Coming to Terms with an Evolved Mind* (London: Granta). (Socialist politics and modern Darwinism.)

Maynard Smith, John, and Szathmáry, Eörs (1995), *The Major Transitions in Evolution* (New York: W. H. Freeman). (The transition to speech and social contracts was one of a series of major transitions punctuating the story of life on earth.)

de Waal, Franz (1996), *Good Natured: The Origins of Right and Wrong in Humans and Other Animals* (Cambridge, Mass.: Harvard University Press). (Do apes have morals?)

REFERENCES

BATES, ELIZABETH, BENIGNI, L., BRETHERTON, I., CAMAIONI, L., and VOLTERRA, L. (1979), *The Emergence of Symbols: Cognition and Communication in Infancy* (New York: Academic Press).

BLOCH, MAURICE (1975), *Political Language and Oratory in Traditional Society* (London: Academic Press).

BLOUNT, B. G. (1990), 'Spatial Expression of Social Relationships among Captive *Pan paniscus*: Ontogenetic and Phylogenetic Implications', in S. T. Parker and K. R. Gibson (eds.), *'Language' and Intelligence in Monkeys and Apes: Comparative Developmental Perspectives* (Cambridge: Cambridge University Press), 420–32.

BOTHA, R. P. (1999), 'On Chomsky's "Fable" of Instantaneous Language Transmission', *Language and Communication*, 19: 243–57.

BOURDIEU, PIERRE (1991), *Language and Symbolic Power* (Cambridge: Polity Press).

BURLING, ROBBINS (1993), 'Primate Calls, Human Language, and Nonverbal Communication', *Current Anthropology*, 34: 25–53.

——(2000), 'Comprehension, Production and Conventionalisation in the Origins of Language', in Knight *et al.* (2000: 27–39).

BYRNE, RICHARD, and WHITEN, Andrew (1988), *Machiavellian Intelligence. Social Expertise and the Evolution of Intellect in Monkeys, Apes, and Humans* (Oxford: Clarendon Press).

CHASE, P. (1994). 'On Symbols and the Paleolithic', *Current Anthropology*, 35/5: 627–9.

CHOMSKY, NOAM (1957), *Syntactic Structures* (The Hague: Mouton).

——(1965), *Aspects of the Theory of Syntax* (Cambridge, Mass.: MIT Press).

——(1976), *Reflections on Language* (London: Temple Smith).

——(1979), *Language and Responsibility* (Hassocks: Harvester).

——(1980), *Rules and Representations* (Oxford: Basil Blackwell).

——(1988), *Language and Problems of Knowledge: The Managua Lectures* (Cambridge, Mass.: MIT Press).

——(1991), 'Linguistics and Cognitive Science: Problems and Mysteries', in A. Kasher (ed.), *The Chomskyan Turn: Generative Linguistics, Philosophy, Mathematics, and Psychology* (Oxford: Blackwell), 26–55.

——(1996), *Powers and Prospects: Reflections on Human Nature and the Social Order* (London: Pluto Press).

——(1998), 'Language and Mind: Current Thoughts on Ancient Problems', Parts I and II; lectures presented at Universidad de Brasilia, published in *Pesquisa Linguistica*, 3, 4. Page references are to the English manuscript.

——(2000), *New Horizons in the Study of Language and Mind* (Cambridge: Cambridge University Press).

DAWKINS, RICHARD (1989), *The Selfish Gene*, 2nd edn. (Oxford: Oxford University Press).

DEACON, TERRENCE (1997), *The Symbolic Species: The Co-evolution of Language and the Human Brain* (London: Penguin).

DESSALLES, JEAN-LOUIS (1998), 'Altruism, Status and the Origin of Relevance', in Hurford *et al.* (1998: 130–47).

——(2000), 'Language and Hominid Politics', in Knight *et al.* (2000: 62–80).

DONALD, MERLIN (1991), *Origins of the Modern Mind. Three Stages in the Evolution of Culture and Cognition* (Cambridge, Mass.: Harvard University Press).

DUNBAR, R., KNIGHT, C., and POWER, C. (1999) (eds.), *The Evolution of Culture* (Edinburgh: Edinburgh University Press)

FERNALD, ANNE (1992), 'Human Maternal Vocalizations to Infants as Biologically Relevant Signals: an Evolutionary Perspective', in J. H. Barkow, L. Cosmides, and J. Tooby (eds.), *The Adapted Mind: Evolutionary Psychology and the Generation of Culture* (New York and Oxford: Oxford University Press), 391–428.

GLUCKMAN, MAX (1954/1963), 'Rituals of Rebellion in South-East Africa', in M. Gluckman (ed.), *Order and Rebellion in Tribal Africa* (London: Cohen and West), 110–36.

GOODALL, JANE (1990), *Through a Window: My Thirty Years with the Chimpanzees of Gombe* (Boston: Houghton Mifflin).

GOULD, STEVEN JAY, and VRBA, E. S.(1982), 'Exaptation: A Missing Term in the Science of Form', *Paleobiology,* 8: 4–15.

HILL, KIM (1982), 'Hunting and human evolution', *Journal of Human Evolution,* 11: 521–44.

HURFORD, J. R., STUDDERT-KENNEDY, M., and KNIGHT, C. (1998) (eds.), *Approaches to the Evolution of Language: Social and Cognitive Bases* (Cambridge: Cambridge University Press).

KING, BARBARA J. (1994), *The Information Continuum. Evolution of Social Information Transfer in Monkeys, Apes, and Hominids* (Santa Fe: School of American Research Press).

KNIGHT, CHRIS (1983), 'Lévi-Strauss and the Dragon: Mythologiques Reconsidered in the Light of an Australian Aboriginal Myth', *Man,* NS 18: 21–50.

——(1988), 'Menstrual Synchrony and the Australian Rainbow Snake', in T. Buckley and A. Gottlieb (eds.), *Blood Magic: The Anthropology of Menstruation* (Berkeley and Los Angeles: University of California Press), 232–55.

——(1991), *Blood Relations: Menstruation and the Origins of Culture* (New Haven and London: Yale University Press).

——(1996), 'Menstruation', in A. Barnard and J. Spencer (eds.), *Encyclopedia of Social and Cultural Anthropology* (London and New York: Routledge), 363–4.

——(1998), 'Ritual/Speech Coevolution: A Solution to the Problem of Deception', in Hurford *et al.* (1998: 68–91).

——(1999), 'Sex and Language as Pretend-Play', in Dunbar *et al.* (1999: 228–9).

——(2000), 'Play as Precursor of Phonology and Syntax', in Knight (2000: 99–119).

——POWER, CAMILLA, and WATTS, IAN (1995), 'The Human Symbolic Revolution:

A Darwinian Account', *Cambridge Archaeological Journal*, 5/1: 75–114.

KNIGHT, CHRIS, STUDDERT-KENNEDY, M., and HURFORD, J. R. (2000) (eds.), *The Evolutionary Emergence of Language: Social Function and the Origins of Linguistic Form* (Cambridge: Cambridge University Press).

KOBAYASHI, HIROMI, and KOHSHIMA, SHIRO (2001), 'Unique Morphology of the Human Eye and Its Adaptive Meaning: Comparative Studies on External Morphology of the Primate Eye', *Journal of Human Evolution*, 40/5: 419–35.

LEE, RICHARD B. (1988), 'Reflections on Primitive Communism', in T. Ingold, D. Riches, and J. Woodburn (eds.), *Hunters and Gatherers*, i. *History, Evolution and Social Change* (Chicago: Aldine), 252–68.

LEWIS-WILLIAMS, DAVID (1981), *Believing and Seeing: Symbolic Meanings in Southern San Rock Paintings* (London: Academic Press).

——and DOWSON, T. A. (1989), *Images of Power: Understanding Bushman Rock Art* (Johannesburg: Southern Book Publishers).

LOCK, ANDREW (1993), 'Human Language Development and Object Manipulation: Their Relation in Ontogeny and its Possible Relevance for Phylogenetic Questions', in K. R. Gibson and T. Ingold (eds.), *Tools, Language and Cognition in Human Evolution* (Cambridge: Cambridge University Press), 279–99.

LOCKE, JOHN L. (1993), *The Child's Path to Spoken Language* (Cambridge: Cambridge University Press).

MARX, KARL, and ENGELS, FRIEDRICH (1845–6/1963), *The German Ideology*; extract trans. in T. Bottomore and M. Rubel (eds.), *Karl Marx: Selected Writings in Sociology and Social Philosophy* (Harmondsworth: Penguin), 85–7.

MAYNARD SMITH, JOHN, and SZATHMÁRY, EÖRS (1995), *The Major Transitions in Evolution* (New York: W. H. Freeman).

MILLER, GEOFFREY (1999), 'Sexual Selection for Cultural Displays', in Dunbar *et al.* (1999: 71–91).

MORGAN, LEWIS HENRY (1881), *Houses and House-Life of the American Aborigines* (Chicago and London: University of Chicago Press).

OCHS, ELINOR, and SCHIEFFELIN, BAMBI B. (1984), 'Language Acquisition and Socialization: Three Developmental Stories and Their Implications', in R. A. Shweder and R. A. LeVine (eds.), *Culture Theory: Essays on Mind, Self, and Emotion* (Cambridge: Cambridge University Press), 276–320.

PARISH, AMY (1996), 'Female Relationships in Bonobos (*Pan paniscus*): Evidence for Bonding, Cooperation, and Female Dominance in a Male-philopatric Species', *Human Nature*, 7: 61–96.

POWER, CAMILLA (1998), 'Old Wives Tales: The Gossip Hypothesis and the Reliability of Cheap Signals', in Hurford *et al.* (1998: 111–29).

——(1999), 'Beauty Magic: The Origins of Art', in Dunbar *et al.* (1999: 92–112).

——(2000), 'Secret Language Use at Female Initiation. Bounding Gossiping Communities', in Knight *et al.* (2000: 81–98).

——and AIELLO, LESLIE C. (1997), 'Female Proto-Symbolic Strategies', in L. D. Hager (ed.), *Women in Human Evolution* (New York and London: Routledge), 153–71.

——and WATTS, IAN (1997), 'The Woman with the Zebra's Penis: Gender, Mutability and Performance', *Journal of the Royal Anthropological Institute*, NS 3: 537–60.

RAPPAPORT, ROY A. (1999), *Ritual and Religion in the Making of Humanity* (Cambridge: Cambridge University Press).

SAUSSURE, FERDINAND DE (1974 [1915]), *Course in General Linguistics*, trans. W. Baskin (London: Fontana/Collins).

SAVAGE-RUMBAUGH, E. SUE, and MCDONALD, K. (1988), 'Deception and Social Manipulation in Symbol-Using Apes', in R. W. Byrne and A. Whiten (eds.), *Machiavellian Intelligence* (Oxford: Clarendon Press), 224–37.

——and RUMBAUGH, D. M. (1993), 'The Emergence of Language', in K. Gibson and T. Ingold (eds.), *Tools, Language and Cognition in Human Evolution* (Cambridge: Cambridge University Press), 86–108.

——WILKERSON, B. J., and BAKEMAN, R. (1977), 'Spontaneous Gestural Communication among Conspecifics in the Pygmy Chimpanzee (*Pan paniscus*)', in G. Bourne (ed.), *Progress in Ape Research* (New York: Academic Press), 97–116.

SEARLE, JOHN R. (1996), *The Construction of Social Reality* (London: Penguin).

SIMONDS, P. E. (1965), 'The Bonnet Macaque in South India', in I. DeVore (ed.), *Primate Behavior* (New York: Holt, Rinehart & Winston), 175–96.

SMITH, W. JOHN (1977), *The Behavior of Communicating: An Ethological Approach* (Cambridge, Mass.: Harvard University Press).

TINBERGEN, NIKOLAAS (1952), '"Derived" Activities: Their Causation, Biological Significance, Origin and Emancipation During Evolution', *Quarterly Review of Biology*, 17: 1–32.

TOMASELLO, MICHAEL (1996), 'The Cultural Roots of Language', in B. M. Velichkovsky and D. M. Rumbaugh (eds.), *Communicating Meaning: The Evolution and Development of Language* (Mahwah, NJ: Erlbaum), 275–307.

——and CALL, J. (1997), *Primate Cognition* (New York and Oxford: Oxford University Press).

——SAVAGE-RUMBAUGH, SUSAN, and KRUGER, A. C. (1993), 'Imitative Learning of Actions on Objects by Children, Chimpanzees, and Enculturated Chimpanzees', *Child Development*, 64: 1688–705.

——CALL, J., NAGELL, K., OLGUIN, R., and CARPENTER, M. (1994), 'The Learning and Use of Gestural Signals by Young Chimpanzees: A Trans-generational Study', *Primates*, 35: 137–54.

TREVARTHEN, C. (1979), 'Communication and Co-operation in Early Infancy: A Description of Primary Intersubjectivity', in M. Bullowa (ed.), *Before Speech* (Cambridge: Cambridge University Press), 321–47.

DE WAAL, FRANZ (1982), *Chimpanzee Politics. Power and Sex among Apes* (London: Unwin).

——(1996), *Good Natured: The Origins of Right and Wrong in Humans and Other Animals* (Cambridge, Mass.: Harvard University Press).

Watts, Ian (1999), 'The Origin of Symbolic Culture', in Dunbar *et al.* (1999: 113–46).

Wrangham, Richard W. (1977), 'Feeding Behaviour of Chimpanzees in Gombe National Park, Tanzania', in T. H. Clutton-Brock (ed.), *Primate Ecology: Studies of Feeding and Ranging Behaviour in Lemurs, Monkeys and Apes* (London: Academic Press), 504–38.

8 Did Language Evolve from Manual Gestures?

MICHAEL C. CORBALLIS

8.1 Introduction

The theory that language evolved from manual gestures rather than vocalizations goes back at least to Condillac in 1746, but was given its modern shape by Hewes in 1973. Since then, supporting evidence has continued to accumulate. However, the theory has not found wide acceptance. One reason may be that it is seen to undermine the huge body of work on phonological aspects of language, and on the notion that 'speech is special' (Liberman 1982: 148). Another is that it may seem to lack parsimony. Speech seems so much a natural part of the human condition that one might ask why it should be necessary to postulate that language emerged from an entirely different channel of communication.

Yet although radio and telephone demonstrate that speech can be autonomous, we all gesture as we speak. McNeill (1985) has shown that gestures are precisely synchronized with speech, arguing that they together form a single, integrated system. Goldin-Meadow and McNeill (1999) suggest that speech carries the syntactic component while gesture carries the mimetic, iconic component. Sometimes speech is simply inadequate to convey the message; when asked to explain what a *spiral* is, most people resort to a manual demonstration. Goldin-Meadow *et al.* (1996) have also shown that if people are prevented from speaking and asked to communicate with gestures, their gestures spontaneously take on syntactic elements.

It must surely also be true that gesture was at least minimally involved in the *evolution* of language. Rousseau (1755/1964) drew attention to the para-

I thank Dick Byrne, Alison Wray, and anonymous referees for helpful comments and suggestions.

dox that 'Words would seem to have been necessary to establish the use of words,'[1] raising the question of how a purely vocal language could ever have *begun*. Any dictionary is testimony to the fact that we generally define words in terms of other words, but to someone who knows nothing of a language to begin with a dictionary is merely an elaborate tautology. There must also be some way to indicate what words mean in terms of real-world entities or events. Gestures would go a long way to accomplishing this.

The most obvious example is pointing. When acquiring language, children start to learn the names of things by having them pointed out while the names or qualities are uttered. Of course, this can apply only to concrete items or actions, but may be sufficient to establish a basic vocabulary, and the system can be bootstrapped from there. It may be that the evolution of language proceeded similarly, although gestures probably went beyond pointing to include iconic representations, leading on from there to abstract representations and syntax. If the origins of language lie in gestures rather than in sounds, Rousseau's paradox is largely resolved, since gestures form a natural link with the physically realized world.

8.1.1 *Sign Languages*

Perhaps the major boost to the gestural theory since Hewes's (1973) article has been the realization that sign languages, especially as spontaneously developed by deaf communities everywhere, have all the essential properties of a true language (e.g. Armstrong *et al.* 1995). Infants exposed to a sign language learn it as naturally as those who learn to speak, and perhaps more quickly (Meier and Newport 1990). The same left-hemispheric brain areas are involved, although there may be a more pronounced right-hemispheric contribution in sign language (Neville *et al.* 1998), perhaps because of the added spatial component.

There are at least two respects in which sign languages map onto real-world events in a more 'natural' way than speech does. First, they make use of the three dimensions of space in addition to the dimension of time, whereas speech is structured along only the time dimension. In American Sign Language (ASL), there is a 'signing space' in front of the signer's body, in which specific spatial locations are assigned to the objects and people to be referred

---

[1] 'La parole paroît avoir été fort nécessaire pour établir l'usage de la parole', Rousseau (1775/1964: 148–9).

to through a stretch of discourse. If a particular location, say to the left of one signer's body, is assigned to a particular individual, then two signers conversing need only point to that location when they want to refer to that individual. Sensory functions are signalled by simply touching the appropriate part of the body, such as ears, eyes, nose, or mouth. Time is represented in terms of a time-line that locates the past behind the signer, the present close to the signer's body, and the future in front (see Neidle *et al.* 2000).

Second, many of the signs themselves may carry some of the physical properties of what they represent. In ASL the shape of the hand may take up a shape representative of some given object, such as a car, and verbs of motion involve movement of the particular handshape along a path representative of the actual motion. In American, Danish, and Chinese sign languages, for example, the signs for tree carry something of the shape of a tree, although they do so in very different ways.

It has long been noted, though, that gestures become less iconic and more arbitrary over time. Charles Darwin quotes a passage from a book published in 1870: '[The] contracting of natural gestures into much shorter gestures than the natural expression requires, is very common amongst the deaf and dumb. This contracted gesture is frequently so shortened as nearly to lose all resemblance of the natural one, but to the deaf and dumb who use it, it still has the force of the original expression.'[2] The conversion to shorter, more arbitrary gestures can be described as one of *conventionalization*, and is a general feature of communication systems, in animals as in humans (Givón 1995). The sign for 'home' in ASL was once a combination of the signs for 'eat', which is a bunched hand touching the mouth, and the sign for 'sleep', which is a flat hand on the cheek. Now it consists of two quick touches on the cheek, both with a bunched handshape, so the original iconic components are effectively lost (Frishberg 1975). Studies of deaf children inventing their own homesign also suggest that signs are initially coined for their resemblances to what they represent, but are later adapted to a more arbitrary form (Morford *et al.* 1995). Iconic resemblance may be necessary to get signs up and running, but loses its importance once the signs are established.

Saussure (1931) argued that the *arbitrary* nature of the symbols is one of the critical features of language, but the advantages of arbitrariness may be more practical than essential. In general, conventionalized, abstract ges-

---

[2] Quoted from W. R. Scott's book *The Deaf and the Dumb*, 2nd edn. (1870: 12) by Darwin (1904: 62).

tures are shorter than iconic ones, so communication is more efficient. More importantly, the use of arbitrary symbols enhances the possibility of distinguishing between labels for different objects. Even to distinguish cats from dogs using iconic gestures would be difficult, if not impossible, and the sheer variety of dog shapes is a further reason for an abstract code. The symbols of language are in general designed to maximize contrast, and it is especially important to keep the symbols for similar objects distinct (Burling 1999). Vocalization itself avoids the potential confusions caused by visual resemblances, and this may well have been a significant factor in the gradual replacement, in evolution, of manual signs by spoken words. The spoken word 'cat', for instance, is quite distinct from the spoken word 'dog', and neither word has any conceivable iconic or acoustic resemblance to the animals they represent. Of course, manual signs also become conventionalized to arbitrary form, although they do retain more of an iconic character overall. There may be something of a trade-off, manual signs being easier to acquire initially, but speech ultimately allowing for greater fidelity of transmission.

Sign languages involve the use of the head and upper body as well as the hands and arms, allowing information to be conveyed in parallel to a far greater extent than is possible in speech. For example, in ASL a negative phrase is signalled in part by shaking the head from side to side for the duration of the phrase. Movements of the head and face are also used to mark types of topics; an example is the rapid head-nodding, with raised upper lip and raised eyebrows, to indicate a 'you know' topic, as in 'You know Fred, he's bought a new car.'

ASL has a grammatical structure with all the essential properties of the grammars that underlie spoken languages (Neidle *et al.* 2000), and it is much easier to understand how grammar itself might have *evolved* from representational and indicative gestures than from, say, animal calls. This point is elaborated by Armstrong *et al.* (1995), who note that syntax is implicit in every gesture. Indeed, individual gestures can often be regarded either as words or as simple sentences. For example, a simple gesture of swinging the right hand across the front of the body to grasp the upraised finger of the left hand can be regarded as a sign for the verb 'to catch'. But it can also stand for a sentence such as 'The cat caught the mouse', if, say, the gesture originates in a location specifying a cat and catches the finger in a location specifying a mouse. Implicit in any simple gesture is the *subject–verb–object* (SVO) relation that represents the structure of a basic sentence, as well as the structure of simple events in the real world. The gesture can be modified to provide the equivalent of adjectives or adverbs. For example, if the catching sign is accompanied by raised eyebrows, a near-universal expression of surprise, the gesture might then be interpreted as 'By a lucky fluke, he caught it.'

Armstrong *et al.* suggest that an understanding of the evolution of language through gesture removes the necessity to suppose that syntax evolved in all-or-none fashion, and depended on the prior invention of words. They also challenge the notion that language is organized in modular fashion, or that it exhibits duality of patterning. Once it is seen that the structure of gesture can mimic the structure of events in the world, both words and syntax are born, and can be progressively extended and conventionalized to produce language of the complexity that we find in both the signed and spoken language of modern humans.

8.2 Precursors to Language in Primates

We need not look only to the present-day characteristics of language to find evidence for gestural origins. Our primate heritage strongly suggests we evolved from primate ancestors with highly developed cortical systems for manual control and a sophisticated visual system, but little voluntary control over vocalization.

There is evidence that a sophisticated, cortically controlled system for manual grasping arose in primates long before our great ape ancestors. Rizzolatti and his colleagues have recorded single cells in area F5 of the motor cortex of the macaque that respond whenever the animal makes particular reaching and grasping movements. Some of these neurons, known as *mirror neurons*, also respond when the monkey observes a human making the same movement that elicited the response when it was made by the monkey itself. Area F5 corresponds at least approximately to Broca's area in the human brain, except that Broca's area is typically restricted to the left hemisphere while mirror neurons have been recorded bilaterally. These discoveries suggest that mirror neurons may well have provided a neural basis for the subsequent emergence of syntactic language (Rizzolatti and Arbib 1998). Mirror neurons also, of course, lend strong support to the notion that language evolved from manual gestures. In addition to its role in vocal language, Broca's area is part of a gestural mirror-neuron system in humans (Nishitani and Hari 2000).

8.2.1 *Manual Versus Vocal Behaviour*

In monkeys, bilateral destruction of cortical areas involved in controlling movements of the mouth, tongue, and lips results in a paralysis making it impossible for the animal to eat. Yet the monkeys' calls are hardly affected, suggesting that these are organized subcortically, and are under emotional rather than intentional control (Deacon 1997). Goodall (1986) tells of a chimpanzee who found a cache of bananas, and evidently wished to keep them for himself. The animal was unable to suppress the excited 'pant-hoot' food call, but attempted to muffle it with his hand over his mouth. His predicament may be similar to that of a person trying to suppress involuntary emotional sounds such as laughter or crying. Conversely, it appears to be equally difficult for chimpanzees to produce a call on demand, just as it is for humans to voluntarily produce convincing laughter or crying. After many years of observing chimpanzees in the wild, Goodall (p. 125) concluded that '[t]he production of sound in the *absence* of the appropriate emotional state seems to be an almost impossible task for a chimpanzee'.

Some primate calls, though, imply *reference*. Vervet monkeys emit separate cries to signal the presence of a snake, a hawk, a leopard, a smaller cat, and a baboon, and when hearing these calls they act in a manner appropriate to the signalled danger (Cheney and Seyfarth 1990). Further, observations of the animals' behaviour suggest that the calls are not simply expressions of emotional state, and that they are modified according to their audience. There is relatively little evidence for referential calls in the great apes, although Hauser (1996), in a summary of research, suggests that chimpanzees emit two calls in reference to the discovery of food. Goodall's example of the chimpanzee unable to suppress the pant-hoot call on discovering bananas suggests that these calls may not be under voluntary control, and it is revealing that the animal attempted to suppress the call with a *gesture*. As far as I know, there is no evidence that primates in the wild use referential calls in the absence of the objects or actions they refer to, in the way that humans use words.

It is therefore likely that the common ancestor of humans and chimpanzees had little voluntary control over vocalization. Knight (1998) notes that this is adaptive, because it makes vocal signals hard to fake. Warning signals must be reliable, and not subjected to the whim of the animal who might cry wolf. But it is precisely the *lack* of voluntary control that makes primate vocal calls ill-suited to exaptation for intentional communication.

8.2.2 *Gestures*

Manual gestures provide a more natural medium for intentional interactions, and typically occur in the wild in contexts with a clear social component, such as play, aggression, appeasement, eating, sex, and grooming (Goodall 1986). Chimpanzees in a captive colony have also been observed to teach gestures spontaneously to a foster baby (Fouts *et al.* 1989). The intentional nature of gestures is indicated by a flexible relation between the signal and its apparent purpose; unlike vocal calls, they are not fixed responses to fixed situations (Plooij 1978).

Tomasello and his colleagues have also reported that chimpanzee gestures are predominantly *dyadic*, involving reciprocal interactions between two individuals (see Tomasello and Call 1997). This distinguishes them from chimpanzee *vocalizations*, which are generally not directed to specific others. Gorillas also gesture freely, and Tanner and Byrne (1996) have shown many of their gestures to be iconic, easily understood by both human and gorilla observers. It may well be that the ability of chimpanzees and gorillas to both produce and interpret gestures depends on a mirror-neuron system similar to that in monkeys.

One gesture of special interest is *pointing*, which plays a critical role in children's acquisition of language. There is no evidence that chimpanzees in the wild ever point to things, but chimpanzees in captivity have been readily *taught* to point, especially in the context of artificial communication systems taught by humans. Apes taught to point have spontaneously generalized their pointing to other situations, such as pointing to objects they want, or to places they want to go to. The habit of pointing appears also to have spread to other chimpanzees not given specific instruction by humans (Hopkins and Leavens 1998).

The spread of pointing may be taken as an example of cultural transmission, and there are many other examples. Whiten *et al.* (1999) have examined the evidence from six different chimpanzee communities, and identified thirty-nine different behavioural patterns where the differences between communities could not be attributed to differences in physical or geographic conditions, and must therefore be culturally determined. These patterns include grooming, courtship, and the use of tools. All of them involve manual activities, but not vocalization.

Chimpanzee gestures also tend to become conventionalized, to the point of losing their iconic nature (Tomasello and Call 1997). However, there seems fairly general agreement that neither chimpanzees (Hopkins and Leavens 1998; Tomasello 1996) nor gorillas (Byrne 1996) learn manual skills by imitation, as human children do. Rather, their learning appears to be accomplished by *emulation*, where the focus is on the ends to be achieved, rather than on the precise actions whereby they are achieved. Imitation may be a human trait, and may explain the heightened effectiveness of cultural transmission in human societies.

8.2.3 *Protolanguage*

Evidence of the ability of great apes to use abstract symbols is most compellingly demonstrated in the efforts over the past fifty years to teach captive animals something resembling human language. Tellingly, an early attempt to teach a baby chimpanzee to *talk* was unsuccessful (Hayes 1952), and all subsequent work has used either manual gestures or visual symbols that the animals point to, with at least moderate success in each of the great ape species. The most impressive performer, perhaps, is Kanzi, a bonobo who has learned to use a keyboard containing 256 symbols, all chosen so as *not* to depict their referents in iconic fashion, and he spontaneously supplements this with gestures that he has himself invented (Savage-Rumbaugh *et al.* 1998). Kanzi is also able to respond to quite complicated *spoken* sentences, such as 'You can have some cereal if you give Austin your monster mask to play with.' It is doubtful whether Kanzi understands this sentence in the way a human does; he probably simply extracts the critical words ('cereal', 'Austin', 'monster mask') and takes it from there. And he is not perfect. In one experiment he was given a list of 660 unusual spoken commands, some of them as many as eight words long, and carried out 72 per cent of them correctly. Kanzi was 9 at the time, and scored a little better than the 66 per cent achieved by a 2½-year-old girl.

Bickerton (1995) has described the level of linguistic ability implied by Kanzi's accomplishments as *protolanguage*. This is essentially language without syntax, except for that inherent in the ordering of symbols. There are no function words, no tenses, no moods, no recursion. According to Bickerton, this is also the language of the 2½-year-old child, of pidgin talk, and of people suffering *agrammatism* from brain injury. The other great apes—gorilla (Patterson 1978), common chimpanzee (e.g. Gardner and Gardner 1969), and orang-utan (Miles 1990)—have also acquired protolanguage, at least to the point where there is some degree of production and comprehension of novel combinations of symbols. There is no evidence, though, that any of these animals use protolanguage in the wild; the only known examples are those in which the animals were taught by humans or, like Kanzi, by observing other animals being taught by humans. The ability to acquire protolanguage may be simply part of a more general cognitive ability to manipulate objects, or representations of objects, combinatorially, as in problem-solving chimpanzees (Köhler 1925; Tomasello 1996) or food-preparing gorillas (Byrne 1996).

Although great apes (with the exception perhaps of the solitary orangutan) are social creatures, their capacity for socialization and imitation remains primitive relative to that in humans. But when intentional communication did emerge, it seems reasonable to suppose that it arose out of manual action, not vocal calls. In the words of Hewes (1973: 9), it followed 'the line of biological least resistance' by achieving expression in a system that was already adapted to intentional motor control, the ability to create multiple representations, and social interaction.

8.3 The Upright Hominin

8.3.1 *The Early Bipedal Hominins*

The main feature that distinguished the early hominins[3] from the other great apes was bipedalism. *Australopithecus anamensis*, dating from some 4.2 million years, was almost certainly bipedal (Leakey *et al.* 1995), as was *Australopithecus afarensis* from over 3 million years ago. There is now controversial evidence from Kenya of an even earlier bipedal hominin, named *Orrorin tugensis* (Senut *et al.* 2001), dating from around 6 million years ago. Bipedalism would have freed the arms and hands from primary involvement in locomotion, and opened up the frontal stance. Armstrong *et al.* (1995) suggest that it was these developments that led the early hominins to discover natural relationships between their own gestures and events in the physical world. Bipedalism would have increased the range and salience of gestures, but the selection of bipedalism may have been due to other survival-enhancing capacities associated with it, such as an ability to throw accurately (Marzke 1996).

[3] The term 'hominid' is now often taken to include the African apes, so I have followed the growing trend to use 'hominin' to refer to humans and their bipedal ancestors.

Donald (1991) has proposed that these early hominins went through a 'mimetic' phase in which they communicated in mime, but he argues that this did not comprise language, or even protolanguage. Rather, it simply established the capacity to program voluntary sequences of acts, setting the stage for the sequencing of vocal acts that later evolved into language. According to Donald, mimesis lives on in dance, mime, body language, ritual, some forms of music, and non-verbal communication, all of which are distinct from language, although complementary to it. It is perhaps more likely that mimed communication *was* a precursor to language, and progressed from mimed sequences to a more abstract and conventional-ized system, as do present-day sign languages. These gestural systems may not have developed syntax, however, until the emergence of the genus *Homo*.

8.3.2 *The Genus* Homo, *Tool-Maker*

Although the australopithecines may have used stones as weapons or ham-mers, there is no evidence that they deliberately shaped stones into tools or weapons. The earliest evidence for stone tools dates from some 2.5 million years ago (Semaw *et al.* 1997), and may be associated with the emergence of *Homo rudolfensis* (now considered separate from, and earlier than, *Homo habilis*). In any event, the continuing manufacture of stone tools is associ-ated with the genus *Homo*, from *rudolfensis* to *sapiens*. The early tools of the so-called Oldowan culture were primitive, consisting of simple stone flakes chipped from a cobble. The later Acheulian industry, associated mainly with *Homo ergaster* and dating from around 1.5 million years ago, shows more evidence of standard design and planning, and includes a greater variety of tools—large cutting tools, picks, cleavers, bifacial hand-axes. Holloway (1969) suggested that the elements of design and forethought inherent in the Acheulian imply a dependence on language. Hewes (1973) argued, how-ever, that tool manufacture is more likely to have facilitated gestural than vocal language, since the tools could be readily represented by miming the actions involved in using them.

Two further characteristics of *Homo* suggest that language may have begun to advance beyond mere protolanguage. The australopithecines had brains little or no larger than those of the great apes, at least when corrected for body size, but *Homo* marks the beginning of a systematic increase. It begins with *H. rudolfensis*, continues with *H. ergaster* and its Asian variant *H. erectus*, and in *H. neanderthalensis* and *H. sapiens* the brain is about three times as large as one would predict from a chimpanzee of the same body size (Passingham 1982). The second characteristic was wanderlust. The first migration of hominins out of Africa may have been that of *H. erectus* to east Asia around 1.8 million years ago, and this was followed by perhaps as many as five migratory waves, with hominins reaching Europe some time within the last million years (Tattersall 1997).

The Acheulian stone industry, increased brain size, and the migrations out of Africa may all signal the emergence of syntax. Planning organized movement while avoiding starvation, for example, would surely involve a fairly sophisticated form of communication. The appearance of a standardized tool industry may also suggest more effective communication, as suggested above, although for long stretches of time there is surprisingly little evidence of innovation. The Acheulian industry lasted over a million years with little significant change, and is even associated with early *Homo sapiens* (Walter *et al.* 2000). I shall argue below that gestural language may have actually *inhibited* manufacture, so the full potential of human mechanical inventiveness was not released until language switched more or less completely to the vocal mode.

8.3.3 *Vocal Language*

Watching interactions of Kanzi with his minders and fellow apes, one cannot but be struck by the excited vocalizations that seem to accompany his communications via the keyboard and other gestures. It is unlikely that vocal language emerged from cries such as these, which are probably largely emotional and immune to intentional modification. MacNeilage (1998) has argued instead that speech evolved from repetitive ingestive activities such as chewing, licking, and sucking, which are widespread in mammals, including primates. The lip-smacking, tongue-smacking, and teeth-chattering of primates are communicative activities that were probably exapted from ingestive movements. Although audible, these visuofacial signals clearly have a strong gestural aspect. The critical question, however, is when in evolution vocalization could have been integrated within this system to produce intentional, articulate speech. MacNeilage cites evidence (Tobias 1987) that there was an enlargement of Broca's area in *Homo habilis* some 2 million years ago, which may signal the emergence of cortical control over vocalization. Remember, though, that the homologue of Broca's area in the monkey contains neurons which have to do with manual gesture rather than vocalization. Consequently the enlargement of Broca's area in *H. habilis* may actually signal an advance in the programming of gesture, and perhaps the beginnings of gestural syntax (Rizzolatti 1998).

Another clue comes from the spinal cord. The muscles of the diaphragm involved in breathing are innervated by the vagus nerve, but speech involves extra muscles of the thorax and abdomen that are innervated through the thoracic region of the spinal cord. This region is considerably enlarged in modern humans relative to that in non-human primates, presumably reflecting the extra demands placed on these muscles by speech. The enlargement was evidently not present in the early hominins or even in *Homo ergaster*, dating from about 1.6 million years ago, but was present in several Neanderthal fossils (MacLarnon and Hewitt 1999). At least a rudimentary form of speech may therefore have evolved in the common ancestor of ourselves and the Neanderthals by some 500,000 years ago.

P. Lieberman (1998) has long argued, largely on the basis of the inferred location of the larynx, that fully articulate language emerged even later, and that the Neanderthals of 30,000 years ago would have suffered speech defects sufficient to keep them separate from *H. sapiens*, leading to their eventual extinction. This work has been controversial (e.g. Gibson and Jessee 1999) and does not appear to be widely accepted as definitive, although it has been recently supported by evidence that the facial structure of *H. sapiens* might have been uniquely adapted to speech (D. Lieberman 1998).

It is clear that, at some point in evolution, Broca's area did become involved in the articulation of speech. This may well have been a gradual process, with vocalizations becoming increasingly integrated with manual and facial gestures, eventually taking the dominant role. This final stage may have occurred with the emergence of *Homo sapiens*, and distinguished that species from other extant hominins, some 100,000 to 150,000 years ago. Some authors have argued that speech itself is best understood as made up of gestures (Browman and Goldstein 1991; Studdert-Kennedy 1998) rather than of abstract entities such as phonemes, so that at first, vocalization may have simply added to the repertoire of gestures serving as communicative symbols.

8.4 The Talkative *Homo sapiens*

It has been claimed that the language emerged suddenly in hominin evolution, probably with the appearance of *Homo sapiens* (e.g. Bickerton 1995; P. Lieberman 1998). Bickerton argues, for example, that syntax did not emerge until cognitive mechanisms unrelated to syntax were suddenly connected, an argument difficult to justify in evolutionary terms.[4] It is much more likely that syntactic language evolved gradually and incrementally (Pinker and Bloom 1990).

So long as one supposes that language evolved solely as speech, there is a dilemma, since most of the evidence suggests that the intentional, cortical control of vocalization, and the articulatory mechanisms to support it, must have emerged relatively late in hominin evolution. Chimpanzee and bonobo seem a very long way from being able to speak, and as we have just seen there is doubt as to whether even the large-brained Neanderthals of 30,000 years ago could have been fully articulate. Much of the difficulty disappears if it is supposed that syntactic language evolved primarily in the context of gesture, accompanied by a late-emerging vocal system. The switch to vocal dominance may then have been a small step in neurological terms, but a giant step psychologically.

8.4.1 *Why Did Language Become Vocal?*

There are a number of compelling advantages to a vocal system. Vocalization can be carried on in the dark, or when obstacles intervene. Auditory signals are less demanding attentionally, since one does not have to look at the source. But more importantly, a language system that was autonomously vocal would have freed the hands for other activities, such as holding infants or other objects, or manufacturing tools or weapons. Hewes (1973) has suggested that gestural language would be more effective than vocal language in transmitting tool-making techniques, but I suggest that this confuses language with demonstration. Vocal language would have greatly enhanced the *instruction* of manufacturing techniques, since the instructor could explain verbally and demonstrate manually at the same time. Any popular TV cooking show demonstrates this.

This scenario may well explain the trajectory of tool development over the past 2 million years. We saw earlier that, although stone tool industries are associated with the genus *Homo*, the tools themselves appear to have changed rather little from the Acheulian culture of *H. ergaster* until some

---

[4] In his more recent writing, Bickerton appears to have modified his view somewhat. Although he appears still to hold that syntax emerged as a sudden event, he suggests that it was progressively refined through a process of Balwinian evolution (e.g. Calvin and Bickerton 2000).

200,000 years ago, though the discovery of sophisticated wooden spears in Germany, dating from 380,000 to 400,000 years ago (Thieme 1997) suggests that the early colonizers of Europe may have developed a more sophisticated hunting culture than previously thought. Even so, it was not really until after the emergence of *H. sapiens* some 100,000 to 150,000 years ago that tool manufacture really took off. Indeed, some have suggested that this did not occur until the so-called 'evolutionary explosion' beginning some 40,000 years ago (Pfeiffer 1985), as evidenced by cave drawings, the crafting of ornaments and objects displaying visual metaphor (White 1989), and more sophisticated manufacture.

Anatomically modern humans probably began to migrate around the coasts of Africa and Asia from at least 125,000 years ago (Walter *et al.* 2000), reaching south-east Asia by about 90,000 years ago. Watercraft must have been developed to carry people from the Asian mainland to New Guinea and Australia (once joined), and *H. sapiens* was probably in south-eastern Australia by 60,000 years ago (Thorne *et al.* 1999). However, there is also evidence from an analysis of mitochondrial DNA that present-day non-Africans share a common ancestry with an African origin dating from around only 52,000 years ago (Ingman *et al.* 2000). This suggests that there was an exodus of *H. sapiens* from Africa at that time, and that these migrants eventually replaced all those who had migrated earlier, including the Neanderthals in Europe, and *H. erectus* in Asia, as well as members of their own species. The arrival of this cohort in Europe from around 40,000 years ago may explain the evolutionary explosion described above.

The success of the invading migrants from Africa may well have been due to a more advanced technology than that possessed by earlier migrants. There are indications that a technological advance had already taken place in Africa; for example, there is evidence of a sophisticated bone industry, including the manufacture of harpoons, in Zaire (now the Democratic Republic of the Congo), dating from about 90,000 years ago (Yellen *et al.* 1995). The advance in technology may have been due in turn to the emergence of a language that could be carried out entirely vocally, although still embellished by gesture. It is possible that the anatomical changes necessary for this had actually evolved some time before autonomous speech was realized—and conceivable that even the Neanderthals were anatomically capable of autonomous speech, but simply did not develop it. Vocalizations may at first have consisted of grunts that accompanied actions, but were increasingly refined through natural selection because they offered an expanded range of potential symbols. Since the meanings of spoken words are not carried by the sound of the word itself, spoken language would need to be sustained in part by culture. Vocal speech may therefore have been in part an *invention*, born of the discovery that manual gestures could be largely dispensed with. Perhaps the invention of autonomous vocal language had consequences that were as dramatic in their way as those of the later invention of writing.

8.5 Conclusions

In summary, the main steps in the evolution of language may have been the following:

1. In the beginning was the gesture. Chimpanzees and other great apes make extensive use of manual and facial gestures in the wild, and these have an intentional, dyadic quality lacking in their vocalizations. Gesture would no doubt have been enhanced by bipedalism in the early hominins.
2. After the emergence of the genus *Homo* about 2.5 million years ago, gesture may have begun to acquire syntactic structure, perhaps reaching the sophistication evident in the present-day signed languages of the deaf by around 1 million years ago. Vocal elements were gradually introduced with enhanced cortical control and changes to the vocal tract.
3. The vocal element gradually became more pronounced, driven partly by the freeing of the hands for other activities, such as carrying and manufacturing. The achievement of autonomous speech may have occurred within the past 100,000 years in Africa—perhaps even as recently as around 50,000 years ago—and may explain the extraordinary explosion of manufacture, art, and culture that has taken place since that time.

FURTHER READING

ARMSTRONG, D. F., STOKOE, W. C., and WILCOX, S. E. (1995), *Gesture and the Nature of Language* (Cambridge: Cambridge University Press). (Argues for the gestural origins of language, including syntax, largely from the point of view of present-day sign languages.)

CORBALLIS, M. C. (1991), *The Lopsided Ape* (New York: Oxford University Press). (This book makes the additional point that the switch from primarily gestural to vocal language may explain why humans are uniquely right-handed and left-cerebrally dominant for speech.)

HEWES, G. W. (1973), 'Primate Communication and the Gestural Origins of Language'. *Current Anthropology*, 14: 5–24. (The classic article on the gestural origins of language.)

RIZZOLATTI, G., and ARBIB, M. A. (1998), 'Language Within our Grasp', *Trends in Neuroscience*, 21: 188–94. (The importance of 'mirror neurons' to an understanding of the gestural origins of language.)

REFERENCES

ARMSTRONG, D. F., STOKOE, W. C., and WILCOX, S. E. (1995), *Gesture and the Nature of Language* (Cambridge: Cambridge University Press).

BICKERTON, D. (1995), *Language and Human Behaviour* (Seattle: University of Washington Press).

BROWMAN, C., and GOLDSTEIN, L. (1991), 'Gestural Structures: Distinctiveness, Phonological Processes, and Historical Change', in I. G. Mattingly and M. Studdert-Kennedy (eds.), *Modularity and the Motor Theory of Speech Perception* (Hillsdale, NJ: Erlbaum), 313–38.

BURLING, R. (1999), 'Motivation, Conventionalization, and Arbitrariness in the Origin of Language', in B. J. King (ed.), *The Origins of Language: What Nonhuman Primates Can Tell Us* (Santa Fe: School of American Research Press), 307–50.

BYRNE, R. W. (1996), 'The Misunderstood Ape: Cognitive Skills of the Gorilla', in A. E. Russon, K. A. Bard, and S. T. Parker (eds.), *Reaching into Thought* (Cambridge: Cambridge University Press), 111–30.

CALVIN, W. H., and BICKERTON, D. (2000), *Lingua ex Machina: Reconciling Darwin and Chomsky with the Human Brain* (Cambridge, Mass.: A Bradford Book, MIT Press).

CHENEY, D. L., and SEYFARTH, R. S. (1990), *How Monkeys See the World* (Chicago: University of Chicago Press).

DE CONDILLAC, ÉTIENNE BONNOT, L'ABBÉ (1746), 'Essai sur l'Origine des Connaissances Humaines', repr. in 1971 in facsimile reproduction of T. Nugent's 1756 trans. as *An Essay on the Origin of Human Knowledge* (Gainesville, Fla.: Scholars' Facsimiles and Reprints).

DARWIN, C. (1904), *The Expression of the Emotions in Man and Animals* (London: John Murray).

DEACON, T. (1997), *The Symbolic Species: The Co-evolution of Language and the Brain* (Harmondsworth: Penguin).

DONALD, M. (1991), *Origins of the Modern Mind: Three Stages in the Evolution of Culture and Cognition* (Cambridge, Mass.: Harvard University Press).

FOUTS, R. S., FOUTS, D. H., and VAN CANTFORT, T. E. (1989), 'The Infant Loulis Learns Signs from Cross-Fostered Chimpanzees', in R. A. Gardner, B. T. Gardner, and T. E. Van Cantfort (eds.), *Teaching Sign Language to Chimpanzees* (New York: State University of New York Press), 280–92.

FRISHBERG, N. (1975), 'Arbitrariness and Iconicity in American Sign Language', *Language*, 51: 696–719.

GARDNER, R. A., and GARDNER, B. T. (1969), 'Teaching Sign Language to a Chimpanzee', *Science*, 165: 664–72.

GIBSON, K. R., and JESSEE, S. (1999), 'Language Evolution and Expansions of Multiple Neurological Processing Areas', in B. J. King (ed.), *The Origins of Language: What Nonhuman Primates Can Tell Us* (Santa Fe: School of American Research Press), 189–227.

GIVÓN, T. (1995), *Functionalism and Grammar* (Amsterdam: Benjamins).

GOLDIN-MEADOW, S., and McNEILL, D. (1999), 'The Role of Gesture and Mimetic Representation in Making Language the Province of Speech', in M. C. Corballis and S. E. G. Lea (eds.), *The Descent of Mind* (Oxford: Oxford University Press), 155–72.

—— McNEILL, D., and SINGLETON, J. (1996), 'Silence Is Liberating: Removing the Handcuffs on Grammatical Expression and Speech', *Psychological Review*, 103: 34–55.

GOODALL, J. (1986), *The Chimpanzees of Gombe: Patterns of Behaviour* (Cambridge, Mass.: Harvard University Press).

HAUSER, M. D. (1996), *The Evolution of Communication* (Cambridge, Mass.: MIT Press).

HAYES, C. (1952), *The Ape in Our House* (London: Gollancz).

HEWES, G. W. (1973), 'Primate Communication and the Gestural Origins of Language', *Current Anthropology*, 14: 5–24.

HOLLOWAY, R. (1969), 'Culture: A Human Domain', *Current Anthropology*, 4: 135–68.

HOPKINS, W. D., and LEAVENS, D. A. (1998), 'Hand Use and Gestural Communication in Chimpanzees (Pan troglodytes)', *Journal of Comparative Psychology*, 112: 95–9.

INGMAN, M., KAESSMANN, H., PÄÄBO, S., and GYLLENSTEN, U. (2000), 'Mitochondrial Genome Variation and the Origin of Modern Humans', *Nature*, 208: 708–13.

KNIGHT, C. (1998), 'Ritual/speech Coevolution: A Solution to the Problem of Deception', in J. R. Hurford, M. Studdert-Kennedy, and C. Knight (eds.), *Approaches to the Evolution of Language: Social and Cognitive Bases* (Cambridge: Cambridge University Press), 68–91.

KÖHLER, W. (1925), *The Mentality of Apes* (New York: Routledge & Kegan Paul).

LEAKEY, M. G., FEIBEL, C. S., McDOUGALL, I., and WALKER, A. (1995), 'New Four-Million-Year-Old Hominid Species from Kanapoi and Allia Bay, Kenya', *Nature*, 376: 565–71.

LIBERMAN, A. (1982), 'On Finding That Speech Is Special', *American Psychologist*, 37: 148–67.

LIEBERMAN, D. (1998), 'Sphenoid Shortening and the Evolution of the Modern Human Cranial Shape', *Nature*, 393: 158–62.

LIEBERMAN, P. (1998), *Eve Spoke: Human Language and Human Evolution* (New York: Norton).

MacLarnon, A., and Hewitt, G. (1999), 'The Evolution of Human Speech: The Role of Enhanced Breathing Control', *American Journal of Physical Anthropology*, 109: 341–63.

MacNeilage, P. F. (1998), 'The Frame/Content Theory of the Evolution of Speech Production', *Behavioural and Brain Sciences*, 21: 499–546.

McNeill, D. (1985), 'So You Think Gestures Are Nonverbal?', *Psychological Review*, 92: 350–71.

Marzke, M. (1996), 'Evolution of the Hand and Bipedality', in A. Lock and C. R. Peters (eds.), *Handbook of Human Symbolic Evolution* (Oxford: Oxford University Press), 126–54.

Meier, R. P., and Newport, E. (1990), 'Out of the Hands of Babes: On a Possible Sign Advantage in Language Acquisition', *Language*, 66: 1–23.

Miles, H. L. (1990), 'The Cognitive Foundations for Reference in a Signing Orangutan', in S. T. Parker and K. R. Gibson (eds.), *Language and Intelligence in Monkeys and Apes* (Cambridge: Cambridge University Press), 511–39.

Morford, J. P., Singleton, J. L., and Goldin-Meadow, S. (1995), 'The Genesis of Language: How Much Time Is Needed to Generate Arbitrary Symbols in a Sign Language?', in K. Emmorey and K. Reilly (eds.), *Language, Gesture, and Space* (Hillsdale, NJ: Erlbaum), 313–32.

Neidle, C., Kegl, J., MacLaughlin, D., Bahan, B., and Lee, R. G. (2000), *The Syntax of American Sign Language* (Cambridge, Mass.: MIT Press).

Neville, H. J., Bavelier, D., Corina, D., Rauschecker, J., Karni, A., Lalwani, A., et al. (1998), 'Cerebral Organization for Deaf and Hearing Subjects: Biological Constraints and Effects of Experience', *Proceedings of the National Academy of Sciences*, 95: 922–9.

Nishitani, N., and Hari, R. (2000), 'Dynamics of Cortical Representation for Action', *Proceedings of the National Academy of Sciences, USA*, 97: 913–18.

Passingham, R. E. (1982), *The Human Primate* (San Francisco: Freeman).

Patterson, F. (1978), 'Conversations with a Gorilla', *National Geographic*, 154: 438–65.

Pfeiffer, J. E. (1985), *The Emergence of Humankind* (New York: Harper & Row).

Pinker, S., and Bloom, P. (1990), 'Natural Language and Natural Selection', *Behavioural and Brain Sciences*, 13: 707–84.

Plooij, F. X. (1978), 'Some Basic Traits of Language in Wild Chimpanzees', in A. Lock (ed.), *Action, Gesture, and Symbol* (London: Academic Press), 111–31.

Rizzolatti, G. (1998), 'What Happened to *Homo habilis*? (Language and Mirror Neurons)', *Behavioural and Brain Sciences*, 21: 527–8.

—— and Arbib, M. A. (1998), 'Language Within Our Grasp', *Trends in Neuroscience*, 21: 188–94.

Rousseau, J.-J. (1755/1964), 'Discours sur l'Origine et les Fondements de l'Inégalité parmi les Hommes', in B. Gagnebin and M. Raymond (eds.), *Œuvres Complètes de Rousseau* (Paris: Gallimard), 131–223.

Saussure, F. de (1931), *Cours de Linguistique Générale*, 3rd edn. (Paris: Payot).

SAVAGE-RUMBAUGH, S., SHANKER, S. G., and TAYLOR, T. J. (1998), *Apes, Language, and the Human Mind* (New York: Oxford University Press).

SEMAW, S., RENNE, P., HARRIS, J. W. K., FEIBEL, C. S., BERNOR, R. L., FESSEHA, N., *et al.* (1997), '2.5 Million-Year-Old Stone Tools from Gona, Ethiopia', *Nature*, 385: 333–6.

SENUT, B., PICKFORD, M., GOMMERY, D., MEIN, P., CHEBOI, K., and COPPENS, Y. (2001), 'First Hominid from the Miocene (Lukeino Formation, Kenya)', *Comtes Rendues de l'Académie des Sciences, Sciences de la Terre et des Planètes*, 332: 137–44.

STUDDERT-KENNEDY, M. (1998), 'The Particulate Origins of Language Generativity: from Syllable to Gesture', in J. R. Hurford, M. Studdert-Kennedy, and C. Knight (eds.), *Approaches to the Evolution of Language: Social and Cognitive Bases* (Cambridge: Cambridge University Press), 202–21.

TANNER, J. E., and BYRNE, R. W. (1996), 'Representation of Action Through Iconic Gesture in a Captive Lowland Gorilla', *Current Anthropology*, 37: 162–73.

TATTERSALL, I. (1997), 'Out of Africa Again . . . and Again?', *Scientific American* (April), 60–7.

THIEME, H. (1997), 'Lower Palaeolithic Hunting Spears from Germany', *Nature*, 385: 807–10.

THORNE, A., GRÜN, R., MORTIMER, G., SPOONER, N. A., SIMPSON, J. J., McCULLOCH, M., *et al.* (1999), 'Australia's Oldest Human Remains: Age of the Lake Mungo 3 Skeleton', *Journal of Human Evolution*, 36: 591–612.

TOBIAS, P. V. (1987), 'The Brain of *Homo habilis*: A New Level of Organization in Cerebral Evolution', *Journal of Human Evolution*, 16: 741–61.

TOMASELLO, M. (1996), 'Do Apes Ape?', in J. Galef and C. Heyes (eds.), *Social Learning in Animals: The Roots of Culture* (New York: Academic Press), 319–46.

—— and CALL, J. (1997), *Primate Cognition* (New York: Oxford University Press).

WALTER, R. C., BUFFLER, R. T., BRUGGEMANN, J. H., GUILLAUME, M. M. M., BERHE, S. M., *et al.* (2000), 'Early Human Occupation of the Red Sea Coast of Eritrea During the Last Interglacial', *Nature*, 405: 65–9.

WHITE, R. (1989), 'Visual Thinking in the Ice Age', *Scientific American* (January), 74–81.

WHITEN, A., GOODALL, J., McGREW, W. C., NISHIDA, T., REYNOLDS, V., SUGIYAMA, Y., *et al.* (1999), 'Cultures in Chimpanzees', *Nature*, 399: 682–5.

YELLEN, J. E., BROOKS, A. S., CORNELISSEN, E., MEHLMAN, M. J., and STEWART, K. (1995), 'A Middle Stone Age Worked Bone Industry from Katanda, Upper Semliki Valley, Zaire', *Science*, 268: 553–6.

9 The Finished Artefact Fallacy: Acheulean Hand-axes and Language Origins

IAIN DAVIDSON

9.1 Introduction

Approaches to the study of the origins of language have three major sources of evidence: (1) from modern humans, including psychology and linguistics; (2) from modern non-human primates, including their communicative abilities; (3) from archaeology. This chapter is about the third of these—the archaeological evidence of what actually happened. Ten years ago, I outlined problems with the traditional framework of understanding stone tools (Davidson and Noble 1993; Gibson and Ingold 1993). In this chapter, I will return to issues I raised on that occasion and present more evidence and argument about Acheulean hand-axes.

The principal point of my previous review was that although the apparent existence of different tool types is often attributed to the deliberate intentions to produce the forms recognized by archaeologists, there are other factors that make that attribution implausible. Without plausible argument about the intentions of tool-makers, we cannot approach an understanding of what tools tell us about the language-based symbolic representations in the mind. The argument in this chapter is principally about this question of intentionality, and suggests that Acheulean hand-axes do not demonstrate

I would like to thank Art Jelinek for access to the Tabun collections and generous assistance during my stay in Tucson. I am also grateful to Heather Burke for her help in converting the photographs into a format suitable for publication. Stephen Kuhn, Kris Kerry, Michael Bisson, Tom Wynn, Nick Toth, and Matt Pope provided stimulating discussion during that period of leave, which was partly funded by a small ARC grant from the University of New England. I also acknowledge a series of interactions with Derek Bickerton that sharpened my perception of the need to recognize the two-stage emergence of language, even if I still believe that his concept of 'protolanguage' is misleading. I doubt that any of these would agree with everything I say in this chapter, so I am happy to absolve them of responsibility.

an intention to produce objects of that form. Most interpretations of them as indicating abilities that depend on language are, therefore, adventurous.

The argument here is based only on the question of the identification of symbolic communication in the archaeological record. Questions of language origins (that lie at the base of all arguments about the evolution of language) need to recognize two elements of the evolutionary emergence of language. The first, which I believe to be prior both in time and as an issue to be understood, is the question of communication using symbols. Noble and I (1996) have shown how such an argument can be developed around the evidence from the archaeological record. Here I am only concerned with evidence relating to this element. The second issue is the emergence of the forms—the languages—by which we recognize language among modern people, particularly through the universal nature of elements of syntax, present in all languages of the world. That issue is beyond the scope of the present account.

Noble and I (1996) have previously argued that the manufacture of tools of preconceived form, produced outside the immediate context of use, must entail a representation of intention, something that we may consider indicative of language as communication using symbols. The issue in this chapter is about the extent to which the forms of stone tools, as they are found in the archaeological record, indicate the prior intentions of their makers. I will argue that the observed patterning of stone tools among human ancestors—early hominins[1]—is not a sufficient indicator of the emergence of language.

9.2 The Finished Artefact Fallacy

In a previous paper, Davidson and Noble (1993) defined a problem with the study of stone tools that we named the Finished Artefact Fallacy. This problem has many facets that directly influence arguments about the intentions of the makers of stone tools. In its briefest form, the Finished Artefact Fallacy states that:

In studying the stone artefacts in the archaeological record it is a fallacy to

---

[1] I use the word 'hominin' for human ancestors in preference to the previously general 'hominid' because it reflects more accurately the phylogenetic closeness between African apes and human ancestors.

assume that we know which were (and which were not) the tools.[2] It is also a fallacy to assume that the form in which a stone artefact is found is a product of an intention to produce that form.

There are (at least) five facets of the fallacy:

1. In choosing materials for analysis, archaeologists sometimes unwittingly bias their analysis towards the observation of patterning. It is a fallacy to attribute intentions to the knappers[3] on the basis of patterning that results principally from the selections made by archaeologists.

2. In knapping stone, there are always at least two products. Most simply, there is a flake which is removed, and a core[4] (or retouched flake[5]) from which it is removed. Both cores and retouched flakes appear to be 'modified' because flakes have been removed from them. It is a fallacy to assume that the removal of flakes from a core or a retouched flake is sufficient evidence to indicate any prior intention on the part of the knapper beyond the removal of a flake.

3. In a process of knapping, there are many products, from the fine dust of micro-debitage to spectacular cores, such as hand-axes. Almost any product that can be held in the hand or fixed in a haft can be used as a tool whether or not it has been modified in the manner of cores or retouched flakes. It is a fallacy to suppose that only those flakes or cores that have been 'modified' were used as tools.

4. All knapping involves the successful application of some simple mechanical principles to the process. It is a fallacy to account for the similarities resulting from such requirements as the products of prior intentions of the knappers.

---

[2] I am using a conventional distinction between all things made by humans or their ancestors—artefacts—and those artefacts which were definitely used—tools. More subtleties could be introduced in this distinction, but this is all that is meant here.

[3] 'Knapping' is the usual term for flaking of stone.

[4] I am following a standard definition here that a *core* is a lump of stone from which flakes have been removed, and which shows only the negative scars of such removals. See Whittaker (1994) for flintknapping generally.

[5] A *retouched flake* is a flake from which further flakes have been removed, affecting the surface that was revealed when the flake was removed from the core (the ventral surface). Unlike a core, it may show signs of both the negative scars from these removals, and the positive features (bulb of percussion) of its own removal from the core. In some stone industries the flakes made by such retouching were intended for use (Hiscock 1993; Moore 2000), so that there can be confusion between retouched flakes and cores.

5. Other constraints, including those in the procedures of knapping, may result in the appearance of patterning of core or flake. It is a fallacy to assume that such patterning must be the product of prior intentions by the knappers.

In this chapter I will present evidence showing that fallacious argument is possible in each of these five categories in the study of Acheulean hand-axes. Combining the alternative interpretations that involve fewest assumptions about intentions allows different conclusions about the early emergence of language. But first I will set out how the formulation of the Finished Artefact Fallacy was arrived at, and some of the reactions to it.

9.3 Tools, Language and Cognition in Human Evolution

Davidson and Noble (1993) sought to show how the received wisdom about stone tools was open to other interpretations. To do this, we took a standard account of the changes in stone tools during the period of hominin and human evolution from one of the standard textbooks for first-year university students (Fagan 1989).[6] We outlined evidence from specialist studies of stone tools that does not appear to fit the standard story.

The earliest stone industries first appearing 2.5 million years ago are known as Oldowan or Mode 1 industries. Toth's (Keeley and Toth 1981; Toth 1985) studies showed that unpatterned and unmodified flakes were used for cutting meat and plant materials. Where there was patterning of the artefacts, Toth showed that the patterning depended on the initial shape of the rock. On other grounds, Wynn and McGrew (1989) showed that the hominins responsible for such industries 2 million years ago did not require mental abilities that differed very much from those documented for other apes.

The subsequent industries are called Acheulean (or Mode 2) industries and are characterized by the presence of spectacular flaked artefacts called hand-axes. These are symmetrical both about a plane and about an axis drawn on that plane (Fig. 9.1). Such industries are now said to begin 1.4 million years ago (Asfaw *et al.* 1992). However, evidence from Potts (1989) showed that the flakes from hand-axes were used whether or not the hand-

[6] This was not intended as a criticism of Fagan, but was a recognition that thousands of students have used such textbooks to learn the basic elements of stone artefact archaeology. All first-year textbooks use such formulations of the standard story.

axes were. Noble and I also countered an argument by Gowlett (1984, 1986) that similarities in the proportions of measurements of hand-axes indicate geometric sophistication of the makers: the similarities are too widespread to be cultural, with very similar statistics found in Europe as in Africa (Rolland 1986). In support of this, replicative experiments by Bradley and Sampson (1986) show that some hand-axe forms occur incidentally within the middle of a knapping sequence, and should not be considered an intentional end product of flaking.

In Mode 3 industries, dating back at least 0.5 million years (e.g. Foley and Lahr 1997), the Levallois technique is said to have involved the removal of flakes from a core with an intention of setting up a final stage of knapping for the removal of a distinctive final flake, the shape of which had been envisaged from the start of knapping. This procedure is said to indicate a stage at which hominins had become able to knap a core with foresight about the end product of their procedures. Gowlett (1986) and I agree that the technique was present at the earliest sites of Olduvai Gorge (Leakey 1971) 1.8 million years ago, with one distinctive difference—the final flake was not removed. There are some sites where the cores were abandoned together with the 'final' flake, which is definitive evidence that there was no initial intention to produce a final flake of predetermined form.

Finally, in our review of the standard story of early stages of artefact variation and patterning, we drew on Dibble's (1987; Rolland and Dibble

FIG. 9.1 Hand-axe from Tabun. Note the three flake scars in the middle of the left side which are similar in size and shape to three scars on the core in Fig. 9.4. Long axis 106 mm. *Photo Iain Davidson, courtesy of Art Jelinek.*

1990) arguments about the Mousterian stone industry. These are the artefacts most commonly associated with Neanderthals, from the period immediately prior to the emergence of modern human behaviour in Europe
and adjacent regions. Such industries are often characterized by large numbers of retouched flakes probably used for scraping skins and wood, which
archaeologists have been accustomed to classify into different types of tools.
Dibble has shown that several of these forms of scraper appear at different
times as a single flake is modified during its use life. The apparent existence
of different tool types is not a product of deliberate intentions to produce
the forms recognized by archaeologists, but an incidental outcome of the
use of flakes as scrapers. Dibble's insight gave rise to our definition of the
Finished Artefact Fallacy. Although it would certainly be possible to account
for all artefact patterning as being the product of design—just as experimental knappers can replicate the forms by design—that may not be the most
appropriate explanation for the patterning.

9.3.1 *Discussions of the Finished Artefact Fallacy*

Gowlett (1996: 196) dismissed the Finished Artefact Fallacy, asserting that
'the concept of using an unfinished tool seems a greater fallacy'. No such suggestion has ever been made. Rather, we are saying that the form in which
archaeologists find artefacts does not, in all cases, represent a form designed
by intention prior to use. Gowlett's misrepresentation of our argument stems

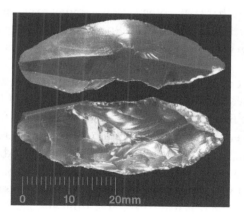

FIG. 9.2 Tula adze slug from Glenormiston Station, Queensland.
Photo Iain MacKay.

from his further statement that: 'It seems inevitable that the maker must have some mental recourse to the "finished tool", or he [*sic*] could not make it' (ibid.). Our objective as archaeologists is to use stone artefacts as evidence in the quest to identify the 'mental resources' of the knappers. Can stone artefacts allow us to distinguish the abilities of hominins from those of damming beavers, or nesting birds, or chimpanzees armed with twigs in pursuit of termites? The archaeological evidence cannot be used to investigate 'mental resources' if those resources are assumed at the beginning of the research.

Ingold (1993) took our concept and provided an *almost* suitable definition: the Finished Artefact Fallacy is 'the assumption that the objects which the archaeologist recovers represent final forms corresponding to the self-consciously articulated, prior intentions of their one-time makers' (p. 340). It is, of course, only a fallacy if that is a false assumption. He illustrated his interpretation by the example of the pencil stub, which is a standardized end product of manufacture and use (through resharpening of the working pencil), but should not be considered the finished pencil intended at the outset of manufacture. A similar uniformity of outcome may be seen in the tree stumps left after beavers have gnawed through trees in the production of logs used in their dams. In Australian archaeology, one of the most recognizable stone artefact forms is the *tula* adze slug (Fig. 9.2), a worked-out woodworking tool discarded at the end of its usefulness (Tindale 1965). It is an almost perfect analogy for Ingold's pencil stub. The final form of the artefact does not represent the prior intentions of the makers. But this is only a partial clarification of the concept of the Finished Artefact Fallacy.

The difficulty is that archaeologists have tended to claim to identify which artefacts are worth studying. By analogy with Ingold's pencil stub, they have generally chosen to ignore the shavings removed in resharpening the pencil, unless the form of them was subsequently modified. But in stone knapping, the flakes—the equivalent of the shavings produced in sharpening a pencil—were also available for use. Part of the importance of Potts's demonstration of the use of flakes from Acheulean hand-axes is that when evidence has been sought, it generally shows that some of the flakes were used. Worse still, archaeologists have a capacity to identify damage to modified and unmodified flakes through use-wear (Keeley 1980) and in some cases residues of the material that was worked still adhering to tools thousands of years after their discard (Loy and Hardy 1992). Yet, time and again, the sharp flakes that have not been blunted by later modification or retouch have been eliminated from the analysis (e.g. Frame 1986).

The results of examining unmodified flakes have sometimes been surprising. Beyries (1987) showed that many unretouched flakes in Mousterian assemblages showed signs of use. Also the patterning of use was not consistent with the assumptions about the Levallois technique in the standard story. Non-Levallois flakes were more often used than Levallois flakes; among used flakes, non-Levallois flakes were more common than Levallois flakes; among Levallois flakes, unused flakes were more common than used; among non-Levallois flakes used flakes were more common than unused. That result does not seem consistent with an intention to make many non-Levallois flakes for the purpose of making a single (or many) Levallois flakes of a supposedly preconceived form. Van Peer (1992) has shown, by fitting flakes from Levallois cores back together, that it is most often the non-Levallois flakes that are missing, presumably removed for use. Similarly, at the site of Boxgrove, generally described as a place where those distinctive cores called hand-axes[7] were made, there were many flakes, including the tranchet flakes from the tips of hand-axes, that appeared to be damaged by use (Roberts *et al.* 1997).

Selective study is at the root of the Finished Artefact Fallacy. From the very beginning, archaeologists have sought evidence of patterning in artefacts to define similarity and to identify variation between clusters of patterning. But Dibble's (1987) demonstration, described earlier, that the continuing process of use and reuse of scrapers produced different patterns within a single process, undermined the significance of the types of stone tools recognized by archaeologists. The 'types' identified are often accidents of the cycle of production, use, and discard, rather than indicators of cultural decisions about tool shape.

Chase (1991) produced an understanding of the Finished Artefact Fallacy. He argued that the appearance of highly standardized tool types could result from:

1. mechanical or conceptual constraints of function;
2. constraints of technology or raw material; or,
3. knappers working with a technological concept of an ideal form.

---

[7] I call them 'cores' here in the strict technological definition of a core in n. 4. I do not intend to imply (and I never have) that anyone can tell by inspection whether the knapping was intended to produce that object through reduction (as Michaelangelo intended to produce *David* by reduction) or that there was an intention to produce the flakes for use (as, for example, in Magdalenian blade cores).

These are fundamental distinctions that have not always been kept apart in some of the discussions of hominin and human artefacts.

I agree with Chase that constraints (1) and (2) need not involve the mental abilities that follow from using language. In any argument that seeks to infer language use from stone artefacts, these explanations of artefact variation and patterning should be investigated first.

On the other hand, Noble and I have argued (1996) that if it could be shown that hominins worked, as in (3), towards an ideal (or intended) form of artefact, then the mental representations involved *were* symbolic. The issue is how we identify such an intention from the form of the artefact.

9.4 Imposed Form

Mellars (1989) tackled the question of intentionality by introducing the phrase 'imposed form'. If archaeologists can find a way to identify that hominins or humans imposed a form on an artefact, then it would be possible to comment on the process of conceptualization among those hominins. It is this, often unexpressed, understanding that led to the emphasis on 'modified' forms that feature so prominently in the Finished Artefact Fallacy—as if modification and the motives for it were sufficient for the identification of the intention to impose form. For Mellars (1996), imposed form was absent from Mousterian scrapers where the modification of the flake is related to its original form, but it was present in the Upper Palaeolithic of Europe where there were flakes modified in ways that are visually distinctive, repetitive, and standardized. Such modifications may or may not have been applied to flakes that were themselves of standardized form, such as the 'blades' of the Upper Palaeolithic.

In our earlier paper, we argued that the first appearance of 'imposed form' was with the distinctive geometric microliths of the Middle Stone Age in southern Africa (Davidson and Noble 1993; cf. Deacon 1989). Here the form was seen to be imposed because the shape of the artefacts did not depend on any aspect of the mechanics of production or use, the modified edge was not that used, and the forms were standardized within a very narrow range of shapes. I would now reinforce this judgement as a result of the documentation of the processes of production of these tools (Wurz 1997).

In addition to the stone tools forms, there are other indicators of the emergence of modern human behaviour from the same time period. There is a now well-documented presence of bone tools (Henshilwood and Sealy

1997) in southern Africa and elsewhere in Africa (Brooks *et al.* 1995). In an argument similar to Chase's, I have been at pains to point out the constraints on artefact form imposed by the mechanics of stone knapping (Davidson 1991). No such constraints apply to the production of bone tools. Among these African artefacts of 90,000 years ago, there are two distinct types. Some are fragments of bone where the only modification is the shaping of an end to form a smoothed and polished point. Arguably these could be produced principally to achieve an immediate goal. The second group of artefacts are bone objects where the whole bone fragment has been modified to produce a standardized artefact type. It is more difficult to argue that the form would be produced in such a similar way at different times and places simply in response to the requirements of function or the contingencies of use.

The working of this second group of African bone tools, therefore, probably involved their shaping before any possible use. This contrasts with many of the earlier bone tools, such as those from Bilzingsleben (in Germany, dated about 280,000 ago), where the standardization of form appears to be directly related to use or to result from being used (Noble and Davidson 1996). I believe an appropriate argument can be constructed that these products of the African Middle Stone Age were made by people who used language. That they are accompanied by quantities of worked ochre is a comfort to some other arguments about language origins (Knight *et al.* 1995). To others it is important that there are also bones at Middle Stone Age sites modified for no apparent utilitarian purpose, possibly indicating the creation of symbolic objects (Davidson and Noble 1998). It remains a puzzle why there is not a continuous sequence between these early indications of the emergence of (what we take to be) modern human behaviour and the later archaeological record.

In Mellars's terms, the Middle Stone Age tools were visually distinctive, repetitive, and standardized. The crucial issue is still whether, without the assumptions of the Finished Artefact Fallacy, there were earlier artefacts that fulfilled those criteria, and, if so, whether they indicate language use. The most obvious case that still needs discussion is the hand-axes called Acheulean which seem to dominate the production of stone tools for 1.3 million years and over most of the world occupied by hominins during that period.[8]

---

[8] One of the novelties of the last ten years has been the increasing recognition that industries which produce hand-axe forms are found in east Asia (Yamei *et al.* 2000, cf. Schick 1994).

9.5 Constraints in the Production of Hand-axes

The most significant exploration of the cognitive implications of the making of hand-axes has been that by Tom Wynn (1993, 1995, 1998). In his initial work on the subject, Wynn (1979) explored implications of hand-axe geometry, and the processes of its creation, for understanding hominin mental abilities, using the stages that Piaget identified in the development of modern human children as they grow up. In this and later work (Wynn 1993), he concluded that there are some robust conclusions about the distinctive abilities of the knappers of hand-axes:

1. symmetry appears to have been deliberately sought;
2. learning to make such objects required an ability to learn a shared standard;
3. a consequence of the presence of such shared standards is that the makers must have had a greater decentration of thought than anything reported for apes;
4. complexities of the form of hand-axes imply an ability to organize hierarchically complex patterns of action, including an ability to hold several concepts in mind at once.

But as Wynn acknowledges, *all* such interpretation depends upon an argument (previously no more than an assumption) that the objects archaeologists choose to study were produced *intentionally*. We began to question this assumption in our previous paper (Davidson and Noble 1993), and the remainder of this chapter will present further reasons for doubt.

One reason for questioning the level of intentionality is given by the selective analysis of hand-axes, as suggested in the first facet of the Finished Artefact Fallacy (sect. 9.2).

9.5.1 *Patterning Due to Factors Other than the Intentions of Knappers*

The fundamental observation is that there is some standardization among hand-axes. Some of this arises from the first example of the Finished Artefact Fallacy—I will argue that some of the appearance of standardization results from practices in the study of Acheulean industries, particularly through the emphasis on hand-axes.

Although Wynn and Tierson (1990) have demonstrated that there is some

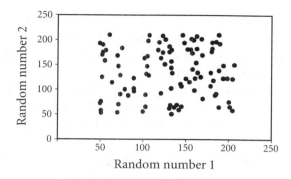

FIG. 9.3a Scatter plot of 100 pairs of random numbers.

regional variation in hand-axe form (but see McPherron 2000), the presence of standardization is one of the persistent observations about hand-axes. Dibble (1989) showed there was some element of the apparent standardization of form of hand-axes that resulted from other simple procedures adopted by archaeologists. I illustrate this (Fig. 9.3a–d) by showing the results of a test similar to that of Dibble to indicate how few manipulations are required to produce the sort of patterning that is taken to be standardization. First, following Dibble, I generated pairs of random numbers (by computer) with only two constraints: a maximum of 210 and a minimum of 50. Plotting them against each other on a scatter plot produced, as expected, a random cloud of points with little or no correlation (Fig. 9.3a). Like Dibble,

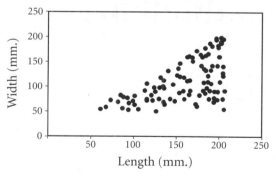

FIG. 9.3b Scatter plot of pairs of random numbers from Fig. 9.3a adjusted to plot larger number of pair on the x-axis, and to label the larger number as length in millimetres and the smaller as width in millimetres.

I then set the larger as 'length in millimetres', because archaeologists define the length of hand-axes as the longer dimension, so hand-axes are always longer than they are wide. Sorting the random numbers to ensure that the larger one of the pair was always in one column and the smaller in the other shows how easily significant patterning can result (Fig. 9.3b). With this one manipulation, the random numbers are now correlated, and at significance levels that would usually draw our attention if we were dealing with archaeological samples.

But I went further and inspected the statistics for 100 samples of 100 specimens generated in this way using a single manipulation of pairs of random numbers. The statistics bear comparison with the results of analysis of real archaeological bifaces: strong correlations between the two randomly generated variables (Fig. 9.3c); tight clustering of the mean values of ratios comparable to those observed in archaeological samples (Fig. 9.3d). These outcomes are a result principally of the computer algorithm that generates random numbers together with one manipulation of those random numbers that is a plausible simulation of a judgement during analysis by an archaeologist.

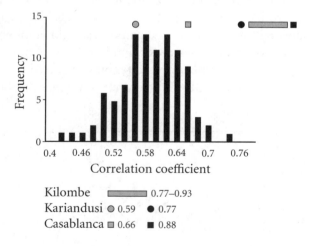

FIG. 9.3c Histogram of correlation coefficients for 100 examples of process illustrated in Figs. 9.3a and 9.3b. For samples of 100 specimens, any value above 0.195 is significant ($p < 0.05$) and above 0.254 is highly significant ($p < 0.01$). All values in this histogram are highly significant. Also shown are ranges of values for hand-axes from Kilombe, Kariandusi, and Casablanca (see Davidson and Noble 1993 for references).

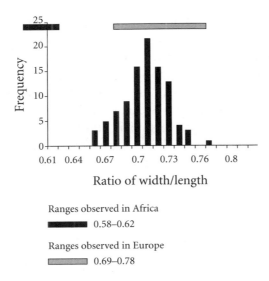

F<small>IG</small>. 9.3d   Histogram of ratios of width/length for samples in Fig. 9.3c, also showing values for samples of hand-axes from Africa and Europe (see Davidson and Noble 1993 for references).

The conclusion here is to reinforce the suggestion that a relatively small number of constraints, not *necessarily* these, could determine the appearance of standardization of Acheulean hand-axes. But several things might be going on. First, it may really be the case that relatively standardized products were the result of a relatively small number of constraints. These constraints may have little or nothing to do with the intentions, if any, of the knappers. The second possibility is that there has been selection by archaeologists of the things they include in their analysis. Hand-axes look alike because archaeologists select for analysis objects that look like hand-axes. There are objects in Acheulean assemblages that have some of the characteristics of hand-axes, but not all. These are excluded from comparison, reinforcing some of the appearance of standardization. Third, if such a simple procedure as that in this simulation can produce the appearance of standardization, we may be rather unsophisticated in identifying standardization.

There are two major reasons why artefacts might have been standardized at the time of their production: either there was a technical, procedural, or cognitive constraint on the possible outcomes (Chase's constraints), or a single option of many available was chosen. Only the latter demonstrates

intention in the knappers. Dibble's observations, together with this extension of it, show that the appearance of standardization may also be a result
of selectivity in analysis. In order to unravel these possibilities further, I have
begun an analysis of cores from the oldest layers at the site of Tabun, the Pal-
estinian site first excavated by Dorothy Garrod. The tools I looked at came
from the meticulous excavations by Art Jelinek (1982*a*,*b*, 1988; Mercier *et
al.* 1995). If I am right in the contention that the form of hand-axes is an outcome of the application of a small number of constraints in knapping, then
some of the features of hand-axes should be present on the non-hand-axe
cores in the related assemblage, because they are not part of the intention to
produce a hand-axe.

9.5.2 *Production of Flakes or Modification of a Finished Core Tool?*

The flakes removed from cores cannot in principle be distinguished from
those removed in the production of a hand-axe. Fig. 9.4 shows a core with
three flakes removed. Because this core is not in the form of a hand-axe,
few analysts would doubt an interpretation that the flakes could have been
removed for use. But comparison with Fig. 9.1 shows that there are hand-
axes with similar flake scars. Nothing about these flake scars indicates that
the flakes were removed for any purpose different from that of the flakes in
Fig. 9.4. The flakes in Fig. 9.4 were produced by the same technique without
any apparent intention to produce a core of a particular form. Under these
circumstances there are no principles to guide the archaeological interpretation of the intentions of the knapper.

FIG. 9.4 Core from Tabun with three flakes removed similar in size and shape to
three flakes removed from the biface in Fig. 9.1. Vertical axis 58 mm. *Photo Iain
Davidson, courtesy of Art Jelinek.*

9.5.3 *Modification and the Patterning of Tools and Other Artefacts*

Wynn (1995) indicated three main reasons why he thinks hand-axe shape was intentionally produced:

1. Removal of 'tiny, trimming flakes' which could not have been useful.
2. Bilateral symmetry, including examples where one margin is flaked and the other is not.
3. Production of hand-axes in a single sequence of knapping (as at the British sites of Caddington and Boxgrove where all steps from obtaining the raw material to abandoning the hand-axe appear to be present).

Leaving aside the question of the minimum size at which flakes might be useful, there are always three possible reasons why 'tiny, trimming flakes' might be removed from the margin of a flaked stone artefact:

1. Overhang removal from the surface adjacent to the point of force application.
2. Preparation of the striking platform prior to the removal of another flake.
3. Shaping of the edge.

My observations at Tabun suggest that very careful analysis is required to distinguish between modifications produced by these three processes. The first two are almost automatic in the mechanical routine of knapping, and need not involve intention beyond the production of the next flake. They are certainly present on the cores, including the hand-axes, at Tabun. Without that analysis both procedures might easily be mistaken for edge shaping. Without eliminating that option, I suggest intention is difficult to infer. In addition, the trimming of the edge for use does not imply anything about the time depth of the intentionality beyond the requirements of the immediate contingencies of use.

9.5.4 *Mechanical Principles in the Appearance of Patterning*

The preliminary analysis of the Tabun artefacts showed that there is a tendency towards production of flakes only (1) from acute angled platforms (as in the production of hand-axes) or (2) from platforms near to the limits of obtuseness (Fig. 9.5). Only when both margins are flaked with acute angles do the artefacts tend to be hand-axes. Symmetry about a plane, one of the dis-

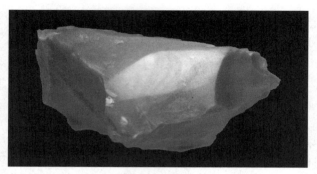

FIG. 9.5 Acute and obtuse angle platforms on the core of Fig. 9.4. Width 64 mm. *Photo Iain Davidson, courtesy of Art Jelinek.*

tinctive features of hand-axes, is partly a result of that convergence. Indeed, when the angles are obtuse all around the core, there may be a tendency to produce cores such as are found in the Levallois technique. It is this pattern that both Gowlett and I pointed out in the artefacts from the lowest levels at Olduvai Gorge.

9.5.5 *Factors in the Appearance of Patterning*

The question of symmetry needs extensive treatment. I have just indicated one of the contributing factors in the production of symmetry about a plane in hand-axes. But hand-axes are also symmetrical about an axis on

FIG. 9.6a Flake scars on margin of flake from Tabun. The flaked margin is on the bottom of photograph. Width 75 mm. *Photo Iain Davidson, courtesy of Art Jelinek.*

FIG. 9.6b Same flake as in Fig. 9.6a after one-flip rotation, showing flake scars on margin of flake on bottom of photograph. Width 75 mm. *Photo Iain Davidson, courtesy of Art Jelinek.*

that plane. In some artefacts, symmetry about an axis may be the outcome of a knapping procedure evident at Tabun—the removal of flakes from opposite margins after a single rotation of the core. In Fig. 9.6a, flakes were removed from one margin of the core which was then rotated once. The flakes removed from the second margin involved precisely the same hand movements following that one change (Fig. 9.6b). The effect of that procedure, when both margins were acute angled, would be to produce a tendency towards symmetry about the line around which the core was rotated. This is obviously not the whole story, but is an illustration of the procedures in operation in these Acheulean industries. The application of such procedures, for which it seems unnecessary to invoke any intention about the final product, had the effect of producing patterning of those products that could be interpreted as intentional.

Finally, in relation to Wynn's criteria for intentional determination of form, it needs to be said yet again that there is no evidence for the full sequence of production of a hand-axe at Caddington (Bradley and Sampson 1978; Noble and Davidson 1996) or Boxgrove (Bergman and Roberts 1988; Bergman *et al.* 1990; Roberts 1986; Roberts *et al.* 1997; Wenban-Smith 1989). Nor should we expect there to be, for that would be knapping for its own sake, what one of my knapping colleagues calls 'therapeutic kinaesthetics'. Refitting artefacts from a single nodule of raw material at Boxgrove has established that cores were roughed out from the cobbles available at the site.[9] Both flakes and hand-axes were used for the activities at the site, which included butchery.

Tabun provides good evidence confirming the claim by Bradley and Sampson (1986; see also Davidson and Noble 1993) that hand-axe forms might be one stage in a reduction sequence—not necessarily the last one. Fig. 9.7 shows the removal of the tip of a hand-axe from Tabun. This extension of the reduction sequence beyond the production of the hand-axe implies that something was being obtained other than the hand-axe as a tool. The hand-axe might still have been an intentional end product that was destroyed in an act of desperation when there was a shortage of material. This seems unlikely, given the abundance of raw material close to the site.[10]

---

[9] I am very grateful to Matt Pope for showing me, in April 1998, the Boxgrove site and the flaked flints he has fitted back together.

[10] Art Jelinek, personal communication, March 1998.

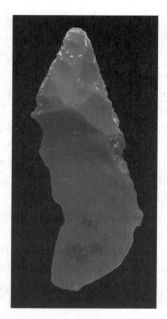

FIG. 9.7 Tip of hand-axe from Tabun. The flake has been removed after the hand-axe shape was achieved, indicating that the hand-axe form was not necessarily an intentional end product. Long axis 128 mm. *Photo Iain Davidson, courtesy of Art Jelinek.*

9.6 Conclusion

Interpretation of the mental abilities of early human ancestors from the evidence of the stone tools requires an understanding of the intentions of the makers of the tools. In this study I have sought to show that the form of early stone artefacts of the Acheulean can be partly understood in terms of selective study by archaeologists, and of the procedural and technical practices of the knappers. Without eliminating the influence of these factors, any interpretation of the intentions of the knappers is impossible. On the other hand, I repeat our earlier observation that some stone artefacts from the Middle Stone Age in South Africa show modification of their form that is unrelated to the procedural or technical limitations of the knappers, and that these are accompanied by bone artefacts for which the same is true. More work needs to be done to explore the contrasts implied here before the intentions of knappers can be said to involve language-based mental representations any earlier than the Middle Stone Age of South Africa.

FURTHER READING

On modern humans, including psychology and linguistics:

CALVIN, W. H., and BICKERTON, D. (2000), *Lingua ex Machina: Reconciling Darwin and Chomsky with the Human Brain* (Cambridge, Mass. MIT Press). (This book attempts to rescue Chomsky's linguistics from the charge of being ahistorical. It consists of a dialogue between a specialist on the brain (Calvin) and a linguist (Bickerton), of somewhat unorthodox views, who has been a pioneer in the reasoned argument about the origins of language.)

DEACON, T. (1997), *The Symbolic Species: The Co-evolution of Language and The Human Brain* (New York: W. W. Norton). (Probably the current definitive work of synthesis on language origins, including a very dense account of neurological studies. Suffers from uncritical approach to the archaeological record.)

On modern non-human primates, including their communicative abilities:

CHENEY, D. L., and SEYFARTH, R. M. (1990), *How Monkeys See The World* (Chicago: University of Chicago Press). (The classic study of communication among wild primates. It is principally concerned with vervet monkeys and their famous calls in the presence of predators, but it also contains detailed studies of the quieter vocalizations among monkeys when not threatened. It also has useful summaries of other studies of primate communication.)

SAVAGE-RUMBAUGH, S., and LEWIN, R. (1994), *Kanzi* (New York: McGraw-Hill). (Popular account of the remarkable studies at the Language Research Centre that made the breakthrough to getting apes to communicate with humans in controlled circumstances. More detailed studies have been published elsewhere, but this volume is also valuable for its frank summary of the successes and failures of other language experiments with apes.)

KING, B. J. (1999) (ed.), *The Origins of Language: What Nonhuman Primates Can Tell Us* (Santa Fe: School of American Research Press). (Symposium volume with important papers by a number of major players (including primatologists, linguists, and anthropologists) in the debates about language origins).

On archaeology:

NOBLE, W., and DAVIDSON, I. (1996), *Human Evolution, Language and Mind* (Cambridge: Cambridge University Press). (The only published attempt that combines the development of psychological theory and a reassessment of the interpretation of the archaeological record to produce an integrated account of the origins of language and its implications for the evolution of human behaviour.)

REFERENCES

ASFAW, B., BEYENE, Y., SUWA, G., WALTER, R. C., WHITE, T. D., WOLDEGABRIEL, G., and YEMANE, T. (1992), 'The earliest Acheulean from Konso-Gardula', *Nature*, 360: 732–5.

BERGMAN, C. A., and ROBERTS, M. B. (1988), 'Flaking technology at the Acheulean site of Boxgrove, West Sussex (England)', *Revue Archéologique De Picardie*, 1–2: 105–13.

————— COLLCUTT, S., and BARLOW, P. (1990), 'Refitting and Spatial Analysis of Artefacts from Quarry 2 at the Middle Pleistocene Acheulean Site of Boxgrove, West Sussex, England', in E. Cziesia, S. Eickhoff, N. Arts, and D. Winter (eds.), *The Big Puzzle: International Symposium on Stone Artefacts* (Bonn: Holos), 265–81.

BEYRIES, S. (1987), *Variabilité de l'industrie lithique au Moustérien* (Oxford: British Archaeological Reports, International Series 328).

BRADLEY, B., and SAMPSON, C. G. (1978), 'Artifacts from the Cottages Site', in C. G. Sampson (ed.), *Paleoecology and Archeology of an Acheulian Site at Caddington, England* (Dallas: Department of Anthropology, Southern Methodist University), 83–137.

————— (1986), 'Analysis by Replication of Two Acheulian Artefact Assemblages', in G. N. Bailey and P. Callow (eds.), *Stone Age Prehistory* (Cambridge: Cambridge University Press), 29–45.

BROOKS, A. S., HELGREN, D. M., CRAMER, J. S., FRANKLIN, A., HORNYAK, W., KEATING, J. M., KLEIN, R. G., RINK, W. J., SCHWARZ, H., LEITH SMITH, J. N., STEWART, K., TODD, N. E., VERNIERS, J., and YELLEN, J. E. (1995), 'Dating and Context of Three Middle Stone Age sites with Bone Points in the Upper Semliki Valley, Zaire', *Science*, 268: 548–53.

CHASE, P. G. (1991), 'Symbols and Paleolithic Artefacts', *Journal of Anthropological Archaeology*, 10: 193–214.

DAVIDSON, I. (1991), 'The Archaeology of Language Origins', *Antiquity*, 65: 39–48.

——and NOBLE, W. (1993), 'Tools and Language in Human Evolution', in K. Gibson and T. Ingold (eds.), *Tools, Language and Cognition in Human Evolution* (Cambridge: Cambridge University Press), 363–88.

—————(1998), 'Two Views on Language Origins', *Cambridge Archaeological Journal*, 8/1: 82–8.

DEACON, H. J. (1989), 'Late Pleistocene Palaeoecology and Archaeology in the Southern Cape, South Africa', in P. Mellars and C. Stringer (eds.), *The Human Revolution* (Edinburgh: Edinburgh University Press), 547–64.

DIBBLE, H. L. (1987), 'Reduction Sequences in the Manufacture of Mousterian implements of France', in O. Soffer (ed.), *The Pleistocene Old World* (New York: Plenum Press), 33–44.

——(1989), 'The Implications of Stone Tool Types for the Presence of Language during the Lower and Middle Paleolithic', in P. A. Mellars and C. B. Stringer (eds.), *The Human Revolution* (Princeton, NJ: Princeton University Press), 415–31.

FAGAN, B. (1989), *People of the Earth*, 6th edn. (Glenview, Ill.: Scott, Foresman).

FOLEY, R. A., and LAHR, M. M. (1997), 'Mode 3 Technologies and the Evolution of Modern Humans', *Cambridge Archaeological Journal*, 7/1: 3–36.

FRAME, H. (1986), 'Microscopic Use-Wear Traces', in P. Callow and J. Cornford (eds.), *La Cotte de St. Brelade 1961–1978: Excavations by C. B. M. McBurney* (Norwich: Geo Books), 353–62.

GIBSON, K. R., and INGOLD, T. (1993) (eds.), *Tools, Language and Cognition in Human Evolution* (Cambridge: Cambridge University Press).

GOWLETT, J. A. J. (1984), 'Mental Abilities of Early Man', in R. Foley (ed.), *Hominid Evolution and Community Ecology* (London: Academic Press), 167–92.

——(1986), 'Culture and Conceptualisation', in G. N. Bailey and P. Callow (eds.), *Stone Age Prehistory* (Cambridge: Cambridge University Press), 243–60.

——(1996), 'Mental Abilities of Early *Homo*', in P. Mellars and K. Gibson (eds.), *Modelling the Early Human Mind*, McDonald Institute Monographs (Cambridge: McDonald Institute for Archaeological Research), 191–215.

HENSHILWOOD, C., and SEALY, J. (1997), 'Bone Artefacts from the Middle Stone Age at Blombos Cave, Southern Cape, South Africa', *Current Anthropology*, 38/5: 890–5.

HISCOCK, P. D. (1993), 'Bondaian Technology in the Hunter Valley, New South Wales', *Archaeology in Oceania*, 28: 65–76.

INGOLD, T. (1993), 'Tools, Techniques and Technology', in K. R. Gibson and T. Ingold (eds.), *Tools, Language and Cognition in Human Evolution* (Cambridge: Cambridge University Press), 337–45.

JELINEK, A. J. (1982*a*), 'The Tabun Cave and Paleolithic Man in the Levant', *Science*, 216: 1369–75.

——(1982*b*), 'The Middle Paleolithic in the Southern Levant, With Comments on the Appearance of Modern *Homo sapiens*', in A. Ronen (ed.), *The Transition from Lower to Middle Palaeolithic and the Origin of Modern Man* (Oxford: British Archaeological Reports, International Series, vol. 151), 57–104.

——(1988), 'Technology, Typology, and Culture in the Middle Paleolithic', in H. L. Dibble and A. Montet-White (eds.), *Upper Pleistocene Prehistory of Western Eurasia* (Philadelphia: University Museum, University of Pennsylvania), 199–212.

KEELEY, L. H. (1980), *Experimental Determination of Stone Tool Uses* (Chicago: University of Chicago Press).

——and TOTH, N. (1981), 'Microwear Polishes on Early Stone Tools from Koobi Fora, Kenya', *Nature*, 293: 464–5.

KNIGHT, C. D., POWER, C., and WATTS, I. (1995), 'The Human Symbolic Revolution', *Cambridge Archaeological Journal*, 5/1: 75–114.

LEAKEY, M. D. (1971), *Olduvai Gorge* (Cambridge: Cambridge University Press).

LOY, T. H., and HARDY, B. L. (1992), 'Blood Residue Analysis of 90,000-Year-Old Stone Tools from Tabun Cave, Israel', *Antiquity*, 66: 24–35.

McPHERRON, S. (2000), 'Handaxes as a Measure of the Mental Capabilities of Early Hominids', *Journal of Archaeological Science*, 27: 655–63.

MELLARS, P. A. (1989), 'Technological Changes across the Middle-Upper Palaeolithic Transition', in P. A. Mellars and C. B. Stringer (eds.), *The Human Revolution* (Princeton, NJ: Princeton University Press), 338–65.

——(1996), 'Symbolism, Language, and the Neanderthal Mind', in P. Mellars and

K. Gibson (eds.), *Modelling the Early Human Mind*, McDonald Institute Monographs (Cambridge: McDonald Institute for Archaeological Research), 15–32.

MERCIER, N., VALLADAS, H., VALLADAS, G., REYSS, J.-L., JELINEK, A., MEIGNEN, L., and JORON, J.-L. (1995), 'TL Dates of Burnt Flints from Jelinek's Excavations at Tabun and their Implications', *Journal of Archaeological Science*, 22: 495–509.

MOORE, M. W. (2000), 'Technology of Hunter Valley Microlith Assemblages, New South Wales', *Australian Archaeology*, 51: 28–39.

NOBLE, W., and DAVIDSON, I. (1996), *Human Evolution, Language and Mind* (Cambridge: Cambridge University Press).

POTTS, R. (1989), 'Olorgesailie', *Journal of Human Evolution*, 18: 477–84.

ROBERTS, M. B. (1986), 'Excavations of the Lower Palaeolithic Site at Amey's Eartham Pit, Boxgrove, West Sussex', *Proceedings of the Prehistoric Society*, 52: 215–45.

——PARFITT, S. A., POPE, M. J., and WENBAN-SMITH, F. F. (1997), 'Boxgrove, West Sussex', *Proceedings of the Prehistoric Society*, 63: 303–58.

ROLLAND, N. (1986), 'Recent Findings from La Micoque and Other Sites in South-Western and Mediterranean France', in G. N. Bailey and P. Callow (eds.), *Stone Age Prehistory* (Cambridge: Cambridge University Press), 121–51.

——and DIBBLE, H. L. (1990), 'A New Synthesis of Middle Paleolithic Variability', *American Antiquity*, 55/3: 480–99.

SCHICK, K. D. (1994), 'The Movius Line Reconsidered', in R. S. Coruccini and R. L. Ciochon (eds.), *Integrative Paths to the Past* (Englewood Cliffs, NJ: Prentice Hall), 569–96.

TINDALE, N. B. (1965), 'Stone Implement Making among the Nakako, Ngadadjara and Pitjandjara of the Great Western Desert', *Records of the South Australian Museum*, 15: 131–64.

TOTH, N. (1985), 'The Oldowan Reassessed', *Journal of Archaeological Science*, 12: 101–20.

VAN PEER, P. (1992), *The Levallois Reduction Strategy*, Monographs in World Archaeology, 13 (Madison, Wis.: Prehistory Press).

WENBAN-SMITH, F. F. (1989), 'The Use of Canonical Variates for Determination of Biface Manufacturing Technology at Boxgrove Lower Palaeolithic Site and the Behavioural Implications of this Technology', *Journal of Archaeological Science*, 16: 17–26.

WHITTAKER, J. (1994), *Flintknapping* (Austin: University of Texas Press).

WURZ, S. (1997), 'The Howiesons Poort at Klasies River', MA Thesis, University of Stellenbosch, Stellenbosch, 73 pp.

WYNN, T. (1979), 'The Intelligence of Later Acheulean Hominids', *Man: Journal of the Royal Anthropological Institute*, 14: 371–91.

——(1993), 'Two Developments in the Mind of *Homo erectus*', *Journal of Anthropological Archaeology*, 12: 299–322.

——(1995), 'Handaxe Enigmas', *World Archaeology*, 27/1: 10–24.

——(1998), 'Did *Homo erectus* speak?', *Cambridge Archaeological Journal*, 8/1: 78–81.

——and McGrew, W. C. (1989), 'An Ape's Eye View of the Oldowan', *Man: Journal of the Royal Anthropological Institute*, 24: 383–98.

——and Tierson, F. (1990), 'Regional Comparison of the Shapes of Later Acheulean Handaxes', *American Anthropologist*, 92: 73–84.

Yamei, H., Potts, R., Baoyin, Y., Zhengtang, G., Deino, A., Wei, W., Clark, J., Guagmao, X., and Weiwen, H. (2000), 'Mid-Pleistocene Acheulean-like Stone Technology of the Bose Basin, South China', *Science*, 287 (issue no. 5458): 1622–6.

PART III

External Triggers to Transition:
Environment, Population, and Social Context

10 Foraging versus Social Intelligence in the Evolution of Protolanguage

DEREK BICKERTON

The cover material of Hurford, Studdert-Kennedy, and Knight (1998) announces a new orthodoxy in no uncertain terms:

[T]his volume ... takes as its starting-point the view of human intelligence as social, concerned with one's own and others' desires and motives, and of language as a device for forming alliances, making friends, and thus achieving successful feeding and mating through a complex social network. From this perspective, phonologists and syntacticians may explore the origins of the sound patterns and formal structures that characterize all language.

This consensus is spelled out by contributors to the volume in a variety of ways. According to Dunbar (1998: 94), 'The need to hold large highly structured groups together has been more important than the need to solve ecological problems ... primates (in particular) are significantly more skilled at solving social problems than they are in solving ecological problems.' According to Worden (1998: 164), language arose 'by reuse of pre-existing structures and operations in the brain for social intelligence and the theory of mind'.

It was not always thus. Citing again the cover material of Hurford *et al.* (1998), '(F)or the past two centuries scientists ... have tended to see language function as largely concerned with the exchange of practical information about the mechanics of the physical world: toolmaking, hunting and so forth.' This previous consensus was overturned due to the apparent convergence of several different lines of evidence, as follows:

1. Ethological studies. Over three decades, a series of studies of primates in the wild (Schaller 1963; Goodall 1986; Smuts 1987; Strum 1987; Cheney

I am grateful for some helpful and insightful comments from four anonymous referees, none of whom should be held responsible for any errors or omissions this chapter may still contain.

and Seyfarth 1990) or under relatively free conditions in zoos (de Waal 1982, 1989) showed that the social life of primates was highly complex, structured, and in many ways comparable to the social life of our own species.

2. Machiavellian intelligence. Humphrey's (1976) suggestion that the growth of human intelligence could be more plausibly attributed to competition between individuals than to interaction with the environment fitted well with the concurrent shift in evolutionary theory from models that allowed for group selection to models strictly limited to individual selection. That such competition existed in other primate species, involving calculated instances of tactical deception, was subsequently demonstrated in several studies (Byrne and Whiten 1985, 1992; Whiten and Byrne 1988).

3. Theory of mind. Whether non-human primates have a theory of mind remains controversial (Heyes 1998), but enough evidence exists to suggest some kind of continuity between human and other-primate recognitions of themselves and of the cognitive or affective states of others (Gallup 1982; Jolly 1991; Povinelli 1994; etc.)

4. Ape 'language' experiments. Although attempts to determine the linguistic capacity of apes (Gardner and Gardner 1969; Premack 1971; Terrace *et al.* 1979; Savage-Rumbaugh 1986; Greenfield and Savage-Rumbaugh 1990, etc.) failed to support the proposal that apes could acquire full human language, these experiments left little doubt as to their possession of some crucial prerequisites for human language.

These lines of evidence taken in conjunction seemed to indicate that language arose as a direct result of increased and intensified social interaction, whether resulting from increasing group size (Dunbar 1993), some form of ritualization (Deacon 1997; Knight 1998), or other factors (or combinations thereof).

Relatively little recent work has pointed in a contrary direction. Although studies beginning with Parker and Gibson (1979; see also Gibson 1993; King 1994) have linked language with foraging behaviour, they generally treat improved cognition as an intervening variable (more diversified foraging improved cognitive skills, which in turn made language possible). Moreover, these views are often embedded in a strongly continuist approach to language evolution, cogently expressed by King (1994: 116): 'Early hominids ... may have functioned similarly to chimpanzees in terms of foraging-related information donation.'

In contrast, this chapter argues that the initial impetus for a means of 'information donation' quite distinct from means employed by other primates—that is, some form of protolanguage—arose directly from the requirements of group foraging, predator avoidance, and instruction of the young, rather than from specifically social interactions between individuals (whether competitive or co-operative). However, this exercise concerns itself solely with the immediate pressure that first triggered some kind of language, and in no way denies the vital roles played by social intelligence once even the crudest form of linguistic communication was up and running. As soon as protolanguage had achieved the necessary critical mass (some dozens or perhaps a few hundred meaningful symbols, whether oral or manual is immaterial to the present argument) it was undoubtedly co-opted for a variety of social purposes, which in turn contributed to its further expansion. Moreover, the present writer has already claimed that the core distinguishing factor of human language—syntax—derives from the exaptation of one particular aspect of social intelligence: reciprocal altruism and the social score-keeping required to make reciprocal altruism work (Bickerton 1998; Calvin and Bickerton 2000). All that is claimed here is that, for a variety of reasons, the selective pressure that started us on the road to modern human language cannot have come from social intelligence *per se*. Five quite distinct and mutually independent lines of argument all point to this conclusion.

10.1 Nature of Selective Pressure

Evidence adduced for the complexities of social structure under (1) above proves a two-edged weapon. While suggesting that social intelligence played an important role in the emergence of language, it also shows that the same social intelligence developed not merely in the hominid line but in a number of closely related species, thereby raising the puzzling question of why the same factor should have operated so differently upon humans and non-humans.

Humans have developed language to a high degree of complexity—unquestionably, far indeed from the humble beginnings it must have had. No other species has developed language *at all*. This is not normally the case where the same selective pressure is concerned. Female selection, for example, has driven the development of peacock's tails to inordinate lengths, but the peacock is only one among many species whose tails are longer than their bodies. We would expect that if social intelligence had driven one primate species to full language, it would have driven one or two others to some form of protolanguage (as proposed in Bickerton 1990 for pre-*sapiens homo*), or at the very least to some system of communication more complex and/or more flexible than the general run of animal call systems. But to date at least, no such system has been discovered. In a study admittedly three decades old (but whose basic conclusions have not been contradicted by subsequent work) Wilson (1972) compared the number of units in the communication systems of a variety of species, fish, birds, and mammals, including primates. Surprisingly, the numbers overlap—there are primate species that have fewer units than some birds, or even fish—and although the richest systems do belong to primates, they exceed the maxima for fish and birds by less than 30 per cent.

In addition, there are a number of qualitative differences, of which perhaps the most significant is predication. Even at its simplest level language involves taking some entity and making a statement about that entity's state or activity: *Mary left, dogs bark, rain fell*. This is possible in no other animal communication systems. Vervet calls (Cheney and Seyfarth 1990) can indicate entities—leopards, pythons, martial eagles—but cannot make statements about those entities' states or activities; there is no *leopard hungry, eagle landing, python gone*. Note that even commands imply a subject–predicate distinction—'[you] do so-and-so'—and that in any case commands are of little use for doing what language uniquely does: transmitting (purportedly) factual information.

When a complex and unique development occurs in only one species, the most logical conclusion is that the selective pressure driving that development must have been unique to that species. Thus the strength of social intelligence in other primates argues against, not for, social intelligence as the force behind the emergence of language.

To maintain the claim that social intelligence did constitute that force, one would have to show that some further factor unique to humans had intervened to change, in our species only, the quality or quantity of social interaction. The most coherent attempt to do this so far is that of Dunbar (1993, 1996), according to which an increase in human group size made mutual grooming too time-consuming an activity, so that language developed as a grooming substitute. However, in addition to numerous weaknesses pointed out by commentators on Dunbar (1993), this approach falls foul of at least two of the other lines of argument developed in this chapter (in sects. 10.4 and 10.5 respectively).

It may be wondered why I have ignored what to some is the most striking difference between the hominid line and other primates: bipedalism (Carstairs-McCarthy 1999). Granted, whether the initial forms of language were signed or spoken, bipedalism (by freeing the hands, by restructuring the vocal tract) was a necessary prerequisite for language. But no one that I know of, certainly not Carstairs-McCarthy, has suggested that it is a sufficient prerequisite. Potential capacity for a particular behaviour will come to fruition only if some specific pressure, social or environmental, confers a selective advantage on that behaviour.

10.2 Nature of Complexity Deficits

The idea that the need to cope with growing social complexity led somehow to the emergence of language comes up against another aspect of the evidence surveyed in (1). If the idea were correct, it would imply that the social life of other primates was significantly less complex than that of humans. If we consider modern human societies, this is undoubtedly the case. There are innumerable factors—cultural, legal, economic—that affect our social relations and make them far more convoluted than anything found outside our species. But the vast majority of such factors are products of the last few thousand years of human development, and even today are largely absent from the few remaining societies that continue to survive with the hunting-gathering technology of earlier epochs. Such modern complexities are, therefore, irrelevant to the present debate.

If we compare the social world of other primates with the social world of pre-agricultural humans, the differences are far less obvious. Chimpanzees, for instance, have complex systems of alliances and manipulate one another shamelessly for their own advantage, just as humans do (de Waal 1982). They have established techniques for resolving conflict and re-establishing social cohesion (de Waal 1989) They have even rudimentary forms of justice and fair dealing (de Waal 1996). Lacking language, they cannot literally lie, but they can deliberately deceive one another (see Byrne and Whiten 1985, 1992; Whiten and Byrne 1988). Just what is lacking?

If we try to answer that question, we find that in every case any deficit in complexity between human and non-human primate social life results from the possession of language, rather than constituting a possible cause for it. If our interactions are more complex than those of apes, that is precisely because we can feed one another with selective or downright false information, which can be countered only by eliciting (again through language) other versions of the same 'facts'. We alone can construct and culturally transmit codes of behaviour that regulate interactions with our conspecifics. None of this is possible without language—indeed, without quite a complex form of language. Increases in the power and subtlety of language would naturally have led to increases in the complexity of social interaction, rather than the reverse being the case.

The contrast between the domains of social and environmental intelligence offers further support for this argument. If there is any significant cognitive deficit as between humans and other primates, it clearly falls within the second sphere, rather than the first. Human hunter-gatherers presently are—and must always have been—highly sensitive to the nature of the environment (reasons why this is so will be explored in the next section). Other primates are not.

Cheney and Seyfarth (1990: ch. 9) contains fascinating data on this issue, both observational and experimental. A troop of baboons totally ignored a buffalo recently killed by lions until they spotted the lions themselves. Vervets ignored both real python tracks and simulated ones. Carcasses of gazelles placed in trees likewise elicited no reaction, although human observers familiar with the area readily interpreted these as signs that there were leopards in the vicinity. No modern hunter-gatherer would fail correctly to interpret and react to such signs, and it is reasonable to assume, for reasons discussed in the next section, that our hominid ancestors would have been at least equally observant. Such contrasts inevitably suggest that any cognitive deficit of other primates lies in the realm of non-social rather than social intelligence, and accordingly that language (whether as cause or result) is more closely associated with the former.

10.3 Comparative Ecology

One striking fact about the literature that seeks to link the emergence of language to social intelligence is that none of it pays sufficient attention to the actual environmental conditions that prevailed while hominids (presumably together with early language) were developing. This deficiency is hardly surprising; the vast bulk of what has so far been written about language evolution is vitiated by a failure to take into account the full range of constraints that a variety of disciplines imposes, or should impose, on all studies in this field. But the particular deficiency illustrated here abstracts away from relevant data even more blatantly than some others.

In the absence of any model of early hominid ecology, social intelligence theories seem implicitly to assume that early hominid societies did not differ significantly (except perhaps in terms of some unspecified type of added social or cultural complexity) from modern ape societies. It is implicitly assumed that there was no significant difference between the two in terms even of such crucial parameters as the time that could be devoted to social interaction or the degree to which predation by other species represented a danger.

In fact, as any good study of hominid ecology (e.g. Foley 1987) will show, the lives of hominids 2–3 million years ago differed widely, and in a wide variety of respects, from the lives of contemporary gorillas, chimpanzees, and bonobos, particularly with respect to the following:

1. Environment: while contemporary apes live for the most part in forested areas, early hominids inhabited relatively dry savannahs with isolated clumps of trees and gallery woods.

2. Diet: in consequence of their environment, contemporary apes eat mainly fruits and nuts, which they supplement with vegetable matter (leaves, flowers, buds, seeds, etc.). Insects, birds' eggs, and meat form a relatively minor part of their diet, and are probably taken more for variety than necessity, since fruit and vegetable supplies are usually freely available; in the Gombe stream area, for instance, sources included a fig crop that 'was plentiful, lasting for eight weeks'; 'the fruit of the ubiquitous *mbula* tree'; bananas that had 'an exceptionally long fruiting in one area'; and trees on which 'yellow blossoms . . . grew in profusion' (van Lawick-Goodall 1971: 26, 61, 95, 165). Early hominids, in contrast, seem to have been ill-adapted to flowery, leafy materials, and, under savannah conditions, quantities of fruit and nuts are likely to be severely limited. The probability is that hominids were forced to avail themselves of a much wider variety of food sources, most of which, far from 'lasting eight weeks' or having 'an exceptionally long fruiting', were probably highly transient as well as widely scattered. Moreover, so far as is known, contemporary apes seldom if ever scavenge, while the tools of early hominids, capable of piercing thick hides and crudely carving up carcasses,

suggest that scavenging, with all its attendant risks, difficulties, and benefits, provided a significant part of early hominid diet.

3. Day range: it follows from the distribution of food supplies in their respective terrains that the day ranges of early hominids must have been considerably larger than those of contemporary apes (Foley 1987: 140; see also McHenry 1994). This in turn would have had consequences in terms of predator risk and foraging patterns that will be further discussed in sect. 10.6.

4. Vulnerability to predation: contemporary apes do not suffer from predation to any significant degree. Their ability to brachiate freely (or, in the case of gorillas, their size) places them effectively beyond the reach of terrestrial predators. In contrast, an environment of savannah, scrub, or scattered woodlands exposes its dwellers to predation to a much greater extent; even assuming that early hominids retained some of their ancestors' brachiating capacity, the scarcity and wide dispersal of trees would have made tree-climbing a relatively rare escape option. Moreover, the savannahs of 2–4 million years ago contained twelve distinct genera of predators (sabretooths, for example), several of which have since become extinct, but many of which were larger and fiercer than most contemporary predators (Lewis 1997). Since in similar areas predation on humans even today is substantial (Treves and Naughton-Treves 1999), we can conclude that it must have been far more severe when hominids were smaller and lethal predators far more numerous.

The cumulative effect of these differences had at least two consequences that are significant for the origin of language. First, the time that was available for purely social interaction was probably more limited (since obtaining food and avoiding predation occupied a greater amount of time). Second, the importance of observing and interpreting the signs of nature was probably much greater, in so far as ignoring such signs was likely to lead much more frequently to loss of life.

Moreover, there is an obvious link between the materials discussed in sects. 10.1 and 10.3. In sect. 10.1 it was concluded that language should have resulted from a selective pressure unique to human ancestors. In section 10.3 it has been shown that the ecology of early hominids differed from that of any contemporary ape. In other words, if we are looking for how language originated, we should be looking not for similarities between hominids and contemporary apes, but for differences, and those differences are most readily apparent in their contrasting ecologies.

10.4 Initial Functionality

If any capacity for language was to develop among human ancestors, that capacity had to be functional from day one. If the very first meaningful symbols, manual or vocal, however few in number (and language could hardly have begun with a ready-made inventory of symbols) were not immediately comprehensible and immediately useful, no hominids would have persisted in their use, much less have developed vocabularies comprehensive enough to be used for gossip, deceit, alliance-building, or other social purposes.

What exactly were those first meaningful symbols? It is sometimes assumed that they could originally have corresponded to holistic utterances that were subsequently factored out to yield the more familiar singly referential symbols universal in language today. Such a supposition is useful to those (e.g. Hauser 1996) who still seek for some form of continuity between language and animal call systems (since many animal calls can more readily be anthropomorphized as complete utterances—e.g. 'Mate with me', 'Stay out of my territory'—than as single words). Moreover, it is supported both by those who follow the belief, originally suggested by Darwin (1871) and developed by Jespersen (1922), that language developed out of song, and by at least some of those who computationally model language evolution (e.g. Batali 1998; Kirby 2000). Wray (1998, 2000) puts forward the most specific proposal that the earliest (protolinguistic) utterances consisted of wholes lacking even the potential of resolution into smaller meaningful units: to take Wray's own examples (2000: 294), *tebima* might have meant 'Give that to her' while *mutapi* might have meant 'Give that to me', but although both utterances include the meanings 'give' and 'to', no single analysable subsegment common to these utterances encodes these meanings.

Wray seriously underestimates two sets of problems: those posed by initial understanding of such units, and those posed by their subsequent segmentation. As for the first, how could creatures with no specific linguistic equipment, without even the experience of anything one could call language, have determined at first utterance (or even after numerous subsequent utterances) the intended meaning of holistic utterances of such a completely novel kind, and why would they have had to? Since gestures are holistic and convey (some kinds of) meaning, a simple add-on to a pre-existing call-and/or-gesture system would have worked as or more efficiently for the kinds of example Wray gives, and no evidence is offered that a new modality was required (by, for example, showing that our ancestors' communicative needs outstripped the capacities of their pre-existing system).

As for the problem of subsequent segmentation (unavoidable, as Wray recognizes, if modern human language is going to result) it is well-known that this is difficult enough for modern human infants, equipped with all the bells and whistles of modern human language. Indeed, when required to analyse sequences from agglutinative languages unknown to them (a common test in linguistics exams), graduate students with years of linguistic training often do rather poorly. Yet in both the 'stream of speech' and agglutinated segments, superficially holistic utterances are in fact composed of discrete units with consistent meanings, so that those units are, in principle, analysable. But the utterances proposed by Wray, Batali, and many others are truly holistic (they do not necessarily include any subunits invariant in meaning) so that the task of segmentation would be orders of magnitude more difficult, if possible at all.

It therefore seems likelier that the original symbols consisted of single units with single meanings—meanings, moreover, that could somehow be ostensibly demonstrated from the immediate environment (by gesture, imitation of sound, pointing out something, or whatever). Only such units would be readily interpretable by creatures that still lacked any task-specific mechanism for interpretation. Moreover, it seems reasonable to suppose that these units would have had to be used (and understood) in isolation, as single-symbol utterances, before they could be combined into even two-symbol utterances. Certainly on most analyses (but see Peters 1983) language acquisition among modern human infants universally exhibits single-unit and dual-unit stages, each usually of several months' duration. It seems asking a lot to suppose that the language-using and language-interpreting capacities of early hominids would have exceeded the capacities of modern 1–2-year-olds, as they would have had to do in order to interpret holistic utterances.

The question 'What could the first utterance have been like?' is actually asked in the title of Whiten (1993) (although it remains unanswered in the subsequent text). Let us therefore try partially to answer it by considering what the first utterance could *not* have been like in terms of content. Take the 'gossip' proposal of Dunbar—how could gossip be possible if a large (and relatively abstract) vocabulary did not already exist? How interesting or useful would be the kind of gossip that could be exchanged with a vocabulary in the single digits? Yet such must have been the vocabulary of the earliest stages of language. To discuss the doings of fellow group members at even the most basic, trivial level, one would require quite a considerable vocabulary, one that would contain a number of proper nouns (names of fellow group-members), a number of abstract expressions conveying feelings ('loves', 'dislikes', 'is angry at') and a number of temporal expressions ('yesterday', 'this morning', 'often') as well as concrete nouns ('meat', 'nuts') and action words ('give', 'mate with', 'fight'), as an absolute minimum. Without such an armoury, gossip would prove impossible.

In fact, nobody has even tried so far to build a detailed scenario showing exactly *how* language could have evolved from social intelligence, including a statement of what the earliest utterances might have been, or how they could have served any social function, yet still have been both utterable and comprehensible. The initial plausibility of a social origin for language has been seen as so overwhelming that while a number of proposals have been made in general terms, not one of these proposals has taken on the humble task of working out just what initial words and expressions their scenario entails (of course the actual first words are probably unknowable in principle, but we could at least check scenario plausibility in this way). Even this brief review suggests that the task may well prove an impossible one. Certainly, as will be shown in sect. 10.6, there are forms of interaction in which, much more plausibly, the kinds of minimal utterance inescapable in the early years of language could have been made and readily understood.

10.5   Cheapness of Tokens

Words are cheap, and primates are quick to gain any advantage that can be obtained by cheating. This has led Deacon (1997), Knight (1998), Power (1998), and others to speculate as to how things as easy to produce and as easy to use deceptively as words could ever have come to be relied upon. As Knight points out (1998: 81), '"Machiavellian" primate politics . . . prompts mistrustful listeners to resist all signals except those whose veracity can be *instantly and directly corroborated*' (emphasis added). But in Power's words (1998: 114–15),

How does the listener know that the information is reliable? By definition, she is not gaining any benefit from listening unless she is acquiring information she would not otherwise acquire . . . If the veracity of a signal cannot be corroborated in the immediate context by the listener, the information has to be taken on trust . . . any evolutionary account of language must explain why the volitional signalling of speech is in general assumed by listeners to be intentionally honest—in direct con-travention of the expectations of the Machiavellian intelligence theory of tactical deception.

The point that these authors raise is indeed an extremely important one, and, as they correctly state, one that any valid theory of language evolution must take into account. One does not have to agree with their solutions, which are somewhat elaborate and require us to make assumptions about hominid behaviour for which we have no empirical evidence, in order to accept the crucial nature of the credibility issue. For if linguistic communica-tion was inherently untrustworthy, how could it have spread and become universal among the species? This could have happened only if, in the earli-est stage of protolanguage, there existed means by which the truthfulness (or otherwise) of any given utterance could be quickly and efficiently tested.

The fact that such testing is exceedingly difficult in any kind of social con-text constitutes yet another argument against embedding the initial emer-gence of linguistic behaviour in social intelligence *per se*. Even if we assume that protolanguage's earliest users could have strung together enough sym-bolic units to yield meaningful social messages, how could those messages have been checked? If they could not be checked, why should they have been believed?

However, the section that follows shows that, if the initial impetus for a protolanguage came from environmental rather than social stimuli, all the problems discussed in previous sections can be resolved.

10.6 An Ecology-Based Theory of Protolanguage Origins

In sect. 10.1 it was argued that for a unique development to become fixed, a unique selective pressure had to be present. There is no evidence that the social life of our earliest ancestors differed in any way from that of other closely related primates, except to the extent that their ecology differed—a factor bound to impact on their social lives. For instance, *contra* Dunbar (1993, 1996), there is no empirical evidence for any increase in hominid group size: this is supported only by a claimed correlation between brain-size and group-size based on extrapolation from a narrow range of much smaller primate brain sizes.

However, there is abundant evidence that hominid ecology *did* differ from that of other primates: our ancestors lived on open savannahs or in marginal woodlands rather than in deep forest, and they were primarily terrestrial rather than primarily arboreal. An even sharper distinction relates to an ecological niche occupied from the time of the Olduwan industry (approx. 2.3 million years ago) onwards. According to Binford (1985), hominids became principally scavengers and were able to compete with other scavengers and predators for the carcasses of large animals across a wide range of habitats (Blumenschine *et al.*1994), since stone tools with a cutting edge allowed early access to the flesh of thick-skinned mammals. Moreover, there are abundant indications that hominids were locating carcasses *before* other scavengers, often leaving little but bare bones for their many competitors (Monahan 1996: 116–17).

How did hominids succeed against fierce competition? Not, surely, by wandering round like a troop of baboons and eating what they happened to stumble on. They must have been able to (1) locate fresh carcasses with extreme certainty and rapidity, and (2) fight off competitors, probably with barrages of flung rocks. The second would require a fairly large group, but such a group would have been inefficient for scouting carcasses because it could not cover as much ground as several smaller groups. It seems highly likely that hominids capitalized on the fission–fusion model of foraging found among chimpanzees and scouted in small (single-digit) subgroups, coming together as a full (double-digit) group to exploit finds. But how could subgroups report on their findings, and if two subgroups both made finds, how could they decide which to exploit?

In such a context, the crudest beginnings of some form of language would have paid off from day one. Any hominid group capable of discriminating food sources (and perhaps also of indicating the relative dangers involved in their exploitation) would have enjoyed an advantage over other hominid groups. Note that the first linguistic communications need not have been monomodal, nor need their units have been arbitrary in the Saussurean sense. Directional gesturing with the hand, accompanied by the imitation of the noise made by a mammoth, could easily have been interpreted as meaning 'Come this way, there's a dead mammoth' ('dead' need not have been explicitly mentioned, for no hominid in his right mind would encourage others to come and see a live mammoth). Although the two symbolic units (the 'come' gesture and the 'mammoth' noise) might seem disjoint— two separate, single-symbol utterances, like the one-word utterances of to 15–18-months-old humans—they could easily have been reinterpreted (just as infant utterances at the one-word stage can often be reinterpreted predicatively, Bloom 1973) as '[dead] mammoth thataway', in other words, as the first true predication. And as pointed out above, predication—focusing on something, then making a comment about that something—is one of the most basic characteristics of human language, one that clearly distinguishes it from all other animal systems.[1]

Such an utterance, and others like it, would avoid all the problems discussed in sects. 10.4 and 10.5. On the one hand, unlike the kinds of social message possible with only a handful of symbols they would have been immediately functional: with a minimum of units they could convey messages regarding the location and nature of available food supplies that would have a direct and immediate impact on the survival of those who heard and correctly interpreted those messages. On the other hand, unlike social messages that would have been hard if not impossible to verify, such messages would have been almost immediately testable. When a band member stated 'Mammoth thataway', there either was a dead mammoth thataway, or there wasn't; within a matter of hours, or even minutes, group members would know the truth or otherwise of the message. This would serve to discourage deceptive messages—one can imagine how the rest of the band would react to a member who led them on some wild goose chase—while repeated incidents in which words, though cheap, were proved reliable would have built up a large measure of trust in this new source of information, so that later, when it began to be used for social ends, there would have been a predisposition to believe what one heard, unless one had good reason to doubt it.

Other common situations in hominid ecology would also have benefited from this minimal kind of protolanguage. In sect. 10.2 we noted the ignorance and indifference to the signs of nature that highly socially intelligent primates evince. Such ignorance and indifference would often have proved fatal to our ancestors, more heavily threatened as they were by predators. Note that under these circumstances (and perhaps only under these circumstances) units from pre-linguistic communication systems might have been absorbed into the protolinguistic system; Cheney and Seyfarth (1990: 144–9) have shown that, whether or not such calls come under limbic con-

---

[1] One anonymous referee feared that such a system, like bee language, might remain irrevocably mired in food information, and could never expand to embrace other topics. However, while bee language is a biological adaptation (and therefore unalterable by individual bees), protolanguage required no specific adaptation (it was cobbled together from pre-existing capacities), and therefore, like full language, it had no genetic restrictions on what it can (potentially) represent, and its inventory of symbols could be expanded to represent anything its users needed to represent.

trol, their utterance is subject to voluntary modification. Assume that some ancestral species had warning calls that related to major predators, as vervet alarm calls do today. Such calls (perhaps with a different inflection), if coupled with pointing at a python-track, pawprint, bloodstain, or other indication of a possible nearby predator, could very likely have been understood as a warning that did not require immediate reaction, but rather a heightened awareness and preparedness for action.

A further function of such a protolanguage might well have been instruction of the young. Given a choice between leaving offspring to discover natural dangers for themselves (and perhaps perish in consequence) or informing them in advance of signs and situations to avoid, any species that invested its future in small numbers of offspring would opt for the latter. Indeed, it is hard to think of any mechanism that would act more decisively towards achieving the genes' goal of self-perpetuation.

10.7 Conclusion

The foregoing considerations suggest that an origin for protolanguage stemming directly from social intelligence and its various uses is relatively unlikely. More probable is an origin deriving from various interactions with the environment—exchange of information gleaned in foraging, interpretation of natural signs, warning of the young against dangers. Any attempt to reconstruct earliest origins must, in the present state of our knowledge, involve the telling of just-so stories—but not all just-so stories are equal, they range from the plausible to the wildly improbable, and where facts run out the best we can do is try to judge amongst such stories in the light of what we do know about prehistory.

None of the above in any way implies a reduction of the role that social intelligence undoubtedly played as soon as protolanguage became established, or the vastly important contributions that such use made to the development of both protolanguage and full human language; these contributions have already been acknowledged elsewhere (Calvin and Bickerton 2000). Moreover, only in a species with a richly developed social intelligence, and with at least some beginnings of a theory of mind and a capacity for intentional communication between group members, could language or even protolanguage ever have developed. But no matter how powerful the social precursors and prerequisites, and how vital the subsequent social uses, these still do not require that the initial spark for protolanguage had to spring directly from social intelligence.

We must beware too of the Fallacy of First Use; the fact that language is most often used nowadays for social purposes does not, *contra* Dunbar (1993, 1996), in any way entail that it originated for such use. Computers provide an illuminating analogy. When these were first built and used, it was believed that their only function would be to carry out complex statistical calculations for government agencies; nobody foresaw that within fifty years they would prove to be preadapted for a variety of completely different functions, from e-mail to video-games to commerce. Like the computer, language is not 'for' this function or that function; it is an all-purpose tool, as efficient for lying as for telling the truth, as good at imparting practical information or conducting logical argument as it is for flattering our friends, insulting our enemies, and manipulating others to suit our own ends. Yet if it had not contributed directly to our physical survival, it might never have been.

FURTHER READING

On hominid ecology:

FOLEY, R. (1987), *Another Unique Species: Patterns in Human Evolutionary Ecology* (London: Longman).

MONAHAN, C. M. (1996), 'New Zooarchaeological Data from Bed II, Olduvain Gorge, Tanzania: Implications for Hominid Behavior in the Early Pleistocene', *Journal of Human Evolution*, 31: 93–128.

On language and social intelligence:

HURFORD, J. R., STUDDERT-KENNEDY, M., and KNIGHT, C. (1998) (eds.), *Approaches to the Evolution of Language* (Cambridge: Cambridge University Press).

On the emergence of protolanguage:

BICKERTON, D. (1990), *Language and Species* (Chicago: University of Chicago Press).

CALVIN, W., and BICKERTON, D. (2000), *Lingua ex Machina: Reconciling Darwin and Chomsky with the Human Brain* (Cambridge, Mass.: MIT Press).

REFERENCES

BATALI, J. (1998), 'Computational Simulations of the Emergence of Grammar', in Hurford *et al.* (1998: 405–26).

BICKERTON, D. (1990), *Language and Species* (Chicago: University of Chicago Press).

——(1998), 'Catastrophic Evolution: The Case for a Single Step from Protolanguage to Full Human Language', in Hurford *et al.* (1998: 341–58).

BINFORD, L. S. (1985), 'Human Ancestors: Changing Views of their Behavior', *Journal of Anthropological Archaeology*, 4: 292–327.

BLOOM, L. (1973), *One Word at a Time: The Use of Single-Word Utterances Before Syntax* (The Hague: Mouton).

BLUMENSCHINE, R. J., CAVALLO, J. A., and CAPALDO, S. P. (1994), 'Competition for Carcases and Early Hominid Behavioral Ecology', *Journal of Human Evolution*, 27: 197–214.

BYRNE, R. W., and WHITEN, A. (1985), 'Tactical Deception of Familiar Individuals in Baboons', *Animal Behavior*, 33: 669–73.

—— —— (1992), 'Cognitive Evolution in Primates: Evidence from Tactical Deception', *Man*, 27: 609–27.

CALVIN, W., and BICKERTON, D. (2000), *Lingua ex Machina: Reconciling Darwin and Chomsky with the Human Brain* (Cambridge, Mass.: MIT Press).

CARSTAIRS-McCARTHY, A. (1999), *The Origins of Complex Language* (Oxford: Oxford University Press).

CHENEY, D. L., and SEYFARTH, R. M. (1990), *How Monkeys See the World* (Chicago: University of Chicago Press).

DARWIN, C. (1871), *The Descent of Man, and Selection in Relation to Sex*, 2nd edn. (New York: Appleton).

DEACON, T. (1997), *The Symbolic Species: The Co-evolution of Language and the Brain* (New York: W. W. Norton).

DUNBAR, R. I. M. (1993), 'Coevolution of Neocortical Size, Group Size and Language in Humans', *Behavioral and Brain Sciences*, 16: 681–735.

——(1996), *Grooming, Gossip and the Evolution of Language* (London: Faber & Faber).

——(1998), 'Theory of Mind and the Evolution of Language', in Hurford *et al.* (1998: 92–110).

FOLEY, R. (1987), *Another Unique Species: Patterns in Human Evolutionary Ecology* (London: Longmans).

GALLUP, G. G. (1982), 'Self-Awareness and the Emergence of Mind in Primates', *American Journal of Primatology*, 2: 237–48.

GARDNER, R. A., and GARDNER, B. T. (1969), 'Teaching Sign Language to a Chimpanzee', *Science*, 165: 664–72.

GIBSON, K. R. (1993), 'Tool Use, Language and Social Behavior in Relationship to Information Processing Capacities', in K. R. Gibson and T. Ingold (eds.), *Tools, Language and Cognition in Human Evolution* (Cambridge: Cambridge University Press), 251–71.

GOODALL, J. (1986), *The Chimpanzees of Gombe: Patterns of Behavior* (Cambridge, Mass.: Harvard University Press).

GREENFIELD, P., and SAVAGE-RUMBAUGH, E. S. (1990), 'Grammatical Combination in *Pan paniscus*: Processes of Learning and Invention in the Evolution and Development of Language', in S. Parker and K. Gibson (eds.), *'Language' and Intelligence in Monkeys and Apes: Comparative Developmental Perspectives* (Cambridge: Cambridge University Press).

HAUSER, M. (1996), *The Evolution of Communication* (Cambridge, Mass.: MIT Press).

HEYES, C. M. (1998),'Theory of Mind in Nonhuman Primates', *Behavioral and Brain Sciences*, 21: 101–48.

HUMPHREY, N. K. (1976), 'The Social Function of Intellect', in P. P. G. Bateson and R. A. Hinde (eds.), *Growing Points in Ethology* (Cambridge: Cambridge University Press), 303–17.

HURFORD, J. R., STUDDERT-KENNEDY, M., and KNIGHT, C. (1998) (eds.), *Approaches to the Evolution of Language: Social and Cognitive Bases* (Cambridge: Cambridge University Press).

JESPERSEN, O. (1922), *Language: Its Nature, Development and Origin* (New York: H. Holt).

JOLLY, A. (1991),'Conscious Chimpanzees? A Review of Recent Literature', in C. R. Ristau (ed.), *Cognitive Ethology: The Minds of Other Animals* (Hillsdale, NJ: Lawrence Erlbaum).

KING, B. J. (1994), *The Information Continuum* (Santa Fe: SAR Press).

KIRBY, S. (2000),'Syntax Without Natural Selection: How Compositionality Emerges from Vocabulary in a Population of Learners', in Knight *et al.* (2000: 303–23).

KNIGHT, C. (1998),'Ritual/Speech Coevolution: A Solution to the Problem of Deception', in Hurford *et al.* (1998: 68–91).

——STUDDERT-KENNEDY, M., and HURFORD, J. (eds.) (2000), *The Evolutionary Emergence of Language: Social Function and the Origins of Linguistic Form* (Cambridge: Cambridge University Press).

VAN LAWICK-GOODALL, J. (1971), *In the Shadow of Man* (New York: Dell).

LEWIS, M. E. (1997),'Carnivorean Paleoguilds of Africa: Implications for Hominid Food Procurement Strategies', *Journal of Human Evolution*, 32: 257–88.

McHENRY, H. M. (1994), 'Behavioral Ecological Implications of Early Hominid Body Size', *Journal of Human Evolution*, 27: 77–88.

MONAHAN, C. M. (1996),'New Zooarchaeological Data from Bed II, Olduvai Gorge, Tanzania: Implications for Hominid Behavior in the Early Pleistocene', *Journal of Human Evolution*, 31: 93–128.

PARKER, S. T., and GIBSON, K. R. (1979),'A Developmental Model for the Evolution of Language and Intelligence in Early Hominids', *Behavioral and Brain Sciences*, 2: 367–408.

PETERS, A. (1983), *Units of Language Acquisition* (Cambridge: Cambridge University Press).

POVINELLI, D. J. (1994),'Comparative Studies of Animal Mental State Attribution: A Reply to Heyes', *Animal Behavior*, 48: 239–41.

POWER, C. (1998), 'Old Wives' Tales: The Gossip Hypothesis and the Reliability of Cheap Signals', in Hurford *et al.* (1998: 111–29).

PREMACK, D. (1971), 'Language in Chimpanzee?', *Science*, 172: 808–22.

SAVAGE-RUMBAUGH, E. S. (1986), *Ape 'Language': From Conditioned Response to Symbol* (New York: Columbia University Press).

SCHALLER, G. B. (1963), *The Year of the Gorilla* (New York: Ballantyne).

SMUTS, B. (1987) (ed.), *Primate Societies* (Chicago: University of Chicago Press).

STRUM, S. C. (1987), *Almost Human: A Journey into the World of Baboons* (New York: Norton).

TERRACE, H. S., PETITTO, L. A., SANDERS, R. J., and BEVER, T. G. (1979), 'Can an Ape Create a Sentence?', *Science*, 206: 891–900.

TREVES, A., and NAUGHTON-TREVES, L. (1999), 'Risk and Opportunity for Humans Co-existing with Large Carnivores', *Journal of Human Evolution*, 36: 275–82.

DE WAAL, F. B. M. (1982), *Chimpanzee Politics: Power and Sex among Apes* (London: Cape).

——(1989), *Peacemaking among Primates* (Cambridge, Mass.: Harvard University Press).

——(1996), *Good Natured: The Origin of Right and Wrong in Humans and Other Animals* (Cambridge, Mass.: Harvard University Press).

WHITEN, A. (1993), 'What Could the First Linguistic Utterance Have Been Like?', *Current Anthropology*, 34: 45–6.

——and BYRNE, R. W. (1988), 'The Machiavellian Intelligence Hypothesis', in R. W. Byrne and A. Whiten (eds.), *Machiavellian Intelligence* (Oxford: Oxford University Press).

WILSON, E. O. (1972), 'Animal Communication', in W. S.-Y. Wang (ed.), *The Emergence of Language: Development and Evolution* (New York: Freeman), 3–15.

WORDEN, R. P. (1998), 'The Evolution of Language from Social Intelligence', in Hurford *et al.* (1998: 148–66).

WRAY, A. (1998), 'Protolanguage as a Holistic System for Social Interaction', *Language and Communication*, 18: 47–67.

——(2000), 'Holistic Utterances in Protolanguage: The Link from Primates to Humans', in Knight *et al.* (2000: 285–302).

11   Methodological Issues in Simulating the Emergence of Language

BRADLEY TONKES AND JANET WILES

11.1 Introduction

One of the features that differentiates language from other forms of communication is the ability to communicate a greater number of meanings than there are basic signals in the repertoire of the speaker. In human languages syntactic and morphosyntactic constructions allow combinations of simpler elements to express complex meanings. With advances in computational techniques it has become possible to model some of the processes by which populations of communicating agents come to agree on a convention for combining smaller linguistic elements into larger ones.

An interesting idea to emerge from computational studies of this issue is that the dynamics of language transmission (i.e. the process through which speakers of a language teach it to the next generation) may be responsible for some of the phenomena that have been solely attributed to an innate linguistic competence. The proposed hypothesis is that languages adapt to become more easily acquired by their learners and that this process of adaptation may be responsible for some of the observed constraints on cross-linguistic variation (Kirby 1999). Thus, syntactic conventions are partly determined by the process of linguistic transmission, rather than simply reflecting an underlying innate grammatical competence.

A major goal of the computational modelling research is to determine the conditions under which syntactic conventions can be established in a population. That is, to determine when language-like systems of communication (i.e. those that combine simpler elements to form larger constructions) can emerge. Humans are alone in their use of structured communication. Which aspects of human brain organization and human social organization allowed humans to make the advance beyond the signalling systems found in other species? A secondary goal is to determine the types of structural conventions that can be established in a population. The set of human languages constitutes the only examples that are evident in the real world. However, it is unknown which aspects of this set of languages are inevitable emergent properties and which are idiosyncratically human.

Batali (1998) has demonstrated the emergence of rudimentary syntactic structures in a population of communicating neural networks. Batali was able to show how, despite the absence of a sophisticated, innate linguistic competence in the networks, the population converged on a language with compositional characteristics. Are there other reasons for the emergence of compositional structures? An alternative candidate explanation is the language transmission dynamic itself. Kirby (forthcoming) has extended Batali's work by showing how compositional structures may be a result of a language transmission dynamic. As languages are passed from one generation to the next, they are filtered through the learning experience. Importantly, the learning experience acts as a bottleneck since a language learner can never observe every sentence in the language. Kirby argues that a consequence of this bottleneck is a pressure for languages to evolve towards forms that are easy generalizable by learners, and he presents some intriguing simulations to demonstrate his point.

It is worth emphasizing at this stage that the goal of this research is not necessarily to determine the particular properties of humans that give rise to every facet of *human* languages. Humans are amazingly complex beings who cannot be modelled accurately, and it is not feasible to separate those aspects that are important for structured communication from those that are coincidental. Rather, the long-term goal of the research is to establish the conditions under which language-like systems *in general* can emerge, and the range of properties that such systems exhibit. While achieving this goal will not inform us of how every feature of human language came to be, it will shed light on the necessary and sufficient conditions for structured communications systems to emerge, of which human languages are but a subset. It will also be informative about the general properties of structured communication systems, such as whether they are necessarily compositional.

Kirby's simulations, like all computational models, consider an idealized system. Consequently, although Kirby shows that a language-learning evolutionary dynamic is sufficient to evolve a learnable language under a particular set of circumstances, the generality of his results is open to debate. For computational models such as Kirby's, it is important to establish the features of the abstraction that lead to the observed results. That is, we should strive to understand the parts of the abstraction that are required, those which are superfluous, and those that must be constrained to a critical range of values.

In this chapter we explore Kirby's simulations in greater detail. Kirby credited his results to the 'learning bottleneck' but didn't examine variations in learners, tasks, or parameters. His choice of language learning mechanism was based on a learning algorithm that had been previously used in computational linguistics. The choice of semantic domain was constrained so as to have combinatorial structure. The question we consider is whether the learning bottleneck is the primary factor when a different kind of learning mechanism and a differently structured semantic domain are adopted.

In previous work, we have considered communication between a pair of agents that try to communicate a meaning, represented by a value between 0 and 1, using an utterance composed of a sequence of symbols. For each meaning one agent produces an utterance which the other receives and processes back into a meaning. Using this framework, we have shown how a language can evolve to mediate the different computational demands of sender and receiver (Tonkes, Blair, and Wiles 1999), and how language evolution can facilitate learning by adapting towards the forms that exploit the weak biases of a general purpose learner (Tonkes, Blair, and Wiles 2000). It is this communication task that we incorporate into Kirby's population model in the simulations presented in this chapter.

In sect. 11.2 we review Kirby's simulations in greater detail and raise issues related to his learning mechanism that we believe are crucial for his results. His learning mechanisms looked for common substrings and inferred generalized rules for generating them. We believe that this assumption is unnecessarily strong, and that a weaker assumption can be tested in an alternative framework. In sect. 11.3 we present our alternative framework and highlight the similarities and differences to Kirby's, particularly the learner, the differently structured domain, and the parameters. These simulations are performed by varying two parameters: the amount of training data supplied to the learners (the size of the bottleneck), and the size of the population. The results of these simulations, presented in sect. 11.4, reveal that the training corpus size has a significant impact on the communicative accuracy in the population, while changes to the size of the population merely alter the rate at which change occurs. Section 11.5 provides an analysis of why the results vary across changes in these parameters. In sect. 11.6 we report a further exploration of how Kirby's results depend upon experimental conditions, in which we varied aspects of the learning environment.

11.2 Kirby Revisited

Kirby (2000) presents a compelling demonstration of the emergence of grammar in the absence of any phylogenetic adaptation. A population of ten language-users, modelled as context-free grammars, are arranged in a ring so that each individual has two neighbours. Individuals are capable of talking about simple meanings (agent/action/patient tuples) using strings produced from a restricted alphabet of five symbols. While individuals are equipped with a learning mechanism, the initial population has no vocabulary and no grammar. That is, the initial population consists of a mechanism for *acquiring* language, but no language to acquire.

To bootstrap the system, Kirby introduces the notion of random invention: if an individual wants to talk about a particular meaning but has no way of expressing that meaning, it either says nothing or, with small probability, produces a random string. The course of a simulation runs as follows.

1. Replace a randomly chosen individual with a new individual.

2. Produce a corpus of training examples from the utterances produced by the new individual's neighbours.

3. The new individual induces a new grammar based on this corpus. During this training phase, the learner is presented with both the utterance *and its intended meaning*, whereas, during normal (i.e. post-training) operation, only the utterance is presented. The learner is thus required to generalize the relationship between utterances and meanings from the subset of observed examples.

4. Return to step (1).

At the start of a simulation run, the training corpora are typically small and contain examples that are more or less random. That is, there is no systematic relationship between utterance and meaning. Gradually, the training corpora become larger as each individual's grammar becomes more expressive. After a period of time, individuals start to *regularize* their grammars in a compositional manner using common substrings for common parts of a meaning. For example, a meaning such as (*mary, john, likes*) may correspond to an utterance such as 'marylikesjohn' while a meaning such as (*mary, fred, likes*) may correspond to an utterance such as 'marylikesfred'. Eventually, the population comes to use a fully compositional language where every utterance can be broken into subcomponents, each representing a part of the meaning tuple.

Kirby deliberately chose the size of the training corpora so that it was highly unlikely that an individual would be exposed to the full set of *(meaning, utterance)* pairs. That is, the only way that an agent could acquire a complete grammar was to generalize from a limited subset of exemplars. Kirby hypothesizes that it was this feature of the simulations—the learning bottleneck—that caused the fundamental shift in the languages produced, from non-compositional to compositional.

If meanings and utterances are randomly associated, then there is nothing on which to base a generalization mechanism. An unobserved association is therefore unlearned. Conversely, with a systematic relationship between meanings and utterances, it is possible to generalize from a limited set of observed exemplars. This dichotomy, Kirby argues, introduces a 'glossogenetic' selection pressure for languages that can be expressed by a few general purpose rules that can be induced from a smaller set of examples. For these languages, it is not necessary to see every *(meaning, utterance)* pair, rather, the language is learnable from any subset of exemplars from which the general rules can be derived.

Although there is no phylogenetic adaptation during the course of Kirby's simulations, the model incorporates phylogenetic adaptation implicitly in the design of the individuals' language-learning mechanisms. That is, the starting point of the simulations is a population of individuals that are innately endowed with a particular learning mechanism. It seems to us that the chosen induction algorithm is highly biased towards language-like, compositional structures, which is perhaps not surprising given that the algorithm was originally developed for computational linguistics. Although Kirby highlights the importance of languages themselves being systems that adapt to their human hosts, inherent in his choice of learning algorithm is a strong form of language-specific learning bias.

11.3   Methodology

The design of the simulations in this chapter owe much to previous work. The overall dynamic of linguistic interactions, outlined above, is taken from

Kirby's (2000) work. The linguistic agents are of the same type used by Batali (1998) and the semantic domain is one that we have used in previous work (Tonkes *et al.* 2000). While we present here an overview of the simulation design, the interested reader is directed to the original sources for a more in-depth treatment.

11.3.1 *Something to Talk About*

Whereas in Kirby's original simulations, the agents attempted to communicate simple predicates denoting agent, action, and patient (who did what to whom), in our simulations we use a much simpler semantic domain. Meanings are represented as values between 0 and 1, which for simplicity are restricted to 100 values of 0.01 increments (i.e. 0.00, 0.01, 0.02, . . ., 0.99). These meanings are numerically related so that is possible to measure the similarity of two meanings by taking their numeric difference (for example, 0.00 is more similar to 0.01 than it is to 0.30). It thus makes sense to introduce the notion of degrees of understanding, rather than deciding that an utterance has been either 'understood' or 'not understood'. To this end, the domain lends itself to a convenient way of measuring communicative error, which we will take to be the squared difference between the meaning intended by the sender and the meaning as interpreted by the receiver.[1] The similarity between items in this space is analogous to similarity between real-world items. For example, the similarity between red and pink may be analogous to the similarity between 0.40 and 0.50. However, we are trying to model the similarity structure between items rather than the labels attributed to particular items. The model may thus be interpreted as an abstract conception of the similarity amongst meanings in a semantic domain.

11.3.2 *Communicative agents*

As noted earlier, our communicative agents are modelled as simple recurrent networks (SRNs) of the same type as those used by Batali (1998, see the enlarged section in Fig. 11.1). SRNs (Elman 1990) are a type of neural network that are particularly well suited to sequential tasks such as language

---

[1] For example, if the sender tries to communicate the meaning 0.45 which the receiver (mistakenly) understands as 0.65, then the communicative error for that interaction is $(0.45-0.65)^2=0.04$.

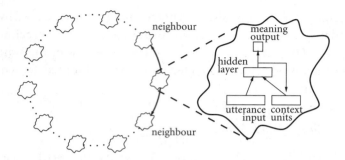

Fig. 11.1 A population of communicating agents. Each agent is modelled by a simple recurrent network and can communicate with two neighbours so that the population forms a ring. The operation of the SRN shown in the enlarged section can be described as follows. Each of the blocks represents a set of simple processing units whose activations are determined by both the activations of the processing units in the previous layer and the strengths of the connections between them (also called 'weights'). The process by which activations flow from the utterance inputs to the output is known as propagation. The activations of the utterance inputs are determined externally by an incoming utterance which is received one symbol at a time. The activations of the context units are copied from the activations of the units in the hidden layer after each symbol is processed. These units are used to provide the network with a working memory and are the characteristic feature of the SRN. The hidden units may be viewed as an internal working space. The meaning that the SRN associates with the utterance is read off the single output unit after the final symbol in the utterance has been propagated through the network.

processing, where they have demonstrated some impressive results (Elman 1991). SRNs can be trained to associate a sequence of patterns (in this case, an utterance that is a sequence of symbols) with an output pattern (in this case, a meaning value).[2]

In previous work (Tonkes *et al.* 1999, 2000), we have differentiated between senders (those agents that generate utterances from meanings) and receivers (those agents that recreate meanings from utterances). For this chapter we use an alternative approach first introduced by Batali, where the same network is used for both sending and receiving. SRNs are not normally capable of such dual-mode operation, so to achieve the desired behaviour,

---

[2] For the simulations in this chapter, we used the back-propagation-through-time algorithm (Rumelhart *et al.* 1986) with a learning rate of 0.01 and a momentum term of 0.9.

Batali used networks that were designed to be receivers and applied a special operation to make them capable of sending (for this reason, Fig. 11.1 shows only a receiving network). The operation that Batali applied is known as an 'obverter' procedure (Oliphant and Batali 1996). The essential idea is that to communicate some meaning M, an agent searches for an utterance U such that if the agent itself were to hear U, it would interpret it as meaning M. (That is, the agent tries to work out the inverse of its own receive function.) Note that understanding the precise mechanics of the obverter procedure is unnecessary for understanding the remainder of the chapter.

Similar to both Batali and Kirby, the utterances themselves consist of sequences of up to six symbols which are taken from an alphabet of four letters. Following common neural network practice, the symbols are represented as four-dimensional binary vectors $[1, 0, 0, 0]$, $[0, 1, 0, 0]$, $[0, 0, 1, 0]$ and $[0, 0, 0, 1]$ which we denote A, B, C, and D respectively. These vectors are used as the activations for the utterance input units in Fig. 11.1.

The communication of a meaning from sender to receiver might proceed in the following manner:

1. The sender decides to communicate a value such as 0.43.

2. Using the obverter procedure outlined earlier, the sender determines the sequence of no more than six symbols (an utterance) that it understands as the best approximation to 0.43. In this example the sender might understand ACDBA to mean 0.41, which is the closest approximation it can find.

3. The utterance, ACDBA, is sent to the receiver.

4. The activations of the processing units of the receiver are initialized to zero so that there is no memory of previous utterances. The vectors of activation values corresponding to each symbol in the utterance are propagated through the receiver's SRN, one at a time. Each SRN has four utterance input units corresponding to the size of the symbol vectors, five hidden units, and a single output unit used for the interpreted meaning.

5. The meaning as understood by the receiver is read from the activation of the receiver SRN's output, in this case it might be 0.46.

6. The next step depends on whether or not the receiver is being trained.

   (a) If the receiver is in its learning phase then it is informed of the intended meaning. It then uses the discrepancy between the intended meaning (0.43) and the interpreted meaning (0.46) to update the weights between processing units so that future presentations of the utterance ACDBA will tend to be understood as a meaning closer to 0.43. Because of the nature of neural network learning, it may take many presentations of the same training material before the learner makes no errors.

(b) If the receiver is not being trained then it is unaware of the intended meaning. It is possible, however, for an external observer to measure the squared communicative error, $(0.43-0.46)^2=0.0009$.

11.3.3 *Population dynamics*

A population of networks is arranged in a ring so that each individual has two neighbours (Fig. 11.1). Simulations are run for 2,500 time-steps. In each time-step of a simulation, the following sequence of events occurs.

1. Replace a randomly chosen network by a new network. Set the connection strengths of that network to small random values.

2. Create a training corpus by using the new individual's two neighbours to generate a set of utterances corresponding to a randomly chosen set of meanings. The training set contains utterances, as well as their intended meanings, produced by both neighbours.

3. Train the new network on the training corpus using the process outlined earlier. The entire training corpus is presented to the network 1,000 times.

4. Evaluate the *communicative accuracy* of the population in the following way. Every combination of sender and receiver, regardless of location, attempts to communicate the 100 meanings. The squared communicative error for each meaning is summed giving a communicative error score for each (sender, receiver) pair. These scores are then averaged, giving a measure of the average communicative error for the population.

We vary two parameters of the simulations—the size of the training corpus and the size of the population—and consider three variations of these parameters. In the first variation we use a population of ten individuals and a training corpus of ten utterances. The second variation increases the size of the training corpus to twenty while keeping the population size at ten. The third variation increases the size of the population to twenty while keeping the training corpus size at ten. We refer to this set of simulations as series 1 and the three combinations of parameter settings as studies 1A (small population, small corpora), 1B (small population, large corpora), and 1C (large population, small corpora). Importantly, the size of the training corpus is chosen to be always significantly less than the size of the full meaning set. Consequently, networks are required to generalize well beyond the examples in the training corpus to communicate about the full set of meanings.

11.3.4 *Putting It All Together*

In this section we briefly describe what happens during a typical run. The initial population of networks are untrained and generally produce uninteresting languages. Networks are unable to produce enough unique utterances to differentiate every meaning. Typically, networks are only able to produce three or four different strings which are reused for many of the 100 meanings. In almost all cases each unique utterance is used for a single contiguous range of meanings. For example, a network may send DDDD for meanings with values between 0.00 and 0.35, DDBD for meanings with values between 0.36 and 0.65, and DBBB for meanings with values from 0.66 to 0.99. Furthermore, the agents in the population disagree on which utterance corresponds to a given meaning. The average communicative accuracy is consequently very poor and agents have little success even in understanding their own utterances. (The degree to which an agent comprehends its own utterances can be tested by taking two copies of the agent, one which acts as sender, the other as receiver, and measuring their communicative error.)

One of the agents is then replaced with a new individual. The new individual is trained on a set of examples produced by its two neighbours. Since the output of the two neighbours is unrelated, the training data for the new network is likely to be a confusing blend. After training, the new network shares some characteristics of the languages produced by its neighbours and is usually able to understand its own utterances. The communicative accuracy of the newly trained network is typically better than the remainder of the population.

After several agents have been replaced and new ones trained, contiguous sections of the population begin to have reasonably high agreement on which utterances to use for which meanings. The consistency is never perfect, but networks do tend towards using similar strings for a given meaning. Often, one contiguous subset of the population will use one convention for a region of the meaning space, while the remainder of the population will use a different convention. For example agents 1–5 may use AAAB to communicate 0.50 while agents 6–10 use DDDC to communicate the same meaning. At this stage, the vocabulary of the agents expands to around twenty unique utterances. That is, agents are capable of differentiating twenty regions of the meaning space where initially they were able to differentiate only three or four. From this point onwards, the course of the simulation is dependent on the choice of parameters. We elaborate on this point in the next section.

11.4 Base Results

For each of the three combinations of population size and training data parameters, three separate runs of the simulation were performed with different seeds of the random number generator producing different sets of initial weights and different choices of training examples. In all cases, simulations performed under the same parameters yielded qualitatively and quantitatively similar results. The results presented here are based on the communicative accuracy of the populations, averaged across the three trials performed for each set of simulation parameters. The communicative error between a sender and a receiver is determined by the squared error between the meaning intended by the sender and the meaning as understood by the receiver, summed across the 100 possible meanings. The communicative error for the population as a whole is taken to be the average communicative error for every possible combination of sender and receiver. From previous studies, we have determined that a communicative error score of one or less corresponds with acceptable communicative accuracy.

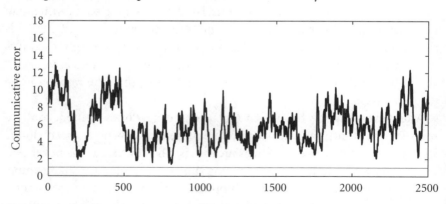

FIG. 11.2 Communicative error over time for a population of ten, using ten examples to train new individuals (study 1A). With these parameters, the population fails to converge on an acceptable language (i.e. one with mean communicative error score lower than threshold at 1.0, shown on the graph).

With a small population size and with small training corpora (study 1A), the populations always failed to reach consensus on a language, as shown in Fig. 11.2. After a brief initial period where communicative error drops quickly, the error increases again. Throughout the course of a run, the communicative accuracy of the population continues to oscillate, and even during the better periods, the populations fail to communicate with an acceptable degree of error. During the initial improvement in accuracy and during subsequent periods of good performance, individual's languages show a reasonable level of agreement with some other members of the population, and there are easily distinguishable families of languages. The populations that are responsible for the periods of high error show little coherence. Although small subsets of the population (two or three individuals) may use languages that are somewhat similar, there is no consensus amongst the population at large.

Keeping the same population size as for the previous study while increasing the amount of training data presented to new agents (study 1B) significantly improves performance (see Fig. 11.3). There is a rapid initial convergence as the population reaches consensus on a language. The languages produced across the population are not identical; however, they are sufficiently similar for accurate communication. While the performance of the population remains on average quite good, there are several transient

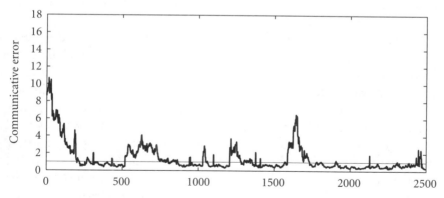

Fig. 11.3 Communicative error over time for a population of ten, using twenty examples to train new individuals (study 1B). Although the population converges to a good language, there are several periods of high error during which two competing languages appear. In these situations the original language may be replaced by a new variant.

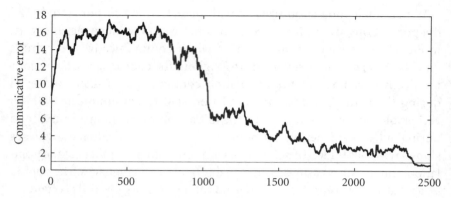

FIG. 11.4 Communicative error over time for a population of twenty, using ten examples to train new individuals (study 1c). The population behaves similarly to that in Fig. 11.3 but on a much slower time-scale. If the population is allowed to run beyond the 2,500 generations shown here, similar intrusions of rogue languages cause intermittent periods of high error.

increases in error. During these periods part of the population uses a completely different language where the population agrees on some regions of the meaning space but not on others. Interestingly, the populations on either side of these transient failures may use languages that are different. That is, following the 'corruption' of the language, the population may reconverge on a different language to the one used previously.

Increasing the population size (study 1c) significantly slows the rate of change of the population (see Fig. 11.4). With the larger population size there is a prolonged period before convergence to an acceptable level of agreement. Indeed, for an initial period the communicative error of the population is substantially higher than at the start. In this region the utterances used by some agents for meanings close to zero are the same as those that other agents use for meanings close to one, and vice versa, giving a worse-than-chance error when they attempt to communicate with one another. Furthermore, under these conditions the population remains unstable in the same way as the case above. Running the simulation for more that 2,500 generations reveals that after the population converges, the same increases in error occur. Moreover, the periods of increased error are of greater duration than those observed in the smaller populations. A representative example of the types of languages found in a population is shown in Table 11.1.

TABLE 11.1 *The utterances used by a neighbourhood of a population for a subset of the meaning space*

Concept	Agent 1	Agent 2	Agent 3	Agent 4	Agent 5	Agent 6
0.00	BBBBBB	BBBBBB	BBBBBB	DDDDDD	DDDDDD	DDDDDD
0.01	BBBBBB	BBBB	BBBBBB	DDDDDD	DDDDDD	DDDDDD
0.02	BBBBBB	BBB	BBB	DDDDD	DDDDDD	DDDDDD
0.03	BBBBBB	BB	BBB	DDDD	DDDDD	DDDDDD
0.04	BBBBBB	BB	BB	DDDB	DDDD	DDDDDD
0.05	BBBBBB	BB	BB	DDD	DDD	DDDDDD
0.06	BBBBBB	B	BB	DDD	DDD	DDDDDD
0.07	BBBBBB	B	B	DDD	DD	DDDDDD
0.08	BBBB	B	B	DDB	DD	DDDDDD
0.09	BBB	B	B	DDB	DD	DDDDDD
0.10	BBB	B	B	DDB	DD	DDDDDD
0.11	BB	B	B	DD	DD	DDDDDD
0.12	BB	B	B	DD	D	DDD
0.13	BB	BDB	B	DD	D	DDD
0.14	BB	BDB	B	DD	D	DD
0.15	BDD	BDB	B	DD	D	DD
0.16	BDD	BDB	BDB	D	D	DD
0.17	BD	BDB	BDB	D	D	DD
0.18	BD	BD	BD	D	D	DD
0.19	BD	BD	BD	D	D	D
0.20	B	BD	BD	DB	D	D
0.21	B	BD	BD	DB	D	D

Note: This small sample shows two competing language forms. Where the first three agents use strings beginning with B for meanings with low numerical values, the other three agents use strings beginning with D. Note that agent 4 shows some familiarities to both families. This example also demonstrates that even within one language family there is significant variability.

11.5 Analysis of Base Results

From observing the change in the languages of the population over time we have been able to conclude that much of the behaviour shown in Figs. 11.2, 11.3, and 11.4, and the differences between them can be attributed to one cause. Namely, that if a learner fails to acquire the language of its neighbours, then nothing prevents that individual teaching its poorly formed language to subsequent learners. The most significant factor in the failure of an individual to learn is the data presented to the learner. If the ten or twenty training examples are chosen poorly (for example, if they are all less than 0.5), it is much harder for the learner successfully to generalize to the remainder of the space. Utterances for similar meanings tend to be similar, so if an agent knows the utterance associated with a meaning such as 0.78 it is more likely to be able to guess the meaning of the utterance associated with 0.75 than it is to guess the meaning of the utterance associated with 0.10.

As the number of training examples increases, the probability of an inadequate sampling of the space diminishes. Hence, the population shown in Fig. 11.2 which uses ten training examples is far less stable than the population shown in Fig. 11.3 which uses twenty training examples. Other factors, such as the initial connection strengths of the learner, may also cause learning failures. However, further simulations (sect. 11.6.1) indicate that the initial weights do not play as significant a role as the distribution of training data.

The differences in time to convergence between Figs. 11.3 and 11.4 can be attributed to greater propagation delays associated with the increase in population size. With a population of ten, individuals are at most five neighbours away from any other individual. Consequently, the speed with which a change in a language can propagate through the entire population is much greater than with the larger population size (twenty). Once a population forms two (or more) distinct languages it also takes a greater time before one comes to dominate. Assuming that the languages are equally learnable, one comes to dominate only through providing a disproportionate number of examples in the training corpora of new individuals. Since there is random selection of which neighbour provides a training example, language dispersal involves a degree of chance. An increase in population size increases the size of the region that must be 'conquered', slowing the dispersal process.

11.6 Varying the Learning Environment

Just as in Kirby's simulations we have seen the emergence of co-ordinated, structured communication as a result of the dynamics of linguistic transmission. While not all Kirby's results have been replicated (we would not expect full replication given the changes made to Kirby's simulation design), we have seen that one of the significant outcomes (structured communication) does replicate with a different learning mechanism and a different semantic domain. We have also seen that a successful outcome can be highly dependent on such factors as the size of the population and the amount of training data available to new individuals. In this section we consider alternative aspects of the learning environment that can influence the outcome of language evolution. The analysis of the first series of simulations indicated that part of the reason why populations could fail to converge was that a single learner with an idiosyncratic language can corrupt future generations. Kirby explicitly sought to simulate language emergence in the absence of selection pressure to explore the power of glossogenetic adaptation alone. Hence, idiosyncrasies could not be eliminated from a language by a mechanism that removed the poorer speakers from the population. Consequently, the three factors that we vary in series 2–4 are chosen for their potential either to prevent learners from failing, or to stop failed learners propagating their half-formed languages.

It is well understood that failures in neural networks to learn a task can often be attributed to the choice of the initial weights (Kolen and Pollack 1990). In simulation series 2, we repeat the simulations of series 1, but instead of generating the initial weights of new individuals randomly, all new individuals start with the *same* weights. In making this change we allow a language to emerge that is learnable from a specific starting point. This technique has proven successful in other work (Tonkes *et al.* 2000; Batali 1994).

Another potential cause of learning failure that we have identified is the selection of training data from which new individuals learn. Learners are presented with a set of *(meaning, utterance)* pairs, where the meaning is a value between 0 and 1. If the selection of meanings in the training sample fails to provide sufficient coverage of the full meaning space, then it is much harder for the learner to generalize to unseen examples as they are dissimilar to the previously seen examples. In simulation series 3, rather than training new learners on different, randomly chosen examples, new learners are trained on the same (randomly chosen) meanings.

In series 4, the variation to series 1 is that we remove the 'neighbourhood' assumption. Instead of using neighbours to provide the training data for new individuals, a 'teacher selection' principle is applied. After every time-step, each individual is given a score based on how well it is understood by the rest of the population (i.e. the portion of error that an individual contributes to the overall error, as plotted in Figs. 11.2, 11.3, and 11.4). This score is used to select which networks generate the examples in a training corpus presented to a learner, based on a proportional selection mechanism (the probability of selection is inversely proportional to error). If a network fails to learn the language of its community then it will be unlikely to be selected to provide examples to train new individuals, thus limiting its impact on future generations.

In summary, the simulations of series 1 (sect. 11.3) are repeated under three different conditions:

1. Using the same set of initial weights for each new learner (series 2: fixed weights).
2. Using the same set of meanings to train each new learner (series 3: fixed examples).
3. Choosing the 'best' networks to generate the training examples for the new learners (series 4: teacher selection).

Again, population size and the training corpus size are varied and the simulations from three different random seeds are repeated under each condition (i.e. we perform studies 2A, 2B, 2C, etc.).

11.6.1 *Results of Varying the Learning Environment*

In all cases, the three repetitions of a condition yielded quantitatively similar results. However, across the conditions, the results varied radically. In the 'fixed weights' condition, the populations rapidly achieved reasonably low communicative error (see Fig. 11.5). This effect may be attributed to the fact that all members of the initial population were identical (having the same, unadjusted connections). However, as in the original series of simulations, the population was unable to maintain this low degree of error and the error fluctuated markedly.

In stark contrast, the populations in the 'fixed examples' condition took longer to converge in each case but showed a remarkable degree of stability (see Fig. 11.6). Although there are some increases in error after the population has apparently converged, the error remains low. Surprisingly, there is no significant difference in the accuracy of the networks when the amount of training data is varied. As before, the C condition results in a slower progression towards the general pattern found in the A condition.

The populations in the 'teacher selection' condition demonstrate yet another pattern of error (see Fig. 11.7). Again, the population rapidly attains

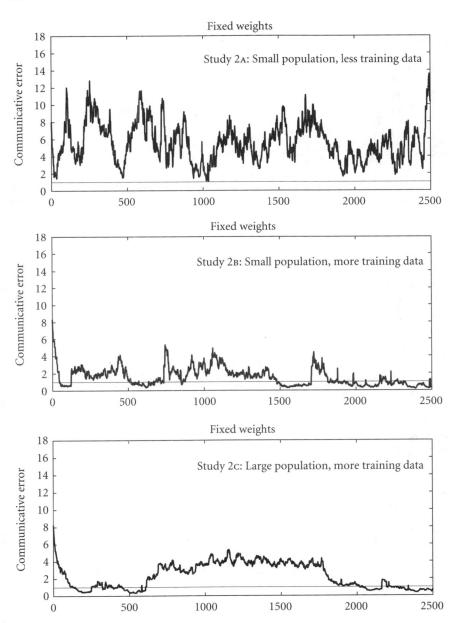

FIG. 11.5 Communicative error of populations over time when new individuals always start from the same initial weights (series 2). Since all individuals are originally identical, the population converges quickly. However, as in sect. 11.4 the population frequently departs from an established convention.

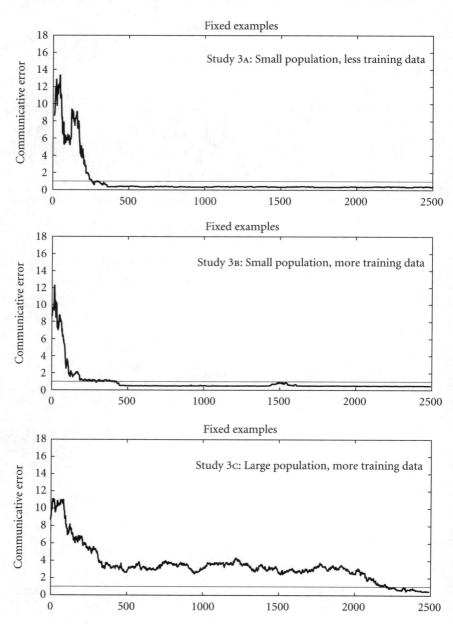

FIG. 11.6 Communicative error of populations over time when new individuals are always trained on the same set of meanings (series 3). In all cases, the population is much more stable than its counterpart in the original simulation. Convergence is still slow for larger populations.

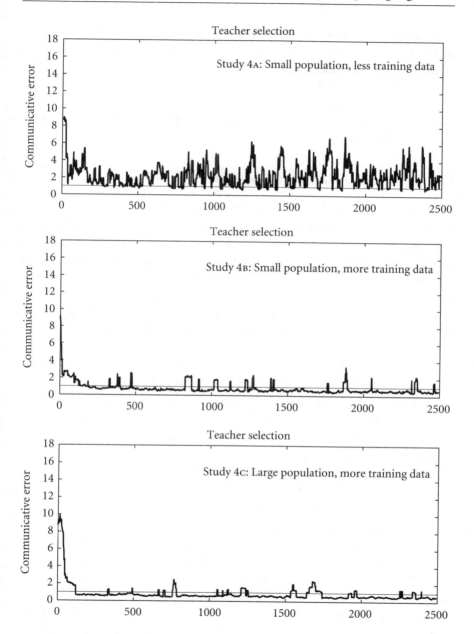

Fig. 11.7 Communicative error of populations over time when new individuals are taught by the better communicators in the population (series 4). Convergence is rapid, even for larger populations. Periods of higher error tend to be transient.

a reasonable degree of communicative accuracy (low error). Any increases in error are very short-lived, far more so than in the original simulations. With a small population and a small amount of training data (study 4A) the population is still unstable, but is much better on average than in the original simulations (Fig. 11.2). Even with a larger size, the population very quickly arrives at a point of low error and tends to remain there, despite the occasional increases in error.

11.6.2 *Analysis of Learning Environments*

Again we performed an analysis of the changes in the population by observing the changes in the languages generated by each population. Apart from the initial improvements in communicative accuracy, the results of the 'fixed weights' populations are effectively the same as in sect. 11.4, indicating that the choice of initial weights is largely irrelevant. Conversely, the performance of populations in the 'fixed examples' condition suggest that the choice of training data is of vital importance. In this condition, only a single training corpus is generated. The probability that this particular corpus is unrepresentative of the meaning space is small, as it is for networks trained in the original simulations. In the original simulations 2,500 different corpora are generated, one for each learner. The probability that some of these corpora are unrepresentative of the meaning space far exceeds the probability that the single corpus in the later simulations is unrepresentative. If, by chance, the single corpus was chosen poorly, we might expect that the population might never be successful. The results of the 'fixed weights' and 'fixed examples' simulations lead us to hypothesize that the populations evolve languages to a point where they are reliably learnable regardless of the initial weights of a network, and that only poorly chosen training samples prevent individuals from learning.

Populations in the 'teacher selection' condition successfully reduced the influence of rogue learners. The impact can be best seen from the length of time that any population experiences high error. Particularly with a population of ten and a training corpus of twenty utterances (study 4B, the middle graph in Fig. 11.7), the length of periods of increased error closely follow the expected lifespan of an individual (10 time-steps on average). This observation suggests that while a rogue learner may lower the communicative error of the population, it does not pass its incompatible language to future generations. Communicative accuracy is thus restored once the rogue learner leaves the population. The effect is much less clear with the smaller training corpus since the probability of multiple successive failed learners is considerably higher. Increases in the number of inconsistent networks in the population increases the probability of further inconsistent networks, hence the instability in this case.

11.7 Discussion and Conclusions

In this final section we consider what correspondences can be drawn between the framework of these studies and characteristics of human language learners and environments. Simulations of populations of communicating simple recurrent networks showed that in favourable circumstances, languages could emerge in the absence of phylogenetic adaptation (sect. 11.4).

Our results demonstrate that one of Kirby's major findings—that a structured communication system can emerge from the dynamics of language transmission—has a generality beyond his original domain. While the kinds of language structures that emerge in our simulations are significantly different to those that emerged from Kirby's simulations, such a result should not be unexpected. The agents will employ the most appropriate structures for their respective communication tasks. Given the structure of the languages produced in our simulations, the results of the simulations may be used to refute claims that classical compositional syntactic structures are the only viable form of linguistic structure. Thus, human languages exhibit compositional structure not because it is the only valid alternative, but because other constraints on human communicative needs (such as the similarity structure of meanings as represented in the human mind) necessitate compositionality.

The effect of manipulating the two parameters in the simulations—population size and training corpus size—suggests some interesting implications for human languages. The results showed that populations converged on languages regardless of the population size, although time to convergence was slowed by the larger population. Conversely, increasing the size of the training corpus (which can be viewed as increasing a learner's exposure to language, perhaps by increasing the critical period) vastly improved the success of populations. While it is not possible to state categorically that the same would be true of human populations, the results suggest an interesting hypothesis for the emergence of human languages.

The modifications to the learning environment made in sect. 11.6 are also suggestive of the desirable conditions for language emergence. The first modification (fixed weights) may be viewed as analogous to a very weak genetic endowment of linguistic knowledge. This modification proved unsuccessful at improving the communicative accuracy of the population. In the second modification (fixed examples), the learning environment is consistent for every individual—every learner has the same set of experiences. With this environment, populations were far more successful at accurate communication. It is not outlandish to suggest that for humans, there is some degree of commonality between learning environments, although no two humans will share the exact same set of experiences.

Preventing failed learners from acting as teachers was also effective in maintaining the language of a population, but still required that learners were given sufficient training data. This condition introduced a selection mechanism, something which Kirby deliberately avoided adding. However, in populations where learners can fail, and then corrupt future learners, our simulations show that some kind of selection mechanism is important to maintain population stability. Such a mechanism may be manifested in a real-world situation by the direction of a learner's attention away from speakers with impaired language abilities, or by the social exclusion of such speakers, so that they do not contribute to learner input to the normal extent (cf. Ragir, this volume).

Although Batali (1998) also used neural networks in his simulations, he did not include any generational component, instead using a static population. In his model, the agents in the population communicate amongst themselves until a consensus is reached. Consequently, after the first round of 'negotiations', agents are no longer naïve about the language of the community, making it difficult to look at changes in the language due to selection pressure for (naïve) learnability. Batali also used a different semantic domain and his population lacked any kind of spatial organization. However, it is interesting to note that Batali's populations were successful in producing basic combinatorial language structures despite the lack of an explicit 'learning bottleneck'—the very mechanism to which Kirby ascribes the success of his simulations. One possible explanation for this disparity is that the learning mechanism itself may provide an implicit bottleneck. One feature of neural networks is their tendency to generalize based on similarity. Consequently, it is much easier for a neural network to learn a regular language than an irregular one; it may even be the case that a neural network will be *unable* to learn some irregular forms. In a series of negotiations, it would thus be expected that the more easily learnable forms (i.e. the regular languages) would persist—networks would compromise on the easier forms. By contrast, in Kirby's simulations, learners were not able to 'forget' associations between meanings and utterances: once a learner acquired an association, it remained for life. Thus, Kirby's learners lack this implicit bottleneck since they will always succeed at finding a grammar that is consistent with the training data.

To provide a comparison between Kirby's explicit bottleneck and the hypothesized implicit bottleneck of the neural network learner, we ran a control study which repeated the first series of simulations (described in sect. 11.3), without removing individuals from the population. Instead, an individual was chosen to be given additional (learning) exposure to the language of its neighbours as in Batali's simulations. With small populations and small training corpus sizes, the population quickly reached a communicative error score of around 1. The languages of these populations were still unstable, although not to the same extent as the population shown in Fig. 11.2. Increasing the amount of training data received in each round resulted in a much more stable population. Even though populations in this condition periodically disagreed, such events were not as catastrophic as those in Fig. 11.3. With a large population and large training corpora, populations were slow to attain reasonable communicative accuracy, much as in Fig. 11.4, though the initial period of very high error was much shorter.

These results, although they are only preliminary, suggest that Kirby's explicit learning bottleneck may not be necessary. Certainly, they indicate that the role of the bottleneck is not as straightforward as Kirby described. Of course, in the case of human languages there clearly is such a bottleneck between generations of learners. Further work may help to determine whether this bottleneck plays a fundamental role, or is merely incidental to the course of language emergence. What seems plausible is a relationship between the implicit bottleneck of the learning mechanism, and the explicit bottleneck in Kirby's simulations.

The major contribution of this chapter is to broaden our ideas of when structured communication systems emerge (and are stable) and when they do not. The chapter also considers the *types* of language structures that emerge from a given situation. Human languages are the only natural example of symbolic structured communication systems that we have. It is difficult to establish the causes for such unique phenomena. Computational models allow us to construct a variety of communication systems and to explore the conditions under which language-like systems can emerge. By examining the conditions under which language does and does not emerge, we can draw conclusions about the significant aspects of the human environment that led to the evolution of human languages. The long-term goal is to deduce the general principles behind the emergence of language and properties of those languages. The work presented in this chapter represents a small step towards that goal.

FURTHER READING

Much of the simulation design used in this chapter was taken from Batali (1998), Kirby (2000), and Tonkes *et al.* (2000).

BATALI, J. (1998), 'Computational Simulations of the Emergence of Grammar', in J. R. Hurford, C. Knight, and M. Studdert-Kennedy (eds.), *Approaches to the Evolution of Language* (Cambridge: Cambridge University Press), 405–26.

ELMAN, J. L. (1991), 'Distributed Representations, Simple Recurrent Networks and Grammatical Structure', *Machine Learning*, 7: 195–224. (The classical introduction to simple recurrent networks with applications for grammatical processing.)

KIRBY, S. (2000), 'Syntax Without Natural Selection: How Compositionality Emerges from Vocabulary in a Population of Learners', in C. Knight, J. R. Hurford, and M. Studdert-Kennedy (eds.), *The Evolutionary Emergence of Language: Social Function and the Origins of Linguistic Form* (Cambridge: Cambridge University Press), 303–23.

STEELS, L. (1997), 'The Synthetic Modeling of Language Origins', *Evolution of Communication*, 1/1: 1–34. (A taxonomy of problems in evolutionary linguistics to which computational approaches have been applied, and a review of the range of different computational approaches.)

TONKES, B., BLAIR, A. D., and WILES, J. (2000), 'Evolving Learnable Languages', in S. A. Solla, T. K. Leen, and K. R. Müller (eds.), *Advances in Neural Information Processing Systems* (Cambridge, Mass.: MIT Press), xii. 66–72.

REFERENCES

BATALI, J. (1994), 'Innate Biases and Critical Periods: Combining Evolution and Learning in the Acquisition of Syntax', in R. Brooks and P. Maes (eds.),

Proceedings of the Fourth Artificial Life Workshop (Cambridge, Mass.: MIT Press), 160–71.

——(1998), 'Computational Simulations of the Emergence of Grammar', in J. R. Hurford, C. Knight, and M. Studdert-Kennedy (eds.), *Approaches to the Evolution of Language: Social and Cognitive Bases* (Cambridge: Cambridge University Press), 405–26.

ELMAN, J. L. (1990), 'Finding Structure in Time', *Cognitive Science*, 14: 179–211.

——(1991), 'Distributed Representations, Simple Recurrent Networks and Grammatical Structure', *Machine Learning*, 7: 195–224.

KIRBY, S. (1999), *Function, Selection, and Innateness* (Oxford: Oxford University Press).

——(2000), 'Syntax Without Natural Selection: How Compositionality Emerges From Vocabulary in a Population of Learners', in C. Knight, J. R. Hurford, and M. Studdert-Kennedy (eds.), *The Evolutionary Emergence of Language: Social Function and the Origins of Linguistic Form* (Cambridge: Cambridge University Press), 303–23.

——(forthcoming), 'Learning, Bottlenecks and the Evolution of Recursive Syntax', in E. J. Briscoe (ed.), *Linguistic Evolution through Language Acquisition: Formal and Computational Models* (Cambridge: Cambridge University Press).

KOLEN, J. F., and POLLACK, J. B. (1990), 'Back-propagation is Sensitive to Initial Conditions', *Complex Systems*, 4/3: 269–80.

OLIPHANT, M., and BATALI, J. (1996), 'Learning and the Emergence of Coordinated Communication', draft MS.

RUMELHART, D. E., HINTON, G. E., and WILLIAMS, R. J. (1986), 'Learning Internal Representations by Error Propagation', in D. E. Rumelhart and J. L. McClelland (eds.), *Parallel Distributed Processing: Explorations in the Microstructure of Cognition* (Cambridge, Mass.: MIT Press), 318–61.

TONKES, B., BLAIR, A. D., and WILES, J. (1999), 'A Paradox of Neural Encoders and Decoders, or, Why Don't We Talk Backwards?', in B. McKay, X. Yao, C. S. Newton, J. H. Kim, and T. Furuhashi (eds.), *Simulated Evolution and Learning*, Lecture Notes in Artificial Intelligence 1585 (London: Springer), 357–64.

——————(2000), 'Evolving Learnable Languages', in S. A. Solla, T. K. Leen, and K. R. Müller (eds.), *Advances in Neural Information Processing Systems* (Cambridge, Mass.: MIT Press), xii. 66–72.

12 Crucial Factors in the Origins of Word-Meaning

L. STEELS, F. KAPLAN, A. MCINTYRE, AND J. VAN LOOVEREN

12.1 Introduction

We have been conducting large-scale public experiments with artificial robotic agents to explore what the necessary and sufficient prerequisites are for word-meaning pairs to evolve autonomously in a population of agents through a self-organized process. We focus not so much on the question of why language has evolved, but rather on how. There are many good reasons to use language once it has come into existence; for example, for establishing and maintaining group coherence, for transmission of cultural knowledge such as tool use, etc. But these reasons only explain why verbal behaviour is reinforced. They do not explain how this verbal behaviour might emerge or become complex. Our hypothesis is that when agents engage in particular interactive behaviours that in turn require specific cognitive structures, they automatically arrive at a language system. This interactive behaviour should be a natural outgrowth of co-operative behaviour (if this were not the case, the behaviour would be unlikely to emerge), and the cognitive structures should be simple enough to have evolved for other purposes as well (pre-

The work that was the foundation of this chapter was carried out at the Sony Computer Science Laboratory in Paris and the VUB AI laboratory in Brussels (financed by a GOA grant). We are extremely grateful to the various sites that hosted physical installations, in particular to Barbara Vanderlinden and Hans-Ulrich Obrist who organized the LABORA-TORIUM exhibition in Antwerpen, to Adam Lowe who organized the N01SE exhibition that led to sites in Cambridge (UK) and London, to Marie Canard and Eric Emery who organized the exhibition on Animal Communication in the Palais de la Découverte in Paris, and to Ben Krose who was instrumental in getting the Amsterdam site operational. We are also indebted to the reviewers and editor of this volume for many useful comments regarding the text.

adaptation). Our main task is therefore to identify precisely what this behaviour is and what cognitive structures are required for it.

Because we study this topic by performing experiments based on artificial systems, our work is comparable with other research attempting to understand the origins of semiotic systems through computer simulations (see Hurford 1989 and MacLennan 1991 for some of the earliest papers, and Steels 1997 for a survey of other work). The research discussed in the present chapter differs primarily from previous work in three respects: (1) The experiments are carried out by agents which have contact with the world through a sensori-motor apparatus. They are therefore grounded in reality. (2) The agents have no direct access to the meanings used by other agents; their only access is indirect, and comes in the form of feedback on interactions taking place in the environment. This is important, because simulations in which the agents are presented with both words and meanings during the lexicon-learning process do not allow certain observed phenomena of natural language such as polysemy or meaning evolution to arise. (3) We do not assume a prior repertoire of concepts given to the agents. Instead, agents must build up their conceptual repertoire in a co-evolutionary process simultaneous with the construction of their lexical system. One of the assumptions underlying the present work is linguistic relativism: the conceptual repertoire of the agents both influences and is influenced by the developing lexicon.

The experiment, known as the Talking Heads Experiment, employs a set of visually grounded autonomous robots into which agents can install themselves to play language games with each other. The language games are centred on scenes containing geometrical figures pasted on a white background (see Fig. 12.1). The software system used has been implemented on top of a generic software infrastructure for exploring language games (McIntyre 1998). The language game played is called the 'guessing game'. One agent plays the role of speaker and the other one plays the role of hearer. Agents take turns playing games so all of them develop the capacity to be speaker or hearer. Agents start without any prior category set or lexicon, and learned knowledge always remains local to the agent. Agents are capable of segmenting the image perceived through the camera into objects and of collecting various sensory data about each object, such as the colour (decomposed in the yellow-blue, red-green, brightness, and saturation channels), average grey-scale, horizontal and vertical position, size, form, etc. The set of objects and their data constitute the context for a language game. The speaker chooses one object from this context, hereafter described as the 'topic'. The other objects form the background. The speaker then gives a linguistic hint to the hearer. The linguistic hint is an utterance that identifies the topic with respect to the objects in the background. For example, if the context contains [1] a red square, [2] a blue triangle, and [3] a green circle, then the speaker may say something like 'the red one' to communicate that [1] is the topic. If the context also contained a red triangle, he would have to be more precise and say something like 'the red square'. Of course, the Talking Heads do not say 'the red square': they use their own language and concepts which are never going to be the same as those used in English. For example, they might say 'malewina' to mean [UPPER EXTREME-LEFT LOW-REDNESS].[1]

Based on the linguistic hint, the hearer tries to guess what topic the speaker has chosen, and he communicates his choice to the speaker by pointing to the object. A robot points by transmitting the direction in which it is looking. The game succeeds if the topic guessed by the hearer is equal to the topic chosen by the speaker. The game fails if the guess was wrong or if a failure occurred earlier in the game (for instance, because the speaker was unable to categorize or describe the topic). If the speaker has no adequate category to discriminate the topic from the other objects, a new category is generated by a learning process. If the speaker has no word to express a desired category, it constructs a random string and associates that in its lexicon with this category. If communication fails, the speaker gives an extralinguistic hint by pointing to the topic it had in mind, and the hearer tries to guess what the possible meaning of the speaker's word might have been in the present context. This meaning is then stored in the hearer's lexicon. At no point is any global knowledge stored anywhere.

The robots are located in different places in the world (Paris, Brussels, Tokyo, Antwerp, Lausanne, Amsterdam, etc.) and are connected through the Internet. Agents travel from one body to another through an 'agent teleportation' infrastructure, and can only interact when at the same physical site. The teleportation infrastructure uses the Internet as a way to transfer the software states of the agents from one location to another. Some of the instal-

---

[1] Meanings can be composed of several 'atomic' meanings when there are no atomic meanings that have enough discriminative power to identify the topic on their own. This means that the topic has to possess all the properties listed in the meaning, while none of the objects in the background may have all the properties. There is no relation between parts of the meaning and parts of the word; words are never decomposed in this system.

lation sites have been at public places: art galleries, museums, and conferences. We estimate that close to 300,000 people have seen the experiment live, most of them at the Paris science museum, le *Palais de la découverte*. Agents are initially launched by human users. Through a web-page (http://talking-heads.csl.sony.fr/), anyone can follow the experiment and interact with the agents. Through the web interface, human users may teach words to their agents and thus influence the evolving lexicon. In this way we have also been able to explore human influence on the emerging artificial language. We estimate that between 10,000 and 15,000 people have visited the experiment's web site and close to 6,000 agents have been launched by sometimes very active human users.

The first Talking Heads experiment ran for four months during the summer of 1999 and showed the validity of the mechanisms that were used for the agent architecture and of the interaction patterns and group dynamics of the agents. A shared lexicon and its underlying conceptual repertoire

Fig. 12.1 Example of a typical Talking Heads set-up. Two steerable cameras are connected to computer equipment and oriented towards a white board on which geometric figures are pasted.

emerged after a few days, enabling successful communication by the agents about the scenes before them. In total, 400,000 grounded games were played. The population of agents rose to just under 2,000, increasing steadily over the period of the experiment. Despite the many perturbations due to grounding, intermittent technical failures, a continuous influx of new agents entering the population, and unpredictable human interaction, the lexicon was maintained throughout the period. A total of 8,000 words and 500 concepts were created, with a core vocabulary consisting of 100 basic words expressing concepts such as up, down, left, right, green, red, large, small, etc. A second experiment cycle was begun at the end of January 2000 and continued until August 2000. After a difficult initial period, in which an excessively high agent influx prevented a shared language from establishing itself, a successful language nevertheless emerged (Kaplan 2001).

The success of the experiment comes from a specific self-organizational dynamic that assumes a positive feedback loop between use and success. Agents keep in their memories scored associations between words and meanings. The score reflects the expectation that the word has a given meaning (one can also say that it reflects the probability that the word will be

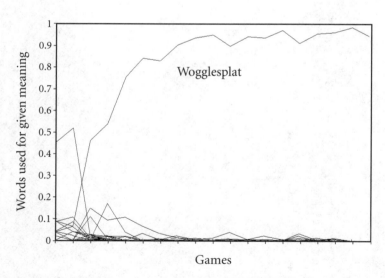

Fig. 12.2 Evolution of word–meaning relations for the same meaning over a period of 90,000 games (as taken from the experiment). The graph shows the average use of all the words per 10 games. One word (*wogglesplat*) comes out as the winner.

used with this particular meaning in the group). When a game succeeds, i.e. when the hearer can correctly identify the topic selected by the speaker through the utterance, speaker and hearer each increase the score of the used association and decrease the score of competing associations. When a game fails, speaker and hearer decrease the score of the association that was used. These dynamics, which are similar to those adopted in other simulation work (e.g. Oliphant 1996), have a winner-take-all structure (Fig. 12.2), in the sense that synonymy (one meaning/many words) is damped.

A situation in which one word form may have multiple meanings (polysemy) occurs naturally in a semiotic system as soon as hearers have to guess the meaning of unknown words. A word can usually have more than one meaning in a given situation and therefore there is no guarantee that the hearer infers the same meaning as the one intended by the speaker. But here too a damping effect occurs. Meanings that are compatible with the same situations will remain entangled until clear situations arise where they are different. This was for example the case for the word *bozopite* (Fig. 12.3). There are two competing meanings: large area (large) and large width (wide). These meanings co-occur often because objects that are large in area typ-

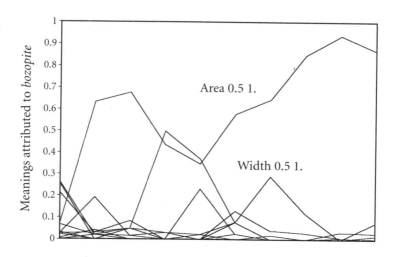

FIG. 12.3 Evolution of word–meaning relations for the same word, *bozopite*, over a period of 250,000 games (as taken from the actual experiment). The graph shows the average use of all the meanings per 10 games. There is a struggle between two meanings—large area and large width—until one emerges as the winner.

ically also have a large width. However, when there are enough situations where the two are incompatible (for example because the object is very tall but not very wide), disambiguation starts and is enforced by the positive feedback loop. Fig. 12.3 also illustrates that lexicons are never completely stable. Evolution continues to take place mostly under the influence of various sources of randomness that are unavoidable in real-world communication (Steels and Kaplan 1998*a*,*b*).

Apart from the damping of synonymy and polysemy, we also see a natural selection towards those concepts and words that are most stable, in the sense that they work perceptually across different environments and are more reliable for picking out the topic from the other objects in the context. Thus, very fine-grained distinctions based on subtle light variations would arise in the system but would have a hard time propagating to the rest of the population because light conditions vary, even when the same set-up is viewed from different angles. The net effect of these tendencies was that the total set of words became progressively restricted to a core of 100 words, with a key vocabulary of 8 words referring to colours (red, green, blue, and bright) and positions (left, right, up, down). Figure 12.4 shows the number of words in frequent use as the experiment progresses. Steels and Kaplan (1999) discuss in more detail the semiotic dynamics that we have seen emerging.

The goal of the rest of this chapter is to identify the factors that we found

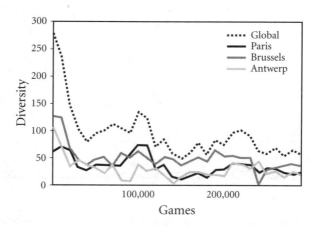

FIG. 12.4 Evolution of word diversity. After an initial period in which many words were used, the system stabilizes around a kernel of about a hundred words which are sufficient to deal with the situations encountered.

to be crucial for the success of these experiments. These can be grouped into two subsets: internal factors relating to the individual architecture of the agents and external factors relating to the group dynamics and the environments encountered. We report not only those factors that we explicitly incorporated in the experiment but also the ones that we expressly omitted in order to prove that they are not needed.

We believe that the same factors must have been in place to allow the origins of human language. Indeed, the role of simulations and experiments is to show the strength and limitations of certain theoretical models (Kaplan 1998). The fact that human language first arose in the very distant past means that direct observation of the origins of human language is impossible; approaches based on simulation thus offer perhaps the best option for a rigorous evaluation of theoretical models.

The simulation described here deals with the formation of a lexicon. Human languages are characterized by having complex grammatical conventions. Although we have been working on the problem of how grammar may arise in a set-up similar to that of the Talking Heads experiment (Steels 1998), this issue is not discussed in this chapter. In any case, a firm vocabulary must be in place before more complex grammatical constructions can be envisioned.

12.2 Internal Factors

Factor 1: Agents must be able to engage in co-ordinated interactions. This means that they must be able to have shared goals and a willingness to co-operate. Each agent must be able to follow a script of actions in agreement with a shared protocol, and have a way to see whether the goal of the interaction has been satisfied. In our experiment, we simply assumed these obvious requirements and explicitly programmed into each agent the scripts achieving the desired co-operative interaction. Emergence of co-operation is not addressed in our research, but it is addressed in other work (see, for instance, Lindgren and Nordal 1991). The emergence of communication as part of co-operation has also been addressed by a number of researchers (e.g. Noble and Cliff 1996). On the other hand, the emergence of shared interaction scripts is—as far as we know—an open problem, not only for human communication but for other forms of social interaction—such as physical co-operation in a shared task—as well.

Factor 2: Agents must have parallel non-verbal ways to achieve the goals of verbal interactions. The communicative goal of the agents in our experiment is to draw attention through verbal means to an object in a visually perceived reality. There are, of course, many other things humans do with language but this is surely an important one and a prerequisite for more sophisticated verbal exchanges, such as requests for action that require reliable identification of the objects involved in the action. We have found that it is crucial that the agents have a non-verbal way to achieve this goal: by pointing, gaze-following, grasping, etc. This alternative way must be sufficiently reliable, at least initially when the system is bootstrapping from scratch. Once the language system is in place, however, external behavioural feedback is less crucial or may be absent altogether. A non-verbal means of communication is a necessity if the hearer has no 'telepathic capacity' to know what meanings are intended by the speaker, no prior innate categories (as in many other experiments in language evolution), or any other way to guess what the meaning might be, independently of language.

Evidence for Factor 2 comes from two sources. (1) In the experiment, the hearer physically points to the object that the speaker indicated through verbal means and the speaker physically points to the object when the speaker made the wrong guess. Pointing is done by moving the camera in the direction of the object and zooming in on the object. We have found that major problems occurred during certain phases of the experiment in which the calibration of the pointing behaviour was inaccurate due to physical movement of the robot that was beyond our control. In these cases the feedback introduced random errors and destroyed the communication system in place. (2) We also carried out some simulation experiments to explicitly test the importance of non-verbal interaction (see Fig. 12.5) (Steels and Kaplan 1998a). In these experiments the accuracy of non-verbal feedback is a parameter that can be varied. We see that in Phase 1, no language formed due to a very high randomness[2] in non-verbal interaction. In Phase 2,

---

[2] In the experiment described by the graph, the robots may indicate topics both verbally and non-verbally (i.e. by pointing). The topic-recognition stochasticity (ET) affects the degree of certainty with which a hearer can recognize a topic indicated by non-verbal means (in simpler terms, how reliably the hearer can identify what the speaker is pointing to). When the value is high, the hearer is more likely to fail to identify the intended topic. So in Fig. 12.5, ET begins high, and the language has difficulty forming (because hearers cannot identify the topic accurately). In the second phase, ET is reduced to 0—perfect accuracy in pointing—and the language bootstraps. In the third phase, the language is maintained, even though ET is reset to the initial high value.

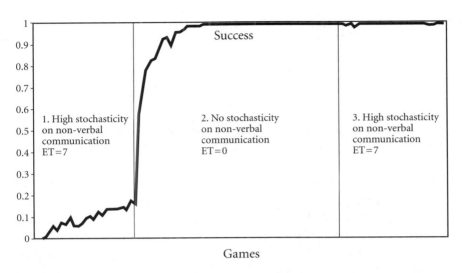

Fig. 12.5 Simulation experiments with 20 agents and 10 meanings for 20,000 games. The x-axis plots consecutive games and the y-axis averages success per 10 games. We see three phases depending on a stochasticity (randomness) factor ET ('error in topic recognition').

we decreased this randomness and a shared lexicon formed. In Phase 3, we increased the randomness of non-verbal feedback and observed that communicative success (and lexical stability) remained at very high level. In other words, the conventions, once established, are strongly enough ingrained in the population to overcome pointing randomness. To determine the referent of an utterance, the hearer uses both knowledge of the language and knowledge about the situation. Rather than simply choosing the word with the highest score, the best interpretation in the current situation will be chosen.

Factor 3: Agents must have ways to conceptualize reality and to acquire these conceptualizations, constrained by the semantic concepts expressed in the emerging lexicon and the types of situations they encounter. Obviously, conceptualization precedes verbalization. A word such as 'left' does not refer to a specific object, but assumes that objects are conceptualized based on their horizontal position and that the object is assumed to be in one subregion along this dimension. So words express categories as opposed to names of specific situations. We believe that it is unrealistic to assume that the repertoire of concepts is fixed and given in advance (as is often done in simu-

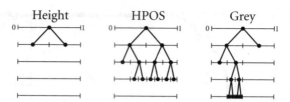

FIG. 12.6 Example of a part of the conceptual repertoires of a single agent. Each tree divides a sensory channel into subregions, associating a concept with each region.

lations) because agents will always be confronted with new situations and new tasks. So there must be a concept-acquisition process coupled to the language process. Which concept-acquisition process is used is not critical. It can be based on neural network techniques such as perceptron-style feed-forward networks, Kohonen networks (Bishop 1995), or symbolic machine learning techniques (Mitchell 1997). We have used a specific method based on the learning of decision trees, more specifically binary discrimination trees (Fig. 12.6)[3] in a selectionist fashion (Steels 1997). Although there are many possible mechanisms for concept acquisition, we found some important constraints for this process:

1. The concept-formation processes of the agents must be based on similar sensory channels and result in similar although not necessarily equal conceptual repertoires.

We have incorporated this constraint at present by giving each agent the same low-level sensory apparatus (vision) and by assuming the same sort of binary discrimination trees for the agent's conceptual repertoires. There are other researchers who have used significantly different types of agents (Yanco and Stein 1993) so that this constraint appears to be less strict, however the vocabularies and concept repertoires of the agents have been too small in these experiments to pose a serious search problem when agents have to guess the meaning of unknown words. Conceptualization schemes based on randomly structured discrimination trees, prototypes, or neural networks are also adequate for finding a distinctive conceptualization, but we found that they result in larger differences between the repertoires of the agents, making it more difficult to achieve lexical coherence in the popula-

[3] HPOS means 'horizontal position' and Grey means 'position on the black–white continuum', where 0.0 is black and 1.0 is white.

tion. Coherence may still be achieved, as shown in the experiments of Vogt (1999) which use a prototype-based categorization, but such systems tend to be less effective than the ones used in this experiment, even when the concept repertoire is small enough to render the search problem negligible.

2. The conceptualization for a particular situation must be constrained to be similar so that the agents have a reasonable chance at guessing the conceptualization that a speaker may have used.

Even if there is a more or less shared repertoire, there will still be many possible ways to conceptualize reality. For example, in a particular scene containing a red triangle to the left and a blue square to the right, three distinctions—red versus blue, triangle versus square, and left versus right—are all adequate. We found that if the search space for possible meanings in a given situation is too large, the agents do not manage to reach a highly coherent lexicon.

In the Talking Heads experiment, we have reduced the search space in two ways. First, by using saliency: sensory differences that stand out more will be preferred for conceptualizing the scene, thus reducing the search space for the meaning of unknown words. Thus if there are three objects all with strongly different colours in the scene, two on the left and one on the right, then colour will be preferred to position because it is more distinctive. The second constraint comes from taking the lexicon into account for conceptualization. When there are two concepts that are equally salient, but one has a stronger lexicalization (i.e. a word with a higher score) than the other, then the first one is chosen. The latter leads to a steadily increasing coherence in the ontological repertoires of the agents, and thus shows how linguistic relativism is possible.

Factor 4: Agents must have ways to recognize word-forms and reproduce them. This is quite obvious, because otherwise words would be confused all the time. In the Talking Heads experiment we have simply given the agents the capability to recognize and reproduce each others' word-forms perfectly. We have also done some simulation experiments (Steels and Kaplan 1998a) to test the validity of Factor 4. by introducing an error rate on the transmission of signals (see Fig. 12.7).[4] When this error rate is too high the communica-

---

[4] EF is the form stochasticity ('error in form recognition'). In the experiment, the word tokens—'forms'—may be perceived with varying degrees of accuracy. For example, if EF is high, the form 'moba' might be misheard as 'mopa'. This, clearly, has an effect on the language and the formation process and on the final composition of the lexicon.

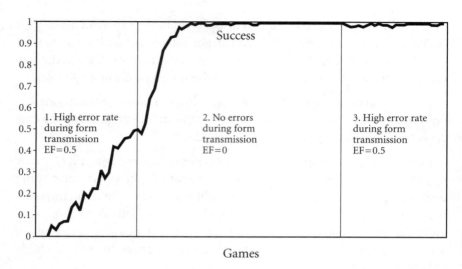

FIG. 12.7 Communicative success measured over number of games. A parameter has been introduced to vary the accuracy with which signals are recognized and reproduced by agents.

tion system does not get off the ground (Phase 1). When the error rate is lowered, so that word-forms are better recognized, we see a communication system forming (Phase 2). When the error rate is increased again, we see that communicative success decreases (Phase 3), but still stays very high. We see again that once a lexical system is in place it can overcome the randomness inherent in verbal communication.

Factor 5: Agents must have the ability to discover and use the strongest associations (between words and meanings) in the group. The associative memory of an agent must be two-way (from words to meanings and meanings to words), must handle multiple competing associations (one word, many meanings; one meaning, many words), and must keep track of a score that represents how well the association has been doing based on their own past experience. When a decision must be made (which word to use, which meaning to prefer), there is an internal competition between different associations in which the one with the highest score wins. There are still many possible ways to achieve each of these behaviours. For example, the score updating can be based on use and success, or on a simple score that goes up and down with every usage, or on more sophisticated mechanisms.

Simulation experiments have been conducted to test each of these claims and explore different variations (Kaplan 1999). A very important outcome of these experiments is that statistical learning is not sufficient to bootstrap a coherent mapping between words and meanings. Such a mapping needs to be efficient for communicating, which means that if, for instance, a meaning is associated with several words, all these words need to be decoded in the same meaning. Agents need to test whether the associations they use actually lead to success in communication. If agents are only using statistical learning they have no reason to agree on an efficient mapping. Their mapping need not even be internally coherent.

Our experiments also show that the convergence towards a shared mapping between words and meanings is a lot easier when the number of words available is greater than the number of meanings. This assumption is realistic in the case of the emergence of human language, because languages typically allow for an open-ended set of potential words within a given phonological framework, but was not made in some other work (cf. Oliphant 1996) in the sense that it assumed a finite set of words, fixed a priori.

Assuming that humans possess a two-way associative memory of this kind makes sense in a wider evolutionary context. Such a memory would be useful also for many other tasks, such as associating physical locations with sources of food. It is therefore reasonable to assume that cognitive structures of this type are likely to evolve, and that they need not do so solely and specifically for language purposes. This justifies the pre-adaptation hypothesis.

It is perhaps important also to point out which factors we did *not* incorporate in the experiment because we feel that they are superfluous:

1. Theory of mind. There is a widespread belief that verbal communication requires a strong theory of mind of the other agents before verbal interactions are possible. In our experiment, this is not the case, although for more sophisticated language games (such as for reference to abstract entities or belief-states) it is obviously required. To support the emergence of a language directly grounded in visual and motor interaction, it is sufficient that agents follow specific protocols of interaction. They do not need to know why these protocols are successful. (Just as a child does not need explicit knowledge of theories of physics to throw a ball but just has to acquire the appropriate behaviours compatible with these laws.)

2. Prior concepts. Another widely made assumption is that concepts (par-

ticularly the perceptually grounded concepts that are the focus of our experiment) need to be shared prior to and independent of language. For some cognitive researchers this implies that they are innate (Fodor 1998). For others, it suggests that they are acquired through a universal inductive mechanism that yields the same concepts for all agents (Harnad 1990). We do not assume a prior set of categories in our experiments and in fact believe this to be impossible given the adaptive nature of verbal communication. Instead we have set up a strong interaction between language acquisition and concept formation. The repertoire of categories develops in a selectionist fashion under pressure from the language and concepts which have no success in verbal interaction are not encouraged.

3. Telepathy. We have not assumed that agents have a way of knowing what meaning the speaker transmits independently of language. Although non-verbal communication, similarity of sensors, shared history of past experiences, saliency, etc. help to restrict the set of possible meanings, the hearer can only guess what the speaker meant. Neither have we assumed that agents have exactly the same perception. Usually raw perception and consequently-derived sensory features are different. Equal perception is of course an unrealistic assumption for embodied agents because each agent sees the scene from a different point of view.

12.3. *External Factors*

Factor 6: There must be sufficient group stability to enable a sufficient set of encounters between agents. We have found that if there is a too rapid in- and outflux of agents, a lexicon will collapse because there is not enough time for new members to acquire the conventions (so they build their own). Similarly, older members leave too quickly, so that there is no memory in the population of the existing conventions. The exact critical levels of the fluxes depend on the size of the population and on the complexity of the environment. Evidence for Factor 6 is borne out by simulation experiments, as shown in Fig. 12.8, concerned with varying the increase in population. In Phase 1 no new agents enter or leave and complete communicative success and lexical coherence is reached. In Phase 2, there is a replacement of 1 agent every 100 games. This lowers success and coherence but the population can cope. In Phase 3, the replacement rate is 1 agent every 10 games. The lexicon collapses. The cumulative change measure increases each time a meaning is coded by a new word in the global lexicon. When no new words are invented for existing meanings the cumulative change is zero. Fig. 12.8 shows that the lexicon is transmitted without alteration in the first two phases but changes rapidly in the last phase.

Factor 7: Initial group size should not be too large, so that there are enough encounters between the same individuals. Obviously when the group size is large, it is going to be more difficult to establish lexical coherence. This is partly because there is a much greater chance that new words will be created by individuals or groups of individuals before the mass effect of self-organization can have an impact, and partly because a minimum number of interactions is required: due to the limited number of sites available, the more agents there are the fewer games they have in the same time period. Once a lexicon is in place, however, there can be an almost unbounded increase in the population. In the second run of the Talking Heads experiment, a very large population was created, causing significant difficulties for language formation. In the first experiment the population grew more gradually so that after a week a solid lexicon had already emerged and remained in place for the remaining months of the experiment, despite an agent population that ultimately contained some thousands of agents.

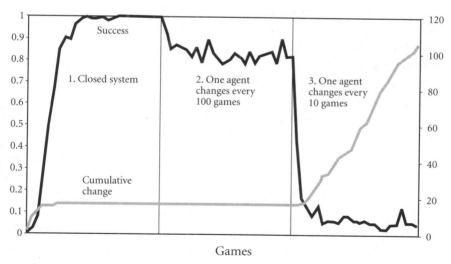

Games

FIG. 12.8 Communicative success of the emergent lexicon and the lexicon change over time in a population of 20 agents over 15,000 games and with different population renewal rates.

Each agent site typically had a population that focused on that site (as directed by their users). Because these agents had more interaction with each other than with agents at other sites sub-lexicons formed that were unique to the site. The geographical separation was never total because other agents (again as directed by their users) travelled a lot in between different sites. In another series of experiments with spatially distributed language games, phenomena familiar in studies of language contact started to appear when the importance of this geographical separation was reduced; under such circumstances, the language from the largest population tends to dominate (Steels and McIntyre 1998).

Factor 8: There must be sufficient environmental stability and different degrees of complexity. The environments encountered by the agents and perceivable by the agents through their sensory apparatus must have certain invariant structural properties so that concepts can form and word-meaning pairs can settle. This does not mean that the environment needs to be closed (indeed it should not be if we want to be realistic), nor even that the sensory space should be closed (new sensory routines surely develop in children even after they have acquired their first words).

We found that if the agents encounter only complex scenes, they cannot settle on a successful repertoire or at least have much greater difficulty in doing so due to unstable concepts. So there must be scenes, at least initially, which can be handled by making simple distinctions (such as between left and right). Such simplified environments can be seen as analogous to the initial environment of infants: because many sensory capabilities are not available at birth, the child learns its initial categorizations in the context of what is effectively a simplified perceptual environment (Elman *et al.* 1996).

We were also able to exclude two external factors which we determined were unnecessary:

1. Global view or central control. A central puzzle in the origins of language is how a population of distributed autonomous agents can reach coherence without a central controlling organism and without giving individual agents access to a global view. A model should never introduce any central control on language or give agents a global view of the language as a whole. Our experiments have shown extensively and convincingly that self-organization is perfectly adequate to explain language coherence without this.

2. Total coherence. It is often assumed that all individuals have exactly the same linguistic competence and that deviations are due only to perform-

ance errors. We have shown that this assumption is unnecessary. The conceptualizations and lexicons of the individual agents in the experiment were *never* exactly the same. They had different degrees of knowledge and there were unavoidable individual differences arising from the absence of a global view. The experiment shows that communicative success can nevertheless be reached without such absolute coherence. For example, words can often be maintained in a polysemous state without causing confusion in a series of environments, while synonyms are tolerated because agents can understand words that they themselves might not necessarily choose to use.

12.4 Conclusion

This chapter aims to show how experiments based on software simulations or robotic set-ups, such as the Talking Heads experiment, can play an important role in the debate on the origin and evolution of human languages. In a field where 'real' experimentation is not possible, this type of experiment allows researchers to compare hypotheses and use models to test which factors are crucial and which are contingent in achieving a communication system. Similar experiments have also studied the emergence and complexification of grammar (Steels 1998).

In summary, we have established the following internal factors for the evolution of a lexical system in a group of distributed agents with neither a prior set of categories nor a lexicon and without the telepathic capability to guess meanings independently of physical action (such as pointing) or language:

1. Agents must be able to engage in co-ordinated interactions.
2. Agents must have parallel non-verbal ways to achieve the goals of verbal interactions.
3. Agents must have ways to conceptualize reality and to form these conceptualizations, constrained by the set of categories underlying the emerging lexicon and the types of situations they encounter.
4. Agents must have ways to recognize word-forms and reproduce them.
5. Agents must have the ability to discover and use the strongest associations (between words and meanings) in the group.

We also established the following external factors:

6. There must be sufficient group stability to enable a sufficient set of encounters between agents.

7. Initial group size should not be too large so that there are enough encounters between the same individuals.

8. There must be sufficient environmental stability and different degrees of complexity in the environment.

These various constraints help us to understand the conditions under which language may have emerged in human societies and what kind of minimal cognitive and sensori-motor architecture is needed to get a lexical system off the ground.

FURTHER READING

STEELS, L. (1997), 'The Synthetic Modeling of Language Origins', *Evolution of Communication Journal*, 1/1: 1–34.

—— (2000), 'The Emergence of Grammar in Communicating Autonomous Robotic Agents', in W. Horn (ed.), *Proceedings of ECAI 2000* (Amsterdam: IOS Publishing), 764–9.

—— (2000), 'Language as a Complex Adaptive System', in M. Schoenauer (ed.), *Proceedings of PPSN VI*, Lecture Notes in Computer Science (Berlin: Springer), 17–26.

—— and BROOKS, R. (1995), 'The Artificial Life Route to Artificial Intelligence', *Building Embodied Situated Agents* (New Haven: Lawrence Erlbaum).

REFERENCES

BISHOP, C. M. (1995), *Neural Networks for Pattern Recognition* (Oxford: Oxford University Press).

ELMAN, J., BATES, E., JOHNSON, M., KARMILOFF-SMITH, A., PARISI, D., and PLUNKETT, K. (1996), *Rethinking Innateness* (Cambridge, Mass.: MIT Press).

FODOR, J. (1998), *Concepts: Where Cognitive Science Went Wrong* (Oxford: Clarendon Press).

HARNAD, S. (1990), 'The Symbol Grounding Problem', *Physica*, D, 42: 335–46.

HURFORD, J. (1989), 'Biological Evolution of the Saussurean Sign as a Component of the Language Acquisition Device', *Lingua*, 77: 187–222.

KAPLAN, F. (1998), 'Rôle de la simulation multi-agent pour comprendre l'origine et l'évolution du langage', in J.-P. Barthès, V. Chevrier, and C. Brassac (eds.), *Systèmes multi-agents: De l'interaction à la socialité* (Paris: Hermès), 51–64.

—— (1999), 'Dynamiques de l'auto-organisation lexicale: Simulations multi-agents et "Têtes parlantes"', *In Cognito*, 15: 3–23.

—— (2001), *La naissance d'une langue chez les robots* (Paris: Hermès).

LINDGREN, K., and NORDAL, M.(1991), 'Cooperation and Community Structure in Artificial Ecosystems', in C. Langton (ed.) *Artificial Life: An Overview* (Cambridge, Mass.: MIT Press), 15–37.

McINTYRE, A. (1998), 'Babel: A Testbed for Research in the Origins of Language', *Proceedings of Coling-ACL 98* (Montreal: ACL), 830–5.

MacLENNAN, B. (1991), 'Synthetic Ethology: An Approach to the Study of Communication', in C. Langton, C. Taylor, J. D. Farmer, and S. Rasmussen (eds.), *Artificial Life* (Reading: Addison-Wesley), 631–58.

MITCHELL, T. (1997), *Machine Learning* (New York: McGraw Hill).

NOBLE, J., and CLIFF, D. (1996), 'On Simulating the Evolution of Communication', in P. Maes, M. Mataric, J.-A. Meyer, J. Pollack, and S. W. Wilson (eds.), *From Animals to Animates 4: Proceedings of Fourth International Conference on Simulation of Adaptive Behavior* (Cambridge, Mass.: MIT Press), 608–17.

OLIPHANT, M. (1996), 'The Dilemma of Saussurean Communication', *Biosystems*, 37: 31–8.

STEELS, L. (1997), 'The Synthetic Modeling of Language Origins', *Evolution of Communication Journal*, 1/1: 1–34.

——(1998), 'The Origins of Syntax in Visually Grounded Robotic Agents', *Artificial Intelligence*, 103: 1–24.

——and KAPLAN, F. (1998*a*), 'Stochasticity as a Source of Innovation in Language Games', in C. Adami, R. Belew, H. Kitano, and C. Taylor (eds.), *Proceedings of Artificial Life VI* (Cambridge, Mass.: MIT Press), 368–76.

—— ——(1998*b*), 'Spontaneous Lexicon Change', *Proceedings of Coling-ACL 98* (Montreal: ACL), 1243–9.

—— ——(1999), 'Collective Learning and Semiotic Dynamics', in D. Floreano, J. D. Nicoud, and F. Mondada (eds.), *Advances in Artificial Life* (Proceedings of ECAL 99); Lecture Notes in Computer Science (Berlin: Springer-Verlag), 679–88.

——and McINTYRE, A. (1998), 'Spatially Distributed Naming Games', *Advances in Complex Systems*, 1/4: 301–24.

VOGT, P. (1999), 'Grounding a Lexicon in a Coordination on Mobile Robots', in E. Postma and M. Gyssens (eds.), *Proceedings of Eleventh Belgium-Netherlands Conference on Artificial Intelligence* (Maastricht: University of Maastricht), 275–6.

YANCO, H., and STEIN, L. (1993), 'An adaptive communication protocol for cooperating mobile robots', in J.-A. Meyer, H. L. Roitblat, and S. W. Wilson (eds.), *From Animals to Animates 2: Proceedings of the Second International Conference on the Simulation of Adaptive Behavior* (Cambridge, Mass.: MIT Press/Bradford Books), 478–85.

13 Constraints on Communities with Indigenous Sign Languages: Clues to the Dynamics of Language Genesis

SONIA RAGIR

13.1 Introduction

A common criticism of language origin hypotheses has been that they are too speculative—that there is no way of proving or disproving them by observing language actually being formed in a languageless community. This is no longer, strictly speaking, true. There are three sources of information that shed significant light on language genesis: recent studies of indigenous sign language formation; historical accounts of the transformation of plantation pidgins into Creoles (Bickerton 1990, 1999; McWhorter 1997); and computer simulations of language genesis (Kirby 1999a, 2000, 2001; Batali 1998, 2000; Steels 1998, Steels et al., this volume). Where sign language is concerned, it is important to realize that the deaf individuals who have created communication systems within hearing–speaking populations did not have access to the existing spoken languages (Kegl et al. 1999); thus, an examination of the formation of sign in their different communities offers a unique glimpse into language genesis in real populations.

Because the formation of language under both innate and epigenetic influences is the result of self-organizing negotiations between individuals and between populations and a selective environment—albeit over different biological timescales—it is difficult to distinguish between them. Such multilevelled negotiations generate similar outcomes whether they are a function of natural selection on populations across generations or a function of selective acquisition of dominant patterns in the language of the

The author gratefully acknowledges the support of the American Museum of Natural History, New York.

current generation (Kress and Ragir 2001). The negotiation of an innate program goes on between generations as a result of natural selection that changes gene frequencies in a fitness landscape that has been transformed by language use. An innate hypothesis presumes that combinations of alleles contributing to the easy comprehension, acquisition, and production of language will lead to the selection of universal parameters of a specialized language faculty. Such innate syntax ought to be relatively insensitive to disruptions during transmission and to limitations on language activity. We might expect to find innate parameters structuring the acquisition of language in young learners regardless of the state of language input and community cohesiveness.

On the other hand, a dynamic, learned system is negotiated within a group and automated during the ontogeny of individual members who participate in and are sensitive to patterns in form and content. In an epigenetic system, successive semantic and syntactic generalizations are stored in the ongoing language environment and become the language input for new learners. It is the operation of basic learning algorithms on the increasingly formal patterns found in the language environment, rather than the selection for specialized language faculties or programs, that accounts for language formation across generations. The morphological parameters of such self-organizing systems are only as stable as the practices that inform the community, and system formation is more sensitive to disruptions of transmission and marginal participation than pre-programmed systems. If social disruption, such as a limited participation in community exchange, can be shown to result in the long-term failure of language formation, then there is good reason to believe that there is no innate language bioprogram. Therefore, I have investigated the literature on communities in which either the distribution of deafness or the social discrimination against the deaf members of a population has inhibited the transformation of signed jargons to fully grammatical languages. Social disruptions that interfere with the transformation of spoken and signed pidgins into languages have profound implications with respect to language formation hypotheses.

13.2 Negotiated Dynamic Systems

Universal features of language, including the regulation of the phonological system, semantic compositionality, and syntax, closely resemble the ordering properties that characterize other self-organized behavioural systems (Kauffman 1993). Self-organizing mechanisms simultaneously regulate multiple levels of interactions in the brain, in the developing organism, and in patterns of community activity (Kelso 1995: 15). Kelso (p. 12) points out that: 'The transitions between one stable order and another are not the smooth, slow, gradual changes of natural selection ... In self-organizing systems, a small change, ... in the number of neurons in the brain, in the amount of information to be processed, or in the number of organisms in an aggregate can produce a huge [abrupt] collective effect.' The two most important dynamic interactions are between (1) the organization of the central and peripheral nervous systems during ontogeny in response to the patterns of participation in communicative exchanges, and (2) the patterns of social exchange in the community wherein the need to exchange information triggers competing demands that communications be easy to produce, comprehend, and learn (cf. Kirby and Hurford 1997).

During an early learning-sensitive period, patterns in sensory input acquire contextual significance through repetition. Both dendritic and synaptic proliferation respond to repetitive activation; as a result, the most active neural connections become stronger and facilitate the rapid discrimination and production of meaningful categories (Koch and Laurent 1999). Thus, language is automated during a period of dendritic proliferation and pruning in which intra-cortical connections are built in response to the discrimination of meaningful variations in sensory input and motor output.

Deacon connected the growth and development of the brain to language genesis in a population by arguing that:

The source of information that is used to 'grow' a language lies neither in the corpus of texts and corrections presented to the child, nor in the child's brain to begin with. It is highly distributed across myriad interactions between children's learning and the evolution of the language community. ... *The mechanisms driving language change at the socio-cultural level are also responsible for everyday language learning.* (Deacon 1997: 115, emphasis added)

He describes a process whereby human language was shaped by developmental constraints on memory and attention, and by systemic delays in foetal developmental timing that caused the prefrontal cortex to become relatively as well as absolutely large compared to rest of the cortex.

The negotiated organization of information-exchange that arose in populations of simulated learners caused Kirby and Hurford (1997; cf. Kirby

1999*a*: 125–7) to propose that learning guided the evolution of language (see e.g. Baldwin 1896: Deacon 1997). However, as Mayley (1996, 1997), Kress and Ragir (2001), and others (Rice 2000; Yamaguchi 2000) have described elsewhere, selective pressure on learned behaviour ceases to affect evolutionary change as soon as every agent is capable of achieving a locally optimal phenotype. Language simulations can generate language syntax in populations without modelling selective mechanisms that affect innate parameters, such as changes in the timing or the mechanisms of learning (Batali 2000; Kirby 1999*b*, 2000, 2001; Steels 1998; Steels *et al.* this volume).

13.3 The Development of Indigenous Sign Languages

There are six communities with indigenous sign systems that have been studied in detail, including one where the actual formation of a sign language was observed over a period of twenty years. In three instances—Martha's Vineyard, Nicaragua, and Enga (New Guinea)—conditions encouraged the growth of well-developed context-independent lexicons and grammars. In three others—Noyha (Guatemala), Grand Cayman Island, and Providence Island—social marginalization inhibited language formation, and, as a result, the indigenous sign systems remained static and context-dependent for many generations. When studied together, these field studies make a convincing case for language formation processes that are epigenetic and self-organizing rather than innate.

The field studies present two kinds of disruptions to language formation: (1) breaks in the transmission of language between speakers and learners, and (2) constraints on speaker participation in the full range of social activity. Hereditary deafness in Martha's Vineyard, Noyha, Grand Cayman Island, and Providence Island led to the easy transmission of sign across generations. The sign language on Martha's Vineyard was well-formed soon after the community was founded, while on Noyha, Grand Cayman, and Providence the signed pidgins never developed grammars. The transmission of sign was inhibited in Nicaragua and Enga because deaf children, born every ten to twenty years as a result of epidemics of measles and meningitis, were scattered throughout relatively large regions (Kendon 1980*a*; personal communication). R. J. Senghas (1997) reported that there were no indigenous Nicaraguan sign languages prior to the formation of schools for the deaf in 1978; on the other hand, Kendon reported the existence of a well-formed

TABLE 13.1 *Communities from which an indigenous signed system of communication emerged*

Sign Language location	Estimated no. of deaf	Number of generations of deaf	Language pool	Etiology of deafness	Sign morphology G/E/I/A	Social relations among deaf (%)	Deaf who are married (%)	Deaf-deaf marriages (%)
Martha's Vineyard (West Tisbury, Gayhead, Chilmark)	>150 at turn of 20th c.	12	Opend	Hereditary	Strongly coded [G]	Fully integrated into the economics and politics on island	80	30
Providence Island, Columbia	20 in 1978 many more in the 19th c.	4–6	Opend	Hereditary	Weakly coded [I] [RV] context-dependent	Deaf kept in the family—considered incompetent	None reported Children common	None reported
Grand Cayman Island, Jamaica	In 1978, 18; in 1965–75: c.40–50 people in 6 families; in 19th c., many more	4–6	Open	Hereditary	Conventional, context-dependent [A] [RV]	Deaf considered incompetent	None reported— 3 women have children	None reported
Nohya, Yucatan	12 in 4 related families	2	Closed	Hereditary	Weakly coded [I] context-dependent	Daily association among males	None	None

Enga, Highland New Guinea	Cohorts of age-mates	3–5	Open	Childhood disease—meningitis	Strongly coded [E]	Informal during visits and at district centres	Unknown	Unknown
USA 19th c. and 1982	1:5,728 2 million deaf	Rarely in same family	Closed	Rarely hereditary	Strongly coded [G] [RV]	Schools and clubs	45 Unknown	79 85
Nicaragua 1979–95	100–500	2	Open	Rubella and meningitis	From weak to strongly coded [A–G]	Schools	Unknown	85
Adamorable, Ghana	c.50 in study site	?	Open	Disease	Strongly coded [G]	?	?	?
Rennel Island	1	—	—	—	Context-dependent	—	—	—

Note: G=grammatically structured; E=extended morphology; I=conventional lexicon and hand shapes, indexing, incipient phrase structure; A=little formal structure; RV=enclave and regional variation sign system among the Enga for perhaps 100 years. If innate parameters significantly guide language genesis, then the transmission of sign between deaf adults and their deaf children, where the sign is used by large numbers of deaf in a community, ought to create an ideal context for the grammaticalization of signed jargons and pidgins. The persistence of weakly coded signed pidgins under such circumstances seriously undermines claims for innate language-specific programming.

Perhaps the best-known community using an indigenous sign language was that of Martha's Vineyard, whose signers contributed substantially to the formation of American Sign Language during the nineteenth century (Groce 1985). Hereditary deafness, concentrated in the endogamous up-Island farming settlements, left almost every large family with at least one or two deaf members. The social context in which signing developed and flourished has been carefully reconstructed. No economic, political, or social prejudices separated deaf from hearing citizens; the majority of the deaf married, and the number of deaf–deaf marriages was substantially lower than on the mainland (35% compared to 85%). Many deaf islanders were literate, held land and political offices, owned businesses, and engaged in trade; they were not marginalized or treated as incapacitated. The immigrant families that settled Martha's Vineyard in 1642 came, via Cape Cod from Weald in Kent, where there was well-documented evidence for congenital deafness in the sixteenth century (cf. Groce 1985: 21–35). Although the lexicon and grammar were not described before the emergence of ASL at the end of the nineteenth century, the expansion of the signed lexicon and a grammatical structure probably occurred as early as 1700 (ibid. 71). Everyone in the up-Island villages learned to sign, and communication was carried on simultaneously and/or interchangeably in English and Sign until the distinction between hearing and deaf became vague in the minds of the islanders (ibid. 51).

Nicaraguan Sign Language also formed relatively quickly, but in a radically different social context. The Sandinista government established the first schools for the deaf in Nicaragua in the late 1970s (Kegl *et al.* 1999; A. Senghas 1994, 1995). The previously socially isolated children used home signs that were more discrete and conventional than mimetic gesture but without the relational signs or morphology that resembled conventional grammar.[1] No instruction or example of a signed language was available

---

[1] A grammar can be defined here as a code structured of relations between signs; in it, discrete linguistic units convey grammatical information independent of the context of speaking (cf. Washabaugh *et al.* 1978).

at the school, yet a peer-group jargon apparently emerged from the chaos of home signs within months of the first schoolyard interaction among the more than 100 deaf children.

Since the schoolyard jargon was the only source of language information, each new child learned to sign from the students who were already familiar with the gesture space, lexicon, and phrase constraints of signing, and the system became increasingly conventional and sophisticated. As the lexicon increased and signing became more fluent, gesture shape became abstract and streamlined. After the sign-shape and lexicon-morphology had developed for ten years, the youngest cohorts (between 5 and 7 years old) began to adapt and abbreviate relatively stable but quite cumbersome expressive forms to mark semantic roles and syntactic function, including object classifiers, number, mode, time, and attitude.

Older students and those who entered the school during the first five to ten years of its operation rarely, if ever, attained the speed or grammatical proficiency of the youngest signers who joined the school in the later half of the study (Kegl *et al.* 1999).[2] There is little in the two decades to suggest that grammaticalization occurred suddenly in a single child or cohort of students. Year after year new groups of children, who knew only mutually unintelligible home signs, learned from students whose sign was acquired during earlier phases of the system's development. Each class of new learners generalized and streamlined the growing lexicon and the many competing semantic structures in the language pool. While the older signers appeared to contribute many of the new lexical items, the younger students conventionalized the gestures and systematized a phrase structure (A. Senghas 1995, personal communication).

The children appeared to sharpen and extend the salient patterns in the language available to them, and created 'rules out of tendencies, and a coher-

---

[2] Kegl *et al.* (1999: 222–3) do not consider the grammaticalization of the peer-group incompatible with Bickerton's bioprogramme. Analogous to Bickerton's innate 'semantic oppositions', they suggest that an individual has an innate set of lexical conceptual structures (LCS), independent of language, that decompose a verb's meaning into semantic concepts such as *go, be, stay*, and *move*. The set also includes elements bearing certain semantic/thematic roles such as event, state, goal, source, theme, place, etc. with respect to the verb. This LCS superset of information becomes encoded into the verb's representation, and the restricted syntax of early NSL sign/pidgin is unable to disambiguate grammatical relations and other material predicated on the verb. Thus, the solution is to allow sequences of verbs fully to express these LCS using a restricted syntax. What puzzles me is why these language-independent conceptual structures are presumed to be innate rather than acquired and organized like so much else, during development, as the organism interacts within the world.

ent system of rules out of conflicting processes' (Newport 1999: 173). The study demonstrated a learning-sensitive developmental phase that ended roughly seven years after birth, and thus explained the difficulty that older students had in learning the new syntax. It seems reasonable, therefore, to propose that innate constraints might not be specific constraints on language learning, but that the children tended to form mapping rules that were more systematic than the input obtained from their communicative experiences (cf. ibid. 172–3). The multiphased and flexible patterns of the growth and use of Nicaraguan Sign Language might be interpreted best as negotiated responses to the increasing size of the lexicon, the rapidly enlarging community of signers, the continual influx of new learners, and the expanding range of activities in which sign was used.

Kendon (1980*a*,*b*,*c*) provided a remarkable study of the sign system of a 20-year-old Enga woman who had been deaf since infancy. The young woman was extremely rapid and fluent in her signing; the signs were highly conventionalized and had undergone the considerable abbreviation that is typical of signed languages (Kendon 1980*b*). Her sentences were consistently constructed, and she was able to tell lengthy narratives (Kendon 1980*c*). Her signs were readily interpreted by a hearing relative, and by an unrelated hearing male interpreter from another village who had a deaf sibling. The fact that a stranger easily understood the lengthy narratives suggests that the semantic and syntactic structure was context-independent. An early film of a 'sign language' and missionaries' accounts provided circumstantial evidence for the existence of a sign system in this region for over eighty years (Kendon 1980*a*).

Kendon made no attempt to examine the social context of deafness in the valley, but did give some indirect indications of it. The local magistrate reported that translators were frequently needed to handle the testimony of deaf people in the district court; thus, we may assume that the deaf were relatively numerous and considered competent enough to testify as responsible adults. Enga deafness was not congenital, and it was said that deafness emerged in the aftermath of epidemics of invasive European childhood diseases (ibid.). Because of the patchy temporal and scattered spatial distribution of deafness, the transmission of the sign language across generations and throughout hamlets could only have been accomplished through the interactions of hearing as well as deaf signers.

Enga sign is important to this discussion because a consistent morphology and a complex grammar emerged despite the disruptions in sign transmission between deaf signers. In New Guinea, where there were until recently more than 800 different languages, many men and women were fluent in three or four spoken languages and in a pidgin lingua franca used for trade and travel outside their district. Such a polyglot social environment would be unlikely to harbour the kind of resistance to the formation, learning, and general use of a signed language that inhibited the growth of sign in Nicaragua prior to 1980. Hearing people with deaf friends or relatives would quite naturally learn to sign—just as readily as they learned the language of their in-laws and other political allies. The Enga context suggests that a symmetrical peer relationship between hearing and deaf may allow the formation of syntax even without extensive deaf–deaf interaction.

Innate language parameters ought to appear readily in the language of deaf children who learn to sign from deaf adults. Nohya in the Guatemalan highlands, Grand Cayman Island, and Providence Island contain significant numbers of congenitally deaf children and adults who have learned to communicate from native signers and have never developed a grammar. Noyha had a deaf population of about twelve; these closely related individuals developed a heavily context-dependent sign that appeared to remain without syntactic structure for two generations (Shuman 1980a,b).

Circumstantial evidence indicates hereditary deafness to have begun in Grand Cayman (Jamaica) and Providence Island (Colombia) relatively soon after the first permanent settlement by Jamaican landowners, slaves, and British sailors in the eighteenth century, and some island villages had large populations of deaf by the nineteenth century. More than five to seven generations of hereditary deafness in four to six related families generated fluent but heavily context-dependent signed pidgins (Washabaugh 1981, 1986). All the deaf children and adults on Providence and Grand Cayman learned the pidgin from older native signers, but they did not generate a syntax, create names for people or places, or reduce indexicality in the process (Washabaugh 1980, 1986: 104; Woodward 1978). On both islands, indexing functioned in lieu of grammatical structure, and the gestures for lexical items often varied between one village and the next.

The hearing members of the Providence and Grand Cayman communities considered the deaf simple-minded and unable to protect themselves; the deaf were not encouraged to socialize or work outside the extended family. The hearing smothered the deaf with a paternalistic care and prevented them from carrying their own weight in communicative interactions. The deaf did not often sign among themselves and did not make room in their lives for a fully functioning sign language (Washabaugh 1986: 145). Washabaugh concluded that sign systems on the two island communities failed to generate an extensive repertoire of nominal signs or a disambiguating grammar because of the marginal status of the deaf.

The static, immature, signed pidgins of Providence Island and Grand Cayman stand in stark contrast to the well-formed language and social integration of Martha's Vineyard and probably that of the Enga as well. The lack of language development in communities in which signed pidgins are passed from deaf parent to deaf child for five or six generations ought to create serious doubts about the existence of universal, innate language-specific parameters. Semantic and syntactic parameters that are sensitive to social marginalization, despite early access to sign, suggest that language formation is dynamic, self-organizing, and epigenetic.

13.4 Creole Genesis

The original Language Bioprogram Hypothesis (LBH) claimed that when single-generation creoles are formed, innate principles of universal grammar help determine their nature; that is, they will have semantic and syntactic properties that are not derived from the pidgins that preceded them (Bickerton 1999: 49). Children in this first generation produce 'both embedded structures and a regular system of grammatical morphemes' while they are still in the early active phase of language acquisition (ibid. 54).

The *process* of acquisition differs not at all in the normal and creole cases. In both, children acquire as much vocabulary as they need, or as exists ... In the normal case, a child of four or five will have acquired a wide range of grammatical items— enough to satisfy the structural requirements imposed by the innate syntax. In the creole case, for most of these requirements the child simply cannot find appropriate grammatical items in the pidgin. Grammatical items therefore have to be created by recruiting lexical items and bleaching them of their normal lexical meaning.   (ibid. 57)

It is not very clear just who in a growing, dynamic population constitutes the 'first generation', or whether creolization requires some minimum number of children and/or a community of a certain critical size or cohesiveness (cf. Kegl *et al.* 1999; McWhorter 1997).

At the centre of the LBH discussion was Bickerton's claim that only an innate program could explain the *abrupt appearance* of universal syntactic parameters found in the emergence of Hawaiian English Creole at the turn of the century. McWhorter (1997) in his study of creole genesis gathered together considerable evidence that this was not so. Pacific plantations and ship pidgins developed among migrant, adult, largely male workers and were gradually, rather than abruptly, expanded between 1800 and 1900 with little or no contribution from children. He saw the spread of an expanded pidgin-English as the result of at least three well-documented contacts with the English language: (1) British and American sailors wintering on the island, (2) migrant workers from the Gilbert Islands using Pacific Island English, and (3) island men working on English trade ships, where South Sea Jargon was spoken (Holm 1988; McWhorter 1997). McWhorter (ibid. 68) concluded that Bickerton's Hawaiian data did not represent a fossil pidgin and its creole descendant side-by-side; instead, it represented a second-language register of HEC that was spoken largely by Japanese immigrants who had arrived long after the formation of the creole.

McWhorter also traced the morphological structures characterizing Atlantic English-based creoles back to a stable, expanded pidgin that formed among African slavers at trading-forts on the West African coast. If his analysis is correct, the creolized register began to appear before those first slave populations were imported to plantations in the West Indies, and long before children could have contributed to grammaticalization (ibid. 123–43, 174). The contribution of children to language structure may be difficult to disentangle from the changes in social conditions that allowed children to live on the plantations in the first place. Contributions to semantic content from more diverse social activities and a more cohesive community, where births rather than migrants or captives replace losses, may well be confounded with such contributions from a 'language acquisition faculty': 'If children are indeed capable of transforming a fragmentary jargon into fluent creole, then pidgins and creoles to date have not offered us a demonstration, and are unlikely to in the future' (McWhorter 1997: 82).

While McWhorter does not speak about self-organization in his proposed model of creole genesis, he does establish parameters central to a dynamic systems theory—such as the changes in the critical mass of participants, the influx of individuals and information into a language pool, and the cohesiveness of a community—as the most important constraints on creole genesis. He clearly emphasizes the self-organizing forces of language formation and change over those of an innate language faculty.

13.5 Computer Simulations of Language Formation

Kirby (1998, 1999*b*, 2001), Batali (1998, 2000), and Steels (1998; Steels *et al.* this volume) simulated the exchange of information in populations of agents in which a shared compositional semantics and syntax was generated using basic learning algorithms and without selection pressure for successful communication. Neo-Darwinian explanations tend to ignore principles of self-organization in biological systems, and thus to assume that the systematicity inherent in language is pre-programmed. The computer simulations of language genesis are powerful counter-examples to arguments that only an innate faculty could produce universal language parameters in a population (Bhalla and Iyengar 1999; Koch and Laurent 1999; Parrish and Edelstein-Keshet 1999; Weng, Bhalla, and Iyengar 1999).

Both biological and physical self-organizing systems standardize, streamline, and produce a hierarchical ordering of rule-like, or syntactic, complexity starting with chaotic or ill-formed input (Steels 1998; Batali 1998, 2000). Kauffman (1993) and Kelso (1995) have presented models and experimental support for the self-organizing properties of neural architectures that constrain the emergent properties in systems of information-exchange between minds. Oyama (1985), Karmiloff-Smith (1992), and Thelen and Smith (1998) described self-organizing cognitive repertoires, while Hemelrijk (1999) modelled self-organizing intra- and interspecies variations in primate social structure. Demolin and Soquet (1999) and de Boer (1999) investigated the role of competing constraints between vocal production and auditory reception in the epigenetic organization of language phonology. Finally, Bates and Elman (1996) and others (Elman *et al.* 1996) proposed that children's language acquisition was a function of the dynamic organization of cognitive development in a language environment.

Kirby (1998, 1999*b*, 2000, 2001), and Steels (1998; Steels *et al.* this volume) confirm that shared form, semantic content, and hierarchically embedded levels of semantic structure emerge in learning populations without preprogrammed, language-specific parameter settings, and without selection. Combinatorial syntax arose out of an exchange of information in a population with limited resources of time, memory, and processing power (Steels 1998). In the simplified landscape of a computer simulation, exchanges of information inevitably generated an easy-to-learn system of representation that included (1) a single communicative modality; (2) negotiated systems of basic forms from which all meaningful patterns were built; (3) shared associations between forms and concepts; and (4) morphologically marked semantic and grammatical functions (Kirby 1998: 379). Considered together with the evidence of sign language and creole formation cited above, these artificial language simulations make a powerful case for an epigenetic, negotiated language genesis. In other words, languages seem able to originate spontaneously in artificial and in natural populations as a result of an exchange of information between individuals and the survival in the language pool of structure and content that is easy to produce, comprehend, and learn.

13.6 Language Origins

The idea that a hierarchically ordered structure would automatically emerge out of initially chaotic exchanges of information in populations of real and artificial life-forms radically alters our understanding of language evolution. I am proposing that we consider 'language-readiness' as a function of an enlarged brain and a prolonged learning-sensitive period rather than a language-specific bioprogram. In other words, as soon as human memory and processing reached a still unknown minimum capacity, indigenous languages formed in every hominine community over a historic rather than an evolutionary timescale (Skoyles 1999). As a result of species-wide delays in developmental timing, a language-ready brain was probably ubiquitous in *Homo* at least as early as half a million years ago (Bermudez de Castro and Rosas 2001; Smith 1993). The earliest languages emerged as social and technological activities diversified, as brain volume and ontogeny approached that of modern humans.[3]

As for what triggered the increase in brain size that supports language-readiness, brain scaling in mammals suggests that selection for large brains and/or rapid learning may not be sufficient to explain encephalization

---

[3] Sign language formation differs from language genesis among hominid populations in that the critical parameter inhibiting sign language growth is not simply the number of deaf or lack of continuity in transmission, but the marginal status of the deaf in some communities. In addition, bilingual, sign, and spoken language users can introduce semantic structure from the spoken language into the sign language depending on the number of bilingual signers, the number of deaf, and the integration of deaf members into the community.

(Finlay, Darlington, and Nicastro 2001; Kress and Ragir 2001; Mayley 1997; Ragir 2001). Even with strong selective pressure for complex, adult cognitive skills, the reduction in birthrate that would be a natural consequence of producing large-brained, slowly maturing offspring meant that competitors bearing more quickly maturing, small-brained offspring would still have predominated (Ragir 2000*a*). Given such intraspecies competition, the number of individuals with large brains would remain small, and a group adaptation such as language that depended on enhanced memory and recall would never have emerged. It seems more reasonable to account for encephalization in terms of the prolongation of the phases of foetal development, caused by changes in the selective pressures on infant morphology and developmental timing, rather than on adult behaviour.

Pelvic adaptations for bipedalism narrowed the anterior–posterior dimension of the birth canal, and although the pelvis became wider as the hominid body became larger, the mechanics of walking inhibited a proportionate increase in this anterior–posterior dimension (Ruff 1995). Foetal size is strongly correlated to the size of the mother; once the pelvis was restructured to accommodate terrestrial bipedalism, any increase in female-neonatal body size would trigger further delays in skeletal maturation (Leigh and Park 1998; Leonard and Robertson 1996; Shea 1990; Trevathan and Rosenberg 2000). Selection for skeletal immaturity during parturition would have eased the passage of the enlarged neonate through the relatively narrow birth canal (Ragir 2000*a*, 2001).[4] Thus, species-wide pelvic constraints on obstetrics would trigger skeletal immaturity, and this in turn would lead to developmental delays. Such delays would create a *species-wide* reduction in female reproductive fitness, rather than a reduced fitness only in females with encephalized infants. In consequence, no intraspecies competitive differences in fertility would inhibit encephalization. In short, the whole population would change together, and encephalization could be relatively rapid and universal.

Language genesis probably required cohesive communities, socially structured exchanges of material goods, personnel, and information between individuals and groups, and foetal growth and postnatal development similar

---

[4] Large body size is highly adaptive in terrestrial mammals occupying environments with nutrient-rich, seasonal, and patchily distributed resources (Godfrey *et al.* 2001; Kozlowski and Weiner 1997). And because behavioural adaptations follow changes in habitat and/or resource availability, environmental variation is likely to have been the independent variable triggering hominid dietary change and increases in body size.

to that found in modern populations. The archaeological evidence suggests that an extraordinary number of complex behavioural repertories, including prepared-core stone technologies, tool-assisted food preparation, and co-operative hunting of large animals, emerged with *Homo ergaster/erectus* subsequent to the second episode of encephalization that accompanied an increase in body size and modern post-cranial body proportions (Milton 1999; O'Connell *et al.* 1999; Ragir 2000*b*). Even without language-specific structures or pre-programming, slowly maturing, large-brained hominids (>1,000cc) would have been 'language-ready' (Ragir 2000*a*; Skoyles 1999). The survival of *information* about neighbours, resources, territories, and technologies depended on generating a readily understood, easily learned, stable system of communication. It is probable that languages organized spontaneously in many different autonomous groups in Africa and Eurasia rather than in one small, unique African population; time, contact, and conquest would then have tended to reduce their original diversity.

13.7 Conclusion

The appearance of universal language parameters cannot discriminate between an innate language program and a self-organized, epigenetic language formation because a relatively abrupt emergence of structure is predicted by both hypotheses. However, unlike innate models, an epigenetic model of language formation entails a systemic sensitivity to the disruption of the language context. Young sign languages provide evidence that marginalization can inhibit language formation, perhaps more permanently than disruptions of transmission. The growth of home sign where everyday activity-related gestures become the basis of the communicative sign suggests that semantic input to children need not be language-like or even intentionally communicative for a process of language formation to be initiated (Morford *et al.* 1995; Singleton *et al.* 1993). The speed at which language emerges appears to be a function of the number and age of the new learners entering the language pool and of the overall number of deaf and hearing signers in the community.

The degree of language complexity and systematicity appear to be negotiated within the social exchange. Participation in a language pool during dendrogenesis lays the foundation for the functional specialization of cognitive infrastructure, while lifelong synaptogenesis permits the acquisition of new meanings, if not new morphological generalizations, to continue through-out life. The inhibition of semantic and syntactic generalization as a result of disruptions in information exchange within the group suggests that lan-guage parameters are epigenetic, negotiated structures, rather than innate parameters.

The tendency to generalize over statistical patterns in input has been observed in the formation of Nicaraguan Sign Language and in the lan-guage acquisition in deaf children when the signed lexicon and grammar are severely depleted (Newport 1999). It appears that when input is relatively unsystematic, basic learning algorithms have a tendency to impose order and schematize responses. Kirby (1999b: 10) has proposed that:

The process of the transmission of learned behavior has certain general properties whatever our assumptions about the learners. These properties will tend to favour the emergence of systems with patterns that can be exploited by learning. Where the behaviour that is being learned is a mapping between two structured spaces, we can expect the process of transmission to give us mappings that preserve structure. For the case of language, where these spaces are propositional meanings on the one hand, and linear strings on the other, the mappings that will inevitably emerge will be syntactic.

The 'rules' of syntax are properties of a dynamic system rather than of pre-programmed cognitive modules, and the specific 'principles' that govern sentence construction are stored in the language pool within which an indi-vidual functions rather than in innate cognitive faculties.

A dynamic exchange of information in open, cohesive human popula-tions during a prolonged childhood appears to be the necessary and suf-ficient condition for language formation in real populations. The more growth and pruning of neural connections there is during a learning-sen-sitive ontogenetic period, the easier it is for everyone in a population to acquire the adult repertory regardless of underlying differences in genetic predisposition. Meaning–form connections and compositional morphol-ogy become automatic as a result of repetitive activation of dendritic and synaptic links. Language genesis is constrained by dynamic interactions at three epigenetic levels; that is, within and between cortical and subcortical structures, between the ontogeny of the brain and activity of the individual, and between the ontogeny of the individual and the adaptation of the group within an ecosystem. The complex organization that emerges from patterns of competitive and co-operative behaviour and the potential for these activ-ities to organize the brain are far more important for language origins and genesis than the basic learning algorithms that govern neural processing across cortical subsystems and species.

FURTHER READING

GROCE, N. E. (1985), *Everyone Here Spoke Sign Language: Hereditary Deafness on Martha's Vineyard* (Cambridge, Mass.: Harvard University Press). (A history of deafness on Martha's Vineyard and a reconstruction of the integrated deaf–hearing community that produced the most influential sign language in the history of American Sign Language.)

KENDON, A. (1980), 'A Description of A Deaf-Mute Sign Language from the Enga Province of Papua New Guinea with Some Comparative Discussion. Part I: The Formational Properties of Enga Signs', *Semiotica*, 31/1–2: 1–34. 'Part II: The Semiotic Functioning of Enga Signs', *Semiotica*, 32/1–2: 81–117. 'Part III: Aspects of Utterance Construction', *Semiotica*, 32/3–4: 245–313. (This is the best description of an indigenous non-Western sign language in the literature and set the standard to which other descriptions aspire.)

McWHORTER, J. H. (1997), *Toward a New Model of Creole Genesis* (New York: Peter Lang). (This is a persuasive discussion of trade and plantation creoles using linguistic and historic evidence to argue against the Language Bioprogram as a significant factor in creolization. McWhorter argues against the abrupt creolization of Hawaiian English Creole at the turn of the century. And he presents an original interpretation of the Atlantic English-based Creoles as being derived from an expanded pidgin originating among the Africans working at slave-trading forts on the coast of West Africa.)

MAYLEY, G. (1996), 'The Evolutionary Cost of Learning', in P. Maes, M. Mataric, J. A. Meyer, J. Pollack, and S. Wilson (eds.), *From Animals to Animates: Proceedings of the Fourth International Conference on Simulation of Adaptive Behaviour* (Cambridge, Mass.: MIT Press), 458–67. (An account of learning costs and how they affect adult fitness.)

WASHABAUGH, W. (1986), *Five Fingers for Survival* (Ann Arbor: Karoma Publishers). (This book is an excellent description of the deaf members of the Providence Island communities and the social constraints that inhibited language formation.)

REFERENCES

BALDWIN, J. M. (1896), 'A New Factor in Evolution', *American Naturalist*, 30: 441–51.

BATALI, J. (1998), 'Computational Simulations of the Emergence of Grammar', in J. Hurford, M. Studdert-Kennedy, and C. Knight (eds.), *Approaches to the Evolution of Language: Social and Cognitive Bases* (Cambridge: Cambridge University Press), 405–26.

BATALI, J. (2000), 'Negotiating Syntax', *Proceedings of the Third Conference on the Evolution of Language: Extended Abstracts* (Paris: École National Supérieure des Télécommunications), 18–20.

BATES, E., and ELMAN, J. L. (1996), 'Learning Rediscovered', *Science*, 274: 1849–50.

BERMUDEZ DE CASTRO, J. M., and ROSAS, A. (2001), 'Pattern of Dental Development in Hominid XVII from the Middle Pleistocene Atapuerca-Sima de los Huesos Site (Spain)', *American Journal of Physical Anthropology*, 114/4: 325–30.

BHALLA, U. S., and IYENGAR, P. (1999), 'Emergent Properties of Networks of Biological Signaling Pathways', *Science*, 283: 381–7.

BICKERTON D. (1990), *Language and Species* (Chicago: University of Chicago Press).

——(1999), 'How to Acquire Language without Positive Evidence: What Acquisitionists Can Learn from Creoles', in M. DeGraff (ed.), *Language Creation and Language Change: Creolization, Diachrony, and Development* (Cambridge, Mass.: MIT Press), 49–74.

DE BOER, B. (1999), 'Evolution and Self-Organization in Vowel Systems', *Evolution of Communication*, 3/1: 79–103.

DEACON, T. W. (1997), *The Symbolic Species: The Co-evolution of Language and the Brain* (New York: Norton).

DEMOLIN, D., and SOQUET, A. (1999), 'The Role of Self-Organization in the Emergence of Phonological Systems', *Evolution of Communication*, 3/1: 21–48.

ELMAN, J. L., BATES E. A., JOHNSON, M. H., KARMILOFF-SMITH, A., PARISI, D., and PLUNKETT, K. (1996), *Rethinking Innateness: A Connectionist Perspective on Development* (Cambridge, Mass.: MIT Press).

FINLAY, B. L., DARLINGTON, R., and NICASTRO, N. (2001), 'Developmental Structure in Brain Evolution', *Behavioral and Brain Science*, 24/2, www.bbsonline.org.

GODFREY, L. R, SAMONDS, K. E., JUNGERS, W. L., and SUTHERLAND, M. R. (2001), 'Teeth, Brains, and Primate Life Histories', *American Journal of Physical Anthropology*, 114/3: 192–214.

GROCE, N. E. (1985), *Everyone Here Spoke Sign Language: Hereditary Deafness on Martha's Vineyard* (Cambridge, Mass.: Harvard University Press).

HEMELRIJK, C. K. (1999), 'An Individual-Orientated Model of the Emergence of Despotic and Egalitarian Societies', *Proceedings of the Royal Society*, London B, 266: 361–9.

HOLM, J. (1988), *Pidgins and Creoles*, i. *Theory and Structure* (Cambridge: Cambridge University Press).

KARMILOFF-SMITH, A. (1992), *Beyond Modularity: A Developmental Perspective on Cognitive Science* (Cambridge, Mass.: MIT Press).

KAUFFMAN, S. A. (1993), *The Origins of Order: Self-Organization and Selection in Evolution* (New York: Oxford University Press).

KEGL, J., SENGHAS, A., and COPPOLA, M. (1999), 'Creation Through Contact: Sign Language Emergence and Sign Language Change in Nicaragua', in M. DeGraff (ed.), *Comparative Grammatical Change: The Intersection of Language Acquisition, Creole Genesis, and Diachronic Syntax* (Cambridge, Mass.: MIT Press), 179–238.

KELSO, J. A. SCOTT (1995), *Dynamic Patterns: The Self-Organization of Brain and Behavior* (Cambridge, Mass.: MIT Press).

KENDON, A. (1980*a*), 'A Description of a Deaf-Mute Sign Language from the Enga Province of Papua New Guinea with Some Comparative Discussion. Part I: The Formational Properties of Enga Signs', *Semiotica*, 31/1–2: 1–34.

——(1980*b*), 'A Description of a Deaf-Mute Sign Language from the Enga Province of Papua New Guinea With Some Comparative Discussion. Part II: The Semiotic Functioning of Enga Signs', *Semiotica*, 32/1–2: 81–117.

——(1980*c*), 'A Description of a Deaf-Mute Sign Language from the Enga Province of Papua New Guinea With Some Comparative Discussion. Part III: Aspects of Utterance Construction', *Semiotica*, 32/3–4: 245–313.

KIRBY, S. (1998), 'Fitness and the Selective Adaptation of Language', in J. R. Hurford, M. Studdert-Kennedy, and C. Knight (eds.), *Approaches to the Evolution of Language: Social and Cognitive Bases* (Cambridge: Cambridge University Press), 359–83.

——(1999*a*), *Function, Selection, and Innateness: The Emergence of Language Universals* (Oxford: Oxford University Press).

——(1999*b*). 'Syntax out of Learning: The Cultural Evolution of Structured Communication in a Population of Induction Algorithms', in D. Floreano, J.-D. Nicoud, and F. Mondada (eds.), *Advances in Artificial Life*, Lecture Notes in Computer Science, 1674 (Berlin: Springer-Verlag), 694–703; www.ling.ed.ac.uk/lec/publications.html.

——(2000), 'Syntax without Natural Selection: How Compositionality Emerges from Vocabulary in a Population of Learners', in C. Knight, M. Studdert-Kennedy, and J. R. Hurford (eds.), *The Evolutionary Emergence of Language: Social Function and the Origins of Linguistic Form* (Cambridge: Cambridge University Press), 303–23.

——(2001), 'Spontaneous Evolution of Linguistic Structure: An Iterated Learning Model of the Emergence of Regularity and Irregularity', *IEEE Transactions on Evolutionary Computation*, 5/2: 102–10.

——and HURFORD, J. (1997), 'The Evolution of Incremental Learning: Language Development and Critical Periods', *University of Edinburgh Occasional Papers in Linguistics* (EOPL-97-2).

KOCH, C., and LAURENT, G. (1999), 'Complexity and the Nervous System', *Science*, 284: 96–8.

KOZLOWSKI, J., and WEINER, J. (1997), 'Interspecific Allometries are By-products of Body Size Optimization', *American Naturalist*, 149: 352–80.

KRESS, M., and RAGIR, S. (2001), 'Can the Baldwin Effect Guide the Evolution of Social Behavior?', *American Journal of Physical Anthropology*, Suppl. 32: 122.

LEIGH, S. R., and PARK, P. B. (1998), 'Evolution of Human Growth Prolongation', *American Journal of Physical Anthropology*, 107: 331–50.

LEONARD, W. R., and ROBERTSON, M. L. (1996), 'On Diet, Energy Metabolism, and Brain Size in Human Evolution', *Current Anthropology*, 37/1: 125–9.

MCWHORTER, J. H. (1997), *Toward a New Model of Creole Genesis* (New York: Peter Lang).

MAYLEY, G. (1996), 'The Evolutionary Cost of Learning', in P. Maes, M. Mataric, J. A. Meyer, J. Pollack, and S. Wilson (eds.), *From Animals to Animates: Proceedings of the Fourth International Conference on Simulation of Adaptive Behaviour* (Cambridge, Mass.: MIT Press), 458–67.

——(1997), 'Guiding or Hiding', in P. Husbands and I. Harvey (eds.), *Proceedings of the Fourth European Conference on Artificial Life* (Cambridge, Mass.: MIT Press), 135–44.

MILTON, K. (1999), 'A Hypothesis to Explain the Role of Meat-Eating in Human Evolution', *Evolutionary Anthropology*, 8/1: 11–21.

MORFORD, J. P., SINGLETON J. L., and GOLDIN-MEADOW S. (1995), 'The Genesis of Language: How Much Time is Needed to Generate Arbitrary Symbols in a Sign System?', in K. Emmorey and J. Reilly (eds.), *Language, Gesture and Space* (Hillsdale, NJ: Lawrence Erlbaum), 313–32.

NEWPORT, E. (1999), 'Reduced Input in the Acquisition of Signed Languages: Contributions to the Study of Creolization', in M. DeGraff (ed.), *Language Creation and Language Change: Creolization, Diachrony, and Development* (Cambridge, Mass.: MIT Press), 161–78.

O'CONNELL, J. F., HAWKES, K., and BLURTON JONES, N. G. (1999), 'Grandmothering and the Evolution of *Homo erectus*', *Journal of Human Evolution*, 36/5: 461–86.

OYAMA, S. (1985), *The Ontogeny of Information: Developmental Systems and Evolution* (Cambridge: Cambridge University Press).

PARRISH, J. K., and EDELSTEIN-KESHET, L. (1999), 'Complexity, Pattern, and Evolutionary Trade-offs in Animal Aggregation', *Science*, 284: 99–101.

RAGIR, S. (2000a), 'Toward an Understanding of the Relationship between Bipedal Walking, Encephalization and Language Origins', in G. Gyori (ed.), *Language Evolution: Biological, Linguistic, and Philosophical Perspectives* (Frankfurt am Main: Peter Lang), 69–104.

——(2000b), 'Gut Morphology and the Avoidance of Carrion Among Chimpanzees, Baboons, and Early Hominids', *Journal of Anthropological Research*, 56: 477–512.

——(2001), 'Changes in Perinatal Conditions Selected for Neonatal Immaturity: Commentary on Finlay, Darlington and Nicastros, "Developmental Structure in Brain Evolution"', *Behavioral and Brain Science*, 24/2: 291–2; www.bbsonline.org.

RICE, S. H. (2000), 'The Evolution of Developmental Interactors: Epistasis, Canalization, and Integration', in J. B. Wolf, E. D. Brodie, and M. J. Wade (eds.), *Epistasis and the Evolutionary Process* (Oxford: Oxford University Press), 82–98.

RUFF, C. (1995), 'Biomechanics of the Hip and Birth in Early Homo', *American Journal of Physical Anthropology*, 98: 527–74.

SENGHAS, A. (1994), 'Nicaragua's Lessons for Language Acquisition', *Signpost*, 7/1: 32–46.

——(1995), 'The Development of Nicaraguan Sign Language via the Language Acquisition Process', in D. McLaughlin and S. McEwen (eds.), *Proceedings of the 19th Annual Boston University Conference on Language Development* (Sommerville, Mass.: Cascadilla Press), 543–52.

SENGHAS, R. J. (1997), 'An ?Unspeakable, Unwriteable? Language: Deaf Identity, Language and Personhood among the First Cohorts of Nicaraguan Signers', Ph.D. Thesis, Department of Anthropology, University of Rochester, Rochester, New York. Ann Arbor MI: UMI Microform # 9808912.

SHEA, B. T. (1990), 'Dynamic Morphology: Growth, Life History, and Ecology in Primate Evolution', in J. C. DeRousseau (ed.), *Primate Life History and Evolution* (New York: Wiley-Liss), 543–52.

SHUMAN, M. K. (1980a), 'Culture and Deafness in a Mayan Indian Village', *Psychiatry: Journal for the Study of Interpersonal Processes*, 43/4: 359–70.

——(1980b), 'A Preliminary Account of Sign Language Use by the Deaf in a Yucatan Maya Village', *Language Sciences*, 2: 144–73.

SINGLETON, J. L., MORFORD J. P., and GOLDIN-MEADOW S. (1993), 'Once is Not Enough: Standards of Well-formedness in Manual Communication Created over Three Timespans', *Language*, 69: 683–715.

SKOYLES, J. R. (1999), 'Human Evolution Expanded Brains to Increase Expertise Capacity, Not IQ', *Psycoloquy* 10(002) Brain Expertise (i) ftp://ftp.princeton.edu/pub/harnad/Psycoloquy/1999.volume.10/psyc.99.10.002.brain-expertise.1.skoyles.

SMITH, B. H. (1993), 'The Physiological Age of KNM-WT 1500', in A. Walker and R. Leakey (eds.), *The Nariokotome Homo erectus Skeleton: Part iii. Analytical Studies* (Cambridge, Mass.: Harvard University Press), 195–220.

STEELS, L. (1998), 'Synthesizing the Origins of Language and Meaning Using Coevolution, Self-Organization and Level Formation', in J. Hurford, M. Studdert-Kennedy, and C. Knight (eds.), *Approaches to the Evolution of Language: Social and Cognitive Bases* (Cambridge: Cambridge University Press), 348–404.

THELEN, E., and SMITH, L. B. (1998), *A Dynamic Systems Approach to the Development of Cognition and Action* (Cambridge, Mass.: MIT Press).

TREVATHAN, W., and ROSENBERG, K. R. (2000), 'The Shoulders Follow the Head: Post-Cranial Constraints on Human Childbirth', *Journal of Human Evolution*, 39/6: 583–6.

WASHABAUGH, W. (1980), 'The Organization and Use of Providence Island Sign Language', *Sign Language Studies*, 26: 65–92.

——(1981), 'The Deaf of Grand Cayman, BWI', *Sign Language Studies*, 31: 117–34.

——(1986), *Five Fingers for Survival* (Ann Arbor: Karoma Publishers).

WASHABAUGH, W., WOODWARD, J. C., and DESANTIS, S. (1978), 'Providence Island Sign: A Context-Dependent Language', *Anthropological Linguistics*, 20/3: 95–109.

WENG, G., BHALLA, U. P., and IYENGAR, R. (1999), 'Complexity in Biological Signaling Systems', *Science*, 284: 92–5.

WOODWARD, J. C. (1978), 'Attitudes towards Deaf People of Providence Island', *Sign Language Studies*, 18: 49–68.

YAMAGUCHI, H. (2000), 'Evolution of LAD and the Baldwin Effect: Epistasis, Pleiotropy, and the Baldwin Effect', Masters dissertation, University of Edinburgh, www.ling.ed.ac.uk/lec/publications .

PART IV

The Onward Journey:
Determining the Shape of Language

14   The Slow Growth of Language in Children

ROBBINS BURLING

14.1 Introduction

A surprisingly broad consensus has grown among scholars who are interested in the origin of language that the ability to speak was a relatively recent and quite rapid development (e.g. Noble and Davidson 1996: 17). Hardly anyone would now go so far as to credit a single mutation for all syntax, as Bickerton once did (1990, 1998), and even Bickerton has moderated his earlier position (Bickerton 2000, Calvin and Bickerton 2000). Carstairs-McCarthy has also proposed a scenario that allows for more than a single stage of syntax (1999, 2000). In spite of this, however, full syntax is still widely presumed to have come quite late (40,000 to 150,000 years ago) and, by the standards of most evolutionary change, very quickly. One support for the presumption of suddenness is the difficulty that some linguists have in imagining a partial syntax. Syntax is presumed to be not only incredibly complex, but highly interconnected. No part, it is sometimes believed, could exist without all the rest, and all its extraordinary complexities are seen as following from a few simple principles (e.g. Berwick 1998).

Anyone who denies even the possibility of a partial or simple syntax would have to deny its existence in any of the varieties of language that we can observe today. Possible candidates for partial syntax include pidgin languages and the imperfect language of feral children, but child language stands out as a particularly promising form of language to consider. If some stage of child language could be shown to exhibit partial syntax it would be

Barbara Pan, Marilyn Shatz, Hanne Gram Simonsen, and Catherine Snow offered their advice and helped me to find my way into some of the literature on the early and late stages of language acquisition. I thank them all for their generosity. Four perceptive anonymous reviewers offered their suggestions for improving the chapter. One of these later admitted to being Alison Wray. All four of these reviewers, but Wray in particular, have earned my profound thanks.

difficult to insist that no system of partial syntax is even possible. This means that anyone who denies partial syntax ought to be driven to interpret child language as jumping abruptly from a stage where it consists of little more than strings of poorly joined individual words (so-called 'protolanguage') to the stage of full syntax. No one has pursued the logic of this argument more forthrightly than Derek Bickerton (1990), and we owe him a considerable debt for presenting the best available evidence for the rapid advance of children from protolanguage to full language.

Unfortunately for those who hold this position, the facts of child language, as we can observe it each day in the behaviour of our own children, do not fit an abrupt scenario. It is true that children frequently appear to achieve complex syntax with enviable speed, but they do not move from the single-word stage, or even from some sort of protolanguage, to full syntax in a few months, let alone in the single day that should be expected by anyone who is unable to imagine a partial syntax. I believe that the abrupt appearance of syntax in children is actually an illusion, but it is an illusion that is helped by our frequent failure to take account of both early and late learning. First, we may not notice the great amount of learning that takes place silently before active production of language even begins, and second, we may fail to recognize that the apparent mastery over syntax with which we sometimes credit 5-year-old children is due in good part to their avoidance of complex constructions. By avoiding mistakes they may fool us into believing that they have learned it all.

In the following pages, I will offer several examples of both the early and late learning of syntax by children. My goal is to show that the development of syntax, as we can actually observe it in children, gives no support for the belief that syntax comes suddenly. It follows from this that the course of child language development does not, as many suppose, support the conclusion that language must have come suddenly in evolution.

14.2 Early Learning

First, I offer some examples of the learning that occurs silently before children actually produce the forms that they have learned, and I cannot resist starting with an example, admittedly anecdotal, from my own grandson. Jamie was very slow to talk. At the age of 2 years and 2 months, when most children are forming full sentences, his parents reported to me that he had used a grand total of three words. The only one of these that I had ever heard was *daʔ-daʔ-daʔ-daʔ* meaning 'I want it'. Unfortunately I was separated from him for some months after this point in his linguistic development, so I missed his burst into productive language, but his parents told me that soon after I had been with him, he seemed to wake up one morning with the attitude, 'Hey, it's time to talk.' Very soon he was not only using large numbers of words, but sentences as well. If ever there was a candidate for demonstrating the abrupt learning of language, it was Jamie.

Such a conclusion, however, would be premature. At the age of 2 years and 2 months, when he said almost nothing, he was able to understand a great deal. He certainly understood many hundreds of words, quite plausibly thousands. When asked, he could point reliably not only to his eyes, nose, and mouth, but to his chin, elbow, and knee. He could point reliably not only to a window or a door, but to the ceiling, wall, and floor. He knew the names of dozens of people. The occasion at which I was with him, at 2 years and 2 months, was a family reunion which gathered a number of people whom Jamie had never known before, one of whom was the girlfriend of my nephew, his father's cousin. She expressed astonishment, one evening, that he was able to comply, with no apparent difficulty, to the request 'Can you give some popcorn to Cindy?' even though many people were present to whom the popcorn might, at that moment, have been passed. Cindy had not supposed that Jamie had seen enough of her to have learned her name. Of course he could use cues both from the social context and from the sentence in which the name was embedded. These certainly could have helped him to interpret the request. The point is, however, that he knew enough language to help him in his interpretation. He must have known that every person has a name. Even if he selected Cindy because he knew the names of everyone else in the immediate vicinity, that would demonstrate his knowledge of all the other names, as well as his ability to pluck the name out from the syntactic context in which it occurred. It was, to be sure, much easier to assess Jamie's knowledge of words than of syntax, but he understood words as they came flowing to him among other words, and he must have learned them in the same way. He was probably helped to learn 'eye' and 'nose' by hearing them in isolation while playing the games that adults enjoy so much, but I doubt if anyone ever drilled him with 'ceiling', 'wall', and 'floor'. He must have learned these words as he heard them among other words, and he would have needed to have at least some passive grasp of syntax just to extract them from the linguistic background. Exactly how much syntax he could understand is very difficult even to speculate about, but he understood a lot of English.

More systematic studies of early language comprehension have been made than my admittedly casual observations of Jamie. Consider, for example, the work of Kathy Hirsh-Pasek and Roberta Golinkoff (1991, 1996). They studied comprehension by playing recorded sentences to small children who could look at either of two TV monitors. One of these monitors illustrated the sentence and the other illustrated a contrasting situation. Hirsh-Pasek and Golinkoff compared the length of time in which the children looked at the two monitors. For example, one of the sentences that the children heard was, *She is kissing the keys.* While this sentence came over the loud speaker, one of monitors showed a woman kissing a bunch of keys that she held in one hand, while she held up a ball in plain view with the other hand. The second monitor showed the opposite situation: a woman kissing a ball, while she held up the bunch of keys.

Children between 13 and 15 months of age who had not moved past the one-word stage and who had an average productive vocabulary of about 25 words, reliably focused for a longer time on the TV monitor whose picture corresponded to the sentence they heard than on the monitor that showed a contrasting scene. To be sure, not much syntax is needed to discriminate between the meanings, but since both pictures in this example show both *kissing* and *keys*, more is needed than simple receptive comprehension of the words. The child must, at least, be able to recognize that some sort of association connects the words *kissing* and *keys* in the sentence that they heard. This experiment suggests that children who are just beginning to talk, can already find associations between the words of the sentences that they hear.

Children who were just slightly older—between 16 and 18 months—but whose productive language had still not passed the one-word stage, were able to respond correctly, with greater than chance accuracy, to sentences such as *Where is Big Bird washing Cookie Monster?* This sentence is 'reversible' in the sense that either of the two characters might have been doing the washing, and the two monitors showed the contrasting actions. When the spoken sentence described Big Bird doing the washing, the children looked longer at the screen that depicted that action than at the screen where Big Bird was being washed. Their preference was reversed when the sentence they heard had the characters reversed. These children, none of whom used more than one word at a time in their production, were able to use word order to interpret the meaning of at least some of the sentences that they heard.

Additional evidence for the precedence of comprehension over production comes from imitation experiments conducted by LouAnn Gerken, Barbara Landau, and Robert E. Remez (1990). This group worked with children who were as young as 24 months, still in the early stages of productive language, but a bit older than the children studied by Hirsh-Pasek and Golinkoff. These children were persuaded to imitate short phrases. Some of the phrases that they heard had four English morphemes arranged according to the following pattern: a verb, such as *push*, to which -*es* 'third singular' was suffixed, followed in turn by the article *the* and a noun such as *truck*. The resulting phrases had the form of *pushes the truck*, with a verb, two function morphemes, and a noun. Other phrases were similar except that some of the English words and affixes were replaced by nonsense forms. In some, the content words, the verb and noun, were replaced by nonsense words, while in others it was the function morphemes, -*es* and *the*, that were replaced. In still other examples all four morphemes were nonsense forms. As in real phrases, the verb base and noun base that framed the examples were given the full stress of content words, while the two morphemes that came in the middle were weakly stressed. The experimental results came from comparing the success of the children in imitating the content words and the function morphemes, both genuine and artificial, under a variety of conditions. One might suppose that children would more reliably imitate genuine English morphemes than nonsense substitutes, but the results were not so simple.

First, other things being equal, the children were notably more successful at imitating the content words (whether English or nonsense) than the function morphemes (whether English or nonsense). That is, they often said things such as *push truck* instead of the full sequence that they heard. If we knew no more, this might be attributed to either of two things. First, the content words received greater stress than the function morphemes, as they do in normal speech, and this ought to have made imitation easier. On the other hand, the more reliable imitation of the English nouns and verbs could mean that the children had not yet learned the function morphemes as well as they had the content words.

More interesting was the fact that children omitted genuine English function morphemes *more* often that they omitted nonsense substitutes for them. Instead of saying *pushes the truck*, some children said *push truck*. When imitating such sentences as *pusheg le truck*, where the nonsense forms -*eg* and *le* have been substituted for -*es* and *the*, more children imitated more accurately. They were more likely to include -*eg* and *le* than they were to imitate the genuine English suffix and article. Apparently they recognized some sort of difference between the familiar English function morphemes and their unfamiliar substitutes, and the very familiarity of the real morphemes made it possible to leave them out. Even on the most cautious interpretation, the children reacted differently to the familiar morphemes than they did to the strange ones, and since they imitated the unfamiliar ones more accurately, their omission of the familiar form must have been the result of some sort of active editing out, not simply a failure to notice them.

In addition, the children imitated the content words, whether these words were genuinely English or nonsense substitutes, more successfully in the presence of genuinely English function morphemes than in the presence of nonsense substitutes. They could imitate *push* and *truck* more successfully when they heard *pushes the truck* than when they heard *pusheg le truck*. In other words, the genuine English function morphemes helped them to imitate the content words, even when they did not actually articulate the function morphemes. Children who failed to imitate the function morphemes were still able to use these function morphemes to help in the identification and isolation of the content words. Gerken *et al.* do not suggest that the children had a full adult understanding of the function morphemes, but it does seem that even at a stage when children are considerably less likely to imitate function morphemes than content words, the function morphemes can still be used to help them extract the meaning, and even the grammatical structure, of the sentences. They used markers of syntax more reliably in comprehension than in their own production.

I have summarized the results of these experiments rather schematically, and I should point out that all the results are statistical trends rather than absolute differences. The children were more likely to imitate content words than function morphemes but imitation of function morphemes did sometimes take place. Nevertheless, the overall trends are so clear that I find it impossible to doubt that comprehension of syntax comfortably precedes its production. It is much more difficult to study language comprehension than language production. When children appear to understand a bit of language, it is often impossible to know to what extent they have depended on words, on syntax, or on the non-verbal context within which the language is embedded, but studies such as these show that the study of comprehension is not impossible. Any study that focuses exclusively on production while failing to recognize the likelihood that comprehension of syntax, like comprehension of words, runs well ahead of production, is bound to give a distorted picture of a child's linguistic skills. Producing a syntactic construction in the appropriate circumstances should be looked upon as only the final stage in a long developmental process.

14.3 Late Learning

The second source for the illusion of very rapid language learning comes with the late stages. It is sometimes asserted that 5-year-old children have mastered their grammar (e.g. McNeill 1966: 99; Rees 1974: 255). By then, it has been supposed, children know all the syntax that they will ever need to know. It is true that 5-year-olds have generally overcome the imperfect phonology of their earlier years, and those who are learning English, at least, no longer make many of the obvious morphological errors of younger children. Still, the illusion of syntactic mastery that 5-year-old children give us is not achieved by knowing all there is to know about syntax, but by the simple expedient of avoiding complex syntactic constructions.

Much less attention has been given to 5 to 10-year-old language learners than to younger children, but those working with older children still point back to the pioneering work of Carol Chomsky (1969). In careful sessions Chomsky asked forty predominantly middle-class 5 to 10-year-old English-speaking children to manipulate dolls in ways that would demonstrate their understanding of various types of sentence. She found that 5-year-olds still lacked mastery over several central aspects of syntax. Few 5-year-olds, for example, could recognize with any consistency that the pronoun *he*, in a sentence such as *He found out that Mickey won the race*, has to refer to someone other than *Mickey*. Chomsky's subjects were asked to manipulate or point to two dolls, one of Mickey Mouse and one of Pluto. When given the sentence *He found out that Mickey won the race* and asked to point to the doll that *found it out*, most of the 5-year-old children in the sample responded quite randomly. They were as likely to point to Mickey as to Pluto. Most children who were 6 or older had no trouble identifying the right doll.

In several other types of sentence, the pronoun was ambiguous. Ambiguous sentences include those where the main clause comes second, as in *After he got the candy, Mickey left*, and those in which the pronoun refers back to an earlier main clause, as in *Mickey said that he was hungry*. In both these cases *he* can refer either to *Mickey* or to someone else. The children of 6 and over often explicitly recognized the ambiguity of the *he* in such sentences. They made such comments as 'It could be either one.' In contrast, the younger children never commented on the ambiguity. Clearly, the 5-year-olds still had some syntax to learn.

Carol Chomsky investigated other bits of syntax that were learned even later. In the presence of a blindfolded doll, children were asked, *Is the doll easy to see or hard to see?* Some children as old as 7 and 8, and more who were 5 and 6, replied that the doll was *hard* to see. Those who responded in this way were then asked *Would you make her easy to see?* Logically and consistently, they then proceeded to remove the blindfold from the doll's eyes. In discussing what they had done, some children even explained that the blindfold made her hard to see but that the difficulty could be solved by removing the blindfold. Children who called the blindfolded doll *easy to see*, were asked to make her *hard* to see and they responded in various ways. Some hid the doll under the table, some put something on top of her, some merely closed or covered their own eyes. As we would expect, a higher proportion of older children answered this question as adults would answer it, but there was considerable overlap in ages, some 5-year-olds responding correctly, some 8-year-olds failing to do so. As Chomsky (1969: 32) commented, 'The fact that there are children of 7 and 8 who have not yet mastered this construction indicates that fairly basic syntactic learning is still going on considerably beyond the age at which it is generally considered to be complete.'

Other evidence indicates that we can be fooled into exaggerating children's knowledge, if they use forms in a way that appears superficially to conform to adult standards of syntax even though they still lack full comprehension of the way these forms are used. Annette Karmiloff-Smith (1986) has shown that French-speaking children do not gain a full understanding of such basic function words as articles and possessives until they are about 8 years old. A difficult feature of articles and possessives is that they combine several functions, and French articles and possessives are even more complex on this score than are those of English. *Les*, for example, not only shows definiteness as does English *the*, and totalization (in contrast to *des*, 'some'), but also pluralization (in contrast to *le/la*). A possessive pronoun such as *mes*, 'my', indicates possession, but, unlike English *my*, it also indicates plurality. More subtly, unless modified in some way, *mes*, like English *my*, refers to all the mentioned objects, as in *give me my books*, or *donnez moi mes livres*, where the pronoun could not refer to only *some* of the *books that are mine*. At the same time *mes* and *my* denote a particular subclass, so *mes livres* distinguishes 'my particular books' from all the books that might be under consideration.

French-speaking children as young as 3½ years old use *les* and *mes* in ways that seem, superficially, to conform to adult standards, but among the children whom Karmiloff-Smith studied it was only those who were older who understood their full array of meanings. By five years of age, children easily used *les* to indicate plurality, but they did not recognize the totalizing sense of 'all that are present'. Both the possessive and pluralizing functions of pronouns such as *mes*, 'my', were understood well enough, but, once again the totalizing function was not. These words were taken to indicate a plural number, but not necessarily all those under consideration.

Part of the evidence for the failure of young children to understand the full implications of *les* and *mes*, came from children between 5 and 8 years old. Unlike younger children they did, at least, demonstrate an awareness of the need to indicate totality but they more often accomplished this by adding *tous*, 'all', (which is redundant to adults) than by exploiting the totalizing function of the plural article or possessive. Karmiloff-Smith summarizes in this way:

Thus, whereas smaller children used *les X* in a given situation but only meant to convey pluralization, children of the second level [5½–8 years old] added in the same situation (*tous les X*) in order to cover totalization also. It was not until the third level [8–12] that children used *les X* to mark pluralization and totalization simultaneously.

A number of studies have shown that children of 5, and even older, have considerable difficulty interpreting passives and some kinds of relative clauses. Sheldon (1974), for example, showed that 5-year-old children, when asked to manipulate toy animals to show what a sentence describes, often misunderstood a sentence such as *The dog bumps into the horse that the giraffe jumps over*. Many children, some of them with great consistency, interpreted such sentences as if it was the subject rather than the object of the main clause that was the object of the relative clause. In this example they made the giraffe jump over the dog rather than the horse. Children did considerably better with co-ordinate expressions that are synonymous with relative sentences. In other words, they were better at interpreting *The dog bumps into the horse and the giraffe jumps over the horse*, than they were with the synonymous *The dog bumps into the horse that the giraffe jumps over*. This shows that it was the construction that was causing the difficulty, not the idea. Of course adults may also find the relative construction more difficult that the co-ordinate construction, but they are far better at understanding it than 5-year-old children are. Five-year-olds simply do not have anything like an adult level of competence. Since 5-year-olds rarely attempt to use constructions of this sort, their lack of adult competence will not be easily observed if we pay attention only to spontaneous production while ignoring comprehension.

14.4 The Middle Years

The examples that I have given suggest that syntax starts to be learned well before it is exhibited in productive speech and that it continues to be refined for several years past 5. Neither of these age periods has been the main focus for studies of syntactic development, however, and it is still the case that the best evidence for the progressive, step by step growth of syntax comes from the classical period for language acquisition, from about 1½ years old to 5. Bickerton has argued that syntax develops very rapidly in children and he has recently (Calvin and Bickerton 2000: 205) referred to 'what some acqui-sitionists have called "the syntactic spurt"'. In my own reading of the litera-ture on child language I have come across little discussion of any syntactic spurt and Bickerton does not give references. A 'word spurt' has, to be sure, been widely discussed, but even that has now been called into question. Paul Bloom (2000: 39–43) carefully dissects the evidence for a word spurt and finds it wanting. Instead of any discussion of a syntactic spurt I find, instead, a pervasive, though rarely explicitly stated, presumption of gradual and con-tinuous syntactic growth. The question of whether or not syntax appears abruptly during this period has not really attracted much attention from stu-dents of child language. They are more likely simply to take it for granted that syntax develops progressively through these years. For example, a fine recent book-length survey of research in child syntax, William O'Grady's *Syntactic Development* (1997), never argues the point explicitly, but the examples give ample evidence that syntax develops progressively from simple beginnings through increasingly complex stages. Of course, the consensus among child language experts does not make it true, but the absence of attention to the question does present a few problems for someone like me who has a point to make. I will limit myself to one example from these middle years that I find particularly persuasive.

Adele Goldberg (1995; 1999) has pointed out that linguists often presume that each verb brings with it the expectation that it will be associated with certain particular arguments such as a subject, direct object, locative, and so

forth. In other words, verbs are presumed to 'project' their argument structures. Thus we suppose that the verb *go* in a sentence such as *Pat goes down
the street*, requires a subject (*Pat*), and a prepositional phrase complement
(*down the street*). We may also take it for granted that it is the verb *go* that
leads us to interpret this sentence as describing motion (Goldberg 1999:
197). These presumptions run into problems with other verbs, however. We
would hardly want to credit *rumble* in *The truck rumbles down the street*
with the same attributes as *go*. *Rumble* does not, by itself, imply any sort of
motion. Nor does *rumble* so strongly push us to use a prepositional phrase
complement as does *go*. Nevertheless, upon hearing *The truck rumbles down
the street*, we immediately understand that motion in involved. How do we
do that?

Goldberg's answer is that in addition to words, children learn constructions that have characteristic meanings and that they first learn these constructions with the help of what she calls 'light' verbs. These are verbs that
are very common, that have quite general meanings, and that typically are
short, all characteristics that make them easy to learn. Examples of English
light verbs, in addition to *go*, are *do, make, give*, and *put*. Light verbs such
as these occur with very high frequency in the speech of children whose
syntax is in its early stages. Sentences with light verbs act as prototypes for
the later acquisition of other verbs, and they continue to act as prototypes
for adults. When we hear the verb *rumble* in the same construction that we
have learned for *go*, as in *The truck rumbles down the street*, we give it a parallel interpretation. Even though no word in this sentence by itself implies
motion, we understand the sentence to imply motion just as clearly as if the
verb were *go*. For present purposes, the point is simply that learning the construction with a light verb takes time. Learning to interpret other sentences
as having the same construction takes more time. Since we can productively
interpret sentences with new words as fitting into this construction, we need
syntactic as well as lexical knowledge. The stages by which this is learned are
not difficult to observe in children once we know what to look for.

14.5 Conclusions

It might be argued that my examples come from the peripheral, language-
specific, areas of syntax, and that they fail to touch the core of Universal
Grammar. Perhaps Universal Grammar comes abruptly, even if the more
peripheral features come gradually. This argument presents the student

of child language with a serious dilemma. Our understanding of binding, subjacency, and the rest of Universal Grammar rests on grammaticality judgements, not on observations of language in use. Since it is futile to ask 5-year-olds for grammaticality judgements, we have no choice, with children, but to study their language in use. So far as I can see, this leaves us with no reliable way to study Universal Grammar in children, but since Universal Grammar consists, by definition, of those aspects of grammar that do not have to be learned, it is, in any case, pointless to ask about its learning. Whether all UG becomes suddenly available to a child some fine Thursday morning, or unfolds gradually over the entire course of childhood, is an intriguing abstract question, but it appears to be seriously resistant to empirical investigation. We are, then, forced to fall back on what we can observe in the talk and behaviour of children. The complexities of the language that we can actually observe develop gradually over many years. If this observable syntax starts to be learned months before it appears in production, and if it continues to be learned as late as the age of 10, its acquisition is not as magically fast as has sometimes been supposed. Partial syntax of many levels of complexity can be observed in our own children.

If syntax can grow gradually in children throughout all the years of childhood, it could surely have grown gradually over many hundreds of thousands or even millions of years of phylogeny. I do *not* mean to imply by this that ontogeny recapitulates phylogeny. The sequence of steps through which children pass need not be the same as that once taken by our species. Obviously, our species did not babble for a hundred thousand years while preparing for the language that was still to come. Even if we become convinced that it takes more than a decade for children to gain full control over the syntax of their first language, this slow acquisition would not demonstrate that syntax developed slowly in evolution.

However, the opposite recapitulationist argument has been made. This is the claim that the abrupt development of syntax in children offers evidence for its abrupt development in evolution. That argument was always suspect because of its recapitulationist assumption. But if its premise of children's abrupt acquisition of syntax turns out to be wrong, the argument will have to be judged doubly deficient. It rests not only on the dubious theory of recapitulation but on a misplaced belief in children's abrupt learning. At the very least, even someone who *does* believe that ontogeny recapitulates phylogeny ought not to use the evidence of children to support the idea that language developed suddenly, or even quickly, in phylogeny. I would argue in favour of the gradual development of syntax in evolution, not on the grounds that children learn gradually, but on the grounds that this is the way evolution works.

FURTHER READING

BICKERTON, DEREK (1998), 'Catastrophic Evolution: The Case for a Single Step from Protolanguage to Full Human Language', in James R. Hurford, Michael Studdert-Kennedy, and Chris Knight (eds.), *Approaches to the Evolution of Language* (Cambridge: Cambridge University Press), 341–58. (A forthright statement of the position that I am arguing *against*.)

GOLDBERG, ADELE (1995), *Constructions: A Construction Grammar Approach to Argument Structure* (Chicago: University of Chicago Press). (A compact source for some interesting ideas.)

HIRSH-PASEK, KATHY, and GOLINKOFF, ROBERTA M. (1996), *The Origins of Grammar: Evidence from Early Language Comprehension* (Cambridge, Mass.: MIT Press). (A rare example of a serious effort to look at very early grammar learning.)

KARMILOFF-SMITH, ANNETTE (1986), 'Some Fundamental Aspects of Language Development After 5', in Paul Fletcher and Michael Garman (eds.), *Language Acquisition*, 2nd edn. (Cambridge: Cambridge University Press), 455–74. (A thoughtful examination of late learning.)

O'GRADY, WILLIAM D. (1997), *Syntactic Development* (Chicago: University of Chicago Press). (A fine review of syntactic development at all ages.)

REFERENCES

BERWICK, ROBERT C. (1998), 'Language Evolution and the Minimalist Program: The Origins of Syntax', in James R. Hurford, Michael Studdert-Kennedy, and Chris Knight (eds.), *Approaches to the Evolution of Language: Social and Cognitive Bases* (Cambridge: Cambridge University Press), 320–40.

BICKERTON, DEREK (1990), *Language and Species* (Chicago: University of Chicago Press).

——(1998), 'Catastrophic Evolution: The Case for a Single Step from Protolanguage to Full Human Language', in James R. Hurford, M. Studdert-Kennedy, and Chris Knight (eds.), *Approaches to the Evolution of Language: Social and Cognitive Bases* (Cambridge: Cambridge University Press), 341–58.

——(2000), 'How Protolanguage Became Language', in Chris Knight, Michael Studdert-Kennedy, and James R. Hurford (eds.), *The Evolutionary Emergence of Language: Social Function and the Origins of Linguistic Form* (Cambridge: Cambridge University Press), 264–84.

BLOOM, PAUL (2000), *How Children Learn the Meanings of Words* (Cambridge, Mass.: MIT Press).

CALVIN, WILLIAM H., and BICKERTON, DEREK (2000), *Lingua ex Machina: Reconciling Darwin and Chomsky with the Human Brain* (Cambridge, Mass.: MIT Press).

CARSTAIRS-MCCARTHY, ANDREW (1999), *The Origins of Complex Language: An Inquiry into the Evolutionary Beginnings of Sentences, Syllables, and Truth* (Oxford: Oxford University Press).

——(2000), 'The Distinction Between Sentences and Noun Phrases: an Impediment to Language Evolution?', in Chris Knight, Michael Studdert-Kennedy, and James R. Hurford (eds.), *The Evolutionary Emergence of Language: Social Function and the Origins of Linguistic Form* (Cambridge: Cambridge University Press), 248–63.

CHOMSKY, CAROL (1969), *The Acquisition of Syntax in Children from 5 to 10* (Cambridge, Mass.: MIT Press).

GERKEN, LOUANN, LANDAU, BARBARA, and REMEZ, ROBERT E. (1990), 'Function Morphemes in Young Children's Speech Perception and Production', *Developmental Psychology*, 26/2: 204–16.

GOLDBERG, ADELE E. (1995), *Constructions: A Construction Grammar Approach to Argument Structure* (Chicago: The University of Chicago Press).

——(1999), 'The Emergence of the Semantics of Argument Structure Constructions', in Brian MacWhinney (ed.), *The Emergence of Language* (Mahwah, NJ: Lawrence Erlbaum), 197–212.

HIRSH-PASEK, KATHY, and GOLINKOFF, ROBERTA M. (1991), 'Language Comprehension: A New Look at Some Old Themes', in N. Krasnegor, D. Rumbaugh, R. Schiefelbusch, and M. Studdert-Kennedy (eds.), *Biological and Behavioral Determinants of Language Development* (Hillsdale, NJ: Lawrence Erlbaum), 301–20.

——(1996), *The Origins of Grammar: Evidence from Early Language Comprehension* (Cambridge, Mass.: MIT Press).

KARMILOFF-SMITH, ANNETTE (1986), 'Some Fundamental Aspects of Language Development after 5', in Paul Fletcher and Michael Garman (eds.), *Language Acquisition: Studies in First Language Development*, 2nd edn (Cambridge: Cambridge University Press), 455–74.

MCNEILL, DAVID (1966), 'The Creation of Language by Children', in John Lyons and R. J. Wales (eds.), *Psycholinguistic Papers: The Proceedings of the 1966 Edinburgh Conference* (Edinburgh: Edinburgh University Press).

NOBLE, WILLIAM, and DAVIDSON, IAIN (1996), *Human Evolution, Language and Mind: A Psychological and Archeological Inquiry* (Cambridge: Cambridge University Press).

O'GRADY, WILLIAM D. (1997), *Syntactic Development* (Chicago: The University of Chicago Press).

REES, NORMA S. (1974), 'The Speech Pathologist and the Reading Process', *American Speech–Language–Hearing Association*, 16: 255–8.

SHELDON, AMY (1974), 'The Role of Parallel Function in the Acquisition of Relative Clauses in English', *Journal of Verbal Learning and Verbal Behavior*, 13: 272–81.

15   The Roles of Expression and Representation in Language Evolution

JAMES R. HURFORD

15.1 Introduction

> We should search for the ancestry of language not in prior systems of animal communication but *in prior representational systems.*
>
> (Bickerton 1990: 23, emphasis added)

This quotation makes a negative point and a positive point, given added emphasis above. The idea that language, and by implication much of its current complex structure, arose from pre-linguistic representational systems has attracted attention and not much criticism. A goal of evolutionary linguistics is to explain the origins of the structure found in language. It can be agreed that little of the distinctively complex structure of modern languages can be attributed to ancestry in animal communication systems.[1] But how much of the complex structure of modern languages can be attributed to ancestry in pre-linguistic representational systems? Sampson (1997: 100) expressed a view opposed to Bickerton's.

it is not plausible that our internal representation of statements, which we use in order to reason and draw inferences in other modes, will map in a simple element-by-element fashion into the words with which we express those statements in speech. . . . Nobody really has the least idea what is physically going on in the head when we reason, but I agree that whatever goes on is likely to relate in a fairly abstract way to the words of spoken utterances, which are adapted to the necessary linearity of speech and to the fact that speaker and hearer are working with separate models of reality.

---

[1] This is not to deny the possible contribution of some limited pre-linguistic ability to string units together into longer calls, as documented, for instance, by Ujhelyi (1998).

Pinker and Bloom (1990: 714) make a similar point:

It is occasionally suggested that language evolved as a medium of internal knowledge representation for use in the computations underlying reasoning. But although there may be a languagelike representational medium—'the language of thought', or 'mentalese' (Fodor 1975)—it clearly cannot be English, Japanese, and so on. Natural languages are hopeless for this function: They are needlessly serial, rife with ambiguity (usually harmless in conversational contexts, but unsuited for long-term knowledge representation), complicated by alternations that are relevant only to discourse (e.g. topicalization), and cluttered with devices (such as phonology and much of morphology) that make no contribution to reasoning.

This chapter will provide extended illustration of these views briefly expressed by Sampson and Pinker and Bloom. The chapter is intended as a counterblast to the view that language has more to do with mental representation than with communication, whether now, as emphasized by Chomsky (e.g. 1980) or in its origins, as emphasized by Bickerton (e.g. 1990, 1998). All the facts that I mention are extremely well known to linguists, but I hope this will be useful in drawing attention to what cannot be explained by way of mental representation, as well as reminding non-linguists that syntax is not all just common sense. Thus, in this chapter, I argue for the two following related propositions:

1. Much of the structure of language has no role in a system for the internal representation of thought.

2. Much of the structure of language has a role in systems for the external expression of thought, which includes communication.

A corollary of these propositions, not pursued in detail here, is:

3. Pressure for effective expression of thought, including communication, may explain much of the structure of language.

In the next section, to start this argument, independent characterizations of non-linguistic mental representations and the structure of language are set out. The following sections conduct a survey of the central layers of the structure of any language, its phonology, morphology, and syntax, arguing in all cases that the structuring concerned plays no role in the representation of thought, but defines, or constitutes, the mapping of thoughts onto linguistic expressions.

15.2 Mental Representation

In a polemic passage, Chomsky (1980: 229–30) disparages the idea of communication as the essential function of language, preferring to see language as enabling the expression of thought. I will not quibble over the term 'essential' here; I will use 'communication' and 'expression of thought' interchangeably in this chapter, but the latter term has the virtue of highlighting a clear separation between language and thought. Linguistic form, in this view, is something different from thought itself, which is 'expressed' in language. Thought that remains unexpressed does not take linguistic form. Much of our thought is of this unexpressed kind, i.e. not in language. Yet unexpressed thought is not formless or contentless, and so one can speak meaningfully of it as a kind of representation.

It is assumed here that the existence of non-linguistic representations is unproblematic, contrary to the views of a few philosophers (e.g. Stich 1983; Judge 1985; Schiffer 1989; Horst 1996). Beyond the assumption of their existence, no particularly strong further assumptions are made here about mental representations. For example, the view of non-linguistic representations taken here is compatible with, but not dependent on, distributed connectionist views of how to code the input to the expression of thought. But the argument pursued here will naturally emphasize dissimilarities between language structure and the structure of non-linguistic mental representation.

Non-linguistic mental representations are possessed by animals and pre-linguistic infants for remembering and thinking about events in the world. They are derived from extero- and intero-perception, such as perceptions of light, heat, touch, sound, thirst, and hunger. Non-linguistic mental representations are often referred to as constituting the 'language of thought' (as in Fodor 1975) or 'mentalese'. The language metaphor, implicit in both Fodor's title and the '-ese' suffix, is attractive because it alludes implicitly to the complex structure of thought. But the language metaphor is also misleading. Fodor's *Language of Thought* clearly does not have much of the structure of a public language such as French or Swahili. Indeed, it is exactly the non-language-like features of non-linguistic mental representations that are at the core of my argument here. The essential differences between an internal (cognitive) representation system and a communication system are as follows.

1. A communication system maps external forms (such as speech sounds or manual signs), via mental structures, to meanings (where many, if not all, meanings relate to external objects, events, or situations). A communication system is typically public, shared by many individuals.[2]

2. A representation system lacks the mapping to external forms, and merely provides mental structures which relate to, or denote, external situations. There would be no practical advantage in having a representation system that was not in some way related to the world outside the mind possessing it.

Thus a communication system properly includes a representation system. There are elements in a communication system that are not part of the inherent representation system. Analogously, there are elements in a computer system that relate only to keyboard and screen functions and not to the core business of computation. Any aspects of a communication system that pertain only to the mapping between external forms (i.e. sounds or signs) and the internal cognitive representation system are not part of the representation system *per se*.

Non-linguistic mental representations are *non-temporal*; all parts of the representation of a remembered event are simultaneously present to the mind. Non-linguistic mental representations are *multi-dimensional*; for example, they are often diagrammed on paper as networks, with hierarchical relationships between the parts, and/or as composed of features (which can be seen as dimensions). Non-linguistic mental representations do not exist in the same medium as the external forms to which they are mapped by the structure of a language; specifically, they are *non-acoustic* and *non-manual*. With non-linguistic mental representations, no issue of *ambiguity* arises; they are what they are (although mental representations may be vague or general).

By contrast, utterances are *temporal*. Utterances in spoken language are *acoustic* events, and in sign language, *manual* events. The raw, unprocessed speech signal that reaches the eardrum is a complex sound wave, no more than a temporal sequence of variations in air pressure. The variations are

---

[2] But this is not crucial, as, for example, the last living speaker of a dying language can still be said to possess a communication system.

more or less strong surges and declines in pressure, with periods of stillness. At any instant in time, the only information immediately available in this signal is the relative strength of the change in air-pressure, a single (positive or negative) number. At bottom, the whole rich linguistic fabric of an utterance, from phonemic oppositions (e.g. what makes a 'b' different from an 's') through syllables, morphemes, words, and phrases to clauses and sentences, is signalled by this temporal sequence of air-pressure variations. Thus utterances are linear or one-dimensional sequences of events; any perceived imposition of further dimensions on the signal (e.g. by intonation) arises from knowledge of the mapping between utterances and the non-linguistic mental representations of their meanings. The term 'one-dimensional' emphasizes that the events or landmarks in the temporal sequence are distinguished by their values on a single parameter, that of relative pressure. (In sign language, admittedly, some degree of simultaneity is present in the manual signals.) Utterances are frequently ambiguous; as computational linguists know to their cost, ambiguity, especially local ambiguity, is rife in language. Ambiguity arises at all levels of linguistic structure. For instance, the utterance 'I'm coming to get you' is ambiguous between a threat and a promise of help; the sentence *Visiting relatives can be boring* can be understood as describing at least two different situations; the word *list*, like many other English words, has many senses; phonetically, in English a plosive where voicing commences simultaneously with release can be interpreted as either voiced, as in *beer*, or voiceless, as in *spear*. These are examples contributing to the many-to-one mapping between non-linguistic representations and linguistic strings. (In fact, given the existence of synonymy and paraphrase, the overall mapping is many-to-many.)

The problem of expressing multi-dimensional mental representations as one-dimensional sequences of sounds is analogous to any problem involving dimension-squashing. Consider the two-dimensional picture in Fig. 15.1. Now, is this a picture of a solid cube or of the inside of a room

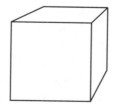

FIG. 15.1 Three dimensions squashed into two.

(showing the ceiling, far wall, and right-hand wall)? As you look at it, the interpretation will probably switch back and forth. The picture is ambiguous, because it has squashed three dimensions into two. Consider now how much further information is lost by trying to depict a cube (or the inside of a room, if you will) in just one dimension. The diagonal line in the Fig. 15.2 is an attempt to represent the solid body one-dimensionally, with the blobs on the line as distinguishable points purporting to correspond to the vertices in the two-dimensional picture.

FIG. 15.2 Three dimensions squashed into one.

As a linguistic example of the dimension-squashing problem faced by the expression of thought, consider argument selection, as discussed by Dowty (1991). Noun phrases in some sentences reflect the Agent (or Patient) role more clearly than the noun phrases in other sentences. For instance, *Jim* is more clearly an active (i.e. agentive) participant in *Jim kicked the editor* than in *Jim admires the editor*. And likewise, the *editor* is more clearly affected (i.e. fulfils the Patient role) by the situation described by the first sentence than in the situation described by the second. This induces Dowty to postulate the 'proto-roles', Proto-Agent and Proto-Patient. A participant in an event can conform to a greater or lesser degree to the set of criteria defining Proto-Agent or Proto-Patient. Another way of putting this is to say that the concepts of Agent and Patient are not atomic, but are clusters of values in a multi-dimensional space. Participants in mentally represented events that conform most closely to the Proto-Agent criteria are near the centre of the Agent region of this multi-dimensional space; likewise, participants that conform most closely to the Proto-Patient criteria are near the centre of the Patient region of this multi-dimensional space. Participants that do not meet many of the criteria are on the outskirts of the regions. Dowty's six criteria are shown in Fig. 15.3.

Proto-AGENT	Proto-PATIENT
Volitional involvement	Non-volitional involvement
Sentience or perception	No sentience/perception
Causing event	Causally affected
No change of state	Change of state
Moving	Stationary
Independent existence	No (independent) existence

Fɪɢ. 15.3 The 6-dimensional space of Agenthood and Patient-hood (after Dowty 1991).

Agent and Patient are thus seen as complex multi-dimensional notions.[3] Let us grant, as proponents of the view I am opposing[4] typically do, that our pre-linguistic ancestors would have represented the events in their social and material environment with concepts hardly less complex than this. They would have had mental representations incorporating information along all these six dimensions, i.e. about who deliberately did what to whom, who felt what, what caused what to happen, what changed somehow, what moved, and what suddenly appeared. I agree that all such information would have been represented by pre-linguistic creatures. The problem is to convey all this in speech. In basic cases, languages solve the problem by rules of argument selection, which map points in this six-dimensional space onto two grammatical polar points of a transitive clause, namely Subject and Object (Fig. 15.4). In the vast majority of languages, if not all, the organization of basic transitive clauses has the Subject preceding the Object. Thus the word-string typically signals information compressed out of the six-dimensional Agent–Patient space by linear order of two major parts of the string.

[3] A somewhat technical, though important, point is that Dowty appears to claim that there are two clusters (his proto-Agent and proto-Patient) in a six-dimensional space. Accepting the six dimensions as approximately correct, it remains an empirical question whether the participants in perceived worldly events do tend to fall into two clusters, or whether they are in fact more evenly distributed all over the six-dimensional space. The appearance of just two clusters may be no more than a projection back into the analysis of the mental representation system of a syntactic distinction between subjects and objects; if this is so, 'proto-subject' and 'proto-object' would be better labels than Dowty's. In any case, the central point made here, about the squashing of information on six dimensions into a linear string, remains.

[4] e.g. Bickerton (1990, 1998)

SUBJECT   OBJECT

Fig. 15.4 Two grammatical polar points of a transitive clause.

The syntactic relations Subject and Object are universally available, and probably universally used, in the grammars of languages.[5] They do not belong to non-linguistic (or pre-linguistic) mental representations, but are rather part of the solution to the problem of mapping 'propositional structures onto a serial channel' (Pinker and Bloom 1990: 713).

In the following sections, a survey will be presented of other such aspects of the structure of language that are parts of the solution to the expression problem, rather than aspects of the pre-existing mental representations. Languages are very complex, highly structured communication systems. The view that linguistic structure derives from representation systems existing prior to language can only be sustained to the extent that there is no structure that is only part of the communicative aspect of a language system. How much of language structure is purely representational, and how much of it is part of the mapping to external forms? One cannot quantify such questions, but the answer advocated here is that almost all the complex structure of languages belongs to their expressive aspect, and very little to their purely representational aspect.

15.3 Language Structure I: Phonology and Morphology

Linguists know that each of the over 6,000 languages in the world is an extremely complex system, with a great wealth of detailed structure at all levels. In an interdisciplinary book such as this, whose readers include anthropologists, psychologists, and biologists with an interest in the evolution of language, it is worth briefly rehearsing some of the details of what linguistic structure consists of.

---

[5] The discussion here relates to transitive sentences, in which both a subject and an object are present. The fact that in ergative languages the subject of an intransitive clause is assigned the same case as the object of a transitive clause does not affect this argument. What this fact shows is that languages may solve some aspects of the mapping problem differently in intransitive clauses, i.e. where only one participant is involved, who may have various of the Agent or Patient properties.

A language is a system of mappings between meanings and external forms (usually sounds but also manual signs), as diagrammed in Fig. 15.5. The bidirectional arrows indicate that the map between meanings and sounds can be followed in either direction—from meanings to sounds when speaking, and from sounds to meanings when listening. The language structure itself (the map) is neutral between speaking and hearing.

15.3.1 *Double Articulation*

Note the 'double articulation' (or 'duality of patterning') in Fig. 15.5, the separation into two distinct levels of organization, phonology and morphosyntax. What this means is that a language has two quite distinct kinds of rules for 'putting things together', and these rules deal in quite different basic units. Phonology, or phonological rules, puts sounds (individual consonants and vowels) together to make syllables and basic units of meaning, called morphemes. Morphosyntactic rules take these elements and put them together to make sentences. The linguistic structure of a sentence is basically two-tier, to put the matter at its simplest. This duality of patterning is a fundamental universal characteristic. It has no motivation in a purely representational system, but plausible arguments can be advanced for its communicative adaptiveness.

It is important, in communication, to be able to locate the boundaries of the elements composing the one-dimensional speech string. In written Eng-

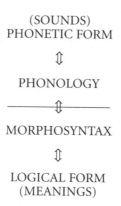

Fig. 15.5 Language as a system of mappings between meanings and external forms.

lish, spaces serve this function. In speech, syllables have characteristic structure, with beginnings and ends, facilitating the location of their boundaries by a hearer. The beginning–end, or onset–coda, structure of syllables, plus the requirement for syllables to be distinctive, is the basic framework on which the rich phonological systems of languages elaborate. Phonology is a syntax of sounds, without any concomitant semantics. Individual consonants and vowels have no meanings of their own, and hence have no counterparts in non-linguistic mental representations, but they play a solid part in an organizational level of language structure, namely phonology.

15.3.2 *Phonological Structure*

The business of phonetics is simply the physical description of sounds (in either articulatory or acoustic terms). The business of phonology, on the other hand, as outlined in the box of Fig. 15.6 below, is to describe how different languages organize their sounds. Such organization includes: which sounds to use, out of the hundreds possible (e.g. English uses sounds not used in French and vice versa); how to combine sounds (e.g. some languages don't allow two consonants together); how sounds are modified in various contexts (e.g. English vowels are longer before voiced consonants than before voiceless ones). To give some impression of the complexity of the phonological aspects of linguistic structure, Fig. 15.6 is a summary of the table of contents of a textbook on phonology.

This example is quite typical of phonology textbooks (although they all have their own characteristic differences of emphasis). Clearly, phonological structure is complex and requires a lot of explaining. The phonological component of a language comprises a very significant proportion of its structure. Phonological structure is (part of) the mapping between internal representations of meanings and their external expressive forms. A purely representational system has no mapping to external expressive form. Obviously, then, all facets of phonological structure belong in the aspect of linguistic structure dealing with the (public) expression of thought.

15.3.3 *Morphology Versus Syntax*

On the morphosyntactic side of the duality of patterning, the universal distinction between morphology and syntax (however that is drawn) plays

The phoneme, including Distinctiveness: phonemes and allophones, and Phonological symmetry. [19 pages]

Distinctive features, including Major class features, Cavity features, Tongue body features, Tongue root features, Laryngeal features, Manner features, Prosodic features, Segment structure redundancy. [25 pages]

Phonological representations [19 pages]

Phonological processes, including Assimilation, Direction of assimilation, Assimilation processes, Palatalisation, Labialisation, Voice assimilation, Place of articulation assimilation, Manner of articulation assimilation, Nasalisation, Dissimilation. [19 pages]

Naturalness and Strength, including Natural segments, natural classes and natural processes. Phonological strength hierarchies. [19 pages]

Interaction between rules, including Introduction to rule formalisation and ordering, Linear rule ordering. [17 pages]

The abstractness of underlying representations. [19 pages]

The syllable, including The representation of syllable structure, the CV-tier, A generative CV-phonology model of syllable structure, Syllabification, Functions of the syllable, The syllable as the basic phonotactic unit, The syllable as the domain of phonological rules, The syllable and the structure of complex segments, Compensatory lengthening, The syllable as indispensable building block for higher phonological domains, Syllable weight, Abstract segments, Extrasyllabicity. [33 pages]

Multi-tiered phonology, including Tone languages, The representation of tone, Contour tones, Tone stability, Melody levels, Tone and intonation, Pitch accent, Vowel harmony, Nasalisation, Morphemic tier. [30 pages]

Stress and intonation, including Stress, Metrical phonology, Metrical trees and grids, Extrametricality, Quantity sensitivity, Intonation, Accentuation function, Intonation and illocutionary force, Grammatical function of intonation, Attitudinal functions of intonation, Discourse function of intonation. [33 pages]

FIG. 15.6 Phonological structure, what's in it? A typical overview (from Katamba 1989).

no role in non-communicative representation. This distinction rests on the discrimination by languages of a level of words, which are small- to middle-sized units distinct from both semantically or grammatically atomic morphemes and higher level syntactic units such as phrases. Here is an example of somewhat complex morphology from Turkish:

sevildirememek, 'not to be able to cause to be loved'

sev	*il*	*dir*	*e*	*me*	*mek*
'love'	Passive	Causative	Ability	Negative	Infinitive

The Turkish expression is a single word consisting of six separate morphemes stuck together ('agglutinated'). The same meaning in English would be expressed by a phrase consisting of at least the same number of separate words. This common meaning, which can be diagrammed as some structured configuration of the elements 'love', Passive, Causative, Ability, Negative, Infinitive is mapped onto linguistic strings quite differently in English and Turkish. The two languages segment the linguistic string into words in radically different ways. The criteria by which we can satisfy ourselves that we are dealing with a single word in Turkish, and not a lot of small ones, are empirically relatively clear. For example in Turkish, all the vowels within a word must harmonize with each other according to strict rules, and the placement of stress is calculated on the basis of word-level units. But word-level units differ in size and number of elements from one language to another. In uninflected languages (e.g. Vietnamese) there is a greater correspondence than in other languages between word-sized chunks and what might be basic units of meaning, or conceptual representation. Segmentation into words is not inherent in non-linguistic representations. This is an aspect of linguistic structure that is part of the expressive apparatus for mapping non-linguistic representations onto strings.

A morpheme is standardly defined as the 'minimal unit of meaning or grammatical function' (Yule 1985: 60) in a language. This carefully disjunctive definition shows that even the basic building blocks of morphosyntax cannot all be taken to serve as plausible candidates for elements of non-linguistic representation, existing before syntactic organization. Of the six morphemes in the Turkish example above, at least two, Passive and Infinitive, are clearly grammatical morphemes, rather than lexical (i.e. semantically contentful), and are thus part of the solution to the expression problem, rather than elements of non-linguistic mental representation.

The volume of work on the morphological structure of language is not far short of the volume of work on phonological structure. Suffice it to say here that, within morphology, various structural features, such as the layering of inflectional morphemes outside derivational morphemes, and the inventory of structural devices used in word-formation (affixation, suppletion, fusion, cliticization, reduplication, compounding) also play no purely representational role. These processes, by which semantically and grammatically functional minimal elements are assembled into word-level units, and which vary from language to language, are not motivated by any structural characteristic that can plausibly be attributed to non-linguistic (or prelinguistic) representations.

15.4 Language Structure II: Syntax

Syntax remains the central focal area of the structure of language. And it is in syntax that the most emphatic claims have been made for deriving modern linguistic structure from the pre-existing structure of mental representations: 'Events, Agents, Themes and Goals ... already formed part of the primate inventory of "Things that there are in the world"' (Bickerton 1998: 351). A creature's knowledge of events, agents, themes and goals belongs to what Bickerton, and linguists more generally, call a 'theta-analysis component'. Descriptive linguists conceive of this component as an integral part of the system mapping meanings to their external expression in modern human languages. For Bickerton, this component also pre-existed the emergence of language, and the move from protolanguage to syntactic language came about as a result of new cerebral connections being established between this theta-analysis component and the mental apparatus representing the phonetic structure of words (which also already existed as part of protolanguage).

The creation of such connections would have enabled information to pass through the theta-analysis component before it reached phonetic representation. Information passing through this area would have been automatically sorted into units consisting of an action and its participants obligatorily represented—exactly those clausal units that constitute the basic units of syntax. (ibid. 352).

... the linkage of theta-analysis with other elements involved in protolanguage would not merely have put in place the basic structure of syntax, but would also have led directly to a cascade of consequences that would, in one rapid and continuous sequence, have transformed protolanguage into language substantially as we know it today. (ibid. 353)

Two claims are made in these quotations. First it is claimed that the pre-existing theta-analysis representations were clear enough to give rise unambiguously to clausal structures. The second claim is the sweeping one that once clausal structure had emerged, all the rest of what we now see as syntactic structure followed automatically. The second claim has been weakened in a recent publication: 'in the millennia that followed the birth of syntax [i.e. the appearance of compulsory argument structure], our ancestors must have been competing with one another to produce devices that would make that syntax more readily parsable, hence easier to understand automatically'

(Calvin and Bickerton 2000: 146). Although the more recent account still leans heavily on non-linguistic predicate-argument structures to yield basic syntax, it does invoke some extra factors, such as a hierarchy of roles, a 'procedure for joining [hence linearizing] meaningful units' and 'a process of binary attachment' (ibid. 215, 218–19). There is no space here for a full discussion of these hypothesized additional factors, but note that it remains to be explained how they originated and how much of modern syntactic structure they account for, anyway. I will argue that predicate–argument structure alone is not enough to guarantee the evolution of all the syntactic complexity of modern developed languages. In order to do that, we need to look at the relationship between internal representation and linguistic expression.

15.4.1 *Non-linguistic Representation and Lexical Subcategorization*

Let us grant, for the sake of this argument, that when a non-linguistic creature witnesses an event, it can form a rich mental representation of this event or state of affairs in terms of categories such as Agent, Action, and Patient, roughly 'who did what to whom'. In particular, let us grant that the action or state involved is clearly categorized as some kind of mental predicate, though not, at this pre-linguistic stage, a predicate associated with any external word or sign. Given this much, it is for Bickerton, as seen above, a simple step to basic clause structure, apparently nothing more than clothing the internal predicate and its arguments, 'units consisting of an action and its participants obligatorily represented', in phonetic form.

Syntactic theory takes the information about the obligatory arguments of a predicate as the basis for wellformedness at all levels of linguistic structure.[6] But the step from internal pre-linguistic representation to lexical entry is not straightforward. Conceptual representation does not fully determine lexical subcategorization. I will argue this with a number of examples.

One of the most frequently cited facts about the subcategorization of verbs in English is that the verb *put* obligatorily takes a direct object and a locative phrase, as shown by these examples:

Morgan puts the ball on the ground
*Morgan puts the ball

---

[6] This is stated in the Projection Principle: 'Representations at each syntactic level (i.e. LF, and D- and S-structure) are projected from the lexicon, in that they observe the subcategorization properties of lexical items' (Chomsky 1981: 29).

In many contexts, the verb *place* is a synonym of *put*, so that *Morgan places the ball on the ground* is used to describe exactly the same event as the first sentence above. But it is common to hear, in rugby commentaries, sentences such as *Morgan places the ball*. In such cases, it is always understood that the player places the ball on the ground, but the locative phrase can be omitted. Here we have the same event, which must be represented by the same internal mental predicate, getting externalized in two different verbs, which have different obligatory arguments.

As another example, take the case of the verbs *rob* and *steal*. A sentence with *rob* always entails some corresponding sentence with *steal*, and vice versa. In this sense, they are synonyms. A robbing event is always a stealing event, and vice versa. If a pre-linguistic creature mentally represents the event of X stealing food from Y, it also necessarily and simultaneously represents the event of X robbing Y of food. Yet *rob* and *steal* have different lexical subcategorizations. *Rob* takes an obligatory argument referring to the person from whom something is illegally taken; an argument referring to this person is not obligatory with *steal*. Conceptual representation does not fully determine lexical subcategorization.

Another example is the pair *win* and *beat*. I once saw two young children racing each other on a beach. The one who reached the goal first shouted triumphantly **I beat!*, where he should have said *I won!* or *I beat you!* The child had a mental representation of a winning/beating event, involving a competition with another person. But he chose the wrong verb, or omitted the obligatory argument of the verb that he did choose. The fact that one of these verbs requires an obligatory object, where the other does not, is an arbitrary fact about English verbs, and cannot be predicted from the nature of the event itself. If a pre-linguistic creature mentally represents an event of X winning in a contest with Y, then it necessarily and simultaneously represents an event of X beating Y in a contest. They are one and the same event. But the different verbs that can be used to describe this event differ in the requirements they impose on syntactic structure.

15.4.2 *Hierarchical (Tree) Structure*

Syntactic theories vary widely in flavour, but all agree that sentences have hierarchical 'tree' structures, of which that diagrammed in Fig. 15.7 is a commonplace, if somewhat old-fashioned, example (from Culicover 1976: 110). Such structures are justified by considerations such as the simplicity of the

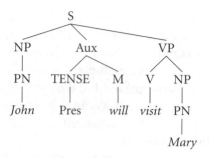

Fɪɢ. 15.7 Typical hierarchical tree structure (from Culicover 1976: 110).

rule-sets generating them and all other well-formed sentences of the language. Note first the presence of syntactic node labels, such as NP, PN, AUX. These labels, although they can be systematically related, in a many-to-many mapping, to semantic or conceptual categories, are clearly not themselves semantic in nature. A completely non-linguistic creature envisaging that John will visit Mary (say for the purpose of anticipating John's next move in the competition for Mary as a sexual partner) would have no use for any of these labels.

Note also the English organization, reflected in this tree structure, of tense. Clearly, the modal verb *will* signals future time, but it is the empty element 'Pres' that receives the label ᴛᴇɴsᴇ. If the modal verb were absent, as in the sentence *John visits Mary*, the ᴛᴇɴsᴇ node would dominate the -*s* suffix, which does indicate present time (amongst other things). The simple conclusion is that the signalling in English of past and present time by verbal suffixes, and of future time by a modal verb, shows a mismatch between morphosyntactic structure and any a priori plausible representation of the timing of events. Such quirky mismatches between morphosyntactic structure and conceptual, or logical, structure are common across languages.

Note next the segmentation of the sentence into higher-level constituents, in particular the VP constituent. Most syntacticians are convinced that the structure of clauses in most languages includes a VP constituent, which contains any grammatical objects of the clause, but does not include its subject. The main motivation for this is that it helps to explain how specific verbs have considerable influence on the form of their objects, but little or no influence on the form of their subjects. For instance, all English verbs take a subject: thus no specific rules are required stating which verbs take subjects and which do not. But verbs do fall into different categories with respect to the number and type of objects that they take: for example, English *sleep* has to be specified as taking no object (i.e. as intransitive), *hit* is specified as taking one object (i.e. as monotransitive), and *give* is specified as taking two objects (i.e. as ditransitive). Furthermore, verbs that take whole clauses as their objects differ in the form they allow such clauses to take: compare *I want Mary to come* with the ill-formed **I want that Mary will come*, as opposed to **I hope Mary to come* versus *I hope that Mary will come*. It seems unlikely that the structure of pre-linguistic thought included a VP-like 'constituent' that bracketed a 2-place predicate with just one of its arguments, but not the other. Analyses in standard predicate logic of 2-place relations treat both arguments of a predicate as elements at the same level, as in VISIT(*john, mary*). It seems likely that the asymmetric treatment of arguments in the typical morphosyntax of languages does not reflect any aspect of the pre-linguistic structuring of thought, but stems from some consideration arising in the expression of thought in linear form.[7]

In several respects some pre-existing hierarchical structure of thought is directly reflected in the tree structures assigned to sentences by linguists. In many cases, the trees drawn by linguists over sentences are motivated by semantic considerations, unlike the case of the VP constituent. There are many familiar instances of structural ambiguity, such as those involving such things as attachment of modifiers (as in *a list of teachers broken down by age and sex*, or *old men and women*), and combinations of different conjunctions (e.g. *John or Mary and Bill*). In such cases, syntacticians draw alternative semantically motivated tree structures over expressions, reflecting their different readings.

Such facts cannot be taken to show that pre-existing hierarchically organized conceptual structure gave rise to hierarchical syntactic structure. To argue that, one would have first to establish the logical independence of the two alleged sorts of hierarchical structure (semantic and syntactic) and then point to the parallelism between them. Genuinely syntactic hierarchical structure is discerned on the basis of the constituents that are posited in grammars designed to account for the distribution of words and morphemes in well-formed strings. But in fact, the tree structures drawn over

---

[7] Perhaps, as is sometimes suggested, grammatical subjects are fossilized topic constituents, placed at the front of the sentence for communicative salience.

sentences in such cases of ambiguity are in parts motivated *only* semantic-ally. The tree structures are actually hybrid representations, showing both syntactic information (e.g. the VP constituent and the syntactic category labels such as NP, etc.) and semantic information about the conceptual groupings of the elements of the expressed thought.

Non-semantic evidence for particular hierarchical structures could involve phonological phrasing or distributional facts about particular sub-strings, as in the case of the arguments for a VP constituent. Very often, phonological phrasing indicates a hierarchical organization of sentences that is at odds with their semantics. For example, if one says a moderately long sentence such as *This is the cat that caught the mouse that ate the cheese that lay in the house that Jack built*, one will typically insert pauses or inton-ation boundaries after *cat*, *mouse*, and *cheese*. But this phrasing cuts across the appropriate semantic analysis of the sentence, in which, for example, *the cheese that lay in the house that Jack built* and *the mouse that ate the cheese that lay in the house that Jack built* are whole referring expressions, one iden-tifying a particular piece of cheese, and the other identifying a particular mouse.

The aspect in which independently motivated hierarchical syntactic struc-ture seems most closely to align with plausible pre-existing hierarchical semantic structure is in the nesting of subordinate clauses within main clauses (and within 'higher' subordinate clauses). Syntax is essentially clause-based. If one were given the task of analysing a large corpus of sentences, without information about their meanings, it is likely that the analysis would recognize units at the level of the clause, purely on distributional grounds, with hierarchical nesting of subordinate clauses.

15.4.3 *Functional Syntactic Categories*

The specific grammatical markers that identify clause boundaries, and affect the internal form of clauses, are functional elements such as the complemen-tizer *that*, as in *I know that you're here*, or the infinitive marker *to*, as in *I want to go*. These provide distributional evidence, independent of semantic con-siderations, for hierarchical phrase structure which often happens to mirror semantically motivated hierarchical structure. However, these indicators of syntactic structure (e.g. *that* and *to*) are not themselves plausible elements of pre-existing mental representations. Rather it seems most likely that they exist just because of the dimension-squashing problem thrown up by the expression of thought. An example in an everyday practical context is: 'If we are told that a pipe has burst in the loft and we start talking about how to deal with the burst pipe, it does not seem likely that our reasoning machinery will contain little bits representing "a" and "the" ' (Sampson 1997: 100).

The prevalence of grammatically functional elements (as opposed to content words) is a hallmark of fully grammatical human language. In most languages, no sentence is grammatically complete without at least one grammatical element, signalling the structure of the sentence. It is hard to make a completely rigid distinction between grammatically functional elements and 'pure content' words, because many words (e.g. conjunctions, pronouns, and prepositions) combine grammatical function with conveying some content. But at a rough estimate, functional elements in English account for about 40 per cent of a typical text. The following is a list of the most frequent word-forms from the 100-million-word British National Corpus, accounting for over 40 per cent of the word-forms in modern English text.

the, is/was/be/are/'s/were/been/being/'re/'m/am, of, and, a/an, in/inside (preposition), *to* (infinitive verb marker), *have/has/have/'ve/'s/had/having/'d, he/him/his, it/its, I/me/my, to* (preposition), *they/them/their, not/n't/no* (interjection), *for, you/ your, she/her, with, on, that* (conjunction), *this/these, that* (demonstrative)/*those, do/did/does/done/doing, we/us/our, by, at, but* (conjunction), *'s* (possessive), *from, as, which, or, will/'ll, said/say/says/saying, would, what, there* (existential), *if, can, all, who/whose, so* (adverb/conjunction), *go/went/gone/goes, more, other/another, one* (numeral).

For most of these word-forms, it seems unlikely that pre-linguistic mental representations would contain anything corresponding closely to them. Yet these word-forms are the major workhorses of English grammar. Similar observations apply to any language.

15.4.4 *Movement, Binding, and Agreement*

Movement

Many models of grammar postulate 'movement' of elements of a grammatical structure from one location in the structure to another. The term 'movement' is a metaphor. No physical movement happens, but the metaphor seems useful in describing, for example, how to form question sentences from the corresponding statement sentences or echo-questions in English, for example (Fig. 15.8). Stylistic movement also occurs for purposes of topi-

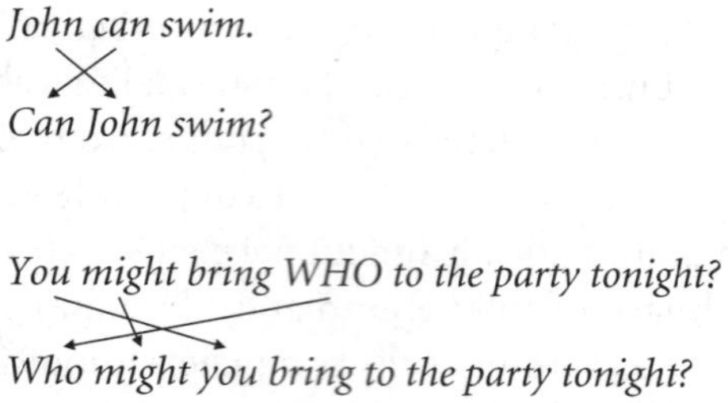

John can swim.

Can John swim?

You might bring WHO to the party tonight?

Who might you bring to the party tonight?

FIG. 15.8 Movement in English question forms.

calization, as in the following sentence where the noun phrases *the dog* and *the cat* are moved from their usual post-verbal positions to the fronts of their respective clauses:

The DOG *we shut in the kitchen, but the* CAT *we left outside*

English makes extensive use of movement rules, but many languages use movement even more productively, effectively achieving by movement many of the effects that English achieves by variations in intonation.

Such phenomena are clearly ways of signalling pragmatic information, such as whether a sentence is intended to elicit information from a hearer, or whether the hearer is assumed to focus attention on one particular referent. With non-linguistic representations, there is no question of a hearer. Such mental representations are private. Even if it could be conceived that a creature could privately 'pose itself a question' or focus its attention on a particular aspect of some mental representation, it is clear that the structural device described by linguists as 'movement' could play no part. Movement is not inherent in pre-linguistic representations. It is part of the apparatus for mapping pre-linguistic representations onto strings.

It follows that universal constraints on movement phenomena in languages, such as the Subjacency Principle, which have attracted much theoretical attention in syntax, are also part of the apparatus for mapping pre-linguistic representations onto strings.

Binding

Pronouns are 'bound' to their antecedents. This means that they are interpreted as having the same referent. Reflexive pronouns provide an example:

John grooms himself

Here, the pronoun *himself* obligatorily refers to the same entity in the world as *John*. The rules for the binding of reflexive pronouns to their antecedents are known to be dependent on details of clause structure; roughly, a reflexive pronoun is bound to a preceding noun phrase only if it occurs in the same simple clause. The antecedence relation cannot violate clause boundaries, as evidenced by the ungrammaticality of **John hopes that himself will win*.

A non-linguistic creature's mental representation of John grooming himself involves only one entity, John. The (English) expression of this event as a string requires repeated mention of John, using *himself* for the second mention, with a consequent requirement to signal the binding of the second mention to the first.

Non-reflexive pronouns are not bound by such tight rules as reflexives, and this gives rise to the ambiguity characteristic of public language. Usually there is ambiguity over whether such a pronoun refers back to an entity recently mentioned in the discourse or to some other entity known by the hearer to be in the contextual frame. For instance, in *John saw Mary look at him* the pronoun *him* might or might not be bound by *John*. That is, *him* could refer to John or to someone else. But a non-linguistic creature's mental representation of either of the possible situations described by this sentence would presumably not be ambiguous, or it would not *be* a representation of the event.

Pronouns, and the quite elaborate grammatical apparatus determining how they can be bound, are not elements of pre-linguistic mental representations. They are part of the apparatus for mapping non-linguistic representations onto strings.

Agreement (concord)

Agreement (or concord) phenomena are very common in languages. An English example is illustrated in Fig. 15.9. In many languages the agreement rules are very elaborate, involving number, gender, and case. Agreement is a purely morphosyntactic phenomenon, and serves the purpose of marking those constituents that are bound together in close grammatical relationships. Such close grammatical relationships often reflect closeness in

The arrows over this sentence show which words agree with which.

FIG. 15.9 Agreement ('concord') in English.

the conceptual representation, but clearly in the mental representation itself such closeness is inherent and does not stand in need of marking. Agreement is part of the apparatus for mapping pre-linguistic representations onto strings.

15.5 Conclusion

The fundamental universal structural characteristic known as 'duality of patterning', whereby languages are organized at two levels of structure, namely phonology and morphosyntax, has no motivation in a purely representational system, but plausible arguments can be advanced for its communicative adaptiveness. Obviously, all facets of phonological structure belong in the communicative aspect of linguistic structure. On the morphosyntactic side of the duality of patterning, the universal distinction between morphology and syntax (however that is drawn) plays no role in non-communicative representation.

Within syntax, some of the main devices that play no role in pre-linguistic representation have been surveyed above. Many of the complex structural phenomena that have attracted study, such as case-marking, anaphor–antecedent relationships, switch-reference devices, control by verbal predicates of the interpretation of their complement clauses, transformations of various sorts (e.g. passivization, topicalization, question formation) and the constraints on such processes, play no role in non-communicative representation. Linear ordering of elements, with which much of syntax is concerned, likewise plays no non-communicative role. Also fundamental to syntactic structure are lexical classes somewhat autonomous of semantics, such as Noun, Verb, Adjective, and Preposition;[8] to the extent that such classes are autonomous, they play no role in semantic representation. Other commonly found grammatico-lexical categories, such as grammatical gender (Noun classes), would seem to serve no representational purpose, although they may contribute to the redundancy of utterances, thereby serving a communicative purpose. Grammatical agreement (concord), which is widespread, also clearly plays no purely representational role.

---

[8] As is well known, some nouns denote actions, rather than objects (e.g. *action, assassination*). The same basic concept can sometimes be expressed by both a verb and an adjective (e.g. *fear/afraid, like/fond*). In many languages there are no adjectives, and concepts expressed in English by adjectives are expressed by verbs.

Some aspects of linguistic structure may indeed plausibly be derived from non-linguistic, representational, structure. These include some (but not all) aspects of hierarchical organization in syntax. But the broad conclusion from the above survey of non-representational aspects of linguistic structure is that attempts to derive linguistic structure, in an evolutionary account, from previously existing cognitive representational structure must fail, for a large slice of linguistic structure. The claim that there was a 'cascade of consequences that would, in one rapid and continuous sequence, have transformed protolanguage into language substantially as we know it today' (Bickerton 1998: 353) is very vague. The idea that linguistic structure derives from pre-existing mental representations is no doubt true *for some very basic aspects* of linguistic structure. But we should not close the investigation prematurely on the sources of linguistic structure, in all its multifarious richness. It is not at all clear what exact 'cascade of consequences' could have led to all the aspects of linguistic structure that I have highlighted in this chapter. Of the few linguists who ponder evolutionary questions, many take the position, not that grammatical structure reflects prior mental representation *per se*, but that it results in part from the need to *interface* representational structure with a phonetic output in order to make communication possible. This is the position taken, sketchily, by Newmeyer (1991: 6–8), for example. Where explanation by derivation from pre-existing mental structure fails, it may be feasible to seek evolutionary explanations (broadly conceived) for much (though not all) of the typical structure of languages in the demands of communication in the human environment.

FURTHER READING

Overall introductions to language structure:

FROMKIN, VICTORIA, and RODMAN, ROBERT (1978), *An Introduction to Language* (New York: Holt, Rinehart & Winston).

O'GRADY, WILLIAM, DOBROVOLSKY, MICHAEL, and ARONOFF, MARK (1997), *Contemporary Linguistics: An Introduction* (New York: St Martins Press).

On 'Mentalese':

FODOR, JERRY A. (1975), *The Language of Thought* (New York: Crowell).

REFERENCES

BICKERTON, DEREK (1990), *Language and Species* (Chicago: University of Chicago Press).

BICKERTON, DEREK (1998), 'Catastrophic Evolution: The Case for a Single Step from Protolanguage to Full Human Language', in James R. Hurford, Michael Studdert-Kennedy, and Chris Knight (eds.), *Approaches to the Evolution of Language: Social and Cognitive Bases* (Cambridge: Cambridge University Press), 341–58.

CALVIN, W. H., and BICKERTON, D. (2000), *Lingua ex Machina* (Cambridge, Mass.: MIT Press).

CHOMSKY, NOAM (1980), *Rules and Representations* (Oxford: Basil Blackwell).

——(1981), *Lectures on Government and Binding* (Dordrecht: Foris Publications).

CULICOVER, PETER (1976), *Syntax* (New York: Academic Press).

DOWTY, DAVID (1991), 'Thematic Proto-roles and Argument Selection', *Language*, 67/3: 547–619.

FODOR, JERRY A. (1975), *The Language of Thought* (New York: Crowell).

HORST, STEVEN W. (1996), *Symbols, Computation and Intentionality: A Critique of the Computational Theory of Mind* (Berkeley: University of California Press).

JUDGE, BRENDA (1985), *Thinking about Things: A Philosophical Study of Representation* (Edinburgh: Scottish Academic Press).

KATAMBA, FRANCIS (1989), *An Introduction to Phonology* (London: Longman).

NEWMEYER, FREDERICK (1991), 'Functional Explanation in Linguistics and the Origins of Language', *Language and Communication*, 11: 3–28.

PINKER, STEVEN, and BLOOM, PAUL (1990), 'Natural Language and Natural Selection', *Behavioral and Brain Sciences*, 13/4: 707–27.

SAMPSON, GEOFFREY (1997), *Educating Eve: The 'Language Instinct' Debate* (London: Cassell).

SCHIFFER, STEPHEN (1989), *Remnants of Meaning* (Cambridge, Mass.: MIT Press).

STICH, STEPHEN (1983), *From Folk Psychology to Cognitive Science* (Cambridge, Mass.: MIT Press).

UJHELYI, MARIA (1998), 'Long-call Structure in Apes as a Possible Precursor for Language', in James R. Hurford, Michael Studdert-Kennedy, and Chris Knight (eds.), *Approaches to the Evolution of Language: Social and Cognitive Bases* (Cambridge: Cambridge University Press), 177–89.

YULE, GEORGE (1985), *The Study of Language* (Cambridge: Cambridge University Press).

16 Linguistic Adaptation without Linguistic Constraints: The Role of Sequential Learning in Language Evolution

MORTEN H. CHRISTIANSEN AND
MICHELLE R. ELLEFSON

16.1 Introduction

The acquisition and processing of language is governed by a number of universal constraints, many of which undoubtedly derive from innate properties of the human brain. These constraints lead to certain universal tendencies in how languages are structured and used. More generally, the constraints help explain why the languages of the world take up only a small part of the considerably larger space defined by the logically possible linguistic subpatterns. Although there is broad consensus about the existence of innate constraints on the way language is acquired and processed, there is much disagreement over whether these constraints are linguistic or cognitive in nature. Determining the nature of these constraints is important not only for theories of language acquisition and processing, but also for theories of language evolution. Indeed, these issues are theoretically intertwined because the constraints on language define the *endpoints* for evolutionary explanations: theories about *how* the constraints evolved in the hominid lineage are thus strongly determined by *what* the nature of these constraints is taken to be.

The Chomskyan approach to language suggests that the constraints on the acquisition and processing of language are linguistic, rather than cognitive, in nature. The constraints are represented in the form of a Universal Grammar (UG)—a large biological endowment of linguistic knowledge (e.g. Chomsky 1986). It is assumed that this knowledge-base is highly abstract, comprising a complex set of linguistic rules and principles that could not be acquired from exposure to language during development. Opinions differ about how UG emerged as the endpoint of language evolution. Some researchers have suggested that it evolved through a gradual process of natural selection (e.g. Newmeyer 1991; Pinker 1994; Pinker and Bloom 1990), whereas others have argued for a sudden emergence through non-adaptationist evolutionary processes (e.g. Bickerton 1995; Piattelli-Palmarini 1989). An important point of agreement is the emphasis in their explanations of language evolution on the need for very substantial biological changes to accommodate linguistic structure.

More recently an alternative perspective is gaining ground, advocating a refocus in thinking about language evolution. Rather than concentrating on biological changes to accommodate language, this approach stresses the adaptation of linguistic structures to the biological substrate of the human brain (e.g. Batali 1998; Christiansen 1994; Christiansen and Devlin 1997; Deacon 1997; Kirby 1998, 2000, 2001). Languages are viewed as dynamic systems of communication, subject to selection pressures arising from limitations on human learning and processing. Some approaches within this framework have built in a certain amount of linguistic machinery, such as context-free grammars (Kirby 2000). In this chapter we argue that many of the constraints on linguistic adaptation derive from non-linguistic limitations on the learning and processing of hierarchically organized sequential structure. The underlying mechanisms existed prior to the appearance of language, but presumably also underwent changes after the emergence of language. However, the selection pressures are likely to have come not only from language but also from other kinds of complex hierarchical processing, such as the need for increasingly complex manual combinations following tool sophistication. Consequently, many language universals may reflect non-linguistic, cognitive constraints on learning and processing of sequential structure rather than an innate UG.

16.1.1 *Exploring Linguistic Adaptation through Artificial Language Learning*

The study of the origin and evolution of language must *necessarily* be an interdisciplinary endeavour. Only by amassing evidence from many different disciplines can theorizing about the evolution of language be sufficiently constrained to remove it from the realm of pure speculation and allow it to become an area of legitimate scientific inquiry. Fuelled by theoretical constraints derived from recent advances in the brain and cognitive sciences, the last decade of the twentieth century has seen a resurgence of scientific interest in the origin and evolution of language. However, direct experimentation is needed in order to go beyond existing data. Computational modelling has become the paradigm of choice for such experimentation (e.g. Batali 1998; Briscoe 2000; Christiansen and Devlin 1997; Kirby 1998, 2000, 2001). Computational models provide an important tool with which to investigate how various types of constraints may affect the evolution of language. One of the advantages of this approach is that specific constraints and/or interactions between constraints can be studied under controlled circumstances.

Here we point to Artificial Language Learning (ALL) as an additional, complementary paradigm for exploring and testing hypotheses about language evolution. Artificial language learning involves training human subjects on artificial languages with particular structural constraints, and then testing their knowledge of the language. Importantly, the ability to acquire linguistic structure can be studied independently of semantic influences. Because ALL permits researchers to investigate the language learning abilities of infants and children in a highly controlled environment, the paradigm is becoming increasingly popular as a method for studying language acquisition (for a review see Gomez and Gerken 2000). We suggest that ALL can be applied to the investigation of issues pertaining to the origin and evolution of language in much the same way as computational modelling is currently being used. One advantage of ALL over computational modelling is that it may be possible to show that specific constraints hypothesized to be important for language evolution actually affect human learning and processing. Below we demonstrate the utility of ALL as a tool for studying the evolution of language by reporting on three ALL experiments that test predictions derived from our evolutionary perspective on language.

In this chapter, we first outline our perspective on the adaptation of linguistic structure. Specifically, we suggest that 'language as an organism' (Christiansen 1994) provides a useful metaphor for understanding language evolution. The idea of linguistic adaptation has been explored previously using computational models of language evolution (e.g. Batali 1998; Kirby 1998, 2000, 2001). Here we report on three ALL studies that corroborate our approach. The first study, conducted by Christiansen, Kelly, Shillcock, and Greenfield (currently unpublished), points to an association between sequential learning and the processing of language. The second study, by Christiansen (2000) with accompanying computational simulations by Christiansen and Devlin (1997), demonstrates how certain word-order constraints can be explained in terms of non-linguistic limitations on sequential learning. The third study, by Ellefson and Christiansen (2000), indicates that processes of linguistic adaptation may explain the emergence of (subjacency) constraints on complex question formation. Finally, we discuss the wider implications of linguistic adaptation for language evolution.

16.2 Language as an Organism

Languages exist only because humans can learn, produce, and process them. Without humans there would be no language (in the narrow sense of *human* language). It therefore makes sense to construe languages as organisms that have had to adapt themselves through natural selection to fit a particular ecological niche: the human brain (Christiansen 1994). In order for languages to 'survive', they must adapt to the properties of the human learning and processing mechanisms. This is not to say that having a language does not confer selective advantage onto humans. It seems clear that humans with superior language abilities are likely to have a selective advantage over other humans (and other organisms) with lesser communicative powers. This is an uncontroversial point, forming the basic premise of many of the adaptationist UG theories of language evolution mentioned above. However, what is often not appreciated is that the selection forces working on language to fit humans are significantly stronger than the selection pressure on humans to be able to use language. In the case of the former, a language can *only* survive if it is learnable and processable by humans. On the other hand, adaptation towards language use is merely *one out of many* selective pressures working on humans (such as, for example, being able to avoid predators and find food). Whereas humans can survive without language, the opposite is not the case. Thus, language is more likely to have adapted itself to its human hosts than the other way round. Languages that are hard for humans to learn simply die out or, more likely, do not come into existence at all.

The biological perspective on language as an adaptive system has a prominent historical pedigree. Indeed, nineteenth-century linguistics was dominated by an organistic view of language (for a review see e.g. McMahon 1994). For example, Franz Bopp, one of the founders of comparative linguistics, regarded language as an organism that could be dissected and classified

(Davies 1987). More generally, languages were viewed as having life-cycles that included birth, progressive growth, procreation, and eventually decay and death. However, the notion of evolution underlying this organistic view of language was largely pre-Darwinian. This is perhaps reflected most clearly in the writings of another influential linguist, August Schleicher. Although he explicitly emphasized the relationship between linguistics and Darwinian theory (Schleicher 1863; quoted in Percival 1987), Darwin's principles of mutation, variation, and natural selection did not enter into the theorizing about language evolution (Nerlich 1989). Instead, the evolution of language was seen in pre-Darwinian terms as the progressive growth towards attainment of perfection, followed by decay.

More recently, the biological perspective on language evolution was resurrected, within a modern Darwinian framework, by Stevick (1963), and later by Nerlich (1989). Christiansen (1994) proposed that language be viewed as a kind of beneficial parasite—a *nonobligate symbiant*—that confers some selective advantage onto its human hosts without whom it cannot survive. Building on this work, Deacon (1997) further developed the metaphor by construing language as a virus. The asymmetry in the relationship between language and its human host is underscored by the fact that the rate of linguistic change is far greater than the rate of biological change. Whereas Danish and Hindi needed less than 5,000 years to evolve from a common hypothesized proto-Indo-European ancestor into very different languages (McMahon 1994), it took our remote ancestors approximately 100,000–200,000 years to evolve from the archaic form of *Homo sapiens* into the anatomically modern form, sometimes termed *Homo sapiens sapiens* (see e.g. Corballis 1992). Consequently, it seems more plausible that the languages of the world have been closely tailored through linguistic adaptation to fit human learning, rather than the other way around. The fact that children are so successful at language learning is therefore best explained as a product of natural selection of linguistic structures, and not as the adaptation of biological structures, such as UG.

From the viewpoint of the UG approach to language, the universal constraints on the acquisition and processing of language are essentially arbitrary (e.g. Pinker and Bloom 1990). That is, given the Chomskyan perspective on language, these constraints appear arbitrary because it is possible to imagine a multitude of alternative, and equally adaptive, constraints on linguistic form. For instance, Piattelli-Palmarini (1989) contends that there are no (linguistic) reasons not to form yes–no questions by reversing the word order of a sentence instead of the normal inversion of subject and auxiliary. On our account, however, these universal constraints are in most cases *not* arbitrary. Rather, they are determined predominately by the properties of the human learning and processing mechanisms that underlie our language capacity.[1] This can explain why we do not reverse the word order to form yes–no questions; it would put too heavy a load on memory to store a whole sentence in order to be able to reverse it.

Our perspective on language evolution also has important implications for current theories of language acquisition and processing. It suggests that many of the cognitive constraints that have shaped the evolution of language are still at play in our current language ability. If this is correct, it should be possible to uncover the source of some of the universal constraints in human performance on sequential learning tasks. In the next three sections, we show how language and sequential learning are intertwined, and how universal constraints on basic word order and complex question formation can be explained in terms of non-linguistic constraints on the learning of complex sequential structure.

16.3 Association between the Processing of Linguistic and Sequential Structure

The theory of language evolution presented here suggests that language has evolved to fit pre-existing sequential learning and processing mechanisms. This points to a strong association between the processing of sequential structure and language. A straightforward prediction from this approach is that one would expect impaired sequential learning and processing to lead to a breakdown of language. Indeed, Grossman (1980) found that Broca's aphasics, besides agrammatism, also had an additional deficit in sequentially reconstructing hierarchical tree structure models from memory. He took this as suggesting that Broca's area not only subserves syntactic speech production, but also functions as a locus for supramodal processing of hierarchically structured behaviour. Another study has suggested a similar association between language and sequential processing. Kimura (1988)

---

[1] Many functional and cognitive linguists also suggest that the putative innate UG constraints arise from general cognitive constraints (e.g. Givón 1998; Hawkins 1994; Lakoff 1987; Langacker 1987). Our approach distinguishes itself from these linguistic perspectives in that it emphasizes the role of sequential learning in the explanation of linguistic constraints.

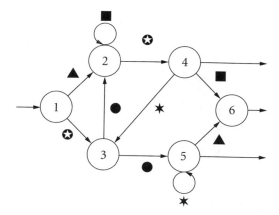

FIG. 16.1 The finite-state grammar used to generate stimuli in Christiansen *et al.* (in preparation). Items are generated by following the arrows between nodes, and writing out their symbols. For example, the item ▲ ■ ✪ ■ is produced by going from node 1 to node 2, then looping back once to node 2, followed by visits to nodes 4 and 6.

reported that sign aphasics often also suffer from apraxia; that is, they have additional problems with the production of novel hand and arm movements not specific to sign language.

More recently, our team has provided a more direct test of the suggested link between breakdown of language and breakdown of sequential learning. We conducted an ALL study using seven agrammatic patients and seven normal controls matched for age, socio-economic status, and spatial reasoning abilities. The subjects were trained on a match–mismatch pairing task in which they had to decide whether two consecutively presented symbol strings were the same or different. The materials consisted of symbol strings (e.g. ✪ ● ■ ✪ ■) generated by the simple finite-state grammar illustrated in Fig. 16.1. Subjects were instructed that they were participating in a memory experiment and that their knowledge of the string patterns would be tested later. After training, the subjects were then presented with novel strings, half of which were derived from the grammar and half of which were not. Subjects were told that the training strings were generated by a complex set of rules,[2] and asked to classify the new strings according to whether they followed these rules or not.

---

[2] The fact that we use rules and syntactic trees to characterize the language to be acquired should not be taken as suggesting that we believe that the end-product of the acquisition process is a set of rules. We merely use rules as convenient descriptive devices, approximating the particular grammatical regularities that we are considering.

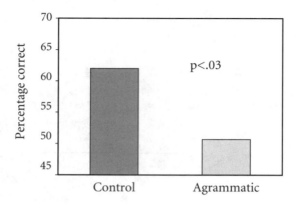

Fig. 16.2 The overall classification performance for the aphasic and normal control subjects in Christiansen *et al.* (in preparation).

The results showed that although both groups did very well on the match–mismatch pairing task, the normal controls were significantly better at classifying the new test strings in comparison with the agrammatic aphasics (see Fig. 16.2). Indeed, the aphasic patients were no better than chance at classifying the test items. Thus, this study indicates that agrammatic aphasic patients have problems with sequential learning in addition to their more obvious language deficits. This point is underscored by a recent study showing that training aphasic patients on non-linguistic hierarchical processing led to improvements in their comprehension of complex linguistic constructions (Dominey *et al.* 2001), indicating a causal link between sequential learning and language. This is, of course, what is predicted by our approach, given the suggested close connection in processing mechanisms between the learning and processing of non-linguistic sequential structure and language.

This close connection in terms of underlying brain mechanisms is further underscored by recent neuroimaging studies of ALL. Steinhauer *et al.* (2001) had subjects play a kind of board game in which two players were required to communicate via an artificial language. After substantial training, event-related potential (ERP) brainwave patterns were then recorded as the subjects were tested on grammatical and ungrammatical sentences from the language. The results showed the same frontal negativity pattern (P600) for syntactic violations in the artificial language as has been found for similar violations in natural language (e.g. Osterhout and Holcomb 1992). Another study by Patel *et al.* (1998) further corroborates this pattern of results but with non-linguistic sequential stimuli: musical sequences with target chords either within the key of a major musical phrase or out of key. When they directly compared the ERP patterns elicited for syntactic incongruities in language with the ERP patterns elicited for incongruent out-of-key target chords, they found that the two types of sequential incongruities resulted in the same, statistically indistinguishable P600 components. In a more recent study, Maess *et al.* (2001) used magnetoencephalography (MEG) to localize the neural substrates that might be involved in the processing of musical sequences. They found that Broca's area in the left hemisphere (and the corresponding frontal area in the right hemisphere) produced significant activation when subjects listened to musical sequences that included an off-key chord. The aphasic studies and the neuroimaging studies of ALL reviewed here converge on the suggestion that the same underlying brain mechanisms are used for the learning and processing of both linguistic and non-linguistic sequential structure, and that similar constraints are imposed on both language and sequential learning. Next, we show how constraints on sequential learning may explain basic word-order universals.

16.4 Cognitive Constraints on Word Order

There is a statistical tendency across human languages to conform to a form in which the head of a phrase is consistently placed in the same position—either first or last—with respect to the remaining clause material. English is considered to be a head-first language, meaning that the head is most frequently placed first in a phrase, as when the verb is placed before the object NP[3] in a transitive VP such as *eat curry*. In contrast, speakers of Hindi would say the equivalent of *curry eat*, because Hindi is a head-last language. Likewise, head-first languages tend to have *prepositions* before the NP in PPs (such as *with a fork*), whereas head-last languages tend to have *post*positions following the NP in PPs (such as *a fork with*). Within Chomsky's (e.g. 1986) approach to language such head direction consistency has been explained in terms of an innate module known as X-bar theory which specifies constraints on the phrase structure of languages. It has further been suggested that this module emerged as a product of natural selection (Pinker 1994). As

---

[3] NP = Noun Phrase; VP = Verb Phrase; PP = Prepositional Phrase.

such, it comes as part of the UG that every child supposedly is born with. All that remains for a child to 'learn' about this aspect of her native language is the direction (i.e. head-first or head-last) of the so-called head-parameter.

Our theory suggests an alternative explanation for word-order consistency based on non-linguistic constraints on the learning of hierarchically organized sequential structure. Christiansen and Devlin (1997) provided an analysis of word-order regularities in a recursive rule set with consistent and inconsistent ordering of the heads. A recursive rule set is a pair of rules for which the expansion of one rule (e.g. NP → N (PP)) involves the second, and vice versa (e.g. PP → prep NP). This analysis showed that head-order inconsistency in a recursive rule set (e.g. the rule set NP → N (PP); PP → NP post) creates centre-embedded constructions, whereas a consistent ordering of heads creates right-branching constructions for head-first orderings and left-branching constructions for head-last orderings (see Fig. 16.3). Centre-embeddings are difficult to process because constituents cannot be completed immediately, forcing the language processor to keep lexical material in memory until it can be discharged. For the same reason, centre-embedded structures are likely to be difficult to learn because of the distance between the material relevant for the discovery and/or reinforcement of a particular grammatical regularity. This means that recursively inconsistent rule sets are likely to be harder to learn than recursively consistent rule sets.[4]

Christiansen and Devlin (1997) also carried out connectionist simulations in which Simple Recurrent Networks (SRNs; Elman 1990, see Fig. 16.4) were trained on corpora generated by thirty-two different artificial grammars with differing degrees of head-order consistency. These networks do not have built-in linguistic biases of the sort envisioned in a UG; rather, they are biased towards the learning of complex sequential structure (e.g. Cleeremans 1993). Nevertheless, the SRNs were sensitive to the amount of head-order inconsistency found in the grammars, such that there was a strong correlation between the degree of head-order consistency of a given grammar and the degree to which the network learned to master the grammatical regularities underlying that grammar: the higher the inconsistency, the worse was the final network performance. The sequential biases of the net-

---

[4] Note that our approach differs from Hawkins's (1994) performance-oriented approach to word order because he focuses exclusively on adult processing of language whereas our emphasis is on language acquisition. Although it may be impossible to tease apart the learning-based constraints from those emerging from processing, we hypothesize that basic word order may be most strongly affected by learnability constraints whereas changes in constituency relations (e.g. heavy NP-shifts) may stem from processing limitations.

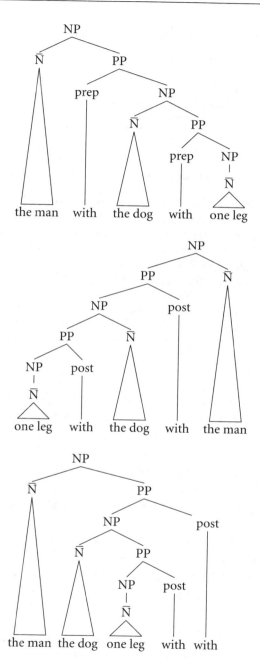

FIG. 16.3 Syntactic trees for a consistent head-first, right-branching NP (top), a consistent head-last, left-branching NP (middle), and an inconsistent NP with centre-embedding (bottom).

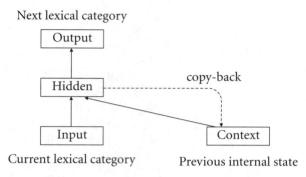

FIG. 16.4 An illustration of the SRN used in the simulations by Christiansen and Devlin (1997) and Ellefson and Christiansen (2000). The rectangles indicate sets of units, solid arrows denote trainable weights, and the dashed arrow the copy-back weights (always 1). An SRN is essentially a standard feed-forward neural network equipped with an extra layer of so-called context units. At a particular time step *t*, an input pattern is propagated through the hidden unit layer to the output layer. At the next time step, *t*+1, the activation of the hidden unit layer at time *t* is copied back to the context layer and paired with the current input. This means that the current state of the hidden units can influence the processing of subsequent inputs, providing a limited ability to deal with sequentially presented input incorporating hierarchical structure.

works made the corpora generated by consistent grammars considerably easier to acquire than the corpora generated from inconsistent grammars. This sequential learnability difference is, *ceteris paribus*,[5] likely to result in different frequency distributions across languages through the adaptation of linguistic structure, a suggestion supported by computational simulations in Kirby (1998), showing how consistent grammars, because of their relative ease of parsing, are selected over inconsistent grammars in linguistic adaptation.

Typological analyses by Christiansen and Devlin using the FANAL database (Dryer 1992) with information regarding 625 of the world's languages further corroborated this account. Languages incorporating fragments that the networks found hard to learn tended to be less well attested than lan-

---

[5] Of course, other factors are likely to play a role in whether or not a given language may be learnable. For example, the presence of concord morphology may help overcome some sequential learning difficulties as demonstrated by an ALL experiment by Morgan *et al.* (1987). None the less, sequential learning difficulties are hypothesized to be strong predictors of frequency in the absence of such ameliorating factors.

guages the network learned more easily. This suggests that constraints on basic word order may derive from non-linguistic constraints on the learning and processing of complex sequential structure, thus obviating the need for an innate X-bar module to explain such word-order universals. Grammatical constructions incorporating a high degree of head-order inconsistency are simply too hard to learn and will therefore tend to disappear. Similar simulations by Van Everbroek (1999) further substantiate this link between sequential learnability of a linguistic fragment and its frequency of occurrence. A variation on the SRN was trained on example sentences from forty-two artificial languages, varying in three dimensions: word order (e.g. subject–verb–object), nominal marking (accusative v. ergative), and verbal marking. The networks easily processed language types that occur with medium to high frequency amongst the languages of the world, while low frequency language types resulted in poor performance. Together, the simulations by Christiansen and Devlin and Van Everbroek support a connection between the distribution of language types and constraints on sequential learning and processing, suggesting that frequent language types tend to be those that have successfully adapted to these learning and processing limitations.

The final line of evidence supporting our explanation of basic word-order universals comes from a recent ALL study by our team. In one experiment, Christiansen took two of the grammars that Christiansen and Devlin had used for their network simulations—a consistent and an inconsistent grammar (see Table 16.1)—and trained forty subjects on sentences (represented as consonant strings) derived from the two grammars. Training and test

TABLE 16.1 *The two grammars used for stimuli generation in Christiansen (2000)*

Consistent Grammar		Inconsistent Grammar	
S	→ NP VP	S	→ NP VP
NP	→ (PP) N	NP	→ (PP) N
PP	→ NP post	PP	→ pre NP
VP	→ (PP) (NP) V	VP	→ (PP) (NP) V
NP	→ (PossP) N	NP	→ (PossP) N
PossP	→ NP Poss	PossP	→ Poss NP

Note: Vocabulary: {X, Z, Q, V, S, M}

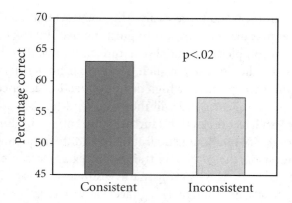

FIG. 16.5 The overall classification performance for the subjects trained on the consistent and inconsistent languages in Christiansen (2000).

materials were controlled for length and simple distributional differences. In the training phase of the experiment, subjects read and reproduced consonant strings on a computer. As in Christiansen *et al.* (in preparation), the subjects were not informed about the rule-based nature of the training items until they were about to commence the test phase.

The results are shown in Fig. 16.5. The twenty subjects trained on strings from the consistent grammar were significantly better at distinguishing grammatical from ungrammatical items than the twenty subjects trained on the inconsistent grammar. Together, Christiansen's ALL experiment and the three lines of evidence from Christiansen and Devlin converge to support our claim that basic word-order universals (head-ordering) can be explained in terms of non-linguistic constraints on sequential learning and processing. This research thus suggests that universal word-order correlations may emerge from non-linguistic constraints on learning, rather than being a product of innate linguistic knowledge. In the next section we show how constraints on complex question formation may be explained in a similar manner.

16.5 Subjacency without Universal Grammar

According to Pinker and Bloom (1990), subjacency is one of the classic examples of an arbitrary linguistic universal that makes sense only from a linguistic perspective. Subjacency provides constraints on complex question formation. Informally, 'Subjacency, in effect, keeps rules from relating elements that are "too far apart from each other", where the distance apart is defined in terms of the number of designated nodes that there are between them' (Newmeyer 1991: 12). Consider the following sentences:

(1) Sara heard (the) news that everybody likes cats.
     N V   N comp N   V N

(2) What (did) Sara hear that everybody likes?
     Wh   N V comp N   V

(3) *What (did) Sara hear (the) news that everybody likes?
     Wh   N V   N comp N   V

According to the subjacency principle, sentence (3) is ungrammatical because too many boundary nodes are placed between the noun phrase complement and its respective 'gap'.

The subjacency principle, in effect, places certain restrictions on the ordering of words in complex questions. The movement of wh-items (*what* in Fig. 16.6) is limited with respect to the number of bounding nodes that it may cross during its upward movement. In English, the bounding nodes are S and NP (circled in Fig. 16.6). Put informally, as a wh-item moves up the

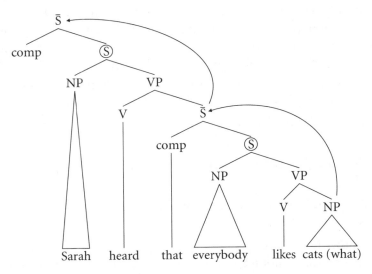

Fig. 16.6 A syntactic tree showing grammatical Wh-movement as in sentence 2.

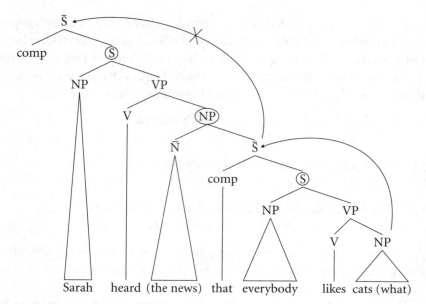

FIG. 16.7 A syntactic tree showing ungrammatical Wh-movement as in sentence 3.

tree it can use comps as temporary 'landing sites' from which to launch the next move. The subjacency principle states that during any move only a single bounding node may be crossed. Sentence (2) is therefore grammatical because only one bounding node is crossed for each of the two moves to the top comp node. Sentence (3) is ungrammatical, however, because the wh-item has to cross two bounding nodes—NP and S—between the temporary comp landing site and the topmost comp, as illustrated in Fig. 16.7.

Not only do subjacency violations occur in NP-complements, but they can also occur in wh-phrase complements. Consider the following examples:

(4)   Sara asked why everyone likes cats.
     N   V   Wh   N   V   N

(5)   Who (did) Sara ask why everyone likes cats?
     Wh   N V Wh   N   V N

(6)   *What (did) Sara ask why everyone likes?
     Wh   N V Wh   N   V

According to the subjacency principle, sentence 6 is ungrammatical because the interrogative pronoun has moved across too many bounding nodes (as was the case in sentence 3).

Ellefson and Christiansen (2000) explored an alternative explanation, suggesting that subjacency violations are avoided, not because of a biological adaptation incorporating the subjacency principle, but because language itself has undergone adaptations to root out such violations in response to non-linguistic constraints on sequential learning. We created two artificial languages to test this idea (including sentence types 1–6 above). As shown in Table 16.2, both languages consisted of six sentence types of which four were identical across the two languages. The two remaining sentence types involved complex question formation. In the natural language the two complex questions were formed in accordance with subjacency, whereas the two complex questions in the unnatural language violated the subjacency constraints. All training and test items were controlled for length and distributional information. As in the previous two ALL experiments, the twenty subjects trained in each condition were not told about the linguistic nature of the stimuli until they received the instructions for the test phase.

The results showed that the subjects trained on the natural grammar were significantly better at distinguishing grammatical from ungrammatical items than were the subjects trained on the unnatural language. As illustrated in Fig. 16.8, subjects in the natural condition were marginally better than the subjects in the unnatural condition at classifying strings related to the two complex questions. Interestingly, the natural group was significantly better at classifying the remaining four sentence types in comparison with the unnatural group—despite the fact that both groups were trained and tested on exactly the same general items. This suggests that the presence of the two unnatural question formation sentence types negatively affected the

TABLE 16.2 *The structure of the natural and unnatural languages in Ellefson and Christiansen (2000)*

Natural	Unnatural
N V N	N V N
Wh N V	Wh N V
N V N comp N V N	N V N comp N V N
N V Wh N V N	N V Wh N V N
Wh N V comp N V	*Wh N V N comp N V
Wh N V Wh N V N	*Wh N V Wh N V

Note: Vocabulary: {X, Z, Q, V, S, M}

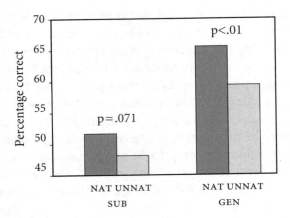

Fig. 16.8 The classification performance on subjacency (SUB) and general (GEN) items for the subjects trained on the natural (NAT) and unnatural (UNNAT) languages in Ellefson and Christiansen (2000).

learning of the other four sentence types. In other words, the presence of the subjacency violations in two of the sentence types in the unnatural language appears to have affected the learning of the language as a whole, not just the two complex question items. From the viewpoint of language evolution, languages such as this unnatural language would be likely to lose out in competition with other languages such as the natural language because the latter is easier to learn.

In principle, one could object that the reason why Ellefson and Christiansen found differences between the natural and the unnatural groups is because the former was in some way able to tap into an innately specified subjacency principle when learning the language. Another possible objection is that the natural language follows the general pattern of English whereas the unnatural language does not, and that our human results could potentially reflect an 'English effect'. To counter these possible objections, and to support the suggestion that the difference in learnability between the two languages is brought about by constraints arising from sequential learning, Ellefson and Christiansen conducted a set of connectionist simulations of the human data using SRNs—a sequential learning device that clearly does not have subjacency constraints built in. We used one network for each subject, and found that the networks were significantly better at learning the natural language than the unnatural language, as measured in terms of the ability to predict the correct sequence of elements in a string. Thus, the simulation results closely mimicked the behavioural results, corroborating the suggestion that constraints on the learning and processing of sequential structure may explain why subjacency violations tend to be avoided: these violations have been weeded out because they made the sequential structure of language too difficult to learn. Even though Ellefson and Christiansen's results do not capture all there is to subjacency, they are nevertheless very encouraging, with future work expected to deal with other variations on subjacency. Based on the current results we therefore venture to suggest that instead of an innate UG principle ruling out subjacency violations, they may have been eliminated through linguistic adaptation.[6]

16.6 Conclusion

In this chapter we have argued that many of the universal constraints on the acquisition and processing of current languages are not linguistic in nature, but rather derive from underlying innate limitations on the learning and processing of hierarchically organized sequential structure. These cognitive constraints defined an important part of the niche within which languages have evolved through the adaptation of linguistic structure. In support of this perspective on language evolution we discussed evidence from three ALL studies. The first study, Christiansen *et al.* (in preparation), demonstrated that language breakdown in agrammatic aphasia is associated with impairment of sequential learning. Along with the other aphasia and neuroimaging studies we reviewed, this helps establish the direct link between language and sequential learning predicted by our account. The next study, Christiansen (2000), showed how constraints on sequential learning can explain basic word-order constraints. The third study, Ellefson and Christiansen (2000), provided a first step towards an explanation, based on sequential learning constraints, for why subjacency violations tend to be avoided across the languages of the world. Together, the results from the three studies (and additional connectionist simulations) suggest that constraints arising from general cognitive processes, such as sequential learning and processing, are likely to play a larger role in sentence processing than

---

[6] Note that whereas Berwick and Weinberg (1984) explain subjacency as a consequence of processing constraints within a linguistically motivated parser, we provide an evolutionary explanation couched in terms of linguistic adaptation constrained to a large degree by *non-linguistic* limitations on sequential learning and processing.

has traditionally been assumed. What we observe today as linguistic universals may be stable states that have emerged through an extended process of linguistic evolution.

When language itself is viewed as a dynamic system sensitive to adaptive pressures, natural selection will favour combinations of linguistic constructions that can be acquired relatively easily given existing learning and processing mechanisms. Consequently, difficult to learn language fragments—such as Christiansen's (2000) inconsistent language and Ellefson and Christiansen's unnatural language—will tend to disappear. If we furthermore assume that the language production system is based conservatively on a processing system acquired in the service of comprehension, then this system would be unlikely to produce inconsistent grammatical structures or subjacency violations because they would not be represented there in the first place. Thus, rather than having innate UG principles to ensure head-direction consistency or to rule out subjacency violations, we argue that such linguistic universals derive from an evolutionary process of linguistic adaptation constrained by prior cognitive limitations on sequential learning and processing.

If language evolution is characterized primarily in terms of the adaptation of linguistic structure to cognitive constraints, it becomes imperative to determine the aspect(s) of language upon which natural selection works. One possibility is that selection takes place at the level of individual utterances; that is, only utterances with high fitness survive. For example, in an exploration of the trade-off between pressures from acquisition and production, Kirby (2001) shows that only utterances that have either a frequent meaning or a compositional syntax survive transmission from one generation to the next. Another possibility is that selection works at the level of grammars; that is, only grammars with high fitness survive. Briscoe (2000) presents simulations in which language evolution is couched in terms of changes over time in the distribution of different grammars that a population of learners acquires through exposure to a body of utterances produced by the previous generation. Based on the studies reported above, we propose that linguistic adaptation may be construed most fruitfully as involving a combination of utterance and whole-language selection. Properties of individual syntactic expressions, such as the degree of recursive inconsistency (as described above) or the frequency of occurrence (as in Kirby 2001), are likely to affect the process of linguistic adaptation. However, the evidence from Ellefson and Christiansen (2000) shows that the existence of less fit utterance types in a language (e.g. the subjacency items in the unnatural language), and not merely the unfit expressions themselves, can affect the learning of the language as whole. From this perspective, a language is more than just a collection of utterances. The relationship between utterances provides an additional source of variation upon which selection pressures can work in the adaptation of linguistic structure. Exactly how the single-utterance and whole-language selection pressures may interact is a question ripe for future research.

Finally, from a methodological perspective, it seems clear that ALL is a useful tool for exploring issues relating to language evolution. It may be objected that the languages used in ALL experiments are simple and deviate significantly from natural language. However, the same objection can be raised against the computational models of language evolution, but this has not diminished their impact, nor their usefulness to the study of language evolution. Moreover, ALL also provides a new tool with which to study other aspects of language evolution, such as creolization (Hudson and Newport 1998) and cross-species comparative aspects of language evolution (Hauser *et al.* 2001). In this way, ALL promises to open up a whole new direction in the search for evidence to rein in scientific theories of language evolution as well as to provide evidence for the adaptation of linguistic structure without linguistic constraints.

FURTHER READING

CANGELOSI, A., and PARISI, D. (eds.) (forthcoming), *Simulating the Evolution of Language* (London: Springer Verlag). (Provides a series of chapters defining the state of the art in simulating the evolution of language.)

GOMEZ, R. L., and GERKEN, L. A. (2000), 'Infant Artificial Language Learning and Language Acquisition', *Trends in Cognitive Sciences*, 4: 178–86. (Provides a cogent overview over the use of artificial language learning to study language acquisition.)

MCMAHON, A. M. S. (1994), *Understanding Language Change* (Cambridge: Cambridge University Press). (Reviews the area of language change, including discussions of different notions of language as an organism.)

MORGAN, J. L., MEIER, R. P., and NEWPORT, E. L. (1987), 'Structural Packaging in the Input to Language Learning: Contributions of Prosodic and Morphological Marking of Phrases to the Acquisition of Language', *Cognitive Psychology*, 19: 498–550. (Presents a series of artificial language learning experiments, demonstrating circumstances under which the presence of multiple linguistic cues, e.g. concord morphology, may help overcome some sequential learning difficulties.)

REFERENCES

BATALI, J. (1998), 'Computational Simulations of the Emergence of Grammar', in J. R. Hurford, M. Studdert-Kennedy, and C. Knight (eds.), *Approaches to the Evolution of Language: Social and Cognitive Bases* (Cambridge: Cambridge University Press), 405–26.

BERWICK, R. C., and WEINBERG, A. S. (1984), *The Grammatical Basis of Linguistic Performance: Language Use and Acquisition* (Cambridge, Mass.: MIT Press).

BICKERTON, D. (1995), *Language and Human Behavior* (Seattle: Washington University Press).

BRISCOE, T. (2000), 'Macro and Micro Models of Linguistic Evolution', in J.-L. Dessalles and L. Ghadakpour (eds.), *Proceedings of the 3rd International Conference on the Evolution of Language* (Paris: École Nationale Supérieure des Télécommunications), 27–9.

CHOMSKY, N. (1986), *Knowledge of Language* (New York: Praeger).

CHRISTIANSEN, M. H. (1994), 'Infinite Languages, Finite Minds: Connectionism, Learning and Linguistic Structure', unpublished doctoral dissertation, Centre for Cognitive Science, University of Edinburgh.

——(2000), 'Using Artificial Language Learning to Study Language Evolution: Exploring the Emergence of Word Order Universals', in J. L. Dessalles and L. Ghadakpour (eds.), *Proceedings of the 3rd International Conference on the Evolution of Language* (Paris: École Nationale Supérieure des Télécommunications), 45–8.

——and DEVLIN, J. T. (1997), 'Recursive Inconsistencies are Hard to Learn: A Connectionist Perspective on Universal Word Order Correlations', in G. W. Cottrell (ed.) *Proceedings of the 19th Annual Cognitive Science Society Conference* (Mahwah, NJ: Lawrence Erlbaum), 113–18.

——KELLY, L., SHILLCOCK, R. C., and GREENFIELD, K. (in preparation). *Artificial Grammar Learning in Agrammatism*.

CLEEREMANS, A. (1993), *Mechanisms of Implicit Learning: Connectionist Models of Sequence Processing* (Cambridge, Mass.: MIT Press).

CORBALLIS, M. C. (1992), 'On the Evolution of Language and Generativity', *Cognition*, 44: 197–226.

DAVIES, A. M. (1987), '"Organic" and "Organism" in Franz Bopp', in H. M. Hoenigswald and L. F. Wiener (eds.), *Biological Metaphor and Cladistic Classification* (Philadelphia: University of Pennsylvania Press), 81–107.

DEACON, T. W. (1997), *The Symbolic Species: The Co-evolution of Language and the Brain* (New York: W. W. Norton).

DOMINEY, P. F., HOEN, M., GOLEMBIOWSKI, M., and GUYOT, E. (2001), *Non-linguistic Training Transfers to Syntactic Comprehension Performance* (Tech. Memo No. 2001–2 (Lyons: Institut des Sciences Cognitives).

DRYER, M. S. (1992), 'The Greenbergian Word Order Correlations', *Language*, 68: 81–138.

ELLEFSON, M. R., and CHRISTIANSEN, M. H. (2000), 'Subjacency Constraints Without Universal Grammar: Evidence from Artificial Language Learning and Connectionist Modeling', in L. R. Gleitman and A. K. Joshi (eds.), *The Proceedings of the 22nd Annual Conference of the Cognitive Science Society* (Mahwah, NJ: Erlbaum), 645–50.

ELMAN, J. L. (1990), 'Finding Structure in Time', *Cognitive Science*, 14: 179–211.

GIVÓN, T. (1998), 'On the Co-evolution of Language, Mind and Brain', *Evolution of Communication*, 2: 45–116.

GOMEZ, R. L., and GERKEN, L. A. (2000), 'Infant Artificial Language Learning and Language Acquisition', *Trends in Cognitive Sciences*, 4: 178–86.

GROSSMAN, M. (1980), 'A Central Processor for Hierarchically Structured Material: Evidence from Broca's Aphasia', *Neuropsychologia*, 18: 299–308.

HAUSER, M. D., NEWPORT, E. L., and ASLIN, R. N. (2001), 'Segmentation of the Speech Stream in a Non-human Primate: Statistical Learning in Cotton-Top Tamarins', *Cognition*, 78: B53–B64.

HAWKINS, J. A. (1994), *A Performance Theory of Order and Constituency* (Cambridge: Cambridge University Press).

HUDSON, C. L., and NEWPORT, E. L. (1998), 'Creolization: Could Adults Really Have Done it All?', in A. Greenhill, H. Littlefield, and C. Tano (eds.), *Proceedings of the 23rd Annual Boston University Conference on Language Development* (Boston: Cascadilla Press), 265–76.

KIMURA, D. (1988), 'Review of What the Hands Reveal about the Brain', *Language and Speech*, 31: 375–8.

KIRBY, S. (1998), 'Fitness and the Selective Adaptation of Language', in J. R. Hurford, M. Studdert-Kennedy, and C. Knight (eds.), *Approaches to the Evolution of Language: Social and Cognitive Bases* (Cambridge: Cambridge University Press), 359–83.

——(2000), 'Language Evolution Without Natural Selection: From Vocabulary to Syntax in a Population of Learners', in C. Knight, J. R. Hurford, and M. Studdert-Kennedy (eds.), *The Evolutionary Emergence of Language: Social Function and the Origins of Linguistic Form* (Cambridge: Cambridge University Press), 303–33.

——(2001), 'Spontaneous Evolution of Linguistic Structure: An Iterated Learning Model of the Emergence of Regularity and Irregularity', *IEEE Transactions on Evolutionary Computation*, 5/2: 102–10.

LAKOFF, G. (1987), *Women, Fire, and Dangerous Things: What Categories Reveal about the Mind* (Chicago: University of Chicago Press).

LANGACKER, R. W. (1987), *Foundations of Cognitive Grammar: Theoretical Perspectives* (Stanford, Calif.: Stanford University Press), i.

MCMAHON, A. M. S. (1994), *Understanding Language Change* (Cambridge: Cambridge University Press).

MAESS, B., KOELSCH, S., GUNTER, T. C., and FRIEDERICI, A. D. (2001), 'Musical Syntax Is Processed in Broca's Area: An MEG study', *Nature Neuroscience*, 4: 540–5.

MORGAN, J. L., MEIER, R. P., and NEWPORT, E. L. (1987), 'Structural Packaging in the Input to Language Learning: Contributions of Prosodic and Morphological Marking of Phrases to the Acquisition of Language', *Cognitive Psychology*, 19: 498–550.

NERLICH, B. (1989), 'The Evolution of the Concept of 'Linguistic Evolution' in the 19th and 20th century', *Lingua*, 77: 101–12.

NEWMEYER, F. (1991), 'Functional Explanation in Linguistics and the Origins of Language', *Language and Communication*, 11: 3–28.

OSTERHOUT, L., and HOLCOMB, P. J. (1992), 'Event-Related Brain Potentials Elicited by Syntactic Anomaly', *Journal of Memory and Language*, 31: 785–806.

PATEL, A. D., GIBSON, E., RATNER, J., BESSON, M., and HOLCOMB, P. J. (1998), 'Processing Syntactic Relations in Language and Music: an Event-Related Potential Study', *Journal of Cognitive Neuroscience*, 10: 717–33.

PERCIVAL, W. K. (1987), 'Biological Analogy in the Study of Languages before the Advent of Comparative Grammar', in H. M. Hoenigswald and L. F. Wiener (eds.), *Biological Metaphor and Cladistic Classification* (Philadelphia: University of Pennsylvania Press), 3–38.

PIATELLI-PALMARINI, M. (1989), 'Evolution, Selection and Cognition: From "Learning" to Parameter Setting in Biology and in the Study of Language', *Cognition*, 31: 1–44.

PINKER, S. (1994), *The Language Instinct: How the Mind Creates Language* (New York: William Morrow).

——and BLOOM, P. (1990), 'Natural Language and Natural Selection', *Brain and Behavioral Sciences*, 13: 707–27.

SCHLEICHER, A. (1863), *Die Darwinsche Theorie Und Die Sprachwissenschaft* (Weimar: Böhlau).

STEINHAUER, K., FRIEDERICI, A. D., and PFEIFER, E. (2001), *ERP Recordings While Listening to Syntax Errors in an Artificial Language: Evidence from Trained and Untrained Subjects*, Poster presented at the 14th Annual CUNY Conference on Human Sentence Processing, Philadelphia.

STEVICK, R. D. (1963), 'The Biological Model and Historical Linguistics', *Language*, 39: 159–69.

VAN EVERBROECK, E. (1999), 'Language Type Frequency and Learnability: A Connectionist Appraisal', in M. Hahn and S. C. Stoness (eds.), *Proceedings of the 21st Annual Cognitive Science Society Conference* (Mahwah, NJ: Erlbaum), 755–60.

17 Uniformitarian Assumptions and Language Evolution Research

FREDERICK J. NEWMEYER

17.1 Introduction

This chapter explores the consequences of the fact that most research into language origins and evolution has taken the 'uniformitarian' position that the general nature of human language has not changed much over the millennia. It concludes that such a position is probably a mistaken one. The chapter is organized as follows. Section 17.2 presents the evidence for uniformitarianism, at least in so far as it governs the languages spoken today. Section 17.3 documents the fact that most language evolution research has assumed the correctness of the principle diachronically, as well as synchronically. Section 17.4 presents reasons to doubt the correctness of uniformitarianism, at least in its strongest form and sect. 5 argues that reasons for such doubt increase the further back we go in time.

17.2 Uniformitarianism in Linguistics

If one quotation captures the essence of twentieth-century linguistics, it would have to be the following from Edward Sapir: 'When it comes to linguistic form, Plato walks with the Macedonian swineherd, and Confucius with the head-hunting savage of Assam' (Sapir 1921: 219). The sentiment expressed, namely that all languages are in some important sense equal, informed most of the linguistic theory carried out in the last century and it looks set to continue to be the bedrock of theorizing in this one.

In what way have languages been considered to be equal? Well, in almost *every* way. First and foremost, linguists have rejected the idea, prevalent throughout most of the nineteenth century, that one language can be characterized as 'more primitive' or 'more advanced', grammatically speaking, than another. By the 1920s, if not earlier, it had become apparent that grammars of all languages are composed of the same sorts of units—phonemes, morphemes, and so on—and therefore all grammars can be analysed by means of the same theoretical tools. As far as bearing on the correct theory of grammar is concerned, a vowel alternation in English is no more or no less relevant than one in Sierra Popoluca.

Furthermore, since the oldest languages that we have on record—the earliest samples of Babylonian, Chinese, Greek, and so on—manifest the same grammatical devices as modern languages, one has typically concluded that there is no overall *directionality* to language change. That, is, human languages have always been pretty much the same in terms of the typological distribution of the elements that compose them.

I will call the conjunction of positions outlined in the previous two paragraphs the 'uniformitarian hypothesis'. This hypothesis has had the very happy consequence of being both evidently factually correct and politically desirable. As far as 'factually correct' is concerned, little needs to be said. Hundreds of languages have been described for the first time since Sapir's statement in 1921. While theories of grammar have changed enormously since then, no language has been encountered with grammatical properties so unusual as to defy the possibility of description within existing theoretical frameworks or within a modest extension of such frameworks. And as far as 'politically desirable' is concerned, little *should* need to be said. If all humans are, at root, the same, then we would expect all their languages to be, at root, the same. All languages are products of the same mind and body.

Uniformitarianist assumptions helped clear the air of nineteenth-century race theories and, as formulated by Sapir's teacher Franz Boas, were a powerful weapon against the various twentieth-century attempts to link race, intelligence, and inherent ability. It is no accident, then, that in the period between the two world wars the governments that condemned structural linguistics outright were fascist Germany and Italy and (for somewhat different reasons) Stalinist Russia (for discussion, see Newmeyer 1986).

Most linguists today are so wedded to uniformitarian assumptions that they hold an even stronger version of the hypothesis than that characterized above. Namely, they maintain that for any given language, there is no correlation between aspects of that language's grammar and properties of the *users* of that grammar. That is, there is no correlation between the grammar of a particular language and the culture, personality, world-view, and so on of the speakers of that language. Again, such a view has a great deal to recommend it. Nineteenth-century historical and comparative linguistics took a qualitative leap forward when researchers stopped trying to link sound changes to the presumed national characteristics of the speakers of the languages undergoing the changes and (a little later) when they stopped trying to correlate grammatical (typically, morphological) properties with racial and cultural characteristics.

In fact, virtually all linguists today would agree that there is no hope of correlating a language's gross grammatical properties with sociocultural facts about its speakers. For example, some languages manifest distinctive phonological tone, others do not. As (1) illustrates, it would be hard to 'link' distinctive tonality to anything external:

(1) *Distinctive tone*   *No distinctive tone*
     Chinese   Korean
     Navajo   Hopi
     Kikuyu   Swahili
     Ewe   Wolof

Languages can also be typologized in terms of the predominant ordering of the verb (V), the subject (S), and the object (O) within the clause. Example (2) illustrates the evident lack of sociocultural implications of the choice of word order:

(2) SVO: English and Zulu
     SOV: Japanese and Siouan
     VSO: Welsh and Quileute

As a final example, consider the property of 'ergativity'. Languages fall roughly into two classes. In nominative–accusative languages, like English, subjects of intransitive and subjects of transitive verbs have the same (nominative) case marking:

(3) Nominative–Accusative Languages:
     Mary-NOM ran
     Mary-NOM threw the ball-ACC

But in ergative–absolutive languages, the subjects of intransitive verbs and the objects of transitive verbs are marked the same. Subjects of transitive verbs have distinctive ergative case marking:

(4) Ergative–Absolutive Languages:
     Mary-ABS ran
     Mary-ERG threw the ball-ABS

As (5) illustrates, one would be hard pressed to correlate ergativity with prop
erties of language users:

(5) *Nominative–Accusative*   *Ergative–Absolutive*
     Spanish   Basque
     Armenian   Chechen
     Hawaiian   Samoan
     Mangarayi   Dyirbal

Now, interestingly, the extension of uniformitarianism to the denial o
links between language, culture, and world-view was manifestly not Sapir's
position. Indeed, he believed strongly that such links exist. Such a belief even
has his name enshrined in it: the Sapir–Whorf Hypothesis. Sapir believed
that the structure of one's language directly shapes one's view of the world
and that different structures impose on the consciousness a different percep
tion of reality:

Language actually defines experience for us by reason of its formal completeness
and because of our unconscious projection of its implicit expectations into the field
of experience . . . Such categories as number, gender, case, tense are not so much
discovered in experience as imposed upon it because of the tyrannical hold that
linguistic form has upon our orientation in the world.   (Sapir 1931: 578)

Sapir's student Benjamin Whorf wrote several articles (collected in Carroll
1956) on how the Hopi's non-Indo-European style system of tenses was at
the root of their (supposedly) not having any sense of time as a smooth flow
ing continuum. Other works in this genre—some by highly regarded lin
guists—have correlated the Navajo set of movement affixes to their nomadic
lifestyle (Hoijer 1964) and the Papago number system to the seeming inabil
ity of speakers of Papago to make black-or-white decisions (Mathiot 1964)
Mathiot notes that the number system of this language is strikingly differ
ent from that of English. Number in Papago is relativistic—their language
forces them to specify whether there are more or fewer objects at some par
ticular place than expected. This fact, she concludes, has helped to deter
mine that 'Papago perception and behavior are along a sliding scale rather
than in terms of a two-valued logic' (p. 160).

It seems safe to state that few theoretical linguists today attach much intellectual value to such ideas. Inevitably, the methodology that led to the conclusions was shoddy, the claims were for the most part untestable, and, where they were tested, they turned out to be simply wrong. In fact, most linguists today regard semantic representations as universal. Such a view, as noted in Bach (1968: 122), constitutes an implicit denial of the Sapir–Whorf hypothesis.

17.3 Uniformitarianism and the Field of Language Evolution Research

Let us now turn to the question of the origins and evolution of language. Uniformitarian assumptions have, in general, been carried over into research on this topic. Specifically, most scenarios of language evolution take uniformitarianism for granted in that they equate the origins of human language with whatever genetic event created human beings. The implication, of course, is that, at least in its grammatical aspects, language has not changed a great deal since that event. Let us now look at the remarks made on this topic by prominent grammarians.

It is well known that Chomsky has been reluctant to speculate on language origins. But what he has said implies that with humans, you get human language. Along these lines, he has written: 'Perhaps [the properties of Universal Grammar] are simply emergent physical properties of a brain that reaches a certain level of complexity under the specific conditions of human evolution' (Chomsky 1991: 50). There is little room for a non-uniformitarian development of the language faculty in such a big-bang scenario.

Robert Berwick, in a specifically minimalist-program oriented approach to language origins, also rejects the idea that human language could ever have been more primitive. As he notes: 'there is no possibility of an 'intermediate' *syntax* between a non-combinatorial one and full natural language— one either has Merge in all its generative glory, or one has no combinatorial syntax at all' (Berwick 1998: 338–9).

Other scholars—most notably Derek Bickerton and Andrew Carstairs-McCarthy—have put forth detailed explicit scenarios on the origins of human grammar. Both point to stages where our ancestors had something more primitive than modern human language. But significantly, it was *Homo erectus*, not *Homo sapiens* that had this more primitive syntax. Bickerton (1990) sees human language as the product of a two-stage process.

The first took place with the rise of *erectus*, approximately 1.6 million years ago. *Erectus* developed protolanguage, a mode of linguistic expression that attaches vocal labels to pre-existing concepts. Protolanguage is quite different from language in a number of respects. First, protolanguage lacks a true syntax. The order of elements in an utterance is determined by the pragmatics of the speech event. Second, it lacks null elements such as traces and null pronominals. Third, predicates do not subcategorize for obligatory arguments. Fourth, recursion is absent. And fifth, there are no grammatical items (i.e. inflections, complementizers, conjunctions, and so on), or at least there are very few of them. A single mutation, coincident with the transition from *erectus* to *sapiens*, created true language from protolanguage. The major linguistic consequence of this mutation was the imposition of recursive hierarchical structure on pre-existing thematic structure, in one swoop transforming protolanguage into true modern human language. However, in his subsequent book (Bickerton 1995), the effects of the mutation are far less evolutionarily catastrophic, in that he explicitly separates out the mutation involved in the linking of pre-existing cognitive subsystems involved in syntax with the other anatomical changes relevant to our full repertoire of linguistic abilities. And Bickerton (1998) posits the single-step creation of a new neural pathway linking thematic structure (now regarded as itself a product of primate reciprocal altruism) and phonetic representation, rather than an actual mutation. Nevertheless, in all three scenarios human language was 'complete' with the birth of the species.

Carstairs-McCarthy (1999) posits a far richer syntax for *erectus* than does Bickerton, but in his view as well, the capstone of modern language—the recursive feature of syntax—comes in with *sapiens* (ibid. 191). In other words, for both Bickerton and Carstairs-McCarthy, uniformitarian assumptions hold throughout the history of *Homo sapiens*.

Computer simulations of the evolution of language have tended to build in uniformitarian assumptions in a rather different way. Consider, for example, Kirby (1998). This work presupposes the performance theory motivated in Hawkins (1994), which sees pressure to identify phrasal and sentential constituents as rapidly as possible as the central force affecting syntactic structure. In one simulation he starts with a hypothetical speech community in which verb–object order and adposition order are 'dysfunctionally' associated. In the course of the simulation, the populations come to converge on the orders preferred by Hawkins's theory, namely, verb–object and prepositional, and object–verb and postpositional. Kirby's take on Hawkins is a thoroughly uniformitarian one. He does not consider the possibility that at an earlier stage of human language, parsing pressure might have been overshadowed by other pressures. If such had been the case, then the typological distribution of grammatical properties would have looked rather different. (See also Tonkes and Wiles, in this volume, which partially replicates Kirby's study.)

In the remainder of this chapter I will first review the evidence for the proposition that, based on existing languages and those for which we have historical records, the strongest form of uniformitarianism might not be correct. I will then go on to discuss how uniformitarian assumptions must almost *surely* be wrong if we expand our time-frame to the whole of human history.

17.4 Some Doubts about the Correctness of Uniformitarianism

There has always been some linguistically informed opposition to uniformitarianism. The bulk of the scepticism that this principle might not be fully correct derives from the very real possibility that there is some overall directionality to language change. That is, using traditional terminology, there is some evidence to support the idea that languages as a whole are 'drifting' in a particular direction. The most frequently encountered claim along these lines is that there has been an overall drift from verb-final to verb-medial order. A dozen different scholars for a dozen different reasons have suggested that verb-final languages are more likely to develop into verb-medial languages than vice versa, suggesting a progressive decline in the overall percentage of verb-final languages (see e.g. Vennemann 1973; Li 1977; Givón 1979; Bichakjian 1991; Bauer 1995; Beaken 1996; Aske 1998; Newmeyer 2000). If such a view is correct, then the typological distribution of grammatical elements must have looked quite different ten, fifty, and a hundred thousand years ago than it does today.

A non-uniformitarian phonological scenario is put forward in Comrie (1992), where it is argued that certain complexities of modern language were not present in the earliest human languages, but arose over historical time. These include morphophonemic alternations (e.g. sound alternations such as we find in *electric* [k] v. *electric* [s] *-ity*), phonemic tone and vowel nasalization, and fusional morphology. Hombert and Marsico (1996) come to the same conclusion. In their view, complex vowel systems are fairly recent historical developments. In particular, they present evidence that seems to suggest that front rounded vowels and nasalized vowels have shown a tendency to increase over the centuries; few reconstructed proto-systems show any evidence of having had them.

Heine and Kuteva (this volume) suggest that the changes that go under the heading of 'grammaticalization' might suggest a non-uniformitarian development of language. Most researchers of this topic (see e.g. Heine *et al.* 1991; Hopper and Traugott 1993), basing their conclusions on internally reconstructed evidence, posit a unidirectional change over time from 'less grammatical' morphosyntactic elements to 'more grammatical' ones, as indicated below:

(6)   lexical categories > functional categories and pronominal elements > clitics > derivational affixes > inflectional affixes > zero

As a simple illustration, *have* in English has developed from a full verb expressing physical possession ('to hold in one's hand') to an auxiliary-like element expressing simple intention to perform an act to an even further reduced clitic form.

Given the unidirectionality of grammaticalization changes, Heine and Kuteva tentatively suggest that the earliest human language might have had lexical categories (nouns and verbs), but no functional categories or affixes. However, they recognize a problem inherent in such a conclusion. The entire progression from full lexical category to affix can take fewer than 2,000 years to run its course. As they note, if there were no processes creating new lexical categories, we would be in the untenable position of saying that languages remained constant from the birth of *Homo sapiens* until a couple of millennia ago, at which point the unidirectional grammaticalization processes began.

What about the shibboleth that grammar and culture are independent? Even here and even looking at the languages spoken today, there is room for doubt as to its total correctness. For example, Perkins (1992) argues that the more complex the culture, the less complex the grammatical system for expressing deixis. Perkins maintains that while European languages may have words for expressing the concepts 'this', 'that', and (possibly) 'that over there', languages spoken by hunter-gatherers tend to have vastly more ways of expressing deictic concepts. In a less ambitious study, Webb (1977) argues that the transitive use of 'have' (as in *I have a car*) is correlated with ownership of property.

Interestingly, quite a few studies have tied properties of language struc-ture to the degree of isolation of the speakers of the language or the amount of contact that speakers have with speakers of other languages. Trudgill (1992), for example, has argued that the languages of small isolated commu-nities tend to have distinctive typological features. For example, they tend to be over-represented by grammatical constructs that pose difficulty for non-native speakers, such as complex inflectional systems, characterized by multiple paradigms for each grammatical class. They also tend to manifest the sorts of features that one might expect to be present in a tight social network, such as weird rules with enough exceptions to mystify non-native learners.

Nettle (1999), by means of computer simulations, has come to very much the same conclusion. His simulations predict that small communities will have languages with more marked structures than will large communities. For example, small-group languages are more likely to have object-initial orders and big segment inventories. Interestingly, these results suggest an alternative explanation to that put forward in Nichols (1990, 1992) for why there is more linguistic diversity in the New World than in the Old World. This fact falls out from the circumstance that linguistic communities in the former tend to be smaller than those in the latter.

There is also the question of language *contact* and its consequences for grammars. In fact, there is no consensus on this point. Trudgill, pointing to pidgins and creoles as support for his position, argues that contact that primarily involves adults leads to simplification of grammars. On the other hand, when whole societies interact, grammatical complications tend to result. By way of example he cites the borrowing by the southern Bantu lan-guages of click sounds from the Koi-San languages with which the Bantus came into contact.

It is not clear that things are as simple as Trudgill would have them. Simi-lar contact situations, it would seem, can lead to either simplification or com-plication. For example, consider the history of English. The prevalent view (see O'Neil 1978) is that the contact between Old Norse and Old English led to the simplification of the latter, in particular to the loss of its complex case system. On the other hand, contact between English and French a few cen-turies later led to complication. As words flooded into English from French, the moderately simple Latin and Old French word stress system was super-imposed on the very simple Old English word stress system, leading to a 'synthesis' (if that is the right word) that was vastly more complicated than either. So it is not clear if there is some overarching generalization as to the relationship between contact and consequences for the grammar.

To complicate matters still further, Dixon (1997) has suggested a model of language change that leads to the conclusion that the typological features characterizing the differences between groups in occasional contact with each other tend to become smaller over time. His model of 'punctuated equilibrium' sees as the norm the diffusion of features across many areas. For Dixon, rapid language change is modellable by classical family trees only when there is dramatic upheaval.

A well-known non-uniformitarian account of language change has been put forward in Givón (1979). He has argued for a transition over time from discourses characterized by a 'pragmatic mode' to those characterized by a 'syntactic mode'. The former, pragmatic, mode employs topic-comment structure, loose conjunction, word order being governed by pragmatic principles, lack of morphology, stress-marked focus, and so on. The latter, syntactic, mode is characterized by subject–predicate structure, tight subordination, predicate–argument structure, lots of grammatical morphology, and the like. Givón suggests that the historical trend has been an overall movement from the pragmatic mode to the syntactic mode. In his view, literate 'more complex' societies speaking languages such as English, Hebrew, Spanish, Japanese, or French exhibit the syntactic mode *par excellence*.

Givón therefore advocates a radically non-uniformitarian view of language change. If the syntactic mode comes in only with literacy, then from the origins of our species to only a few thousand years ago, all communication took place in the pragmatic mode. Indeed, even today, the grammars of the great majority of the world's 5,000 or so languages would be primarily 'pragmatic', rather than 'syntactic'. Such a view, however, seems to me to be riddled with problems. Chinese and Vietnamese, for example, exhibit many features of pragmatic mode, yet there is no sense in which one could characterize their societies of speakers as 'primitive'. Likewise, there are any number of languages spoken in pre-literate societies that seem to manifest the syntactic mode. For example, most of the Cushitic languages spoken in the Horn of Africa have subject–predicate structure, tight subordination, and so on, yet are to this day unwritten.

But one might still make the case that *some* grammatical features are more characteristic of literate than of pre-literate societies. Givón, for example (ibid. 306), suggests that use of referential indefinite subjects is such a case. I have no idea whether he is right or wrong on this point. More importantly, he and many others have suggested that the use of subordinate clauses increases dramatically with literacy. The major study along these lines is Kalmár (1985), which maintains that Samoyed, Bushman, Seneca, and various Australian languages rarely employ subordination. According to Kalmár: 'It is quite likely that the number of subordinate clause types grew as narrative developed and accelerated with the advent of writing. Typical is the development of subordination in Greek, which hardly existed in Homer but was well developed in the classics (Goodwin 1912)'. Mithun (1984) has made the same point in a Berkeley Linguistics Society paper. She undertook text counts on a number of languages with respect to the amount of subordination that one finds in discourses carried out in those languages. All languages manifest *some* subordination (in fact Tlingit manifests a lot of it) but there is a strong correlation between its rare use and the pre-literate status of their speakers.

It is important to stress that nobody—at least one would hope nobody—has claimed that there exists a language for which subordination is literally *impossible*. That really would be a 'primitive language'. All languages seem to allow the possibility. In fact, as societies 'modernize', the use of subordination becomes more frequent. For example, Kalmár observes that Inukitut is now developing subordinate clauses. Nevertheless, it appears that the correlation of the frequency of this key grammatical feature with a purely cultural development challenges uniformitarianism in its strongest form.

17.5 The Consequences of Non-uniformitarianism for Language Evolution Research

The basic problem for language evolution research, as far as the principle of uniformitarianism is concerned, is that if grammar is tailored to the needs and properties of language users (to whatever degree), and language users now are not what they used to be, then it follows that grammar is probably not what it used to be. How might language users have changed over time? In the first place, there are vastly more of them than there were in the earliest stages of human history. For example, if it is safe to assume that in early *sapiens* times, small, relatively isolated bands were the norm, then, as we have seen, the typological distribution of grammatical elements was probably different.

Along the same lines, we have to consider the question of the degree of language contact in early human societies and its typological consequences.

And this question demands in turn an answer to the epistemologically prior question of whether the human species (and hence its languages) has mono-genetic or polygenetic origins. If the latter, then early humans probably lived in small, far-flung groups, resulting in a lot less language contact. What effect would this lack of contact have had on the typological distribution of grammatical elements? Perhaps, following Trudgill and Nettle, complex and (from today's point of view) typologically rare grammatical features were the norm. On the other hand, following Dixon, if in early *sapiens* days the norm was independently functioning small groups that encountered each other from time to time, there would have been stasis and an evening out of typological properties. If the former, monogenetic, possibility is correct, then the relative patterns of typology might carry traces of this one ancestor language, potentially jeopardizing the validity of our modern perspective on what is typologically 'rare'.

Not only would early human groups have been smaller than societies today, but more importantly, their *needs* might have been different from those of modern times. And, if needs are reflected to any significant degree by language structure, then that structure would have been different as well. So we should now turn to the external (functional) factors that might plausibly be said to affect syntactic structure and see if the balance among them might have changed over time. Functional linguists and functionally minded gen-erative grammarians have generally pointed to the following three factors as the most important determinants of grammatical form: parsing pressure, pressure to keep form and meaning in alignment ('structure–concept iconic-ity'), and discourse pressure. Let us examine them briefly in turn.

Parsing pressure, or pressure to identify the constituents of a sentence as rapidly as possible, has clearly left its mark on grammatical structure. We see it, for example, in the fact that in VO languages, long (or 'heavy') grammati-cal elements tend to follow short (or 'light' ones). For example, the ordering of the constituents [verb–object noun phrase–prepositional phrases–sen-tential complement], in which there is a gradual increase in length, is very common, while other orderings of the same four elements is much rarer. And Hawkins (1994) has demonstrated that parsing pressure explains why VO languages tend to be prepositional and OV language postpositional.

Structure–concept iconicity embodies the idea that the form, length, com-plexity, or interrelationship of elements in a linguistic representation reflect the form, length, complexity, or interrelationship of elements in the concept that that representation encodes. The effect of pressure for iconicity can be illustrated by the fact that, typically, syntactic constituents line up with semantic units. Consider also the cross-linguistic distribution of causatives and possessives.Lexical causatives (e.g. *kill*) tend to convey a more direct causation than periphrastic causatives (e.g. *cause to die*). So, where cause and result are formally separated, conceptual distance is greater than when they are not. There are two types of possessives in the world's languages: alienable possession (as in *John's book*) and inalienable possession (as in *John's heart*). Structure–concept iconicity is illustrated by the fact that in no language is the 'distance' between the possessor and the possessed greater for inalienable possession than for alienable possession. That is, many languages have rather complex circumlocutory ways of saying *John's book* and simple direct ways of saying *John's heart*, while the reverse is never true.

Finally, pressure from discourse has been argued to play a role in shaping grammatical structure. Grammars seem to be organized so as efficiently to convey information in an orderly manner about the topicality of the contribution of the participants in the discourse. Consider, for example, elements that serve as discourse focus, i.e. those that play the role of new or especially important information. Such elements tend to occur in a special position in the sentence (often the very beginning or the very end) or to be marked off by heavy stress.

Now, what is the 'balance' between these forces? My view is that parsing and iconicity predominate, but with the former presenting a somewhat stronger influence on grammars than the latter. And Hawkins has shown that pressure from discourse plays a relatively minor role in shaping syntax. Many computer simulations of language evolution have explicitly or implicitly made the same assumptions. But such assumptions are based on an examination of language spoken today. What reason do we have for thinking that the balance of functional forces was the same 10,000 or 50,000 years ago? The simple and honest answer to that question is that we have no way of knowing. Indeed, the balance might have been very different. For example, one popular scenario for language evolution holds that the roots of syntactic structure are in conceptual representation, which at some point in human evolution was neurally linked with that part of the brain controlling the vocal tract, thereby enabling verbal communication (see Pinker and Bloom 1990; Newmeyer 1991; Wilkins and Wakefield 1995). If so, then the effects of iconicity might well have been more evident in early human language than today. Parsing pressure would have begun to shape language only gradually over time.

Parsing pressure would certainly have been weaker if—as seems plausible—subordination was a rarely used grammatical device in the earliest period of human language. One of the more common scenarios for language evolution combines, in a sense, Chomsky-style innateness with functional utility. Kirby and Hurford (1997), for example, suggest that the constraints of universal grammar (UG), while innately determined, did not arise via a genetic mutation (as suggested in Newmeyer 1991). Rather, they owe their origins to genetic assimilation (the Baldwin effect). That is, they were nativized because it was in the interests of language learners to learn their languages fast (and therefore to learn them young). The nativization of subjacency, binding, and so on would help them to do just that. Subjacency, however, manifests itself only in sentences with complex embedding. If our illiterate ancestors had little or no subordination, they would have had little or no need for this UG constraint. So if subjacency is a product of genetic assimilation, then it must have appeared rather late in the course of language evolution. Such is a non-uniformitarian conclusion, to be sure.

Another scenario—and one that we have already pointed to—holds that proto- or early language was subject to what Givón calls the 'pragmatic mode', that is, one in which discourse pressure was the primary determinant of the ordering of grammatical elements. If so, then effects of parsing and iconicity would have been less manifest than those deriving from pressure to convey information in some orderly and unambiguous fashion.

Finally, we have to think about the *time-frame* for human evolution. It is not at all obvious that the origins of the human species and the origins of 'complete' human language are contemporaneous. Published speculation on this topic shows a wild divergence of opinion. Aiello (1996) and Dunbar (1996), citing evidence for social interaction as the crucial factor, tie language to the appearance of the most archaic varieties of *Homo sapiens*— perhaps 250,000 years ago. On the other hand, Noble and Davidson (1996) link the origins of language to archaeological evidence for artefacts with symbolic significance—tens of thousands of years later. But of course, in non-uniformitarian fashion, they could all be right. Just as humans evolved over the past quarter of a million years, their language might have done so as well.

At this point, it would be desirable to write, in traditional scholarly fashion: 'In conclusion . . .' But, of course, no firm conclusion is possible, given the speculative nature of the enterprise. My feeling is that it will not be linguists who provide the next important contributions to our understanding of the degree to which language evolution and change have held true to a uniformitarian scenario. Rather, advances in our understanding will result from studies of human evolution as a whole, both biological and cultural. The more that *these* areas provide evidence for evolutionary continuity within our species, the more the evidence for a uniformitarian development of language. The more breaks in our evolutionary history there are, the more a non-uniformitarian view of language gains in plausibility. In any event, it must always be kept in mind that even if uniformitarianist assumptions are correct for linguistic studies carried out on languages existing today, it is by no means obvious that they are correct for studies of language change over evolutionary time.

FURTHER READING

Uniformitarianism in linguistics:

CARROLL, J. B. (1956) (ed.), *Language, Thought, and Reality: Selected Writings of Benjamin Lee Whorf* (Cambridge, Mass.: MIT Press).

COMRIE, B. (1992), 'Before Complexity', in J. A. Hawkins and M. Gell-Mann (eds.), *The Evolution of Human Languages* (New York: Addison-Wesley), 193–211.

NEWMEYER, F. J. (1986), *The Politics of Linguistics* (Chicago: University of Chicago Press).

SAPIR, E. (1921), *Language* (New York: Harcourt, Brace & World).

REFERENCES

AIELLO, L. C. (1996), 'Terrestriality, Bipedalism, and the Origin of Language', in W. G. Runciman, J. Maynard-Smith, and R. I. M. Dunbar (eds.), *Evolution of Social Behaviour Patterns in Primates and Man*, Proceedings of the British Academy, 88 (Oxford: Oxford University Press), 269–89.

ASKE, J. (1998), *Basque Word Order and Disorder: Principles, Variation, and Prospects* (Amsterdam: John Benjamins).

BACH, E. (1968), 'Nouns and Noun Phrases', in E. Bach and R. Harms (eds.), *Universals in Linguistic Theory* (New York: Holt, Rinehart, & Winston), 91–124.

BAUER, B. L. M. (1995), *The Emergence and Development of SVO Patterning in Latin and French* (Oxford: Oxford University Press).

BEAKEN, M. (1996), *The Making of Language* (Edinburgh: Edinburgh University Press).

BERWICK, R. C. (1998), 'Language Evolution and the Minimalist Program: The Origins of Syntax', in Hurford *et al.* (1998: 320–40).

BICHAKJIAN, B. H. (1991), 'Evolutionary Patterns in Linguistics', in W. v. Raffler-Engel and J. Wind (eds.), *Studies in Language Origins* (Amsterdam: John Benjamins), ii, 187–224.

BICKERTON, D. (1990), *Language and Species* (Chicago: University of Chicago Press).

——(1995), *Language and Human Behavior* (Seattle: University of Washington Press).

——(1998), 'Catastrophic Evolution: The Case for a Single Step from Protolanguage to Full Human Language', in Hurford *et al.* (1998: 341–58).

CARROLL, J. B. (1956) (ed.), *Language, Thought, and Reality: Selected Writings of Benjamin Lee Whorf* (Cambridge, Mass.: MIT Press).

CARSTAIRS-MCCARTHY, A. (1999), *The Origins of Complex Language: An Inquiry into the Evolutionary Beginnings of Sentences, Syllables, and Truth* (Oxford: Oxford University Press).

CHOMSKY, N. (1991), 'Some Notes on Economy of Derivation and Representation', in R. Freidin (ed.), *Principles and Parameters in Comparative Grammar* (Cambridge, Mass.: MIT Press), 417–54.

COMRIE, B. (1992), 'Before Complexity', in J. A. Hawkins and M. Gell-Mann (eds.), *The Evolution of Human Languages* (New York: Addison-Wesley), 193–211.

DIXON, R. M. W. (1997), *The Rise and Fall of Languages* (Cambridge: Cambridge University Press).

DUNBAR, R. (1996), *Grooming, Gossip, and the Evolution of Language* (Cambridge, Mass.: Harvard University Press).

GIVÓN, T. (1979), *On Understanding Grammar* (New York: Academic Press).

HAWKINS, J. A. (1994), *A Performance Theory of Order and Constituency*, Cambridge Studies in Linguistics, 73 (Cambridge: Cambridge University Press).

HEINE, B., CLAUDI, U., and HÜNNEMEYER, F. (1991), *Grammaticalization: A Conceptual Framework* (Chicago: University of Chicago Press).

HOIJER, H. (1964), 'Cultural Implications of Some Navaho Linguistic Categories', in Hymes (1964: 142–53).

HOMBERT, J.-M., and MARSICO, E. (1996), Unpublished paper, Université de Lyon.

HOPPER, P. J., and TRAUGOTT, E. C. (1993), *Grammaticalization* (Cambridge: Cambridge University Press).

HURFORD, J. R., STUDDERT-KENNEDY, M., and KNIGHT, C. (1998) (eds.), *Approaches to the Evolution of Language: Social and Cognitive Bases* (Cambridge: Cambridge University Press).

HYMES, D. (1964) (ed.), *Language in Culture and Society: A Reader in Linguistics and Anthropology* (New York: Harper & Row).

KALMÁR, I. (1985), 'Are There Really No Primitive Languages?' in D. R. Olson, N. Torrance, and A. Hildyard (eds.), *Literacy, Language, and Learning: The Nature and Consequences of Reading and Writing* (Cambridge: Cambridge University Press).

KIRBY, S. (1998), *Function, Selection and Innateness: The Emergence of Language Universals* (Oxford: Oxford University Press).

——and HURFORD, J. (1997), 'Learning, Culture, and Evolution in the Origin of Linguistic Constraints', in P. Husbands and H. Inman (eds.), *Proceedings of the*

Fourth European Conference on Artificial Life (Cambridge, Mass.: MIT Press), 493–502.

Li, C. N. (1977) (ed.), *Mechanisms of Syntactic Change* (Austin: University of Texas Press).

Mathiot, M. (1964), 'Noun Classes and Folk Taxonomy in Papago', in Hymes (1964: 154–63).

Mithun, M. (1984), 'How to Avoid Subordination', *Berkeley Linguistics Society*, 10: 493–523.

Nettle, D. (1999), 'Is the Rate of Linguistic Change Constant?' *Lingua*, 108: 119–36.

Newmeyer, F. J. (1986), *The Politics of Linguistics* (Chicago: University of Chicago Press).

Newmeyer, F. J. (1991), 'Functional Explanation in Linguistics and the Origins of Language', *Language and Communication*, 11: 3–28.

——(2000), 'On Reconstructing "Proto-World" Word Order', in C. Knight, J. Hurford, and M. Studdert-Kennedy (eds.), *The Emergence of Language* (Cambridge: Cambridge University Press), 372–88.

Nichols, J. (1990), 'Linguistic Diversity and the First Settlement of the New World', *Language*, 66: 475–521.

——(1992), *Linguistic Diversity in Space and Time* (Chicago: University of Chicago Press).

Noble, W., and Davidson, I. (1996), *Human Evolution, Language, and Mind: A Psychological and Archaeological Inquiry* (Cambridge: Cambridge University Press).

O'Neil, W. (1978), 'The Evolution of the Germanic Inflectional Systems: A Study in the Causes of Language Change', *Orbis*, 27: 248–86.

Perkins, R. D. (1992), *Deixis, Grammar, and Culture*, Typological Studies in Language, 24 (Amsterdam: John Benjamins).

Pinker, S., and Bloom, P. (1990), 'Natural Language and Natural Selection', *Behavioral and Brain Sciences*, 13: 707–84.

Sapir, E. (1921), *Language* (New York: Harcourt, Brace, & World).

——(1931), 'Conceptual Categories in Primitive Languages (Abstract)', *Science*, 74: 578.

Trudgill, P. (1992), 'Dialect Typology and Social Structure', in E. H. Jahr (ed.), *Language Contact* (New York: Mouton de Gruyter), 195–211.

Vennemann, T. (1973), 'Explanation in Syntax', in J. Kimball (ed.), *Syntax and Semantics* (New York: Seminar Press), ii. 1–50.

Webb, K. E. (1977), 'An Evolutionary Aspect of Social Structure and a Verb "Have"', *American Anthropologist*, 79: 42–9.

Wilkins, W. K., and Wakefield, J. (1995), 'Brain Evolution and Neurolinguistic Preconditions', *Behavioral and Brain Sciences*, 18: 161–226.

18   On the Evolution of Grammatical Forms

BERND HEINE AND TANIA KUTEVA

18.1 Introduction

A number of approaches are available to the linguist for studying earlier phases in the evolution of human language or languages. This chapter explores the potential for grammaticalization theory to throw light on language evolution. Grammaticalization theory relies on regularities in the evolution of linguistic forms, drawing on the unidirectionality principle and its implications for the reconstruction of earlier language states (Traugott and Heine 1991; Heine, Claudi, and Hünnemeyer 1991; Hopper and Traugott 1993). The main purpose of this chapter is to show that there are certain classes of grammatical forms that can be assumed to presuppose other grammatical forms in time. An attempt is made to reconstruct sequences of grammatical evolution with a view to establishing how language may have been structured at earlier stages of human evolution. While there are a number of interesting scenarios for how early human language may have been structured (e.g. Bickerton, this volume; Wray, this volume), it is hard to find convincing hypotheses for how functional categories evolved out of other items or structures that may have been used in early human communication.

Work based on classical methods of historical linguistics has brought about a number of insights into the form and structure of earlier forms of human languages. It would seem, however, that this work gives us access to only a fairly small phase in the evolution of human languages: linguistic reconstruction becomes notoriously fuzzy once we are dealing with a time depth exceeding 10,000 years. While there exists a wide array of opinions

This chapter is based on research carried out by Bernd Heine while he was a fellow at the Center for Advanced Study in the Behavioral Sciences, Stanford, USA, to which he wishes to express his gratitude. Our thanks are also due to comments received from the participants of the Paris 2000 conference, to the anonymous referees for this book, and, most of all, to Alison Wray for many valuable suggestions.

on how far back reconstruction can be pushed and on what the genetic and areal relationship patterns among earlier languages may have been, there appears to be general agreement on one point: the languages that were spoken 10,000 or more years ago were typologically not much different from present-day languages.

Here we want to argue that it is possible to push back linguistic reconstruction to earlier phases of linguistic evolution, that is, to phases where human language or languages can be assumed to have been different in structure from what is found today. The approach that we adopt here is one of *intergenetic grammaticalization comparison*, that is, comparisons across the boundaries of language families (or phyla). This approach differs from other linguistic approaches in that it deals neither with language typology nor with areal or genetic relationships. Like genetic linguistics, it uses etymology as a tool for historical reconstruction. But instead of dealing with genetic relationships among languages, that is, with comparisons within a single language family, it is concerned with principles of grammatical evolution. The goal is to reconstruct grammar at an earlier stage in human history—a stage that is not accessible by using classical methods of historical linguistics, i.e. a stage where language was not yet developed the way we know it from past and present-day records—let us call it *Stage X*.

The approach used here is not entirely new, it has been used—implicitly or explicitly—in some works dealing with the subject matter under scrutiny (see e.g. Sankoff 1979; Comrie 1992; Aitchison 1996). It is concerned with the development of grammatical categories and uses the methodology and findings of grammaticalization theory in order to describe grammatical evolution.[1] In addition, it draws on, but is not confined to (see sect. 18.2), a principle that is commonly ascribed to another method of historical linguistics, namely, internal reconstruction.

18.2 The Present Approach

Grammaticalization concerns the evolution from lexical to grammatical forms and from grammatical to even more grammatical forms. This evolu-

---

[1] With the term 'evolution' we refer to regularities in the development of linguistic forms and structures based on crosslinguistic observations. The development from a numeral 'one' to an indefinite article, for example, is an instance of an evolution since it can be observed to occur regularly and independently across languages. Thus, when talking of

TABLE 18.1 *Mechanisms of the grammaticalization process*

Mechanism	Effect
Desemanticization ('bleaching')	Loss of meaning
Decategorialization ('downgrading')	Loss of categorial properties
Erosion ('phonetic reduction')	Loss of phonetic substance

tion, which is essentially unidirectional,[2] involves a number of interrelated mechanisms, in particular the ones listed in Table 18.1.

In fact, things are slightly more complex than Table 18.1 implies. In particular, there are not only losses but also gains. For example, a loss of meaning may be compensated for by new meanings arising in the context in which the relevant form is used (see Heine *et al.* 1991 for details). However, for our present purposes it will suffice to adopt the simpler framework in Table 18.1. The three mechanisms are interrelated in the sense that desemanticization is a *sine qua non* for erosion and decategorialization to happen, that is, loss in meaning is immediately responsible for triggering the other two mechanisms.

The effects of this evolution can be illustrated with example (1) from Swahili, the national language of Tanzania and Kenya.

(1)   Swahili (Bantu, Niger-Congo[3])
    (a) a- ta- jenga nyumba
          C1 FUT build house
          'he will build a house'
    (b) a-   taka ku- jenga nyumba
          C1:PRS want INF-build house
          'she wants to build a house'

'evolution' we are concerned not with what happens to a given language as a whole, but rather to a given grammatical category.

  [2] This process is not without exceptions: a number of examples contradicting the unidirectionality principle have been found (see e.g. Joseph and Janda 1988; Campbell 1991; Ramat 1992; Frajzyngier 1996; and especially Newmeyer 1998: 260 ff.). Still, as acknowledged by most of the scholars who have identified exceptional cases, they are few compared to the large number of cases that conform to the principle (cf. Haspelmath 1999; 2000: 249). Furthermore, such examples can frequently be accounted for with reference to alternative forces. Finally, no instances of 'complete reversals of grammaticalization' have been discovered so far (cf. Newmeyer 1998: 263; see also Newmeyer, this volume).

  [3] In the examples, the information given after the language name is: sub-family, family, and, where appropriate, a reference to the published source.

(c) a- taka- ye-   jenga nyumba
    C1 want C1:REL build house
    'he who will build a house'

There is a future tense marker -*ta*- in (1a) which is historically derived from the full verb -*taka*, 'want', illustrated in (1b). That this is so can be deduced, first, from the fact that the future marker -*ta*- has retained its earlier form -*taka* in certain contexts, for instance, in relative clauses, as can be seen in (1c). Second, the same process, from volition verb to future marker, has occurred independently in quite a number of genetically and areally unrelated languages, perhaps in hundreds. English is one of them. In English, the future marker *will* is also historically derived from a volition verb and, as in the case of Swahili, more conservative features have been retained in subordinate clauses. The volition meaning of English *will* can still be found in uses such as *Do it as you will*.

Largely predictably, the process from a full verb -*taka* to future tense marker -*ta*- involved a number of individual mechanisms, most of all the ones listed in Table 18.1:

1. Desemanticization: the erstwhile verb lost its lexical meaning (acquiring grammatical meaning).
2. Decategorialization: the verb lost properties characteristic of verbs, such as the capacity to form the predicate nucleus of the clause and to take arguments. Decategorialization has a number of different manifestations:
   (a) Cliticization: being reduced to a grammatical marker, the erstwhile main verb lost its independent status and became dependent on another verb, in example (1) the new main verb -*jenga* 'build'. It turned into a clitic and eventually a prefix.
   (b) Paradigmatic narrowing: verbs are open-class items while grammatical markers are closed-class items. With the transition from verb to future marker, -*taka* shifted from the open class of verbs to the class of tense-aspect markers, which has a membership of less than a dozen.
3. Erosion: the item -*taka* lost phonetic substance, being reduced to -*ta*.

To conclude, the Swahili example is an instance of a more general evolution whereby lexical items, and the structures associated with them, turn into grammatical items as the result of a network of interrelated mechanisms summarily referred to as grammaticalization.

The second part of the approach used here can be described by means of the schema presented in Fig. 18.1.

Past situation: X

Present situation: X   Y

FIG. 18.1 Principle of reconstruction.

Languages reveal layers of past changes in their present structure—they recapitulate their past development, as Greenberg (1992: 155) puts it. Suppose we know that a linguistic structure X under specific conditions develops regularly into Y and, conversely, Y can regularly be traced back to X. Now, if we find that a given language has both X and Y, then we can conclude that at some earlier development stage of that language there was X but no Y. The approach that can be derived from this observation has been described by Comrie (1992) thus: 'Certain kinds of present linguistic alternation can be reconstructed back to earlier states without that alternation.'[4] This procedure is well known from earlier studies in internal reconstruction: 'wherever we find an instance of morphophonemic alternation, we reconstruct an earlier stage where there is no corresponding morphophonemic alternation, and a plausible environment conditioning the alternation on an allophonic basis (ibid. 205).

Comrie uses this approach to argue that certain complexities of all or many presently attested languages were not present in early human language (see below).[5] Applied to our Swahili example we arrive at the following conclusion. There are two morphemes in modern Swahili: a future tense

---

[4] It might be argued that this approach works in cases where appropriate historical evidence exists, but not necessarily in other cases. In other words, our claim that the presence of two structures X and Y can be traced back to an earlier situation where there was X but no Y cannot be generalized. It is a common analytic procedure, we would argue, to describe the unknown in terms of the known given appropriate correlations between the two, and not much is gained by rejecting such a generalization.

[5] It may happen of course that X is lost in the process, so that all we have left would be Y. Usually, such cases can be detected on the basis of comparative evidence. For instance, the English lexical meaning of *will*, 'want, wish' (= X) has almost disappeared, with the result that we are left with a situation where synchronically there is the grammatical marker *will* (= Y) but essentially no more X. On the basis of evidence from other languages, however, it is possible to establish that we are dealing with a special case. There are languages where there is polysemy involving a verb meaning 'want, wish' (= X) on the one hand, and a future tense marker (= Y) on the other (see example (1); see also Bybee *et al.* 1994).

marker *-ta-* and a verb *-taka,* 'want'. Since there is a regular evolution from volition verbs to future tense markers, we can reconstruct an earlier situation where there was the verb but not the future tense marker.[6] However, unlike internal reconstruction, our approach is not restricted to the analysis of language-internal processes; rather, it is comparative in nature and allows for reconstructions across languages.[7]

In the remainder of this chapter we will use this combined approach to discuss some traits of grammatical evolution.

18.3 Some Findings

On the basis of the approach just sketched we will now present some findings on the evolution of grammatical forms. These findings are based on Heine and Kuteva (forthcoming) and involve generalizations on more than 300 instances of grammatical evolution.

18.3.1 *Morphosyntactic Categories*

In the first instance, we shall focus on just one of the mechanisms identified in Table 18.1, namely decategorialization. The effect of this mechanism in the process of grammaticalization is that linguistic forms tend to lose properties characteristic of the morpheme class or syntactic category to which they belong, and to become members of other, more grammatical, categories. With reference to our Swahili example, the effect was that a fully fledged verb lost, in some of its uses, most of its verbal properties and joined a more grammatical morpheme paradigm, i.e. that of tense-aspect inflections. The consequences can be further illustrated with example (2), where a noun

---

[6] An anonymous referee of this chapter observes that the reader is left wondering what would happen if form Y leads on to something else, e.g. to form Z or indeed nothing at all. There is a straightforward answer. In the case of Y > Z, we would be dealing with a new change of the kind (X > Y), hence, we would expect it to behave the same way as X > Y. If 'nothing at all' means that Y takes on a zero formal expression then it may be more difficult, if not impossible, to achieve reconstruction. Such situations may arise in a given language; however, since we are dealing here with crosslinguistic regularities, such situations are special cases and can be identified as such on the basis of findings in other languages having undergone the same grammaticalization process.

[7] An argumentation that is in line with the present approach is found in some of Greenberg's works (Greenberg 1992: 154; see also Greenberg 1966; Croft 1991).

(NOUN), exemplified in (2a), turned into a complex pronoun (PRON) (2b), and eventually a voice marker (PASS) (2c).

(2)   !Xun (North Khoisan, Khoisan)
    (a) mī shē mī |'é (Ju dialect)
        I   see my body
        'I see my body' (or 'I see myself')
    (b) yà kē   !hún yà |'é
        he PAST kill   his self
        'he has killed himself'
    (c) g‖ú má ké   tchì̧ ká'ŋ |'é kē mí
        water TOP PAST drink its   self by me
        'the water has been drunk by me'

For a better understanding of the generalizations we are going to present, there are a few *caveats*. First, the evolutions are unidirectional, that is, a reflexive marker may assume the function of a passive marker while a passive marker is unlikely to develop into a reflexive marker or a noun.

Second, one and the same item may, and frequently does, give rise to more than one path of grammatical evolution, the technical term to refer to this phenomenon being polygrammaticalization. In (2) we observe that there is a noun (NOUN) that gives rise to a pronoun (PRON) and finally to a passive (PASS) category. In example (3), another noun (*megbé*, 'back'), also relating to the human body, illustrates quite a different path of evolution: we are dealing with a noun in (3a) that, in some of its uses, turns into an adverb (ADV) (3b) on the one hand, and an adposition (ADP) (3c) on the other.

(3)   Ewe (Kwa, Niger-Congo)
    (a) éʃé megbé fa
        his back   be-cold
        'his back is cold'
    (b) é- megbé é- yi aʃé
        its back   s/he go home
        'then she went home'
    (c) é- le xɔ- a   megbé
        s/he be house DEF back
        'he is behind the house'

In a similar fashion, adverbs may be part of yet another pathway of grammaticalization. As example (4) from Buang illustrates, involving the item *ken*, locative adverbs ('here' in 4a) may give rise to demonstrative (DEM) markers (4b), which again may develop further into relative clause markers (REL) (4c).

(4)　Buang (Austronesian, Austric; Sankoff 1979: 35–6)

　　(a)　Ke mdo ken
　　　　 I　live　here
　　　　 'I live here'

　　(b)　Ke mdo byaŋ　ken
　　　　 I　live　house this
　　　　 'I live in this house'

　　(c)　Ke mdo byaŋ　ken gu　le　vkev
　　　　 I　live　house that you saw yesterday
　　　　 'I live in the house that you saw yesterday'

These are just a few examples out of roughly 350 common pathways of grammaticalization that have been identified in recent research. Taken together, they can be conflated into a more general evolutionary structure, presented in Fig. 18.2.

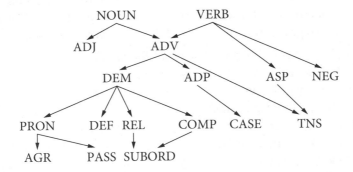

FIG. 18.2 Some salient paths of categorial shift in grammaticalization.

For a better understanding of Fig. 18.2, the following notes need to be taken into account:[8]

---

[8] Abbreviations: ADP = adposition, ADJ = adjective, ADV = adverb, AGR = agreement, ASP = aspect, COMP = complementizer, C1 = noun class 1, DEF = definite marker, DEM = demonstrative, F = feminine gender, FOC = focus, FUT = future tense, HAB = habitual, INF = infinitive, NEG = negation, PASS = passive, PRON = pronoun, PRS = present, PURP = purpose, Q = question, REL = relative clause marker, SUBJ = subjunctive, SUBORD = subordination marker, TNS = tense, TOP = topic.

1. The structure it represents is *non*-transitive, that is, unlike in a tree diagram, a given category can be derived from more than one other category;[9] we have alluded to this fact earlier. For example, (4) illustrates the evolution from adverb (ADV) via demonstrative (DEM) to relative clause marker (REL). But adverbs may go back to at least two different sources: nouns and verbs. And they themselves may give rise to several different form classes, namely demonstratives, adpositions, and tense markers.

2. The processes depicted in Fig. 18.2 are salient ones but they are not the only ones that have been found. For example, there are other sources for passives and also for relative clause markers than the one of each that we have illustrated here (see e.g. Lehmann 1984; Haspelmath 1990).

3. The structure is highly abstract in that it conflates a number of somewhat disparate evolutions. A given pathway of evolution need not involve all intermediate categories found in Fig. 18.2, but may jump over or ignore categories. For example, adpositions may be, and more often than not are, immediately derived from nouns or verbs without an intermediate adverb stage. Perhaps more dramatically, consider example (5). The pathway illustrated in (5) involves a verb *bé* meaning 'say' in (5a), which developed further into a complementizer (5b), and finally into subordinating conjunction, that is, a marker of adverbial clauses of cause and purpose (5c). There are no intermediate stages linking the verb and the complementizer stages.

(5) Ewe (Kwa, Niger-Congo; Heine *et al.* 1991: 237)
 (a) é- bé Kofí vá
    s/he say Kofi come
    'He said that Kofi came'
 (b) me- nyá bé e- li
    I   know that you be
    'I know that you are there'
 (c) bé (ná) wo- á- ʄle agbalē̃ ta- é me- tsɔ́ ga
    that (HAB) you SUBJ buy book PURP FOC I   take money
    nê
    give-him
    'In order for him to buy a book I gave him money'

It is not possible here to address the question of how to account for the various chains or pathways of evolution; once again, we refer to the relevant literature (especially Heine *et al.* 1991; Hopper and Traugott 1993; Bybee *et al.*

---

[9] In other words, the representation in Fig. 18.2 shows all possible routes, not, as a tree diagram would, the specific route for a particular outcome.

1994; Heine 1997*b*). In more general terms, one may say that these evolutions lead:

1. from concrete meanings to more abstract ones,[10]
2. from open-class to closed-class items,
3. from fairly independent, referential meanings to less referential, schematic grammatical functions having to do with relations within the clause or between clauses.

18.3.2 *Some Basic Functions*

Grammatical change has been characterized in Fig. 18.2 in terms of some formal properties of language structure, that is, in terms of a classification of grammatical categories. It goes without saying that there are other aspects to the development than just those mentioned above. Focusing now on the mechanism of desemanticization (in Table 18.1 above), we shall consider what the approach sketched in sect. 18.2 can tell us about some of the salient functions of linguistic communication. In doing so, we will be confined to a few examples, which concern the expression of interrogation, spatial orientation, possession, and personal deixis.

Questions
It would seem that all languages that have been studied in some detail display grammatical forms for asking questions (cf. Aitchison 1996: 177). The evidence available suggests that markers for polar questions are derived from forms for concepts other than interrogative ones. One common source consists of constructions containing negative or alternative markers, or both. Alternative conjunctions, in particular (e.g. 'or'), not uncommonly develop into question markers. Example (6) illustrates this source. The Hausa phrase conjunction *kō* meaning 'or', 'either (... or)', presented in (6a), appears to have given rise to the question particle *kō*, as can be seen in (6b) (see Heine and Kuteva (forthcoming) for more examples).

(6) Hausa (Chadic, Afroasiatic; Cowan and Schuh 1976: 216)
   (a) kō   nī kī kai
       either I or you
       'either you or I'

---

[10] Conceptual shift from concrete to abstract, as understood here, is anthropocentric in nature, in that it leads from meanings that are close to human experience and easy to describe, to meanings that are more difficult to understand and describe.

(b) kō kā sămi gyadã mài yawà?
    Q you get peanuts many
    'did you get a lot of peanuts?'

While the evidence available is still far from satisfactory, it would seem to suggest that the presence of question markers can be reconstructed back to a situation where such markers did not exist, at least not in this capacity. This may suggest that segmental forms for marking questions may not have been part of the inventory of the grammar of human language at Stage X.

Location
Spatial orientation is viewed by some as constituting one of the primitive domains of human conceptualization, and there is a wealth of data to show how locative constructions can provide, and have provided, a convenient conceptual source for encoding other concepts. Studies in grammaticalization suggest, however, that terms for spatial orientation themselves tend to be derived from other domains, almost invariably from terms for concrete objects. Fig. 18.3 describes the network of historical sources for linguistic forms for spatial orientation.

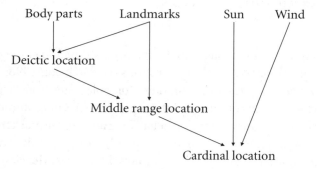

FIG. 18.3 The main source domains of spatial orientation (see Heine 1997*b*).

The human body provides an outstanding structural template for describing spatial concepts, and in many languages terms for body-parts such as 'back', 'face', 'head', or 'belly' have been used to develop expressions for the deictic spatial notions 'behind', 'in front', 'above', and 'inside', respectively. In addition, there is a pool of environmental landmarks (e.g. rivers, mountains, terms for earth/ground or sky) that tend to be grammaticalized to terms for locative concepts (Heine 1997*b*), and finally there are two natural phenomena, the sun and regular wind directions, that provide templates for expressing absolute references, essentially for cardinal directions.

An example from Maa may illustrate the kind of grammaticalization paths involved (7). There is a concrete noun, *n-kɔ́p*, denoting 'earth, ground, country' in (7a). This noun has given rise to a couple of new meanings: as in many other languages, it is used as a landmark concept to denote the 'space below' (7b), and eventually, in some Maasai dialects it has developed into a term for the cardinal direction term 'north' (7c).

(7) Maa (Maasai, Chamus dialect; Nilotic, Nilo-Saharan)
  (a) n- kɔ́p
    F- land
    'soil, earth, country' (Chamus)
  (b) (tɛ́) n- kɔ́p
    (at) F- land
    'below' (Chamus)
  (c) kɔ́pɪ kɔ́p
    land- land
    'north' (Maasai)

What such observations seem to suggest is that spatial orientation is a derived domain, that is, terms for spatial concepts are likely to go back to terms for concrete objects, typically encoded as nouns, to a minor extent also to motion and postural verbs.

Possession

Possession is a concept that appears to be distinguished in all human societies, even if there is some cross-cultural variation in the way this concept is understood. This universality is suggested by a couple of interrelated observations. First, all languages that have been studied in some detail appear to have conventionalized expressions for both predicative possession (e.g.

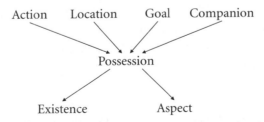

Fig. 18.4 The main source and target domains of predicative possession (see Heine 1997*a*).

I have a dog) and attributive possession (*my dog*) (Heine 1997a). Second, we know of no language that does not have some lexical means of expressing concepts such as 'to steal' or 'theft'. Third, we also know of no society where there is no legalized means of dealing with theft—however 'theft' may be defined in a given culture.

Observations on languages for which there is some diachronic evidence suggest that linguistic expressions for possessive concepts are derived from other conceptual domains. The main sources for 'have'-constructions are summarized in Fig. 18.4.

What Fig. 18.4 suggests is that predications of the form *I have a dog* are historically derived from structures like *I get/hold/keep/take a dog* (= Action), or *A dog is where I am* (= Location), or *A dog is to/for me* (Goal), or *I am with a dog* (Companion) (the examples are from Heine 1997a). But expressions for possession may themselves give rise to other grammatical meanings, most of all to existential copulas and verbal aspect markers.

In (8) we see an example of the action part of the schema in Fig. 18.4, from Chinese, involving the Old Chinese verb *de* 'to obtain'. In (8a) *de* appears in its earliest attestable use as a lexical item ('obtain'). A later use of possession is illustrated in (8b), and one of existence in (8c).[11]

(8)   Chinese
  (a)   Old Chinese (300 BC; *Shijing Guangsui*; quoted from Sun 1996: 112)
    qiu zhi bu de
    want her NEG obtain
    '(The lord) wished (for) her, (but) did not get (her)'
  (b)   tenth-century Chinese (*Zutangji* 1/74; quoted from ibid. 122)
    yi ren   de   wo rou
    one person obtain I   flesh
    'One (of them) has my flesh'
  (c)   tenth-century Chinese (*Zutangji* 1/80; quoted from ibid. 122)
    de san bai   wu-shi jiu nian yi
    have three hundred fifty   nine years ASP
    'There had been 359 years'

---

[11] Among the various grammaticalization processes that the verb *de* underwent in the history of Chinese (see Sun 1996: 108–62), the present one constitutes only a minor, less common pattern.

Thus, we appear to be dealing with an evolution from the Action schema, involving a full verb 'obtain', to a Possession schema, and finally to an existential construction.

On the basis of our approach we are led to conclude that there must have been a stage where a given possessive construction was used for purposes other than designating possession and, hence, that at some earlier state in the history of human languages there were no conventionalized expressions for possession. However, by no means can one conclude from this observation that the relevant speakers did not have a *concept* of possession. Such a conclusion would be clearly beyond the scope of the approach used here.

Personal deixis

One may wonder whether there is any functional domain of grammar to which the above kind of reconstruction does not apply. If there are such domains then personal deixis must surely be one of them. Comparative work on language families where early written documents are available suggest that distinctions in personal pronouns belong to the small pool of what one is tempted to call 'prehistorical primitives'. For example, they have been used by Joseph Greenberg as primary evidence to formulate hypotheses on early genetic relationship.

Nevertheless, there is evidence to suggest that even personal pronouns can be traced back to form–meaning pairings other than personal pronouns. Third-person pronouns can often be reconstructed back to demonstrative pronouns—the development from Latin to the modern Romance languages illustrates this process.[12] First- and second-person pronouns appear to have human nouns as their primary historical source (see Moravcsik 1972: 272; Heine 1997*b*: 15 for details).[13] For example, a number of genetically and areally unrelated languages, such as !Xun of the Khoisan family, and Kono of the Mande family, have used nouns for 'person, people' to develop first-

---

[12] That demonstratives may also have given rise to first- and second-person pronouns has been argued for by Blake (1934), who noted some correspondences between proximal demonstratives and first-person forms, and distal demonstratives and second-person pronouns in a number of languages. The evidence adduced by him is, however, not entirely convincing.

[13] Once a personal pronoun has evolved, it may under certain circumstances give rise to yet another category of personal pronouns. For example, second- or third-person plural pronouns not uncommonly acquire second-person singular reference, as has happened in a number of European languages (e.g. English, German, French).

person plural pronouns ('we'; Heine and Kuteva, forthcoming), and in some south-east Asian languages, nouns denoting persons of inferior social status ('servant', 'slave', 'disciple') have given rise to first-person pronouns, while nouns for persons of superior status ('master', 'king') were grammaticalized to second-person pronouns.[14]

Without wishing to overrate the significance of such evidence, the data available is sufficient to suggest that personal pronouns can be derived from other concepts and we are therefore led to assume that there may have been an earlier stage in the evolution of language or of languages where there were no conventionalized expressions for personal pronouns.

18.4 The Earliest Conceivable Language Structure

The view we take here on language change *processes* is uniformitarian, that is, we assume that the forces and processes of language change were the same in the past as they are in the present. Our proposal relates, however, not to language processes but to language *structure*, and the hypothesis we put forward about language structure is radically non-uniformitarian. We propose that what we refer to as Stage X—that is, language at the point at which current forces of historical language change came into being—had a structure different from the structure that present languages have. Thus, the observations made so far allow us to set up a few properties that might have been characteristic of earlier forms of human language(s), that is, of Stage X:

1. First, all evidence on grammatical evolution suggests that there were no more than two types of linguistic entities: one type denoting thing-like, time-stable entities, that is, nouns, and another one denoting non-time-stable concepts such as actions, activities, and events, i.e. verbs (cf. Aitchison 1996).

2. This would mean that there must have been something corresponding to the notion of a word.

3. It also means that at Stage X there was no morphology.

4. It also follows that there were no items whose primary function it

---

[14] Malay *sahaya*, 'I', is said to go back to a noun for 'servant', and in a similar fashion are Burmese *dabeq-*, 'disciple', and *tyunv-*, 'slave', claimed to have developed into first person pronouns, while Malay *tuan*, 'you', is said to be derived from 'master' and Burmese *minx*, 'king', and *hyinv*, 'master', are considered to be sources for second-person pronouns (see Blake 1934: 244; Cooke 1968: 74–6; Stolz 1994: 78–9).

was to express relations among words; hence the only productive means of syntax must have been word order.

5. While it is quite possible, or even likely, that there were *concepts* for notions such as spatial orientation or possession, we can assume that there were no grammaticalized forms to express these concepts.

6. In a similar fashion, we are led to conclude that there were no forms at Stage X whose primary function it was to express distinctions of personal deixis—in spite of the fact that all available linguistic reconstructions suggest that personal deixis can be traced back to the earliest strata accessible to linguists.

In addition to these observations derived from findings on grammaticalization, one may add some phonological properties that must have characterized Stage X, such as those identified by Comrie (1992: 206–8) using an approach similar to the one employed here. These properties are:

7. There may have been oral vowels and nasal consonants, but no nasalized vowels. Since loss of an earlier vowel or other nasalizing consonant is the ultimate origin of all nasalized vowels, there must have been a stage in the history of human language in which the complication of having a distinction between nasalized and non-nasalized vowels was non-existent.

8. Since all tonal oppositions in language can be shown to have non-tonal origins, tone was not a distinguishing feature.

18.5 The Structure of Pidgins

In languages used in stress situations, where linguistic communication is seriously impaired, where people have only 'inadequate' linguistic models at their disposal, everything that is not vital tends to be stripped off and hence language structure may be reduced to its most essential, and least dispensable, characteristics. Such characteristics are the ones most likely to have been present also in earlier forms of human language.

Pidgin languages offer a paradigm example of such a situation: 'In pidginization the acquisition process involves the learning of a second language by speakers of different language backgrounds, who have limited access to the language of the dominant group' (Romaine 1992: 234; cf. Bickerton 1981, 1984). What may happen in such a situation is described by Sankoff (1979) and Aitchison (1996) with reference to Tok Pisin, but their observations can be extended to other pidgins. A survey of pidgins in different parts of the world suggests that the most likely effects of early pidginization can be summarized as follows (cf. Heine 1979; Romaine 1992; Boretzky 1983; Tosco and Owens 1993; etc.):

1. In phonology, the number of phonemic distinctions is reduced, distinctions in vowel length and tone tend to be given up.
2. Inflectional morphology tends to disappear, derivational morphology is drastically reduced or lost entirely.
3. Grammatical distinctions of tense and aspect, number, gender, definiteness/indefiniteness, case marking, clause embedding, etc. tend to be lost.
4. The lexicon shrinks to a fraction of the size it has in the source language.

The result is a language:

(a) which has virtually no affixal morphology, hence hardly any distinction between morphemes and words,
(b) hence where words are unanalysable entities,
(c) where grammatical functions tend to be expressed either by lexical material or word order, or else are not formally expressed,
(d) which has only a limited number of lexical items, and
(e) where context plays a central role in utterance construction and interpretation.[15]

A structure that characterizes the situation of early pidgins thus resembles the one we proposed in sect. 18.4 as likely to have characterized the earliest conceivable language structure: there is essentially no distinct grammatical morphology and no formal apparatus to signal syntactic relations. But there are also differences. All pidgins beyond the jargon stage on which we have conclusive information appear to display some or all the following grammaticalizd forms:

(1) markers distinguishing personal deixis (i.e. personal pronouns)
(2) demonstratives

---

[15] This stripping process, as Romaine (1992: 232) calls it, tends to be confined to the early stages of pidginization. In their more advanced stages, pidgins develop new grammatical structures. Sankoff (1979) shows, for example, how in Tok Pisin new grammatical categories evolved, such as markers for number, tense, and causativity, or complementizers and relative clause markers, and how meaningful morphemes, such as personal pronouns, may develop into largely obligatory and redundant elements of clause structure.

(3) adpositions
(4) elements expressing negation
(5) elements for conjoining clauses
(6) adverbs and interjections
(7) productive patterns for forming questions
(8) some forms of circumlocution or periphrasis, e.g. to refer to concepts for which there are no appropriate lexical or grammatical means.

Thus, although pidgin languages are strongly reduced in their phonological, morphosyntactic, and lexical inventory *vis-à-vis* the languages from which they can be said to be derived, they still are not without structure, a structure that in some way links them typologically with analytic-isolating languages (see e.g. Boretzky 1983: 21). Compared to this, the language structure that surfaces as the earliest conceivable one on the basis of grammaticalization work is distinctly more 'primitive': There are but two word types, nouns and verbs, and a number of properties characteristic of pidgins, including functional categories such as personal pronouns, demonstratives, negation, can be assumed to have been absent.

As a result, while some authors have drawn attention to the similarities found between pidgins and early human language structure (see in particular Sankoff 1979), we do not see how the two can be related to one another in a systematic way, especially since it remains unclear how the structure of pidgins is affected by the presence of the various lexifier and substrate languages that characterize the genesis of pidgin languages.

18.6 Conclusions

The present chapter challenges some views that have been maintained on the evolution of earlier human language (see especially Newmeyer, this volume; Bickerton, this volume). It is hoped that such views need to be reconsidered in the light of observations arising from the findings on the evolution of functional categories. In the study of language evolution, two partially compatible standpoints can be taken:

(1) The forces and processes of language change were the same in the past as they are in the present.
(2) Languages in the past were structurally the same in principle as languages in the present.

Standpoint (1) has acquired the status of a fundamental principle of historical linguistics. It is very tempting to assume that (1) logically entails (2). In fact, there exists general agreement that in a historically reconstructible time depth, earlier languages were typologically not much different from present-day ones. Nichols (1992: 276) concludes, for instance, that no evidence has been uncovered to indicate that morphosyntactic structure has been subject to increasing complexity since the earliest recoverable stage of language. While we do not contest the assumption in (1) above, in this chapter we have taken a standpoint that differs from the one articulated in (2). More precisely, on the basis of findings in grammaticalization studies, we have argued that languages in the historically non-reconstructible past may have been different—in a systematic way—from present-day languages. We have proposed particular sequences of the evolution of grammatical structures that enable us to reconstruct earlier stages of human language(s). As Fig. 18.2 illustrates, such evolutions lead in a principled way from concrete lexical items to abstract morphosyntactic forms. Thus Fig. 18.2 suggests, on the one hand, that grammatical forms such as case inflections or agreement and voice markers did not fall from heaven; rather they can be shown to be the result of gradual evolutions. Much more importantly, Fig. 18.2 also suggests that at the earliest conceivable stage, human language(s) might have lacked grammatical forms such as case inflections, agreement, voice markers, etc., so that there might have existed only two types of linguistic entities: one denoting thing-like, time-stable entities (i.e. nouns), and another one for non-time-stable concepts such as events (i.e. verbs). We are thus dealing with a situation that does not appear to have a parallel in modern language forms such as pidgins or other structures arising in situations of communicative stress.

   In concluding, we wish to draw attention to a couple of problems that are associated with the approach proposed here. First, we argued that linguistic reconstruction based on grammaticalization theory can be traced back to two kinds of linguistic items, nouns and verbs. The linguistic and philosophical literature of the past two centuries is rich in arguments on why these two kinds of items are more basic, more concrete, and/or more communicatively and pragmatically salient than other morpheme types; still, none of these arguments is entirely satisfactory, and more research is required. The second problem relates to suprasegmental grammatical structures. As mentioned earlier, grammaticalization theory is concerned with the evolution of segmental grammatical forms. This means that non-segmental phenomena such as tone, intonation, or word order are not normally within its scope. In some cases this may affect the results obtained. For example, when dealing with interrogation, we observed that segmental forms for marking polar (or yes–no) questions may not have been part of the inventory of earlier grammar. However, questions are frequently expressed by such phenomena as intonation or word order, instead of or in addition to segmental forms. Our reconstruction must therefore of necessity remain fragmentary.

FURTHER READING

BYBEE, JOAN L., PERKINS, REVERE D., and PAGLIUCA, WILLIAM (1994), *The Evolution of Grammar: Tense, Aspect, and Modality in the Languages of the World* (Chicago: University of Chicago Press).

HEINE, BERND (1997), *Cognitive Foundations of Grammar* (Oxford and New York: Oxford University Press).

——and KUTEVA, TANIA (forthcoming), *World Lexicon of Grammaticalization* (Cambridge: Cambridge University Press).

HOPPER, PAUL J., and TRAUGOTT, ELIZABETH C. (1993), *Grammaticalization* (Cambridge: Cambridge University Press).

REFERENCES

AITCHISON, JEAN (1996), *The Seeds of Speech: Language Origin and Evolution* (Cambridge: Cambridge University Press).

BICKERTON, DEREK (1981), *Roots of Language* (Ann Arbor: Karoma).

——(1984), 'The Language Bioprogram Hypothesis', *The Behavioral and Brain Sciences*, 7: 173–220.

BLAKE, FRANK R. (1934), 'The Origin of Pronouns of the First and Second Persons', *The American Journal of Philology*, 55: 244–8.

BORETZKY, NORBERT (1983), *Kreolsprachen, Substrate und Sprachwandel* (Wiesbaden: Harrassowitz).

BYBEE, JOAN L., PERKINS, REVERE D., and PAGLIUCA, WILLIAM (1994), *The Evolution of Grammar: Tense, Aspect, and Modality in the Languages of the World* (Chicago: University of Chicago Press).

CAMPBELL, LYLE (1991), 'Some Grammaticalization Changes in Estonian and their Implications', in Traugott and Heine (1991: 285–99).

COMRIE, BERNARD (1992), 'Before Complexity', in Hawkins and Gell-Mann (1992: 193–211).

COOKE, JOSEPH R. (1968), *Pronominal Reference in Thai, Burmese, and Vietnamese*, University of California Publications in Linguistics, 52 (Berkeley: University of California Press).

COWAN, J. RONAYNE, and SCHUH, RUSSELL G. (1976), *Spoken Hausa*, I. *Hausa Language-Grammar* (Ithaca: Spoken Language Services).

CROFT, WILLIAM (1991), 'The Evolution of Negation', *Journal of Linguistics*, 27: 1–27.

FRAJZYNGIER, ZYGMUNT (1996), *Grammaticalization of the Complex Sentence: A Case Study in Chadic* (Amsterdam: John Benjamins).

GREENBERG, JOSEPH H. (1966), 'Synchronic and Diachronic Universals on Phonology', *Language*, 42: 508–17.

——(1992), 'Preliminaries to a Systematic Comparison Between Biological and Linguistic Evolution', in Hawkins and Gell-Mann (1992: 139–58).

HASPELMATH, MARTIN (1990), 'The Grammaticalization of Passive Morphology', *Studies in Language*, 14/1: 25–72.

——(1999), 'Why is Grammaticalization Irreversible?', *Linguistics*, 37/6: 1043–68.

——(2000). 'Why Can't We Talk to Each Other?', *Lingua*, 110/4: 235–55.

HAWKINS, JOHN A., and GELL-MANN, MURRAY (1992) (eds.), *The Evolution of Human Language*, Proceedings of the Workshop on the Evolution of Human Languages, August 1989 (Santa Fe: Addison-Wesley).

HEINE, BERND (1979), 'Some Generalizations on African-based Pidgins', in Ian F. Hancock, Edgar Polomé, Morris Goodman, and Bernd Heine (eds.), *Readings in Creole Studies* (Ghent: E. Story-Scientia PVBA).

——(1997a), *Possession: Sources, Forces, and Grammaticalization* (Cambridge: Cambridge University Press).

——(1997b), *Cognitive Foundations of Grammar* (Oxford and New York: Oxford University Press).

——and KUTEVA, TANIA (forthcoming), *World Lexicon of Grammaticalization* (Cambridge: Cambridge University Press).

—— CLAUDI, ULRIKE, and HÜNNEMEYER, FRIEDERIKE (1991), *Grammaticalization: A Conceptual Framework* (Chicago: University of Chicago Press).

HOPPER, PAUL J., and TRAUGOTT, ELIZABETH C. (1993), *Grammaticalization* (Cambridge: Cambridge University Press).

JOSEPH, BRIAN, and JANDA, RICHARD (1988), 'The How and Why of Diachronic Morphologization and Demorphologization', in Michael Hammond and Michael Noonan (eds.), *Theoretical Morphology: Approaches in Modern Linguistics* (New York: Academic Press), 193–210.

LEHMANN, CHRISTIAN (1984), *Der Relativsatz: Typologie seiner Strukturen, Theorie seiner Funktionen, Kompendium seiner Grammatik* (Tübingen: Narr).

MORAVCSIK, EDITH A. (1972), 'Some Crosslinguistic Generalizations About Intensifier Constructions', *Chicago Linguistic Society*, 8: 271–7.

NEWMEYER, FREDERICK J. (1998), *Language Form and Language Function* (Cambridge, Mass.: MIT Press).

NICHOLS, JOHANNA (1992), *Linguistic Diversity in Space and Time* (Chicago: University of Chicago Press).

RAMAT, PAOLO (1992), 'Thoughts on Degrammaticalization', *Linguistics*, 30: 549–60.

ROMAINE, SUZANNE (1992), 'The Evolution of Linguistic Complexity in Pidgin and Creole Languages', in Hawkins and Gell-Mann (1992: 213–38).

SANKOFF, GILLIAN (1979), 'The Genesis of a Language', in Kenneth C. Hill (ed.), *The Genesis of Language*, First Michigan Colloquium, 1979 (Ann Arbor: Karoma), 23–47.

STOLZ, THOMAS (1994), *Sprachdynamik: Auf dem Weg zu einer Typologie sprachlichen Wandels*, ii. *Grammatikalisierung und Metaphorisierung* (Bochum: Brockmeyer).

SUN, CHAOFEN (1996), *Word Order Change and Grammaticalization in the History of Chinese* (Stanford: Stanford University Press).

TOSCO, MAURO, and OWENS, JONATHAN (1993), 'Turku: A Descriptive and Comparative Study', *SUGIA (Sprache und Geschichte in Afrika)*, 14: 177–267.

TRAUGOTT, ELIZABETH C., and HEINE, BERND (1991) (eds.). *Approaches to Grammaticalization* (Amsterdam: John Benjamins), i.

Contributors

Derek Bickerton
Department of Linguistics, University of Hawaii, Honolulu, Hawaii 96822, USA.
bickertond@prodigy.net
Derek Bickerton received his Ph.D. in linguistics from Cambridge University (1976) and taught for 24 years at the University of Hawaii. His research has centred on creole languages and the evolution of language. His most recent books are *Language and Human Behaviour* (1995) and *Lingua ex Machina* (2000, with William Calvin).

Robbins Burling
Department of Anthropology, University of Michigan, 1020 LSA Building, Ann Arbor, Michigan 48109, USA.
rburling@umich.edu
Robbins Burling is Professor (Emeritus) of Anthropology and Linguistics, University of Michigan. Ph.D. Harvard (1958). Interested in kinship and social organization, ethnography of eastern Southern Asia and western South-east Asia, Tibeto-Burman linguistics, sociolinguistics, human origins, and the evolution of culture and language.

Morten H. Christiansen
Department of Psychology, Cornell University, Ithaca, NY 14853, USA.
mhc27@cornell.edu
Morten H. Christiansen is an Assistant Professor of Psychology at Cornell University. His research integrates connectionist modelling, statistical analyses, behavioural experimentation, and event-related potential (ERP) methods in the study of the learning and processing of complex sequential structure, in particular as related to the acquisition, processing, and evolution of language.

Michael C. Corballis
Department of Psychology, University of Auckland, Private Bag 92019, Auckland, New Zealand.
mcorballis@psynov1.auckland.ac.nz
    Michael C. Corballis completed first degrees in New Zealand, and his Ph.D. in Psychology at McGill University in Montreal. He taught for 10 years at McGill before taking up his present post as Professor of Psychology at the University of Auckland. His books include *The Psychology of Left and Right* (1976), *The Ambivalent Mind* (1983), *Human Laterality* (1983), *The Lopsided Ape* (1991), and *The Descent of Mind* (1999).

T. J. Crow
POWIC, University Department of Psychiatry, Warneford Hospital, Oxford, OX3 7JX, UK.
timc@gwmail.jr2.ox.ac.uk
    Tim Crow is on the Medical Research Council External Scientific Staff, a Professor of Psychiatry, and Honourary Director of the SANE Prince of Wales International Centre for Research on Schizophrenia and Depression. He believes that language and psychosis have a common evolutionary origin in the speciation of modern *Homo sapiens*.

Iain Davidson
School of Human and Environmental Studies, University of New England, Armidale, New South Wales, Australia.
Iain.Davidson@une.edu.au
    Iain Davidson is Professor of Archaeology and Palaeoanthropology at the University of New England in Armidale, NSW, Australia. Since 1988 he has published a book (*Human Evolution, Language and Mind*, 1996) and more than twenty-five other publications on the evolutionary emergence of language, mostly jointly with psychologist William Noble. His other research work has been concerned with the Upper Palaeolithic, particularly of Spain, and with the archaeology of Australia including its stone artefacts and rock art.

Michelle R. Ellefson
Department of Psychology, Southern Illinois University, Carbondale, IL 62901-6502, USA.
ellefson@siu.edu
    Michelle R. Ellefson is a graduate student in Brain and Cognitive Sciences at Southern Illinois University. She is working on her dissertation with her

adviser Morten H. Christiansen on a computational model of a sequential learning task of hierarchical structures in adults and children.

W. Tecumseh Fitch
Department of Organismic & Evolutionary Biology, Harvard University, 33 Kirkland Street, Room 982, Cambridge, MA 02138, USA.
tec@wjh.harvard.edu

Tecumseh Fitch studies the evolution of cognition in animals and man, focusing on the evolution of communication. Originally trained in ethology and evolutionary biology, he has a keen interest in all aspects of vocal communication in terrestrial vertebrates. He has applied his graduate training in speech science to animal vocal communication, particularly aspects of vocal production that bear on questions of meaning in animal communication systems including language.

Bernd Heine
Institut für Afrikanistik, Universität zu Köln, 50923 Köln, Germany.
bernd.heine@uni-koeln.de

Bernd Heine is Professor of African Studies at the University of Cologne, and President of the Permanent Committee of World Congresses of African Linguistics. He has been a visiting professor in the USA, Africa, and Australia, and a fellow at the Centre for Advanced Study in the Behavioral Sciences, Stanford. His latest books include *Possession* (1997), *Cognitive Foundations of Grammar* (1997), *African Languages: An Introduction* (2000) and, as co-author, *World Lexicon of Grammaticalization* (2001).

James R. Hurford
Language Evolution and Computation Research Unit, Department of Theoretical and Applied Linguistics, University of Edinburgh, Adam Ferguson Building, Edinburgh, EH8 9LL, UK.
jim@ling.ed.ac.uk

Jim Hurford has a broad interest in reconciling various traditions in linguistics which have tended to conflict. In particular, he has worked on articulating a framework in which formal representation of grammars in individual minds interacts with statistical properties of language as used in communities. The framework emphasizes the interaction of evolution, learning, and communication. He is perhaps best known for his computer simulations of various aspects of the evolution of language.

Frédéric Kaplan
Sony CSL (Paris), 6 Rue Amyot, Paris 75005, France.
kaplan@csl.sony.fr
Dr Frédéric Kaplan is a graduate of the École Nationale Supérieur des Télécommunications in Paris. He joined Sony CSL Paris in 1997 to work on evolution of language. His doctoral dissertation has been published by Hermes under the title, *La Naissance d'une Langue chez les Robots*.

Chris Knight
Department of Sociology and Anthropology, University of East London, Longbridge Road, Barking, Dagenham, RM8 2AS, Essex, UK.
c.knight@uel.ac.uk
Chris Knight is Reader in Anthropology at the University of East London. His first book, *Blood Relations: Menstruation and the Origins of Culture* (1991), outlined a new theory of human origins. He has also authored many book chapters and journal articles on human cognitive and linguistic evolution and was co-editor of *Approaches to the Evolution of Language* (1998), *The Evolution of Culture* (1999), and *The Evolutionary Emergence of Language* (2000).

Tania Kuteva
Heinrich-Heine-Universität Düsseldorf, Anglistik III, Universitätsstraße 1, 40225 Düsseldorf, Germany.
tania.kouteva@phil-fak.uni-duesseldorf.de
Tania Kuteva is Professor of English Linguistics at the University of Düsseldorf. She has published in the areas of grammaticalization, typology, and second language acquisition. Her most recent works are *Auxiliation: An Enquiry into the Nature of Grammaticalization* (2001) and, as co-author, *World Lexicon of Grammaticalization* (2001).

Joris van Looveren
Laboratory for Artificial Intelligence, Vrije Universiteit Brussel, Pleinlaan 2, 1050 Brussels, Belgium.
joris@arti.vub.ac.be
Joris van Looveren studied computer science at the Vrije Universiteit Brussel before joining the Artificial Intelligence laboratory at the VUB. He has been involved in the development of the Talking Heads project, and works now on a similar project on the emergence of more complex expressions.

Angus McIntyre
Sony CSL (Paris), 6 Rue Amyot, Paris 75005, France.

Angus McIntyre studied linguistics and artificial intelligence at the University of Edinburgh. After graduation he worked for AI companies in Italy and Belgium, before joining Sony CSL Paris in October 1996. His work at CSL involves the development of supporting software for experiments in evolution of language.

Frederick J. Newmeyer
Department of Linguistics, University of Washington, Seattle, WA 98195-4340, USA.
fjn@u.washington.edu

Frederick J. Newmeyer has taught in the Department of Linguistics at the University of Washington since 1969, the year that he received his Ph.D. from the University of Illinois. He is the author or editor of twelve books on syntactic theory and the history of linguistics. Newmeyer is an editor of the journal *Natural Language and Linguistic Theory* and, during 2002, President of the Linguistic Society of America.

Kazuo Okanoya
Department of Cognitive and Information Sciences, Faculty of Letters, Chiba University, 1-33 Yayoi-cho, Inage-ku, Chiba 263-8522, Japan.
okanoya@cogsci.L.chiba-u.ac.jp

Kazuo Okanoya earned his Ph.D. in biopsychology from the University of Maryland in 1989. He is now an Associate Professor in the Faculty of Letters, Chiba University. He also has a research appointment at the Japan Science and Technology Corporation. His research interests include neuroethology, behavioural ecology, and computational biology.

Sonia Ragir
Department of Sociology and Anthropology, College of Staten Island (CUNY), 2800 Victory Boulevard, Staten Island, New York 10314, USA.
ragir@ulster.net

A Research Associate in Anthropology at the American Museum of Natural History, New York, and a Professor of Anthropology at the College of Staten Island (CUNY), Sonia Ragir has written about the changes in developmental timing, encephalization, and hominid diet in pursuit of a better understanding of language genesis. Her current research includes simulations of the interaction between epistasis, learning, and selection, and the negotiation of shared representational form and meaning in children's play and games.

Luc Steels
Sony CSL (Paris), 6 Rue Amyot, Paris 75005, France
Laboratory for Artificial Intelligence, Vrije Universiteit Brussel, Pleinlaan 2, 1050 Brussels, Belgium.
steels@arti.vub.ac.be

Professor Luc Steels is the founder and director of two laboratories, the AI Laboratory of the Vrije Universiteit Brussel and the Sony Computer Science laboratory in Paris. His work has spanned many areas of AI. Since 1996 he has focused on robotic experiments in the origins of language.

Herbert S. Terrace
Columbia University, Department of Psychology, 406 Schermerhorn Hall, New York, NY 10027, USA.
terrace@columbia.edu

Herbert Terrace obtained his Ph.D. in 1961 from Harvard University as a student of B. F. Skinner. He then joined the faculty at Columbia University where he has since conducted a research programme on the evolution of intelligence. His experiments have shown that the animal mind can solve complex problems without language to a much larger extent than previously thought possible.

Bradley Tonkes
School of Computer Science and Electrical Engineering, University of Queensland, 4072, Queensland, Australia.
btonkes@csee.uq.edu.ac

Bradley Tonkes is a research student in the School of Computer Science and Electrical Engineering at the University of Queensland. He is currently working on a doctoral thesis on the computational prerequisites for language emergence.

Janet Wiles
School of Psychology/School of Computer Science and Electrical Engineering, University of Queensland, 4072, Queensland, Australia
janetw@csee.uq.edu.au

Janet Wiles is at the University of Queensland, jointly appointed in the School of Computer Science and Electrical Engineering and the School of

Psychology. She is Director of the Cognitive Science Programme, and Co-director of the Centre for Research in Language Processing and Linguistics. Her research interests are in cognitive and linguistic modelling, artificial neural networks, and evolutionary computation.

Alison Wray
Centre for Language and Communication Research, Cardiff University, PO Box 94, Cardiff, CF10 3XB, UK.
wraya@cf.ac.uk

Alison Wray is Senior Research Fellow in the Centre for Language and Communication Research, Cardiff University. She researches the nature of formulaic language and ways of accommodating it in models of lexical and grammatical processing. Books include *The Focusing Hypothesis* (1992), *Formulaic Language and the Lexicon* (2002) and *Projects in Linguistics* (with Trott and Bloomer, 1998).

Index